DATE DUE

AUG 1 3 1997		
MAR 2 8 1998		
GAYLORD		PRINTED IN U.S.A.

Ethnic and Cultural Diversity Among Lesbians and Gay Men

PSYCHOLOGICAL PERSPECTIVES ON LESBIAN AND GAY ISSUES

editors

Beverly Greene
Gregory M. Herek

▼ 1. Lesbian and Gay Psychology:
Theory, Research, and Clinical Applications
Edited by Beverly Greene and Gregory M. Herek

▼ 2. AIDS, Identity, and Community:
The HIV Epidemic and Lesbians and Gay Men
Edited by Gregory M. Herek and Beverly Greene

▼ 3. Ethnic and Cultural Diversity Among
Lesbians and Gay Men
Edited by Beverly Greene

▼ 4. Stigma, Prejudice, and Violence Against
Lesbians, Gay Men, and Bisexuals
Edited by Gregory M. Herek

EDITORIAL BOARD

Ethnic and Cultural Diversity Among Lesbians and Gay Men

▼

editor

Beverly Greene

Psychological Perspectives on Lesbian and Gay Issues

Volume 3

Sponsored by the Society for the Psychological Study of Lesbian and Gay Issues, Division 44 of the American Psychological Association

SAGE Publications
International Educational and Professional Publisher
Thousand Oaks London New Delhi

For information:

SAGE Publications, Inc.
2455 Teller Road
Thousand Oaks, California 91320
E-mail: order@sagepub.com

SAGE Publications Ltd.
6 Bonhill Street
London EC2A 4PU
United Kingdom

SAGE Publications India Pvt. Ltd.
M-32 Market
Greater Kailash I
New Delhi 110 048 India

Printed in the United States of America

Library of Congress Cataloging-in-Publication Data

Main entry under title:

Ethnic and cultural diversity among lesbians and gay men / editor,
Beverly Greene.
    p. cm. — (Psychological perspectives on lesbian and gay
issues; v. 3)
    Includes bibliographical references (p.) and index.
    ISBN 0-8039-5362-3 (cloth: acid-free paper). —
ISBN 0-8039-5363-1 (pbk.: acid-free paper)
    1. Minority gays. 2. Minority gays—United States. 3. Gays—
Identity. 4. Gays—United States—Identity. I. Greene, Beverly.
II. Series.
HQ76.25.E82   1997
305-9'0664—dc21   96-45891

97 98 99 00 11 10 9 8 7 6 5 4 3 2 1

Acquiring Editor:	C. Terry Hendrix
Editorial Assistant:	Dale Mary Grenfell
Production Editor:	Michèle Lingre
Production Assistant:	Karen Wiley
Print Buyer:	Anna Chin

When citing a volume from **Psychological Perspectives on Lesbian and Gay Issues**, please use the following reference style:

Greene, B. (Ed.). (1997). *Psychological perspectives on lesbian and gay issues: Vol. 3. Ethnic and Cultural Diversity Among Lesbians and Gay Men.* Thousand Oaks, CA: Sage.

Evelyn Gentry Hooker, Ph.D.
1907-1996

After this volume went to press, we learned of the death of Dr. Evelyn Hooker. In her passing, the community of gay and lesbian scholars in psychology and the lesbian and gay community as a whole loses an historically important advocate and friend. Dr. Hooker's pioneering research was the first to provide empirical evidence to contradict the prevailing pathological models of homosexuality in mental health. She presented her findings at the 64th Annual Meeting of the American Psychological Association in 1956 at a time when homosexuality was characterized and widely accepted as a condition that was inherently pathological. Her work was instrumental in altering that perception among mental health professionals and in the eventual removal of homosexuality as a diagnostic entity from the American Psychiatric Association's *Diagnostic and Statistical Manual* in 1973.

I last spoke to Dr. Hooker at the 1994 working conference of the Wayne Placek Trust Fund of the American Psychological Foundation in Chicago. The University of Chicago recognized her contributions by giving its Center for the Mental Health of Lesbians and Gay Men her name. In accepting the honor she eschewed both the importance and special nature of contributions that garnered her many accolades. Instead, she offered that her work was the simple result of intellectual curiosity and empathy and that neither required any particular courage. Her modest assessment of her contributions notwithstanding, it is out of gratitude for her pioneering work and fondness for her person that this volume is dedicated to her memory.

Contents

On what basis could we form a coalition is still an open question. The idea of basing it on sexual preference strikes me as somewhat dubious, strikes me as being less than a firm foundation. It seems to me that a coalition has to be based on the grounds of human dignity. . . . There's nothing in me that is not in everybody else, and nothing in everybody else that is not in me. . . . I'm saying I have nothing to prove. The world also belongs to me.

. . . If you don't live the only life you have, you won't live some other life, you won't live any life at all.

—JAMES BALDWIN

From an interview by Richard Goldstein
Village Voice, June 26, 1984

Preface

This is the third volume of the annual series Psychological Perspectives on Lesbian and Gay Issues, sponsored by the Society for the Psychological Study of Lesbian and Gay Issues (Division 44 of the American Psychological Association). Previous volumes have addressed a broad range of topics, including the effect of the AIDS epidemic on the lesbian and gay community. This volume focuses on lesbians and gay men as a heterogeneous, culturally diverse group of men and women who, despite their common bonds, have diverse identities. Such diversity transforms and expands the meanings of gay, lesbian, and bisexual identities.

Culture may be defined as the behaviors, values, and beliefs that characterize a particular social group and perhaps distinguish it from others. Social groups may be distinguished by such factors as ethnicity, age, socioeconomic class, religion, skin color, gender, regional affiliation, and sexual orientation. They may also be distinguished by the uniqueness of their collective experience, such as their colonization, political oppression, or physical or emotional disability. The diverse group of authors who have contributed to this volume explore some of the varied experiences of lesbians and gay men from these and many other perspectives. I have chosen to define culture broadly in this volume to facilitate moving beyond the assumption that cultural diversity is concerned only with the ways that people of color differ from white persons. The authors represent, both in themselves and in their work, some of the wide range of experiences and dilemmas confronting lesbians and gay men as well as the complex interconnections among culture, sexual orientation, and psychological development.

The chapters here were also chosen with the intent of conveying the richness and diversity in ways of knowing within our discipline and, accordingly, empirical studies, clinical and theoretical papers, and personal narratives are included.

In Chapter 2, Letitia Anne Peplau, Susan Cochran, and Vickie Mays present the results of their extensive national survey of the intimate relationships of African American lesbians and gay men, continuing their pioneering collaborative work in this area. Marta Alquijay (Chapter 12) provides an examination of the relationships among self-esteem, acculturation, and lesbian identity formation for Latina lesbians. Both studies contribute significantly to the paucity of empirical research with these populations.

Ethnicity, culture, and sexual orientation are salient aspects of human identity about which most people have strong feelings but often find difficult to discuss openly. Attempting to understand these issues and their interactive effects is challenging. This was evident in the responses of many people who were invited to contribute chapters to this volume. Many elected not to contribute, confiding that they were afraid of assuming a heightened level of visibility in their ethnic communities as lesbians or gay men. Despite the fact that those who were invited are "out" professionally as well as within their families, many perceived addressing the combined effects of these issues publicly as being more out than they cared to tolerate. Moreover, they voiced their concerns that discussing "family business"—matters that take place within their respective cultures that are not generally known to outsiders—with people who do not belong to the group would be perceived as being critical of ethnic communities that have already been historically victimized and then stigmatized by psychology. Although this was a frequent response from lesbians and gay men of color, it was not limited to them. For many white Americans, ethnicity represents something that one must get rid of or something that one must pretend to be rid of in order to be regarded as an authentic "American" as well as to avoid being a target of ethnic discrimination. Thinking about these issues can require revisiting losses, pressure to hide integral parts of one's identity, and painful feelings about both. Sari Dworkin captures the essence of this dilemma in her discussion of Jewish lesbians in Chapter 4. She gives a moving account of the ongoing need to come out, both as a Jew and as a lesbian, in a society that presumes everyone is Christian just as it presumes heterosexuality. Leah Fygetakis, in Chapter 8, discusses Greek American lesbians; she touches on the difficulty of sharing secrets outside of one's culture and shatters some illusions about the perceived historical acceptance of homosexuality by Greeks. In Chapter 6, Armand Cerbone eloquently reveals the dissonance of being a white male symbol of privilege on the one hand and simultaneously devalued as an Italian in postwar Boston and as a gay man who is Catholic. He provides an important glimpse into the struggles that ensue from such starkly contradictory messages and the personal struggle required to reconcile them in healthy ways. In this revealing narrative Cerbone also sensitizes clinicians to the importance of understanding the nature of world political events at the time of a client's birth and development and the role of those events in shaping a community as well as a person's individual identity. Clarence Adams and Douglas Kimmel address the issue of age more directly in Chapter 7, as they report on their study of older African American gay men. Their work focuses on an important but often neglected and invisible segment of our community, older lesbians and gay men and their struggles in both a subculture and dominant culture that idealize youth.

Although many of the names of the contributors to this volume will be familiar to readers, many will be new, and I feel fortunate to be able to introduce their work. Cheryl Potgieter offers us a rare glimpse into the lives of Black South African lesbians in pre- and postapartheid South Africa (Chapter 5). She presents moving personal accounts of the women she interviewed for her study as well as a discussion of the integral role South African psychologists played in both the criminalization of homosexuals as well as the support of apartheid. In Chapter 9, Oliva Espin introduces the concept of crossing borders and boundaries, both psychologically and geographically. Like Potgieter, Espin introduces the narratives of women in her study to highlight the effects of immigration on the process of coming out. Althea Smith focuses in Chapter 14 specifically on the influence of culture and ethnicity in the coming-out process. She raises important questions about what coming out means in a cross-cultural context and challenges its construction as a dichotomous and singular event. In Chapter 11, Connie Chan explores these issues for Asian American lesbians and the culture's broad effects on the development of sexual identity and expression. In Chapter 13, Carla Trujillo examines heterosexism in the Latino/a community and the rigidity of identity boundaries that can occur within the lesbian community despite its marginalization from the broader culture.

Espin also examines the significant role of the narrative in research and its importance in the reconstruction of a life story. The richness of the narrative as a tool used to tell one's story is captured uniquely by Bonnie Strickland in Chapter 3, where she recounts the development of her identity as someone growing up in the "redneck Riviera" of the rural South, among poor, uneducated folk, juggling multiple identities on her life's journey North, to live among "Yankees." The complexity of her life's journey challenges many of the superficial but commonly held assumptions about growing up poor, southern, white, and lesbian.

No attempt to depict a range of cultural perspectives among gay men and lesbians would be complete without an examination of what Terry Tafoya (Chapter 1) refers to as the "Two-Spirited." He makes important observations about lesbians and gay men, and perhaps whether or not those terms are conceptually accurate among Native American peoples. In Chapter 10, I provide a review of salient mental health and treatment issues from the perspective that the history of multiple levels of discrimination, stigma, and visibility creates a range of special challenges for lesbians and gay men of color that psychotherapists must appreciate if they are to offer effective treatment.

Another theme that emerged during this volume's development was that for many people, racism, sexism, and heterosexism, when considered individually, are emotionally challenging enough, but when considered simultaneously, they often provoke feelings of anger, sadness, or of being overwhelmed. There was a sense that engaging these issues intellectually and professionally also requires engaging them personally. For many, these issues represent a painful and challenging aspect of their everyday lives. Unlike other intellectual endeavors, the examination of the combined effects of these social ills requires the confrontation and management of personal feelings that often emerge, and this complicates the task of writing about them. Many authors who were invited to contribute felt too personally vulnerable and declined the invitation. Of those who declined, many were doctoral candidates and untenured faculty members at what they described as "inhospitable" institutions. They acknowledged feeling vulnerable about writing and conducting research on gay or lesbian issues, citing their concerns about potentially negative effects on their tenure, promotion, or candidacy. Lesbians and gay men of color in these situations reiterated their feelings of an even heightened vulnerability as well as a reluctance to take on yet another issue in addition to race. Despite the many gains in lesbian and gay psychology and in the expansion of civil rights to women and to members of ethnic minority groups over the past decade, such occurrences remind us of the continuing legacy of racism, sexism, and heterosexism and the realistic lack of safety that many members of our community are required to negotiate routinely. This speaks to the courage of this volume's contributors, who, in telling their stories and conducting this research, increase their vulnerability. We owe them our gratitude.

Although I have attempted to make this volume inclusive, it in no way represents the full range of diversity among lesbians, gay men, and bisexuals. The omission of some groups should not be taken to suggest that they or their concerns are not worthy of our attention. It is my hope that this volume will represent the first of many to follow that together will contribute to an inclusiveness not only in gay and lesbian psychology, but in the broader psychological literature as well.

I would like to express my appreciation to a few of the many people who have been instrumental in the completion of this volume. Among them, special thanks go to Dorith Brodbar of the New School for Social Research in New York City; to Shanee Stepakoff and Ruby Eddy-Quartey of St. John's University, for crucial research assistance; and to St. John's University, for its ongoing and generous support of my research. Dale Grenfell and Terry Hendrix of Sage Publications have been loyal supporters of this series and have been of invaluable help in bringing it to fruition. Some of the chapters in this volume had their origins in a symposium titled "Ethnic and Cultural Diversity in the Coming Out Process for Lesbians," organized by Adrienne Smith and convened at APA's 1990 meeting in Boston. Even in her absence, Adrienne's influence continues to be felt in the division. Finally, I thank James Baldwin and Audre Lorde, whom I have given the first and last words.

—BEVERLY GREENE

1

Native Gay and Lesbian Issues
The Two-Spirited

TERRY TAFOYA

L ong ago, when the world was young, Coyote was going along..."
(or perhaps it was Raven, or Wiskijiac, or Dukwebah, or Rab-
bit . . .)—with these words, a number of the Native stories of the
Americas begin to tell of an unbroken connectiveness of past, present,
and future.[1] The stories provide a framework for understanding how
the world works, how one identifies oneself as a member of a tribe, a
clan, a community; what to value and what to avoid. These include
issues of sexuality and gender.

Coyote, someone common to many tribes, plays with everything—
sexual behavior, gender identity, boundaries, and bodies. This trickster
always challenges an audience to think and to deal with concepts of
transformation. Often in the stories, when "Evil" (and this term seems
inappropriate, but it is a term forced by English usage and convention
—*disharmonic* might be a more accurate term) is encountered, it is not
seen as something to be destroyed in some final Armageddon, but as
a force or energy that is to be transformed.

For example, in a Pacific Northwest legend, Coyote confronts the
Blood Monster Wawa-yai, a giant who kills people by draining them

AUTHOR'S NOTE: This chapter is excerpted from *Positively Gay*, copyright 1992 by
Betty Berzon, Ed. Reprinted by permission of Celestial Arts, P.O. Box 7123, Berkeley, CA
94707.

of blood. Offering him baskets full of blood soup, Coyote tempts him into excess, until Wawa-yai has ingested so much blood that he can barely move his enormous bloated body. Coyote then taunts the monster into chasing him, but Wawa-yai's belly is now so huge that he cannot fit through the longhouse door, and he bursts as he runs against the thorn-lined door frame. As Coyote watches, the exploding bits and pieces of the monster turn into mosquitoes. "Evil" is not eradicated, but turned into something that is more in balance with the universe, and indeed, the universe would not be in balance without the "Evil." Coyote's action is to stabilize the world by playing with the excess until harmony is restored. If this story is used to form a metaphor for AIDS or substance abuse (contemporary monsters that steal and destroy loved ones in the manner of Wawa-yai), a European worldview of this story (e.g., Hansel and Gretel destroying the witch) would focus on the eradication of the enemy—the dragon is slain, and everyone else lives happily ever after. But just as in substance abuse and real life, where "Evil" doesn't disappear when treatment begins, the "Evil" takes on a more manageable form that a person can live with on a daily basis. A mosquito may be a problem, but not of the significance of the Blood Monster. There is a place for everything in Creation—a fundamental belief of most Native communities.

Most Native communities tend not to classify the world into the concrete binary categories of the Western world—good/bad, right/wrong, male/female, gay/straight—but rather into categories that range from appropriateness to inappropriateness, depending on the context of a situation.

For example, a Navajo man asked a non-Indian man for food to feed his family, including his wife, who was about to give birth. The non-Indian agreed, but asked why the man's family was going hungry when it was well-known what a good hunter he was. The Navajo replied, "Because it is not appropriate that I who am about to receive a life should be taking life at this time." In other words, hunting is not seen as right or wrong, but only understandable in the context of a relationship.

This worldview is critical in understanding Native concepts of sexuality and gender, which do not always fit comfortably and neatly into general American concepts of gay/straight, or male/female. Indeed, even the discrete categories that exist for social science research will not always make conceptual sense to Native people, who may have a far more sophisticated taxonomy addressing spirituality and function, rather than appearance. For example, how does a Euro-American system of "gay/straight" classify a man who wants to be anally penetrated by a woman wearing a dildo?

When Native American people discovered Columbus five centuries ago, they presented a unique conundrum of identity. Not only did most tribes not organize themselves by kings and queens in European tradition, but the majority classified members as having more than two genders. This radical (for Europeans) way of seeing the world brought swift and tragic responses. The 16th-century Spanish explorer Balboa, for example, declared such individuals who were not considered male or female to be "sodomites," and literally had them torn apart by his dogs. Thus from the very beginning of European contact, Native people learned not to discuss openly matters of sexuality and gender with the newcomers, because they could be killed for being "different." Most U.S. citizens are unaware of Native history and reality. For example, American Indians did not become citizens of the United States until 1924. When the reservations were created by the federal government, the superintendents of the reservations were all appointed Christian missionaries of various denominations, with the mandate to "civilize" American Indians by converting them to Christianity, often by withholding food and starving the Indians into submission. Federal boarding schools were set up for Natives (American Indian and Alaskan). Natives were not permitted to attend public schools until the mid-1930s. There are still a number of Indian boarding schools operating today. Children were forcibly removed from their parents, sometimes at gunpoint, deliberately to prevent them from growing up with the influence of their culture and language.

This forced segregation and isolation had a devastating impact on Native communities as a whole. Critical teachings and attitudes regarding sexuality and gender that would have been provided at the time of puberty, for example, were never passed on in many families and tribes because the young persons were away at boarding school. Such things were not permitted to be discussed. In addition, there was an incredible loss of Native lives through exposure to European diseases to which Native people had no immunity (a situation that has a number of parallels to the AIDS epidemic—newspaper editorials of the 1880s in the Pacific Northwest condemned Native Americans for having unacceptable sexual behaviors and multiple partners, and declared their deaths by infectious disease to be "God's punishment"). It is estimated that in the Pacific Northwest, 80% of the Native population died within two generations of European contact.

It is fascinating in working with the Native "gay and lesbian" community to discover how often even those individuals who were denied access to their tribal histories of alternative gender roles and identities manifest the "duties and responsibilities of office" that were an integral part of being "different" before and after European contact. These traditional roles include teaching, keeping the knowledge of the elders, healing, child care, spiritual leadership and participation, herbal wisdom, interpretation, mediation, and all forms of artistic expression.

Of the 250 or so Native languages still spoken in the United States, at least 168 have been identified as having terms for people who are not considered male or female. In the anthropological literature, the most common word used to describe such an individual is *berdache*. This is an unfortunate historic choice, reflecting as it does an old Persian term for a male sexual slave. The word was picked up in the Middle Ages by Europeans during the Crusades, and its pronunciation and spelling evolved into its contemporary form.

When the French fur traders, explorers, and missionaries encountered Native people in North America who did not fit European standards of gender roles, they used the term *berdache* to describe them. In the 17th century, the word in French implied someone who engaged in receptive anal intercourse. It also has a connotation of someone with a biologically male identity, and so tends to exclude Native people who are biologically female. Some modern writers suggest the term *amazon* to discuss biological females who take on an alternative gender role. *Berdache* also indicates a sexual behavior that may or may not be relevant to a particular individual. Neither of these foreign terms is well known to traditional Native people.

In other words, asking a tribal member, "Do you have a *berdache* or amazon tradition in your community?" may bring about a confused stare. Asking a Navajo, "Do your people have *Nadle*?" or asking a Lakota, "Do your people have *Winkte*?" may get a very different response, as people recognize their own language's terms for such people. Many contemporary Native people have difficulty being comfortable with identifying themselves as gay, lesbian, or bisexual, feeling as though they are being "herded" into such categories by the power of English. In response to this, the term *Two-Spirited* or *Two-Spirited people* seems to be gaining greater acceptance for many of today's Native people in lieu of *berdache*, amazon, or gay/lesbian/bisexual. *Two-Spirited* indicates that someone possesses both a male and a female spirit.

A number of non-Native gay, lesbian, and bisexual researchers and writers have suggested the Two-Spirited tradition as a historic "gay" role model because it often carries with it a sense of positive acceptance or even celebration within many Native communities. For example, a European American gay male nurse reported being surprised and delighted to be visiting a Catholic priest on an Apache Indian reservation when a proud mother came in and told the priest, "My 16-year-old son is attracted to other men. We need to arrange for him to be initiated with the medicine men." The nurse was amazed to discover that there was a respected and sanctioned role for such a young person among the Apache, and to note that the mother's response was somehow different from his own mother's when his own sexual orientation became known.

Unfortunately, the simplistic reductionism (*berdache* = gay) of many non-Native writers often fails to see that although Two-Spirited people's and gay/bisexual/lesbian people's experiences and worldviews overlap, they are not the same thing. The Two-Spirited position is not one determined primarily by sexual orientation. The role is one of a spiritual/social identity for Native people, as opposed to psycho-sexual identity. Paula Gunn Allen (1986) (Laguna/Sioux) suggests seeing the *berdache* as a gender role, rather than a sexual identity. Tribal concepts do not stress individuality in the manner of Euro-American concepts, but instead focus on relationships, contexts, and interactions. In short, *gay* can be seen as a noun, but *Two-Spirit* as a verb. (This is meant as a metaphoric statement, meaning that a noun is a person, place, or thing, whereas a verb deals with action and interaction.)

The rigidity of the English language prevents even many self-identified gay/lesbian/bisexual Natives from dealing with fluidity of gender and sexual roles if the only categories that exist in a valued way are "homosexual/heterosexual." Native tradition emphasizes transformation and change, and the idea that an individual is expected to go through many changes in a lifetime. Indeed, many tribes anticipate that someone will change his or her name more than once, since a person at age 45 is not the same person he or she was at 10. Hence a name change seems most appropriate.

While hardly identifying as "asexual" (a lesser-used category employed by some researchers to indicate a gay or lesbian who is not active with males or females), some Two-Spirited people will not be involved on a sexual level with a biologically same-gendered partner, although an emotional/affectionate bonding can occur. This may be a matter of personal choice, an individual's medicine path (a traditional Native term that indicates one's spiritual behavior and connotes a combination of destiny and free choice), or a result of a specific spiritual vision/perception of his or her appropriate behavior. This should in no way distract from the fact that a number of Native people very strongly identify as members of the gay/lesbian/bisexual community. But to see "gay/straight" as the only possible categories of sexual identity for Native people (and certain other ethnic groups in India, Burma, the Middle East, and so on) is grossly misleading and out of touch with historic and contemporary reality. It is also seen as very reasonable that Two-Spirited people can be heterosexual, and that their partnering may change over a period of time. In many tribes there is a history of polygamy or polyandry—multiple spouses. This may still have an influence on how Native Two-Spirited people deal with relationships.

One of the impacts of the gay/lesbian/bisexual movement has actually been to limit the options of younger Native people who are now (in English) informed that they are "gay" or "lesbian" when they begin showing behaviors that in earlier times would indicate they were *Lamana* or *Bote* or another traditional category. Native concepts of masculinity and femininity are so significantly different from European American concepts of gender that they confuse the issue even more. For example, Jamake Highwater (1990) suggests:

> In hypermasculine societies, machismo is of the utmost importance in both heterosexual and homosexual males. In social systems that place less importance on distinction of sex, like those of many North American Indian tribes, there is a full spectrum of acceptable sexual behavior that makes the dualistic connotation of heterosexuality as opposed to homosexuality meaningless, and which therefore does not place a stigma on women who behave in a masculine manner or on men who behave in a feminine manner. (p. 82)

Interviews and research data that I have obtained with more than 200 interracial same-sex couples indicate a higher rate of bisexuality (as defined by behavior rather than identity) among Native populations in the United States than in any other ethnic group studied, which may reflect a more fluid concept of gender relations and sexual expression (Allen, 1986; Tafoya, 1989; Tafoya & Rowell, 1988). Indeed, unpublished data from my own work based on interracial same-sex partners show a higher reported rate of heterosexual experience among self-identified gay and lesbian Natives than among other ethnics, even after the Native subjects had entered into long-term (more than a year's duration) same-sex relationships.

Native individuals may be quite comfortable with their presented identity shifting its emphasis on so-called masculine/feminine behavior, depending upon social context and the behavior/identity of a partner. In other words, a Two-Spirited person may become increasingly "masculine" within a specific environment, or when in a relationship with a "feminine" partner, regardless of biological gender. This appears increasingly complex, simply because the English language does not permit this discussion in a useful manner, with its emphasis on gendered pronouns and fundamental categories of male/female. Jay Miller (1992) offers a six-gendered Native model of (a) hypermasculine (warriors and athletes, often reared away from women), (b) ordinary males, (c) *berdaches*, (d) amazons (or biological female *berdaches*), (e) ordinary females, and (f) hyperfeminine. This model would also take into consideration a very strongly femininely identified (e.g., hyperfeminine) individual who would partner an amazon. At issue with risk reduction in HIV prevention, this has significance, because in the two presented examples, the traditional communities would not consider such partnerships to be "homosexual," because they involve individuals classified as different genders. As a result, a commonly asked question, "Are you a man who has sex with other men?" will honestly be answered no by someone who has sex with a *berdache* or, in some cases, with some Two-Spirited people. (At the risk of being tedious, it should be emphasized that in HIV transmission, "sex" with any gender is not at issue—rather, certain forms of sexual expression carry risk factors and then only if one or more partners are HIV-positive.)

Yet another alternative would be to see European concepts of gender and sexuality as being polar opposites, or different ends of the same stick. One is either/or male or female, gay or straight. Native American concepts usually prefer circles to lines. If one takes the line of male/female, gay/straight, and bends it into a circle, there are an infinite number of points. Just so, there are theoretically an infinite number of possible points of gender and sexual identity for an individual that can shift and differ over time and location.

Historically, the status of the Two-Spirited person was valued in many Native communities, since an ordinary male sees the world through male eyes and an ordinary female sees the world through female eyes. However, a Two-Spirited person (who possesses both a male and a female spirit, regardless of the flesh that is worn) will always see further. For this reason, many Two-Spirited people have become medicine people, leaders, and intermediaries between men and women and between tribal communities and non-Native people. Their greater flexibility provides them with greater possibilities of discovering alternative ways of seeing themselves and the world.

Because of the influence of the federal boarding school system and certain forms of Christianity, some tribal groups may be as homophobic as any other rural community, although Native attitudes tend toward a much greater tolerance and respect for personal choice than found in most Euro-American groups. For some individual Native people, their first contact with the formal category of *berdache* or Two-Spirited may be in a college course on anthropology or in a gay pride presentation. In those communities where the traditional role of the Two-Spirited has declined, many younger Native people report seeking partners and experiences off the reservation, believing they are "the only ones" in their communities. As adults, they discover the frequency of same-gender sexual and emotional involvement that had been happening on the reservation all the time.

Finally, the role of the Two-Spirited person is critical in its relationship to those who are not Two-Spirited. The alternative behaviors and creative options of the gay and lesbian community inform the entire society of what possibilities exist and, like the Coyote legends, offer guidelines and directions for exploring and living life to its fullest potential. A man or a woman is more clearly and accurately defined by the existence of Two-Spirited persons, just as a straight person may more fully understand him- or herself in coming to know and understand gays and lesbians.

Appendix: Suggested Reading and Resources

Unfortunately, there are simply not many materials available that specifically address Native gay and lesbian issues. Among the most relevant are the following:

Roscoe, Will. (1980). *Living the spirit: A gay Native American anthology*. New York: St. Martin's.
Roscoe, Will. (1991). *The Zuni man-woman*. New York: St. Martin's.
Williams, Walter. (1987). *The spirit and the flesh: Sexual diversity in American Indian culture*. New York: Harper & Row.

Resources

Gay American Indian Association
3004 16th Street, Suite 203
San Francisco, CA 94103
(415) 255-7210

WeWah and BarCheAmpe
111 E. 14th Street, Suite 141
New York, NY 10003

American Indian Gays and Lesbians
P.O. Box 10229
Minneapolis, MN 55458

National Native American
 AIDS Prevention Center
3515 Grand Avenue, No. 100
Oakland, CA 94610
(800) 283-AIDS

American Indian AIDS Institute
333 Valencia Street, Suite 200
San Francisco, CA 94103

Tahoma Two-Spirits
P.O. Box 4402
Seattle, WA 98104

Vancouver Two-Spirits
P.O. Box 598, Station A
Vancouver, BC
Canada V2S 1V4

Two-Spirited People of the 1st Nations
476 Parliament Street, No. 202
Toronto, ON
Canada M4X 1P2

Nichiwakan N.G.S.
616 Broadway Avenue
Winnipeg, MB
Canada R3C 0W8

Note

1. *Native* is the term deliberately chosen here over *Native American*, because many of the experiences discussed are relevant to the aboriginal peoples of Canada and Central and South America.

References

Allen, P. G. (1986). *The sacred hoop: Recovering the feminine in American Indian traditions.* Boston: Beacon.

Highwater, J. (1990). *Sex and myth.* New York: Harper & Row.

Miller, J. (1992). A kinship of spirit. In A. M. Josephery (Ed.), *America in 1492.* New York: Alfred A. Knopf.

Tafoya, T. (1989). Pulling coyote's tale: Native American sexuality and AIDS. In V. M. Mays, G. Albee, & S. Schneider (Eds.), *Primary prevention of AIDS* (pp. 280-289). Newbury Park, CA: Sage.

Tafoya, T., & Rowell, R. (1988). Counseling Native American lesbians and gays. In M. Shernoff & W. A. Scott (Eds.), *A sourcebook of lesbian/gay health care* (pp. 63-67). Washington, DC: National Lesbian and Gay Health Foundation.

2

A National Survey of the Intimate Relationships of African American Lesbians and Gay Men

A Look at Commitment, Satisfaction, Sexual Behavior, and HIV Disease

LETITIA ANNE PEPLAU

SUSAN D. COCHRAN

VICKIE M. MAYS

L ove and companionship are essential ingredients for a happy life. A national survey of Americans found that most people, both heterosexual and homosexual, consider love to be extremely important to their overall happiness (Freedman, 1978). Empirical research amply documents that intimate relationships are vital to psychological health (Cohen & Willis, 1985). In a recent review, Myers (1992) concludes, "Whether young or old, male or female, rich or poor, people in stable, loving relationships do enjoy greater well-being" (p. 156). There is also growing evidence that supportive personal relationships contribute to physical health and longevity (Schuster, Kessler, & Aseltine, 1990;

AUTHORS' NOTE: The research reported in this chapter was supported by a grant from the Chicago Resource Center (W8560621) to all three authors, as well as by grants from the National Institute of Mental Health and the National Institute on Allergy and Infectious Diseases (RO1MH42584, RO1MH44345) to the second and third authors and an NIMH Scientist Development Award (K211MH00878) to the second author.

Taylor, 1995; Willis, 1985). Researchers and others have long known about the positive aspects of having intimate close personal relationships (Rook & Pietromonaco, 1987). Intimate interactions with others tend to enhance our moods and feelings of self-worth, and provide the context for emotional health and happiness. They challenge, stimulate, and reward us in our everyday lives, and also serve as buffers during times of stress and upheaval. They allow us to feel secure that we can handle life stressors. Intimate relationships provide us with others we can turn to for help, emotional intimacy, and guidance (Rook & Pietromonaco, 1987). As Bowlby (1973) has noted, people function most effectively "when they are confident that, standing behind them, there are one or more trusted persons who will come to their aid should difficulties arise" (p. 359). In contrast, researchers and health care professionals find that persons who lack intimate relationships tend to be vulnerable to a host of emotional problems, such as anxiety, diminished feelings of self-worth, depression, and psychosomatic symptomatology (Perlman & Peplau, 1984). What emerges from the available evidence is that having a good, close, intimate relationship is important to overall health and well-being.

However, current knowledge about personal relationships is based on research that has largely focused on couples who are White and heterosexual. Little is known about the intimate relationships of ethnic minority lesbians and gay men, particularly African Americans. Studying the intimate relationships of African American lesbians and gay men seems particularly warranted, as African Americans in general tend to have higher rates of morbidity and mortality (Cochran & Mays, 1994; Reed, Darity, & Roberson, 1993; U.S. Department of Health and Human Services, 1985). If intimate relationships can in any way contribute to enhancing or promoting better physical and/or psychological health, then studies of such relationships among African American gays and lesbians are well worthwhile (Cochran & Mays, 1994).

In this chapter we take a look at the intimate relationship experiences of African American lesbians and gay men—a population that is virtually invisible in U.S. society, not only in the eyes of the general public but also in the eyes of scientific researchers (Cochran & Mays, 1994; Mays, Cochran, & Rhue, 1993). Researchers who study Black families typically acknowledge a diversity of family forms and write that African Americans are less likely than other populations in the United States to be in heterosexual marriages, but they rarely mention the existence of enduring same-sex couples (e.g., Hatchett, Cochran, & Jackson, 1991; Mays, Chatters, Cochran, & Mackness, in press; Staples, 1981; Taylor, Chatters, Tucker, & Lewis, 1990). This occurs despite the fact that mothers and other close female relatives in African American families may be quite aware that members of their families are gay or lesbian (Mays et al., in press). Discussions of alternative lifestyles and patterns of friendships among African Americans have not considered same-sex gay and lesbian relationships (e.g., Cazenave, 1980; Ericksen, 1980). Similarly, reviews of the slowly growing literature about same-sex lesbian and gay couples typically focus on Whites (e.g., Harry, 1983; Peplau & Cochran, 1990). Even in very large studies, such as Blumstein and Schwartz's (1983) report *American Couples*, the number of African Americans has been small; among the 1,930 gay men in Blumstein and Schwartz's study, only 39 were Black, and among the 1,549 lesbians, only 15 were Black. The result is that we know very little about the experiences of African Americans whose intimate relationships are with same-sex partners (Cochran & Mays, 1988b; Cochran, Nardi, Mays, & Taylor, 1997; Mays & Cochran, 1988a; Mays et al., 1993).

In this chapter we report findings from the first large-scale empirical study of the same-sex relationships of more than 700 coupled homosexually active African American men and women. Because of the general lack of knowledge about African Americans in same-sex relationships, one of our objectives is to provide basic descriptions of these relationships. Our second goal is to explore relationship satisfaction and its correlates among members of our sample. Finally, our third goal is to compare the experiences of African American gay men and lesbians, noting their similarities and differences as members of both the gay and lesbian community and the African American community. Throughout the presentation of our findings, we refer to previously published research when relevant as a way of learning more about how ethnicity/culture, sexual orientation, and gender affect the relationships of African Americans in same-sex intimate relationships.

Study Participants

As part of two national studies, more than 1,400 homosexually active African American women and men were recruited across the United States to fill out an anonymous questionnaire (Cochran & Mays, 1994;

Mays & Cochran, 1988a; Mays & Jackson, 1991). In order to ensure a heterogeneous sample, we employed a variety of recruitment methods. Questionnaires were mailed to the members of national Black gay and lesbian political, social, and health care organizations, such as the National Coalition of Black Lesbians and Gays. Each nondescript, brown manila envelope contained a questionnaire as well as a stamped, preaddressed envelope with which to return the questionnaire. Also included was a postcard that could be returned separately if the respondent wished to request additional questionnaires for friends or flyers to be distributed or posted in the meeting places of local social and political organizations. In addition, information about the research was distributed nationally via flyers to lesbian and gay bars listed in publications geared toward homosexually active adults and through announcements in gay and lesbian newspapers and gay male erotic publications (see Mays & Jackson, 1991, for methodological discussion).

Participants responded voluntarily to the self-administered, anonymous questionnaires, which, in part, assessed their same-sex relationship experiences. A cover letter informed subjects about the purpose of the study and the protection of their privacy. Men and women completed different, but similar, questionnaires. Male and female versions included identical questions about a current serious, committed, intimate same-sex relationship. Items were drawn from our previous work on primarily White lesbians (Peplau, Cochran, Rook, & Padesky, 1978) and gay men (Peplau & Cochran, 1981). We describe specific items below, as we present the findings.

We conducted several focus groups and pretests of preliminary instruments in locations throughout the United States, including both rural and urban areas, to assist us in the modification of our previous instruments. Our goals in the focus groups and pretests were (a) to determine areas of specific concern in the lives of African American lesbians and gay men; (b) to develop language that would be reflective of the culture of African American lesbians and gay men regardless of regional, education, and class differences (see Mays et al., 1992, for discussion); (c) to determine the best ordering of items, tolerable length of questionnaire, and format of the instrument; and (d) to learn more about methodological parameters for reaching "hidden" African American gays and lesbians who, despite being homosexually active,

Table 2.1 Demographic Characteristics of African American Lesbians and
Gay Men

	Women (n = 398)	Men (n = 325)
Mean age in years	33.5 (7.8)	32.9 (8.2)
Mean years of schooling	15.4 (2.4)	15.0 (2.1)**
Median annual income	$17,500	$22,500***
Employment status (%)		
Professional/technical	30.1	24.3
Management/administrator	12.9	17.4
Sales/clerical	22.1	25.6
Other	17.7	15.1
Employed less than half-time or unemployed	17.2	17.7
Mean age when first had sex with a partner of the		
same gender	19.7 (6.9)	15.1 (5.5)
Self-reported sexual orientation (%)		
Gay or lesbian	85.3	84.6
Bisexual	11.7	10.2
Other	3.1	5.2

NOTE: Standard deviations are given in parentheses.
**$p < .01$; ***$p < .001$.

did not identify as such and were not likely to be reached through organized gay and lesbian networks.

Respondents (846 men and 605 women) to the finalized questionnaire were included in the larger project if they indicated that they (a) were African American and that they (b) had had at least one homosexual sexual experience at some point in their lives, or indicated some intention to do so in the future, or (c) identified as lesbian, gay, or bisexual. The analyses reported in this chapter are based on examination of responses from the subsample of study participants who indicated that they were currently involved in a "committed, romantic/sexual relationship" with a same-sex partner. Demographic characteristics of the participants are presented in Table 2.1.

Women

A total of 398 Black women reported being in a committed, romantic relationship with another woman at the time they completed the survey. Their average current age was 33.5 years, with a range from 18 to 60 years. On average, these women first had sex with another woman at age 20. They had completed an average of 15 years of school, and most (83%) were employed full-time; nearly one-third held professional or technical positions. There was a considerable range of incomes, with 25% of the women earning less than $11,000 per year and 18% earning $30,000 or more. The women's median income was less than $18,000 per year. All female study participants indicated that they were currently in a committed relationship with another woman, but they differed somewhat in their self-reported sexual orientations. The vast majority of our participants (85%) indicated that they were lesbian or gay, but almost 12% said they were bisexual, and 3% preferred some other designation.

Men

A total of 325 African American men indicated that they were currently in a committed, serious relationship with a man. The average male participant was just under 33 years old, although sample members ranged in age from 18 to 70 years. The men reported that they first had had sex with another man at an average age of 15. The average years of schooling completed by the men was similar to that reported by the women participants. They had typically completed 15 years of schooling, or the equivalent of 3 years of college. Most (82%) were employed full-time, and one-fourth held professional or technical jobs. There was considerable variation in the men's annual incomes, with 20% of the sample earning less than $11,000 and 31% earning $30,000 or more. The median annual income was $22,500. Most of the men considered themselves gay (84.6%) or bisexual (10%). Another 5% said they were neither gay nor bisexual but were sexually active with men. By self-report, 34% of the men did not know their HIV status, 37% were HIV-antibody negative at their most recent testing, and 25% were HIV infected, including 41 men (13% of the total sample) diagnosed by a physician with HIV-related disease. (The women's questionnaire did not include questions about HIV status.)

As can be seen in Table 2.1, the men and women in the sample were very similar in their backgrounds. Only three statistically significant demographic differences emerged between the men and women. First, women reported significantly more education than did men, $t(710) = 2.79, p < .01$. Although reliable, the magnitude of this gender difference was quite small, amounting to less than half a year of school. Second, although there was no significant difference between the occupational status of men and women, as might be expected given the prevailing gender gap in wages, men reported significantly higher annual incomes, $t(712) = -3.58$, $p < .001$. The average income difference amounted to roughly $5,000 per year. In addition, women reported having had their first sexual experience with a same-sex partner at a significantly older age than did men, $t(710) = 9.62$, $p < .001$. This age difference at first sexual experience was more than 4 years.

This sample, as in all volunteer studies of partially hidden populations, may not be representative of all African American lesbians and gay men in the United States. Nonetheless, the size and relative diversity of demographic backgrounds among participants suggest that these data can provide a valuable window into the lives of a segment of the African American population about whom few studies examining close relationships exist. A good place to begin this exploration is by looking at what characteristics and attributes are important to African American lesbians and gay men in their selection of intimate partners.

Partner Selection

A general principle of interpersonal attraction is that similarity tends to bring people together. In general, married partners tend to be matched on demographic characteristics such as age, ethnicity, and education (Glick, 1988). Is this pattern found among same-sex partners? Harry (1983) has speculated that a more restricted pool of potential partners from which to choose might lead to less similarity among gay male partners in age, education, employment, and income. Kurdek and Schmitt (1987) tested this idea in a study comparing White gay, lesbian, and heterosexual couples (without children). They found that heterosexual partners were highly matched on age, income, and education, and that lesbian couples were also matched on age ($r = .79$) and education ($r = .39$) and marginally on income ($r = .29$)—although the magnitude of these correlations was smaller than for heterosexual partners. Gay male couples were significantly similar only on age ($r = .38$), supporting the hypothesis of less homogamy in gay male relationships.

In our study, we asked respondents to describe the background characteristics of their current partners with whom they were in a "serious, committed" relationship. As can be seen in Table 2.2, partners for the most part were generally similar to respondents in age, educational attainment, and employment. There were significant correlations between partners in age ($r[394] = .53$, $p < .001$ for women; $r[318] = .42$, $p < .001$ for men), and partners were significantly matched in educational attainment ($r[387] = .33$, $p < .001$ for women; $r[304] = .22$, $p < .001$ for men). Partners also tended to be similar in their employment status. In 76% of our Black male couples, both partners were employed full-time, and in 4% both were employed half-time or less; 20% of partners had different work statuses ($\chi^2[1] = 14.4$, $p < .001$). Among the Black female couples, both partners were employed full-time in 77% of cases, 3% both were employed half-time or less, and, as with the men, 20% of the women partners had different job situations; however, this pattern of association for women was not statistically significant. Looking at similarities and differences in jobs classified based on typical labor market categories in Table 2.2, we found significant matching in types of jobs held by partners for both the women ($\chi^2[16] = 56.4$, $p < .001$) and the men ($\chi^2[16] = 36.7$, $p < .003$) participants. In sum, we found for the African American lesbians and gay men in our study a fair degree of demographic similarity with their partners. This stands in marked contrast to results reported by Kurdek and Schmitt (1987) for White gay men and lesbians. Whether this finding of greater similarity in our study of African American lesbians and gay men is the result of ethnic, cultural, or class differences between the two samples or the greater size of our sample (and hence the greater power to achieve statistical significance) is unclear and remains a question for further study.

There are several questions raised by the greater demographic similarity of African American gay men and lesbians compared with Whites, but one can only speculate as to the answers. One such question concerns the importance or influence of class and/or cultural differences on African American gay men's and lesbians' relationships. Scholars continue to debate the primacy of race/ethnicity versus social class in the experiences of Blacks in the United States today. This debate could well be relevant to our examination of the relationship choices of African American gay men and lesbians.

Table 2.2 Partner Characteristics of African American Lesbians and
Gay Men

	Women (n = 398)	Men (n = 325)	
Demographic characteristics			
Mean age in years	33.0 (7.6)	33.9 (8.6)	
Mean years of schooling	14.9 (2.7)	15.2 (2.8)	
Employment status (%)			
Professional/technical	28.3	39.2 ⎤	
Management/administrator	12.0	15.7	
Sales/clerical	20.8	18.0	**
Other	25.1	15.4	
Employed less than half-time or unemployed	13.9	11.8 ⎦	
Ethnic background (%)			
Black	70.3	57.6 ⎤	
White	20.8	36.8	***
Other	8.9	5.6 ⎦	

NOTE: Standard deviations are given in parentheses.
$**p < .01$; $***p < .001$.

Another interesting pattern to emerge in our study was that more than one-third of the participants were in interracial relationships. As shown in Table 2.2, 30% of the women and 42% of the men had non-Black partners (most often, these partners were White). The greater tendency for the Black gay male participants to have non-Black partners, compared with the Black lesbians in the sample, was statistically significant: $\chi^2(2) = 23.35, p < .001$. (This tendency for more men to have White partners may help explain, in part, the observed difference between the occupational achievement of men's and women's partners—$\chi^2[4] = 16.70, p < .01$—despite the absence of significant gender differences in the partners' ages or years of schooling.)

To our knowledge, only one previous study has examined interracial relationships among African American lesbians and gay men. In *Homosexualities*, Bell and Weinberg (1978) report data from a survey that included 111 Black gay men and 64 Black lesbians, as well as several hundred White gay men and lesbians. These respondents, all from Northern California, were somewhat younger than those in our sample (by 1 year for women and 6 years for men). Although, unfortunately, Bell and Weinberg do not report the races of their subjects' partners at the time of their study, they did ask what proportion of each respondent's gay/lesbian sexual partners had been of a different race.

They found that interracial sexual partners were relatively common among their African American respondents. Two-thirds (67%) of the Black gay men in Bell and Weinberg's San Francisco sample said that half or more of their sexual partners were non-Black, and only 2% had never had sex with a person of another race. In our sample, 14% of the men said they had never had sex with a partner of another race. Among Black lesbians, 30% of Bell and Weinberg's sample said that more than half their sexual partners were non-Black, and 22% had never had a White partner. In our sample, 38% of the women said they had never had sex with a White partner. Hence both studies found that interracial sexual partners were more common among African American gay men than among African American lesbians.

A further context for considering interracial sexual relationships is provided by data on heterosexuals. A recent national sex survey based on a predominantly heterosexual sample gathered by an opinion poll research group found that only 3% of Black women who reported sexual partners reported having a non-Black partner, compared with 18% of Black men (Laumann, Gagnon, Michael, & Michaels, 1994). If we look at U.S. Census data on interracial marriages, a similar pattern emerges. Nationally, about 4.6% of heterosexual Black men marry non-Black women, compared with 2.1% of Black women who marry non-Black men (Taylor et al., 1990). On the West Coast of the United States, which was the site of the Bell and Weinberg (1978) study, the rates of outmarriage among Black men (over 12%) are higher than the national average. The factors that promote interracial marriages are not fully understood. Based on census data for Los Angeles County, Tucker and Mitchell-Kernan (1990) found that such marriages are more common among individuals living away from their place of birth.

It is possible that in a similar way, interracial relationships among African American lesbians and gay men may be fostered when these individuals move into urban gay social communities that may hold more tolerant attitudes than are found in the larger society and provide opportunities for meeting partners of other races. Interracial relationships may also be a function of limited partner choice (Mays et al., 1993). Within the African American community, where homosexuality is often more hidden in comparison to among White gays and lesbians (Cochran & Mays, 1988a, 1988b; Mays et al., 1993), finding a partner of the same ethnicity may be relatively difficult. Whereas White gay men and lesbians can draw upon a number of social organizations, bars, and organized political activities to meet potential partners, organized meeting places for openly gay and lesbian activities are less likely to be a path for partner selection for African Americans. This is particularly a problem for homosexually active African Americans who may not self-identify as gay or lesbian. Parks and Eggert (1993) hold that although individuals may be free to choose whomever they like as partners, relationship initiation is often contextually constrained by dynamics of physical proximity, social norms regarding appropriate and inappropriate relational partners, the position of the initiator in the potential pool of partners, and the actions of third parties. African American gay men and lesbians are likely to find their relationship choices constrained by some of these factors, particularly the problem of physical proximity, if they prefer to choose among other African Americans.

Studies of the role of social norms within the gay community of African Americans about choosing same-ethnicity versus interracial same-sex partners would be useful to our understanding of influences on the relationships of African American lesbians and gay men. Equally interesting would be studies that determine same-sex/same-ethnicity ratios of available partners for African Americans. We already know from researchers studying sex ratio imbalances in the heterosexual African American community that this phenomenon has an influence on the initiation, maintenance, and dissolution of relationships (Staples, 1981). Such behaviors as man sharing, power imbalances (Mays & Cochran, 1988b), and infidelity (Staples, 1981) are viewed as consequences of the unequal ratio of females to available males within the heterosexual African American population. It would be worthwhile to study further whether such influences occur in the same-ethnicity relationship choices of African American gay men and lesbians, and, if so, what behaviors are associated with this socially constructed imbalance in partner choices.

In general, our findings indicate that committed interracial relationships occur at a higher rate among African American lesbians and gay men than among Black heterosexuals. In our sample, African American men were more likely than African American women to have partners of other races, but this gender gap in interracial relationships appears smaller among our sample of homosexually active African Americans than the rate reported in the literature for African American heterosexuals.

Table 2.3 African American Lesbians' and Gay Men's Reasons for Choosing Relationship With Current Partner

	Factor I	Factor II	Factor III	Mean (SD) Scale Scores	
	(32%)	(15%)	(10%)	Women	Men
Instrumental resources (alpha = .79)				2.0 (0.9)	2.1 (0.9)
Type of job	.87	−.01	−.02		
Type of home	.81	.04	.01		
Income	.79	−.00	−.03		
Friends	.61	−.00	.07		
Inner attributes (alpha = .69)				4.0 (0.8)	3.7 (0.8)***
Intelligence	.01	.88	−.06		
Personality	−.16	.79	.00		
Cultural sophistication	.35	.54	.03		
Spiritual energy	.16	.50	.14		
Physical attributes (alpha = .54)				3.1 (1.0)	3.0 (1.0)
Sexual ability	.15	−.12	.76		
Ethnicity	.02	−.03	.70		
Physical attractiveness	−.14	.15	.68		

NOTE: Each attribute was rated on a scale from 1 (*not at all important*) to 5 (*very important*). Factor analyses combined data from men and women. Factors were extracted by principal components analysis and rotated by oblique rotation. Table presents factor loadings; the percentage of variance accounted for by each factor is given in parentheses. Cronbach's alpha was calculated using items loading .50 or above. Mean scores and standard deviations (*SD*) on each factor are given separately for women and men.
***$p < .001$.

We also investigated more personal factors that had led the study participants to select their current partners. Specifically, participants were given a list of partner attributes (e.g., the person's physical attractiveness, the type of job he or she has) and were asked to rate how important each attribute was "in your decision to have a serious/committed relationship with your lover" on a scale from 1 (*not at all important*) to 5 (*very important*). These items were subjected to a principal components factor analysis combining responses for women and men. Three factors emerged that accounted for 57% of the variance. Factors were rotated using the OBLIMIN procedure in SPSS. Factor loadings are given in Table 2.3. As the table shows, the first factor (instrumental resources) indexed the partner's personal resources, including his or her type of job, the "kind of place" he or she lived in, income, and friends. The second factor measured inner personal attributes of the partner, including intelligence, personality, cultural sophistication, and spiritual energy. A final factor appeared to index more physical attributes of the partner, including sexual abilities, ethnic background, and physical attractiveness. Estimates of internal reliability of the items associated with each factor were high. (Identical factor analyses conducted separately for women and men yielded the same three factors.) Mean scores for each of the three scales were calculated by summing those items loading above .5 for each scale and then dividing by the number of items in each scale.

As can be seen in Table 2.3, respondents tended to give greatest weight in selecting their partners to inner attributes (means close to 4 on the 5-point scale); the next highest weight was given to physical attributes (means of about 3), and the lowest to resources (means of about 2). This general pattern of emphasizing socioemotional aspects of a relationship over economic and instrumental concerns replicates previous findings from other samples. For example, in a predominantly White sample of lesbians, gay men, and heterosexuals, Laner (1977) found that all groups gave greatest importance to honesty, affection, and intelligence, and less importance to good looks and money.

Despite the general similarity in men's and women's responses, one gender difference was found. Women gave significantly greater importance to a partner's psychological qualities, such as intelligence and personality, than did men: $t(706) = 3.81, p < .001$.

It is also informative to note some common sex differences that did *not* emerge in these data. In studies of White college students and adults in 37 countries, two consistent findings have emerged for heterosexuals. First, when initially selecting opposite-sex partners, men tend to give greater emphasis to physical attractiveness than do women (e.g., Buss, 1994; Matlin, 1993). Blumstein and Schwartz (1983) also found this gender difference in their sample of predominantly White gay men and lesbians, with substantially more gay men than lesbians indicating that it was important that a partner be "sexy-looking" (59% v. 35%) or be "movie star" good-looking (17% v. 6%). They conclude that although "some lesbians respond to the dictates of fashion, many inhabit a culture scornful of what they consider male standards of female attractiveness, which they reject as indicators of women's worth" (p. 250). In contrast, in our study of African American gay men and lesbians we found no such sex differences in ratings of the importance of a partner's physical attractiveness or other external attributes. Among our African American participants, both men and women gave moderate importance (3.3 on a 5-point scale) to physical attractiveness. The reasons for our unusual findings are not entirely clear, especially given that previous studies have often used single-item measures such as ours. A closer examination of the meaning of physical attractiveness among African Americans gay men and lesbians is warranted.

Second, studies of predominantly White heterosexuals have found that women tend to give greater emphasis to the financial resources of their partners than do heterosexual men (e.g., Buss, 1994; Matlin, 1993). A recent analysis of data from the National Survey of Black Americans also addressed this issue. Hatchett (1991) examined the reasons that African American men and women gave for living with a person of the other sex. She concludes that "black women seem to value the instrumental aspects of marriage—particularly financial security—more than black men" (p. 99). In contrast, African American men gave greater emphasis to "socioemotional" factors, such as companionship and children. In our sample of African American gays and lesbians, we found no gender differences in the importance of instrumental resources. Women did not rate any of the four resource attributes more highly than did men.

We can only speculate about the absence of these gender differences in our sample. Unfortunately, comparative data are not available that would tell us whether the similarities we found stem from differences in the attitudes of lesbians (giving answers more like men's) or differences in the attitudes of gay men (giving answers more like women's) or differences in both. One interpretation of the typical gender pattern is economic. As sociologist of the family Willard Waller (1938) has explained: "A man, when he marries, chooses a companion and perhaps a helpmate but a woman chooses a companion and at the same time a standard of living. It is necessary for a woman to be mercenary" (p. 243). In other words, women's financial dependence on men forces them to emphasize a husband's economic resources; men's financial independence permits them to emphasize other criteria in a mate, such as good looks. From this perspective, a major difference between traditional heterosexual marriages and same-sex relationships is that most homosexual couples have a dual-worker relationship. So it may be that lesbians' greater financial independence reduces their concern about a partner's instrumental resources. Blumstein and Schwartz (1983) conclude, "Our data have told us that lesbians hold up, as the ideal relationship, one where two strong women come together in total equality" (p. 310).

It is worth noting that Buss (1994) interprets the commonly found heterosexual sex differences in valuing appearance versus economic resources from the perspective of evolutionary psychology. He asserts that "men and women have evolved powerful desires for particular characteristics in a mate [that are] highly patterned and universal" (p. 249). Our findings appear to challenge this assertion of human universality.

In summary, we have found that partner selection among African American lesbians and gay men reflects the well-established principle that similarity leads to attraction. Our look at the partner selection of African American gay men and lesbians highlights the need for further studies to investigate how ethnicity and culture influence the ethnic choices of partners and to explain the absence of gender differences in the importance for partner selection of factors such as instrumental resources and physical attractiveness.

Satisfaction and Commitment

Stereotypes often depict gay and lesbian relationships as unhappy. For example, one study found that heterosexual college students expected lesbian and gay relationships to be less satisfying, more prone to discord, and "less in love" than heterosexual relationships (Testa, Kinder, & Ironson, 1987). Contrary to such stereotypes, the available research indicates that most gay and lesbian couples are happy (Peplau, Veniegas, & Campbell, 1996). Studies of the quality of lesbians' and gay men's relationships have found generally high levels of love and satisfaction (e.g., Eldridge & Gilbert, 1990; Peplau & Cochran, 1981; Peplau et al., 1978; Peplau, Padesky, & Hamilton, 1982). Comparative studies indicate that the quality of relationships is generally similar for lesbian, gay male, and heterosexual couples (e.g., Duffy & Rusbult, 1986;

Table 2.4 Comparisons of the Current Intimate Relationships of African American Lesbian and Gay Men Study Participants

	Women	*Men*
Length of current relationship (median months)	28.2	26.0
In love with partner (%)		
Yes	74.2	61.3 ⎤
Unsure	16.2	27.8 ⎬ ***
No	9.6	10.9 ⎦
Mean closeness of relationship	5.9 (1.3)	5.6 (1.4)***
Balance of satisfaction in relationship (%)		
Partner more satisfied	37.4	40.3
Equal	43.0	44.8
Respondent more satisfied	19.6	14.9
Mean overall satisfaction	5.3 (1.4)	5.0 (1.5)*
Currently living with partner (%)	53.8	43.9**
Median months lived together	34.7	27.0*
Mean likelihood relationship will exist		
in 1 year	5.6 (1.5)	5.4 (1.6)
in 5 years	4.9 (1.9)	4.6 (1.9)

NOTE: Standard deviations are given in parentheses.
$*p < .05$; $**p < .01$; $***p < .001$.

Kurdek, 1994; Kurdek & Schmitt, 1986). Unfortunately, none of this work has examined the same-sex partnerships of African Americans.

The current research extended these earlier studies by examining aspects of the quality of intimate relationships among African Americans with same-sex partners. We asked participants to assess satisfaction, commitment, and other dimensions of the quality of their current relationships. The results are presented in Table 2.4. The median length of the current relationship was a little more than 2 years. For the women, the relationships ranged in duration from less than a month to nearly 21 years. For the men, relationship duration varied from less than a month to more than 35 years.

Satisfaction

Several questions assessed respondents' personal satisfaction with their current relationships. Overall, most said that they had a close and satisfying relationship, although women gave somewhat more favorable reports about their relationships than did men (see Table 2.4).

When asked if they were "in love" with their partners, 74% of women and 61% of men said yes. Only about 10% were definitely not in love, and the rest were unsure. Women were more likely than men to report being in love with their partners: $\chi^2(2) = 15.92$, $p < .001$. In general, respondents reported high levels of closeness in their relationships, with mean scores approaching 6 on a 7-point scale. Women reported somewhat greater closeness than did men (mean of 5.9 v. 5.6, $t[714] = 3.38$, $p < .001$).

Another question asked if one partner was more satisfied with the relationship than the other. Roughly 44% of respondents indicated that both partners were equally satisfied. When the balance of satisfaction was unequal, it was more common for study participants to say that their partners were happier than they were. Whether this reflects an accurate perception of the relationship or a tendency to perceive one's own discontents more readily is unknown. Finally, a question asked, "Overall, how satisfied are you with your relationship?" Mean scores were above 5 on the 7-point scale, indicating better-than-moderate satisfaction. Once again, women's scores were significantly higher than men's (mean of 5.3 v. 5.0, $t[712] = 2.23$, $p < .05$). Although the magnitude of the gender differences in satisfaction was small, the pattern consistently favored women.

Commitment

Several questions attempted to gauge the study participant's degree of commitment to the current relationship. Living together rather than apart can be one sign of commitment; roughly half the participants currently lived with their partners. Women were significantly more likely than men to cohabit: 54% of women versus 44% of men, $\chi^2(1) = 6.91$, $p < .01$. Among those living together, women reported having done so for significantly longer periods of time than did men, Mann-Whitney $U = 11,575$, $Z = -1.97$, $p < .05$; this difference amounted to about 8 months. Whether this sex difference in cohabitation reflects greater commitment in women's relationships or women's generally lower incomes (which might require shared housing) is uncertain.

Another question assessed perceptions of commitment more directly by asking participants to estimate the likelihood that their relationships would still exist in 1 year and in 5 years, using a 7-point scale (from *not at all likely* to *definitely will exist*). On average, both men and women were relatively certain that their relationships would continue for 1 year: Nearly two-thirds of participants gave scores of 6 or 7 on this item. Not unexpectedly, they were somewhat less confident about the longer-term outlook (5 years or greater) for their relationships, with 42% scoring 6 or 7. Men and women did not differ in their estimates of likely future duration.

In summary, although there was variation among respondents in their current relationship satisfaction and commitment, a majority of both women and men indicated that they were in love with their partners, that their relationships were highly satisfying, and that they expected the relationships to continue into the future. In a later section, we will consider some of the factors that were correlated with relationship satisfaction.

Sexual Behavior and Satisfaction

Several questions addressed the nature of the respondent's sexual relationship with the current partner as well as sexual contacts with others outside the primary relationship.

Sex With the Current Partner

The questionnaire asked if the respondent had had sex on his or her first meeting or date with the current partner. As shown in Table 2.5, only a minority of respondents said yes: 17.5% of women and 30.7% of men. Women were significantly less likely than men to report having had sex on the first occasion that they went out with their partners, $\chi^2(1) = 16.7, p < .001$. Another question asked how often the couple had had sex during the past month. Sexual frequency was quite variable. Some couples had not had sex in the past month; others reported having sex more than three times a week. Reports of current sexual frequency did not differ significantly between men and women, $\chi^2(4) = 3.82, p < .10$. Despite similar frequency of sexual activity within the relationship, women reported greater levels of sexual satisfaction than did men—a small but statistically significant difference, $t(713) = 2.09$, $p < .05$.

Table 2.5 African American Lesbians' and Gay Men's Sexual Behavior
and Satisfaction With Current Partner

	Women	Men
Sex with current primary partner		
Had sex with partner at first meeting/date (%)	17.5	30.7**
Sexual frequency with partner in past month		
Never	10.7	12.8
Less than once a week	30.5	27.7
Once a week	16.0	20.6
2-3 times a week	31.3	29.0
More than 3 times a week	11.4	10.0
Mean sexual satisfaction	5.7 (1.5)	5.5 (1.4)*
Current agreement with partner: Is sex with		
others permitted? (% not permitted)	56.5	49.4
Since current relationship began: Has respondent		
had sex with someone else? (% yes)	45.8	65.3**
Same-sex affairs (%)		
None	12.6	2.5 ⎤
One partner	52.2	29.9 ⎬ **
More than one partner	35.2	67.6 ⎦
Other-sex affairs (%)		
None	73.1	90.6 ⎤
One partner	19.8	5.0 ⎬ **
More than one partner	7.1	4.5 ⎦
Partner knows about last affair (%)		
No	35.2	71.2 ⎤
Yes, but issue not talked about	10.1	9.8 ⎬ **
Yes, discussed with partner	54.7	19.0 ⎦
Since current relationship began:		
Has partner had sex with someone else? (%)		
No	48.4	30.7 ⎤
Not sure	22.4	36.3 ⎬ **
Yes	29.2	32.9 ⎦
Same-sex affairs by partner (%)		
None	12.8	16.2 ⎤
One partner	53.8	23.8 ⎬ **
More than one partner	33.3	60.0 ⎦
Other-sex affairs by partner (%)		
None	71.8	77.5 ⎤
One partner	20.5	8.8 ⎬ *
More than one partner	7.7	13.7 ⎦

NOTE: Standard deviations are given in parentheses.
*$p < .05$; **$p < .001$.

Sex Outside the Primary Relationship

Several questions concerned the participants' attitudes and experiences about sexual exclusivity in their relationships. Previous research has found considerable variation in attitudes toward monogamy. For example, Blumstein and Schwartz (1983) assessed attitudes about the personal importance given to being monogamous among their large, predominantly White, couples sample. They found that 36% of gay men and 71% of lesbians thought it was important to be monogamous, as did 75% of husbands and 84% of wives. Although differences were evident based both on gender and sexual orientation, the most striking finding was the endorsement of sexual openness by a large percentage of gay men. Other studies have also found tolerant attitudes toward sexual openness among gay men (e.g., Blasband & Peplau, 1985). Participants in our study were asked about their current understandings with their partners concerning sex with other people. As shown in Table 2.5, roughly half indicated that the current agreement was that sex with others was prohibited. There was a trend for more women (56.5%) than men (49.4%) to say their relationships were closed to sex with others ($\chi^2[1] = 3.56$, $p < .06$), but this difference did not achieve statistical significance. Why didn't we find the gender difference reported by Blumstein and Schwartz? One possibility may be that a heightened awareness of the dangers of AIDS has reduced men's enthusiasm about sexual openness and thus narrowed the gender gap in attitudes about monogamy. The reasons for the somewhat lower endorsement of monogamy by lesbians in our sample, compared with Blumstein and Schwartz's, are less clear and merit further study.

When it came to actual behavior, a gender difference was found: Women were more likely than men to report sexually exclusive behavior (see Table 2.5). Since the current relationship began, two-thirds of men had had sex with someone other than their primary partners, compared with less than half of the women, $\chi^2(1) = 27.08$, $p < .001$. These figures—65% for men and 46% for women—differ somewhat from those reported by Blumstein and Schwartz for a White sample. They found that 82% of gay men and 28% of lesbians had had non-monogamous sex since their primary relationships began. Again, our data seem to suggest a greater convergence between the African American women and men in our sample.

If a respondent had had sex with someone else, the questionnaire then asked about the gender of the sex partner(s). As shown in Table 2.5, most of the extrarelationship sex occurred with same-sex partners: 91% of men and 73% of women had sex only with same-sex partners. Although heterosexual affairs were relatively uncommon, they were more often reported by women (27%) than by men (9%), $\chi^2(2) = 22.35$, $p < .001$. Further, more women (15%) than men (7%) reported having had affairs with *both* men and women, $\chi^2(2) = 7.66$, $p < .01$. As the data in Table 2.5 also indicate, men tended to have had more outside partners than had women. Half of the women indicated that they had had sex with only one other woman. In contrast, two-thirds of men who had had affairs reported multiple male partners, $\chi^2(2) = 44.98$, $p < .001$. This gender difference is similar to that reported by Blumstein and Schwartz (1983).

Finally, respondents who had had extrarelationship sex were asked if they had told their partners about their most recent sexual affairs. More than half the women (55%), compared with only 19% of the men, had discussed their last affairs with their partners, $\chi^2(2) = 56.98$, $p < .001$. Most of the men (71%) believed that their partners did not know about the sexual contact.

Participants were also asked if their partners had had sex with someone else since their relationships began (see Table 2.5). Most respondents expressed confidence in their knowledge of their partners; only 22% of women and 36% of men said they were unsure about their partners' behavior. About 48% of women and 31% of men believed their partners had not had sex with anyone else since their relationships began, $\chi^2(2) = 26.44$, $p < .001$. These proportions are similar to those found for participants' reports of their own behavior: 54% of women and 35% of men said they had not had sex with another person. Women were significantly more likely than men to report that their partners had had sex only with other same-sex partners, $\chi^2(2) = 21.60$, $p < .001$. Men reported more frequent heterosexual affairs by their partners than did women, $\chi^2(2) = 7.06$, $p < .05$. These beliefs about the partner differ from respondents' own behavior, in which women were more likely than men to have heterosexual affairs. Approximately 9% of the women and 8% of the men reported that their partners had had sexual contact with both men and women since the beginning of their relationships.

Table 2.6 Correlates of Relationship Satisfaction for African American Lesbians and Gay Men

	Women	Men
Partner attributes		
Resources	.02	.01
Inner attributes	.16*	.16*
External attributes	.06	−.04
Length of relationship	.00	−.02
Live together	.16**	.08
Love and commitment		
In love with partner	.48**	.52**
Closeness in relationship	.74**	.73**
Likelihood relationship will exist		
in 1 year	.69**	.66**
in 5 years	.63**	.65**
Sexual behavior		
Sexual satisfaction with partner	.46**	.44**
Sexual frequency with partner	.35**	.19**
Sex with others not permitted	.18**	.10
Participant has had sex with others	−.20**	−.21**
Partner has had sex with others	−.23**	−.18*

$*p < .01; **p < .001.$

In summary, most participants reported satisfying sex lives with their current partners. Sexual frequency varied greatly among couples, but did not differ systematically between women and men. The sexes differed most on the issue of sexual exclusivity. Although about half of both men and women had agreed with their partners to be sexually monogamous, men were more likely than women to have had sex with other partners and to have had a greater number of partners.

Correlates of Relationship Satisfaction

Our final purpose in undertaking these analyses was to investigate the correlates of participants' general satisfaction with their relationships. These data are presented in Table 2.6. In this study, as in an earlier study of White gay and lesbian couples (Kurdek, 1988), the correlates of relationship quality were usually similar for women and men.

In general, demographic characteristics of the study participant and the partner, such as age, education, and type of job, were unrelated to satisfaction. In this African American sample, the partner's race was unrelated to relationship satisfaction: Interracial couples were no more or less satisfied, on average, than same-race couples. In contrast, participants' ratings of their partners' psychological attributes were important. Of the three types of partner attributes considered, only inner attributes, such as the partner's intelligence and spiritual energy, were significantly associated with satisfaction. For both sexes, evaluating a partner higher on these personal qualities was linked to higher satisfaction.

Neither the length of the relationship nor how long a couple had been living together was related to current satisfaction. In contrast, subjective evaluations of being in love and feeling emotionally close were significant correlates. In addition, perceiving that partners were equally satisfied with the relationship (rather than one person being more satisfied) predicted higher levels of satisfaction for both men ($F[2, 307] = 28.72, p < .001$) and women ($F[2, 388] = 28.48, p < .001$). Sexual behavior both inside and outside the relationship was associated with personal satisfaction. Greater sexual frequency, higher sexual satisfaction, and monogamy correlated positively with overall relationship satisfaction for both women and men. In all of these patterns of association, the direction of causality is uncertain. It is plausible, for example, that believing a partner is smart and good-looking enhances satisfaction with the relationship. It is also possible that finding a relationship gratifying leads to positive perceptions of one's partner.

Finally, in these difficult times, when AIDS and HIV infection threaten the lives of so many Americans, it is important to consider the possible effects of this disease on the relationships of gay men and, in some instances, lesbians. Remarkably, in this sample, men's own HIV status (HIV-negative, untested, HIV infected but asymptomatic, and HIV disease diagnosed) was not related to their ratings of relationship satisfaction ($F[3, 313] = .60, p > .10$), to the frequency of sex with their partners in the previous month ($F[3, 316] = .59, p > .10$), or to their sexual satisfaction ($F[3, 317] = .65, p > .10$). Similar findings were observed when the partner's HIV status (HIV-negative, HIV infected, and status unknown) was considered. Partner's HIV status was not associated with relationship satisfaction ($F[3, 307] = 1.80, p > .10$), frequency of sex with partner in the previous month ($F[3, 308] = 1.19, p > .10$), or sexual satisfaction ($F[3, 310] = 1.83, p > .10$). Another perspective on HIV and men's relationships considered the combined

HIV status of the couple. The gay men in our sample included couples in which both partners were believed to be HIV infected ($n = 33$, 11%), both were believed to be HIV negative ($n = 74$, 24%), both partners' HIV statuses were undetermined ($n = 70$, 23%), one partner was infected and the other was not ($n = 73$, 24%), and one partner was infected and the other's status was unknown ($n = 58$, 19%). Overall, relationship satisfaction was unrelated to the couple's HIV classification, $F(4, 303) = 1.20$, $p > .10$. Also unrelated to couple HIV status were levels of sexual satisfaction ($F[4, 306] = 1.01$, $p > .10$) and sexual frequency in the previous month ($F[4, 304] = 1.09$, $p > .10$).

Although some might imagine that the threat of HIV and AIDS would invariably detract from the satisfaction derived from an intimate relationship, this was not the case. In our sample, all men were currently in a "serious, committed" relationship. Apparently those men who had tested positive for HIV or who were diagnosed with HIV disease found ways to cope with their situation without diminishing the perceived quality of their primary relationships. Indeed, it may be that the support of a caring partner proved especially valuable to men confronting HIV. Information about when men learned of their HIV status (before beginning a relationship versus after a relationship was established) and about ways in which couples cope with HIV would help us to understand the links between HIV status and the quality of intimate relationships. This seems important in a time when some men correctly fear that if they reveal a positive serostatus to a seronegative partner the relationship either will not progress or, if long-term, will dissolve due to the disconcordant serostatuses. Yet findings from our study hint at a more positive picture among Black gay men: that a satisfying relationship and sex life are possible between HIV-disconcordant men.

At the time we were in the field with our study of Black lesbians, we did not ask their HIV status. In recent years, little has appeared in the literature about the HIV concerns of this population, due to small numbers of cases of AIDS and HIV infection among lesbians. This should not deter us from thinking about the impact of HIV on Black lesbians, particularly as they struggle with issues concerning safer sex and injection drug use (Cochran, Bybee, Gage, & Mays, 1996; Mays, Cochran, Pies, Chu, & Ehrhardt, 1996). This seems especially salient for those lesbians and bisexual women who are sexually active not only with women but also with men (Cochran & Mays, 1988a; Cochran, Nardi, et al., 1997).

Our brief look at the close, intimate relationships of African American lesbians and gay men confirmed several previous findings on the relationships of heterosexual African Americans and White lesbians and gay men. However, our study also found variations that suggest unique dimensions to the intimate relationships of African American lesbians and gay men. For example, we found African American lesbians and gay men to be more alike than different in the rating of attributes important in partner selection. This convergence in similarity also seems greater for African American lesbians and gay men in other areas, such as attitudes about sexuality exclusivity and episodes of sex outside of primary relationships. Research that clarifies the gender similarities found in the relationships of African American lesbians and gay men may help us to gain a better understanding of the role of ethnicity and culture in intimate relationships. Further studies into the intimate relationships of African American lesbians and gay men are also one important means of determining the universality of our theories about close relationships. For African American gay men and lesbians, efforts by behavioral scientists to understand more fully how gender, ethnicity/culture, sexual orientation, and social status function in the structuring and maintenance of intimate relationships will strengthen efforts to enhance their emotional well-being and physical health.

References

Bell, A. P., & Weinberg, M. S. (1978). *Homosexualities: A study of diversity among men and women*. New York: Simon & Schuster.

Blasband, D., & Peplau, L. A. (1985). Sexual exclusivity versus openness in gay male couples. *Archives of Sexual Behavior, 14*, 395-412.

Blumstein, P., & Schwartz, P. (1983). *American couples: Money, work, sex*. New York: Simon & Schuster.

Bowlby, J. (1973). *Attachment and loss: Vol. 2. Separation: Anxiety and anger*. London: Hogarth.

Buss, D. M. (1994). The strategies of human mating. *American Scientist, 82*, 238-249.

Cazenave, N. A. (1980). Alternate intimacy, marriage, and family lifestyles among low-income Black Americans. *Alternative Lifestyles, 3*, 425-444.

Cochran, S. D., Bybee, D., Gage, S., & Mays, V. M. (1996). Prevalence of HIV-related self-reported sexual behaviors, sexually transmitted diseases, and problems with drugs and alcohol in three large surveys of lesbian and bisexual women: A look into a segment of the community. *Women's Health: Research on Gender, Behavior and Policy, 2*(1-2), 11-33.

Cochran, S. D., & Mays, V. M. (1988a). Disclosure of sexual preferences to physicians by Black lesbians and bisexual women. *Western Journal of Medicine, 149,* 616-619.

Cochran, S. D., & Mays, V. M. (1988b). Epidemiologic and sociocultural factors in the transmission of HIV infection in Black gay and bisexual men. In M. Shernoff & W. A. Scott (Eds.), *A sourcebook of gay/lesbian health care* (2nd ed., pp. 202-211). Washington, DC: National Lesbian and Gay Health Foundation.

Cochran, S. D., & Mays, V. M. (1994). Depressive distress among homosexually active African American men and women. *American Journal of Psychiatry, 151,* 524-529.

Cochran, S. D., Nardi, P. M., Mays, V. M., & Taylor, R. J. (1997). *Close friendship networks of gay-identified African-American women and men.* Manuscript submitted for publication.

Cohen, S., & Willis, T. A. (1985). Stress, social support, and the buffering hypothesis. *Psychological Bulletin, 98,* 310-357.

Duffy, S. M., & Rusbult, C. E. (1986). Satisfaction and commitment in homosexual and heterosexual relationships. *Journal of Homosexuality, 12*(2), 1-24.

Eldridge, N. S., & Gilbert, L. A. (1990). Correlates of relationship satisfaction in lesbian couples. *Psychology of Women Quarterly, 14,* 43-62.

Ericksen, J. A. (1980). Race, sex, and alternate lifestyle choices. *Alternative Lifestyles, 3,* 405-424.

Freedman, J. (1978). *Happy people.* New York: Harcourt Brace Jovanovich.

Glick, P. (1988). Fifty years of family demography. *Journal of Marriage and the Family, 50,* 861-873.

Harry, J. (1983). Gay male and lesbian relationships. In E. Macklin & R. Rubin (Eds.), *Contemporary families and alternate lifestyles: Handbook on research and theory* (pp. 216-234). Beverly Hills, CA: Sage.

Hatchett, S. J. (1991). Women and men. In J. S. Jackson (Ed.), *Life in Black America* (pp. 84-104). Newbury Park, CA: Sage.

Hatchett, S. J., Cochran, D. L., & Jackson, J. S. (1991). Family life. In J. S. Jackson (Ed.), *Life in Black America* (pp. 46-83). Newbury Park, CA: Sage.

Kurdek, L. A. (1988). Relationship quality of gay and lesbian cohabiting couples.*Journal of Homosexuality, 15*(3-4), 93-118.

Kurdek, L. A. (1994). The nature and correlates of relationship quality in gay, lesbian, and heterosexual cohabiting couples. In B. Greene & G. M. Herek (Eds.), *Lesbian and gay psychology: Theory, research, and clinical applications* (pp. 133-155). Thousand Oaks, CA: Sage.

Kurdek, L. A., & Schmitt, J. P. (1986). Relationship quality of partners in heterosexual married, heterosexual cohabiting, and gay and lesbian relationships. *Journal of Personality and Social Psychology, 51,* 711-720.

Kurdek, L. A., & Schmitt, J. P. (1987). Partner homogamy in married, heterosexual cohabiting, gay, and lesbian couples. *Journal of Sex Research, 23,* 212-232.

Laner, M. R. (1977). Permanent partner priorities: Gay and straight. *Journal of Homosexuality, 3*(1), 21-39.

Laumann, E. O., Gagnon, J. H., Michael, R. T., & Michaels, S. (1994). *The social organization of sexuality.* Chicago: University of Chicago Press.

Matlin, M. W. (1993). *The psychology of women* (2nd ed.). New York: Harcourt Brace Jovanovich.

Mays, V. M., Chatters, L. M., Cochran, S. D., & Mackness, J. (in press). African American families in diversity: Gay men and lesbians as participants in family networks. *Journal of Comparative Family Studies.*

Mays, V. M., & Cochran, S. D. (1988a). The Black Women's Relationship Project: A national survey of Black lesbians. In M. Shernoff & W. A. Scott (Eds.), *A sourcebook of gay/lesbian health care* (2nd ed., pp. 54-62). Washington, DC: National Lesbian and Gay Health Foundation.

Mays, V. M., & Cochran, S. D. (1988b). Issues in the perception of AIDS risk and reduction by Black and Hispanic/Latina women. *American Psychologist, 43,* 949-957.

Mays, V. M., Cochran, S. D., Bellinger, G., Smith, R. G., Henley, N. F., Daniels, M., Gear, T., Victorianne, G. D., Osei, O. K., & Birt, D. K. (1992). The language of Black gay men's sexual behavior: Implications for AIDS risk reduction. *Journal of Sex Research, 29,* 425-434.

Mays, V. M., Cochran, S. D., & Rhue, S. (1993). The impact of perceived discrimination on the intimate relationships of Black lesbians. *Journal of Homosexuality, 25*(4), 1-14.

Mays, V. M., Cochran, S. D., Pies, C., Chu, S. Y., & Ehrhardt, A. (1996). The risk of HIV infection for lesbians and other women who have sex with women: Implications for HIV research, prevention, policy, and services. *Women's Health: Research on Gender, Behavior, and Policy, 2*(1 & 2), 119-139.

Mays, V. M., & Jackson, J. S. (1991). AIDS survey methodology with Black Americans. *Social Science and Medicine, 33,* 47-54.

Myers, D. G. (1992). *The pursuit of happiness.* New York: Avon.

Parks, M. R., & Eggert, L. L. (1993). The role of social context in the dynamics of personal relationships. *Advances in Personal Relationships, 2,* 1-34.

Peplau, L. A., & Cochran, S. D. (1981). Value orientations in the intimate relationships of gay men. *Journal of Homosexuality, 6*(3), 1-19.

Peplau, L. A., & Cochran, S. D. (1990). A relationship perspective on homosexuality. In D. P. McWhirter, S. A. Sanders, & J. M. Reinisch (Eds.), *Homosexuality/heterosexuality: Concepts of sexual orientation* (pp. 321-349). New York: Oxford University Press.

Peplau, L. A., Cochran, S. D., Rook, K., & Padesky, C. (1978). Women in love: Attachment and autonomy in lesbian relationships. *Journal of Social Issues, 34*(3), 7-27.

Peplau, L. A., Padesky, C., & Hamilton, M. (1982). Satisfaction in lesbian relationships. *Journal of Homosexuality, 8*(2), 23-35.

Peplau, L. A., Veniegas, R. C., & Campbell, S. M. (1996). Gay and lesbian relationships. In R. C. Savin-Williams & K. M. Cohen (Eds.), *Developmental, clinical, and social issues among lesbians, gays, and bisexuals* (pp. 250-273). New York: Harcourt Brace Jovanovich.

Perlman, D., & Peplau, L. A. (1984). Loneliness research: A survey of empirical findings. In L. A. Peplau & S. E. Goldston (Eds.), *Preventing the harmful consequences of severe and persistent loneliness* (DHHS Publication No. 84-1312, pp. 13-46). Washington, DC: Government Printing Office.

Reed, W. L., Darity, W., & Robertson, N. L. (1993). *Health and medical care of African-Americans.* Westport, CT: Auburn House.

Rook, K. S., & Pietromonaco, P. (1987). Close relationships: Ties that heal or ties that bind? *Advances in Personal Relationships, 1,* 1-35.

Schuster, T. L., Kessler, R. C., & Aseltine, R. H. (1990). Supportive interactions, negative interactions, and depressed mood. *American Journal of Community Psychology, 18,* 423-437.

Staples, R. (1981). *The changing world of Black singles*. Westport, CT: Greenwood.

Taylor, R. J., Chatters, L. M., Tucker, M. B., & Lewis, E. (1990). Developments in research on Black families: A decade review. *Journal of Marriage and the Family, 52*, 993-1014.

Taylor, S. E. (1995). *Health psychology* (3rd ed.). New York: Random House.

Testa, R. J., Kinder, B. N., & Ironson, G. (1987). Heterosexual bias in the perception of loving relationships of gay males and lesbians. *Journal of Sex Research, 23*, 163-172.

Tucker, M. B., & Mitchell-Kernan, C. (1990). New trends in Black American interracial marriage: The social structural context. *Journal of Marriage and the Family, 52*, 209-218.

U.S. Department of Health and Human Services. (1985). *Report of the Secretary's Task Force on Black and Minority Health*. Washington, DC: Government Printing Office.

Waller, W. (1938). *The family: A dynamic interpretation*. New York: Dryden.

Willis, T. A. (1985). Supportive functions of relationships. In S. Cohen & L. Syme (Eds.), *Social support and health* (pp. 61-82). New York: Academic Press.

3

Leaving the Confederate Closet

BONNIE RUTH STRICKLAND

Some 40 years ago, I joined the "great migration" North. The Ohio State University clinical program was already into affirmative action. The faculty had to assume that a kid named Bonnie Ruth from a school only slightly more imaginative than its name, Alabama College, was African American. Ohio State had a good record of graduating Black scholars and scientists, but I was neither. In fact, I was probably the first person from the Deep South most of the faculty and students had ever met. Of course, I had never met any Yankees, either. If the program was committed to diversity, they found it in me, although I wasn't exactly what they had in mind. But then, I'm beginning to think I never was what others expected, and I usually don't know what to expect of myself.

I still have two memorable items that I took with me on that journey: a book, *Clods of Southern Earth* by Don West, and a small Confederate flag that I keep on my desk at home. I don't know why I have the flag where I can see it every day. Perhaps it simply reminds me of where I came from and where I could return. But I suspect that the reasons aren't that simple and are as complex as the southern culture that spawned me. The flag reminds me of growing up in the South, torn

AUTHOR'S NOTE: A much-abbreviated version of this chapter was published as "Reading, Writing and Talking to People" in E. Mintz and E. Rothblum (Eds.), *Lesbians in Academia* (New York: Routledge).

across boundaries of Black and White, male and female, pride and shame, hospitality and hate. Raised in a southern city (Birmingham, Alabama) distinguished by the vehemence of its violence and the "redneck Riviera" of the panhandle of Florida, how did I find my way to the urbane, sophisticated, gentle Pioneer Valley of Massachusetts? The first of my family to go to college, how did I become a professor in a five-college system at a major university? Reared in racism, prone to violence, and steeped in religion, how did I join a scholarly world dedicated to humane values and the freedom of ideas? Immersed in an extended family of more cousins than I could count, what prepared me to read and write and study alone among the Yankees of whom I had always been suspicious? Most of all, how did the dark secret of being different, of crossing sexualities and loyalties and sin and salvation, shape my life? On this snowy winter morning in New England, with a Confederate flag on my desk, how did I come to be half a century, 2,000 miles, and 40 degrees from home?

Ask a southerner what time it is and she or he will tell you how to build a clock. We are storytellers reaching, perhaps, too far into the past to inform the present. We grow up with a powerful sense of place, living on the land, with fierce loyalties to family. So this is my story, telling it the best I can about my life as a southerner and a lesbian.

Both my mother's and father's forebears were predominantly English—not the royalty of the courts or the dons of the universities, but debtors and prisoners who sailed to the southern United States on the condition that they never return to England. My forefamilies never lingered in the gracious coastal cities but rather seized the great southeastern frontier, confiscating the inland Appalachians from the Cherokees, the red clay of Georgia from the Creeks, and the sandy shores of southern Alabama and Florida from the Seminoles. Escaping the tyranny of one government, they replaced it with another—their own, which included eventually mobilizing an army to defend their independence. I will not argue the true causes and consequences of the Civil War (I certainly never learned them in the Alabama history that I was required to take as a schoolgirl); I will simply note that I was raised in a land still bitter over losing the "War of Northern Aggression," humiliated by having been occupied by foreign troops, and unwilling to forgive a faraway federal government remembered primarily for the savagery of its rampage across a rural landscape and the rampant corruption of Reconstruction. Although I grew up during the

Second World War, the War Between the States was more real to me than the fighting in Asia or Europe. I saved my Confederate money; I knew of the daring horseback escape of my great-great-uncle after he was captured by Yankee soldiers. I remember my daddy, drunk and crying, telling me about my great-granddaddy being wounded by a rifle ball as he knelt for a drink of water from a creek at Chickamauga. I hated Yankees with a passion that left all other minority people models of trust and compassion. Living in a totally segregated society, I had little personal contact with Black citizens. I did have a large number of Jewish friends, and finally met a Catholic when I was a high school junior. To my knowledge, I never knew a Republican—nor did I want to.

My mother was the 12th of 13 children in a family that made a living from the Apalachicola River. Her father ran a general store but spent most of his time on the river with my uncles, cutting cypress logs, cultivating Tupelo honey, and making illegal whiskey. If there was any law in those swamps it was enforced by my grandfather, an undertaking that eventually led to his being jailed for murder along with one of my uncles. Death and violence were a natural part of living on this frontier, not the ferocity of alligators and snakes in the swamps, or the panthers and bears on the shores, but the accidental human cruelties of gunshot wounds and burns from open fires. Once I counted close to 15 violent deaths that occurred in my extended Florida family, mostly from shotgun wounds and drownings. My father, the second of three sons, lived in the community eventually made famous by Fannie Flagg in *Fried Green Tomatoes at the Whistle Stop Cafe*. It was a typical railroad family: My grandfather worked on the trains and his sons were expected to do the same. Typical, as well, was the fact that my grandmother suffered from "nervous breakdowns." In the South, we seldom ask which side of the family is mentally ill; we simply compete as to who is the most crazy. My father's family easily won this one. My grandmother's episodes were characterized by her tearing off her clothes and running through the neighborhood in a frenzy. She would be hauled off to the asylum until she calmed down and then she would be returned to the family.

My mother met my father at a party in Birmingham in 1934, during the depths of the Great Depression. It was love at first sight; they married within 3 weeks, and my 24-year-old father took his 18-year-old bride to live with his family. My grandmother, already taking care of four grown men, didn't particularly welcome the woman who had seduced her second son. In fact, at one point, my mother woke to find my grandmother standing over her bed with a knife. Their rather ambivalent relationship resolved somewhat as my mother joined my grandmother in cleaning, cooking, and assuming her role as a caretaker for men. When my mother became pregnant with me, my grandmother asked that if I were a girl, I be named for her. She died 2 months before I was born, but my middle name is Ruth, as she requested.

As my mother approaches her 80th year, her remembrance of my birth and her labor with me increases in duration. She now maintains that I was in the birth canal for 37 hours. If she lives to be a hundred, her span of labor will exceed all known medical history. My mother says that finally the doctor told the waiting family that he could save one or the other of us, but not both. Naturally, they chose her; the physician delivered me with forceps and handed me, misshapen and not breathing, to a waiting nurse. Using the highest technology of 1936, she first dipped me in cold water and then in hot (or vice versa). I began to cry, no surprise under those conditions, and have been generally healthy ever since.

My mother maintains that my daddy was set on a boy, and that he had no intention of taking a girl child home from the hospital. With great concern, she asked him how he felt about having a girl. He was holding me and looking down at my crooked head and the port wine stains on my face from the forceps. He announced happily that he had no idea that I would be "so pretty." I was my father's child from that day on. My brother was born 4 years later, but my father had evidently forgotten his wish for a boy. According to my mother, he did not even go to the hospital to see his namesake. The ardor of their love at first sight had quickly cooled when they took a second look. Their fights were stormy, and my mother regularly left my father and returned to Florida. Thus began my trips between the river swamps of my mother's family and the streets of Birmingham with my daddy.

Growing up in the panhandle of Florida was a young boy's dream. Life was noisy and active and outdoors. I had cousins of every age— lap babies, yard babies, teenagers, and grown-ups. We were all happily parented by innumerable aunts, uncles, and grandparents. My great-grandfather had run off with his pregnant wife's sister, and my grandmother was the first progeny of this union. This seemed to begin (or extend) a family tradition in which the men were always philandering and the women coming home with extra babies. We never quite knew who belonged to whom, but we were all welcomed and well loved, so it didn't seem to matter.

When I visited Florida I stayed at my grandparents' home close to the Apalachicola River, which drains hundreds of square miles of swampland and empties into the Gulf of Mexico. The house, probably built in the late 1800s, had a dogtrot—a wide hall running through the middle, from the sandy, swept front yard to the outside pump and smokehouse in the back. There was no electricity or indoor plumbing, and I still remember the chilly outhouse on winter mornings, baths in a no. 2 washtub at the pump, and the metallic taste of water from the dipper in the basin next to the kitchen door. I also remember alternately cuddling and kicking various cousins as we giggled and finally fell asleep stacked in bed head to foot. Before dawn, we'd often jump in the back of my Uncle Jennings's pickup truck to go grubbing for fish bait. He would find a field of scrub pine and palmetto, drive a stob into the ground and rub another stick over it. We would run around picking up the worms that came to the surface, drop them into old tin cans, and deliver them by early morning to the bait stores.

The family grew most of our food. With my cousins, I slopped the hogs, fed the chickens, and even learned to wring a chicken's neck, a not particularly useful talent for these days. We had cows for milk and beef, and meat was supplemented with wild game, including turkey, boar, deer, squirrel, and coon. Of course, we always had freshwater fish and occasionally alligator meat. When we didn't eat it fresh, the meat was cured in the smokehouse, which also held the gator skins that Uncle Jennings poached. Some nights, a cousin and I, with lights on our heads, would float the swamp banks looking for frogs, gigging them when we would catch their eyes in our lights. We skipped the gators, whose eyes were spaced too far apart to be those of a friendly frog.

At times, some aunt or uncle would drive as many cousins as were around the few miles to the Gulf. We would scamper through the freshwater bays, feeling for oysters with our bare feet, or float face down, looking for scallops. But the times I remember the best were the long, lazy summer days I spent alone in the swamps in a flat-bottomed bateau with a rifle. I'd walk down a sandy road that led to the landing, picking blackberries along the way. I'd throw some bait and a fishing pole in the boat, but would mostly float with my fantasies. I'd watch the sun slant through the Spanish moss, lighting the dust motes in the water so that they danced like golden flakes. Jesus bugs walked silently on the water, bees swarmed around bright blossoms, cranes and herons scattered through the palmetto bush, and lazy turtles sunned themselves on fallen logs. I knew every slough and waterway and daydreamed that the cypress knees and Tupelo trees were ornamental hedges on the liquid lawn of the house that I would eventually build. All of my uncles built their homes near the river, and I assumed that I would do the same. Like them, I would live off the land—well, at least the water.

Life in the city of Birmingham was very different. My brother and I were the only grandchildren in a family of men. My grandfather cooked holiday meals. My father and his brothers would take us downtown or to watch them play baseball. We would go to the train yards, where I would be hoisted into the engine to blow the whistle. Uncle John also read important books to me and let me read to him. We produced our own plays, and he let me have the best parts. We had electricity and a radio, and it was at their home that I heard about the attack on Pearl Harbor. Although the men had only finished high school, they read books and seemed to have a sense of wonder about the world, perhaps their attempt to escape the trains that they rode, back and forth, between the yards of Birmingham and the small-town stations of Alabama.

Growing up in the South, I came to know any number of interesting and benignly eccentric folks who might now be called gay or lesbian. In the 1940s, however, the term *lesbian* was reserved for a minor Greek poet, and few of us were reading the classics. When the Second World War began, eager to reclaim military honor, southern boys, Black and White, joined up in vast numbers, although they were not particularly eager to share their barracks and bunkers with Yankees, Republicans, gay men, or each other. Southern girls had little to do but plant victory gardens, sleep safely protected from invasion, and dream of the boys who would be coming home. My dreams were also of a war hero, but it was me, easily vanquishing the enemy and returning in triumph to the breathlessly waiting southern belles. I think that I always knew that I preferred girls as my romantic interests. At age 6, when I began first grade, I promptly fell in love with my teacher, a woman, and have been enthusiastically returning to school every September for more than 50 years.

The fall I entered the third grade (I skipped the second and have always wondered about that teacher), my mother left my father for good. We moved to the south side of the steel mills, across the street from a public park with tennis courts and a library. The librarian, as attentive and attractive as my teachers, told me that "books were my friends" and gave me my first paying job, assisting her. My other neighborhood institution, the Southern Baptist Church, was devoutly devoted to saving and keeping me from sin through innumerable meetings and organizations. I was a Sunbeam and a G.A. (member of the Girls' Auxiliary), although I would have much preferred to be an R.A. (a member of the Royal Ambassadors—the equivalent group for boys). I attended Sunday-morning and -evening worship, Wednesday-night prayer meetings, the Baptist Training Union, Vacation Bible School, and church camp. I was also quite taken with the notion of becoming a missionary and traveling around the world to save the heathen. I had no idea why the heathen would want to become Southern Baptists, but I liked the idea of traveling.

In spite of the best efforts of the church, I still found time to sin. I cheated on Bible drills, beat up my little brother, and lusted in my heart after other girls. Although I had no experiences of the flesh, I surely wished for some. I searched the Scriptures for anything I could find on sin and sexuality, especially homosexuality. Much was made of "Men shouldn't lie with men," but I thought this meant that guys weren't supposed to sleep in the same bed together. The Bible was a little weak on women, except that Ruth could forsake all others and live with Naomi. I did get the distinct impression that every kind of sexuality, whether of the spirit or the flesh, was sinful, and I resigned myself to everlasting hell. This in spite of the fact that the whole of my rather limited sexual activities consisted of having been fondled by a church deacon and the man who ran our neighborhood dry cleaners.

My mother tried in vain to curl my hair and dress me in frilly clothes, a struggle that succeeded only for some best-forgotten piano recitals. Boys had all the fun and wouldn't be caught dead in a dress, an attitude I fully endorsed. While I couldn't change my physical sex, I could at least act, think, feel, and pretend that I was a boy. Boys were my preferred playmates, colleagues in adventure, and best friends. Girls were rather exotic creatures who needed to be pampered, protected, and impressed.

My boyish competition knew no bounds. I spent hours in the back-yard pounding a leather punching bag, shooting basketball hoops, and methodically hitting a tennis ball back and forth against the house. I learned to box and played war games in the hot summer evenings after supper, never distracted by television, because there was none. My mother worked from 11 in the morning until 11 at night, so my brother and I were mostly on our own. I was supposed to do the grocery shopping and cooking, but I would usually show up at a neighbor's at supper time, little brother in tow. Southerners invariably want you to eat with them, and my brother and I gave them opportunity to bring new meaning to the word *hospitality*. One neighbor also taught me to play tennis on the park courts. I eventually was nationally ranked and won a state title at Birmingham's most prestigious country club. My mother, having heard me practicing the piano for years, knew imme-diately that tennis was a better investment and paid for lessons from the club pro.

Perhaps in contrast to most southern boys, I also enjoyed school and found another avenue of competition. I struggled to be the best in class whether through grades, spelling bees, drama, poetry reading, or essay writing. At home, I built crystal radios and brewed rather exotic explosive concoctions with my chemistry set. A female Unabomber in the making, I blended homemade bombs from various ingredients and then detonated them in the backyard. No doubt, in my attempts at science, I was rapidly becoming a public menace. I gave up looking to the heavens for God and decided to become an astrophysicist instead of a missionary, exploring the planets instead of people's souls. Actu-ally, I would have preferred to be an astronaut, but they existed only in science fiction. School and books and science gave me a potential escape from what I perceived as the dreary world of my hardworking parents. My mother was a cocktail waitress, for a time in a gay bar, and my father a brakeman on the trains. I yearned for a life beyond the soot of the steel mills and the sludge of the swamps, picturing myself a medical scientist in a clean white lab coat, finding a cure for cancer, or an astronomer discovering a new star. But I knew in my heart that the closest I would ever get to the stars was in a sports arena. I thought about a career in professional tennis, especially after another kid from the South, Althea Gibson, became the first African American to win at Wimbledon. I knew I could join the military like my cousins and other poor southerners, Black and White, but girls were more likely to be military wives than soldiers and I couldn't picture that as my path to philosophy, poetry, and science, nor to other women. Higher education was a completely foreign concept to me. I didn't know anyone who had ever gone to college, except schoolteachers.

My Uncle John seemed to be one who had been able to cross boundaries and bring diverse worlds together, although at some cost. Uncle John had been drafted at the beginning of the Second World War. The family thought he was fighting in Europe when we learned that in basic training he had taken his rifle apart and refused to put it together again. He further refused to talk to anyone. The army resolved this dilemma by pronouncing him paranoid schizophrenic and sending him home to the V.A. hospital in Alabama. On one of his visits to my grandfather's home, my mother invited him to come over and see us sometime. The next day, he packed an old metal suitcase, walked across town, and moved in with us. I don't think this is exactly what my mother had in mind, although she was always inviting people to come live with us. At that time, my cousin Charles from Florida was staying with us and attending public schools in Birmingham. Uncle John simply joined the long parade of cousins, aunts, uncles, housekeepers, friends, and neighbors who were my immediate family from time to time.

Uncle John was with us for a few glorious weeks. He made me a gift of his baseball shoes, which I still have, showing me how to clean the cleats and various other baseball intricacies known only to the initiated. Uncle John often thought himself to be the manager of the New York Yankees—they were always winning then—and considered me another budding baseball star, conveniently ignoring the fact that I was a girl. He would also sit at a card table on the front porch and write long letters to the president of the United States. If Uncle John could direct the president as to how to run the country, I had no doubt that he could turn me into a major sports figure. This happy state of affairs lasted until one evening when my cousin Charles didn't come home for supper. Close to midnight, my mother found Charles hiding. He explained that Uncle John had threatened to bash his brains in and boil them in a dishpan for supper. Charles decided to avoid the evening meal, and mother decided that Uncle John needed to go back to the hospital.

Losing Uncle John interrupted my baseball training, and about that time, my mother embarked on her efforts to discover and/or develop some sense of femininity in me. She thought I should bathe and wash my hair more often. For a while, she tried to model glamour, describing the proper use of cosmetics and constantly asking me if her face powder was caked. How would I know? I could easily calibrate the ratio of oil to gas for a two-cycle engine, but I had absolutely no idea of how to apply powder and lipstick, nor did I want to learn. One of the most fearful moments of my generally fearless life was a time when I had to deliver a telephone message to my mother while she was under the hair dryer in a neighborhood beauty parlor. I still remember the feeling of panic as I opened the door, an illegal alien entering a women's world.

My mother was particularly distressed when I was named center on the 90-pound YMCA boys' football team; she renewed her attempts at a sex change, mine. She announced that I could no longer play with the boys in the park. Actually, she would have been thrilled if I "played" with boys the way most girls did, the shy giggles, the flirting, the flattery. But my play was the rough-and-tumble touching of young males still more interested in physical contact than sexual innuendo. I sat on the steps of our front porch, looking across the street to the park, a familiar but now distant shore to which I could not return. Hurt and helpless, all my boyish bravado vanished; I sobbed like the sissy girl my mother wanted me to be.

As my lucky life would have it, however, I found a grown-up women's softball team, with lots of folks who looked like me. The women, most of whom worked in the mills, cross-dressed and were as good at brawling as they were at softball. Because I already knew how to play ball, I enthusiastically applied myself to a new endeavor, fighting. Skilled in boxing, I now learned more specific techniques of bare-fisted combat, keys between fingers, well-placed knees, and so on. Like most southern boys my age, I learned to cover any feelings of fear and affect a fierceness that I actually came to enjoy. Physical competition was clear to me; I understood the dictates of brute strength and could gauge the caliber of my opponents, including the police who were often called to break up our softball fights. I knew the thrill of contact and the benefits of cease-fire. Indeed, the long-term physical abuse that I visited on my little brother ended abruptly one day when he flexed his muscles and slammed me through a door. No parental interference, no psychotherapy and/or mediation, just immediate conflict resolution and simple justice through one well-placed punch. I knew how to hit people, but I didn't know how to hug them.

My sullen, silent conflict with my mother continued. I begged her to let me leave home and live somewhere else. She suggested the girls' reformatory, but, barring that, insisted that I stay with her until I graduated from high school. I pleaded to live with my father, who had remarried. My brother and I met him weekly in downtown Birmingham. We would walk through the streets, the change jingling in his pockets, and visit the dime stores to look at the toys. Before we got on the bus to go home, we would have a banana split at Lane's drugstore. I don't think he ever knew how much those visits meant to me or how much I adored my stepmother. At one point, it was arranged that I might move in with them, a plan that crashed around me when my stepmother thought it better that I not live with my father. She could tolerate his drinking and womanizing, but she didn't think that I should have to. I escaped to softball, where my teammates appreciated and applauded my athletic skills, and to high school, where my interests were girls, sports, and cars, in that order. I dated boys from school, and although we were too shy to talk about girls, we spent long hours working on cars and discussing high school football and our beloved minor league baseball team, the Birmingham Barons.

Another resource for me was that eternal lesbian savior, the gym teacher. Louise Pope happened to be straight, but she took a special interest in me and how well I did in school. When I barely missed being inducted into the National Honor Society, she went roaring into the principal's office to demand an explanation. Aside from Uncle John, no one else had ever seemed that interested in my grades. Mrs. Pope changed my life. Although I had no plans or money for college, she simply applied to her old school for me. I signed the applications enthusiastically when I received a physical education scholarship, which she arranged, and realized that I would be attending an all-women's college.

The day I graduated from high school, I left home and rented a room in north Birmingham so I could take a summer job at what we would now call an inner-city public swimming pool. Here again I had other run-ins with the police, as my new friends at the pool were constantly being questioned about their assaults, shoplifting, and various other questionable adventures. One guy I dated for a while, Pete, was convicted of vehicular homicide and statutory rape (not with me). A few years later, I visited him at the state penitentiary, grateful but confused that he was behind the brick walls of the prison while I strolled the brick walks of Alabama College.

Attending college meant coming home to a loving family. My first weekend, I was invited to a Baptist Student Union retreat that was held at the campus lake house and developed my first college crush on a prayer date. Then, one of the seniors tucked me into bed, leaned over, and kissed me good night (although only on the forehead), a completely new and joyous event for me. I happily settled into a warm world where I was financially independent and well taken care of emotionally. Scholarships and a job waiting tables gave me funds to cover my tuition, fees, room and board, health care, and laundry. During the summers I lived on campus while I worked as a lifeguard and taught swimming at the town creek. I had a paper route and delivered movie announcements for the local theater. I never returned to my mother's home. I had found a new family of women that satisfied my every longing; I would stay in school the rest of my life.

Surrounded by women students and women faculty, it never occurred to me that men were necessary or useful in the life of the school. We ran our student government (I was elected recreational director), wrote and produced our own plays, dissected cadavers, learned opera, and generally completed the usual academic requirements and extracurricular activities with a sense of self-sufficiency and pride. My junior year, I was devastated to learn that my college would become coeducational to increase enrollment and avoid financial disaster; I preferred bankruptcy.

The addition of men to the student body threw my college life into disarray. I now had to compete with men for a woman's time, and I was no longer cast as the male romantic lead in our theatrical productions. I tried dating some of the male jocks. We hiked the hills around the college, swam the creeks, and explored caves and the old mines that had played out years before. Once, on an outdoor adventure, as we were about to stumble on an illegal still, a bearded man with a shotgun, who could have starred in *Deliverance*, blocked our path. We quickly decided on another direction—one of the few times I was delighted to be with a guy instead of a girl.

In college, I discovered women, reading, and writing, in that order. In the South, one does not admit to being intellectually inclined, nor did I ever discuss my divergent sexual patterns. I did spend a great deal of time wondering in what ways I was similar to and/or different from others. I was comforted by the fact that southerners are actually very good about accepting the peculiarities of family members, friends, and people they like. As far as I could tell, most unusual activities on the part of people I knew personally didn't seem to get them into too much trouble, except for my Uncle John, who kept being carted off to the hospital, and my Uncle Cliff, who was killed by a tax revenue agent. Still, I was increasingly curious about how someone comes to be the person she or he is, especially me. I gave up my earlier questions about the faraway worlds of stars and galaxies and began to wonder about people rather than planets. Sports also became less precious to me. My physical education classes were fun, but classes in camp craft gave me no clues as to why my grandmother became psychotic, fly casting no hints as to whether families needed fathers. Volleyball and synchronized swimming taught me something about getting along with others, but little of the dynamics of interpersonal interactions.

Physical education majors didn't usually go on to graduate school, but the two faculty members (50% female) in our Philosophy, Psychology, and Religion Department encouraged me to pursue psychology and apply to graduate school. Professor Herb Eber, whom I had met on the tennis courts, convinced me that a year in graduate school might not be as much fun as coaching high school sports, but it would be a chance to travel and a year of adventure in a foreign culture. I had never been further north than Tennessee. Once again, a teacher filled out applications for me; Professor Eber assured me that assistantship support would match the full-time salary that I would receive teaching physical education. He also assured me that I could always return South if I didn't like psychology and living with Yankees. The idea of 4 more years of school was compelling, even if I had to move North. At that time, I didn't realize that the further one went in school, the fewer women one encountered, as either teachers or students.

Attending the Clinical Psychology Program of the Ohio State University was another dream come true. I was in classes with famous faculty, and the university was a premier football and basketball powerhouse. Jules Rotter and I played tennis, and he supported me on a research assistantship. These were the heady days of the beginning research on locus of control and need for approval. Graduate students were expected to involve themselves immediately in research and to aim for an academic position. Further, the Ohio State clinical program, especially through Rotter's efforts, prided itself on the diversity of its students and its large proportion of women. Surrounded by Yankees and Republicans and fitting no known minority category, I immediately found a Black southern woman to room with. We both had double names, spoke the same language, and ate the same food. I felt discriminated against only once, when Rotter denounced the hundred thousand "noodle heads," which included me, who filled the football stadium every Saturday afternoon.

Having been in school for 19 of my 25 years, and having received my Ph.D., I was now faced with another life dilemma. I could remain in school by changing majors once again or by finding a job in academia. A faculty position in clinical psychology was clearly tempting. As a teacher in psychology, I could spend my life reading, writing, and talking about human behavior. Perhaps I could finally learn why my Uncle John had become schizophrenic and whether I would as well. I was troubled, however, that being lesbian had already marked me as mentally ill and distressed that clinical psychology seemed to designate any number of differences as disorders and deficiencies. Although not quite diagnosable, being a woman was no big help either. I was considered for faculty positions at several major universities only to be told that although my record was very good, they had decided to hire a *man* instead. Little did they know that they could have hired me and never noticed the difference. Dr. Rotter finally found me a job at Emory University. I welcomed the chance to return South, where I reverted to my first language and could stay outdoors all year.

My public and private lives were distinct and disconnected in my early years in Atlanta. The suburban manicured elegance of Emory, with its well-mannered students, was a far cry from the noisy downtown streets where demonstrations, predominantly by Black protesters, launched the civil rights movement. I longed for another kind of integration that merged the classroom with the lessons of the streets; I never realized until much later how torn I felt about the lack of integration in my professional and personal lives. My teaching, research, and clinical practice never overlapped with my social world of playing on yet another women's softball team and partying with my predominantly lesbian friends and lovers. With few exceptions, my work colleagues and close women friends never met. My partner's picture was *not* on my office desk, and my friends preferred the sports pages over my research articles. I attended faculty events with handsome, charming gay men who were judged by my colleagues to be high-quality husband potential. My faculty acquaintances, like my family, were happily matchmaking, benignly indifferent to the fact that I would rather have a wife than be one.

At times, there were magic moments of centering and integration. One of my first projects, which eventually became a Citation Classic, found Black college student activists, in contrast to those less involved in the civil rights movement, to be significantly more internal than external in their beliefs about locus of control. And perhaps the most welcomed blending of my personal and professional boundaries was our early research on the mental health status of socially functioning gay men and lesbians. My women friends, although not altogether sympathetic to psychology, became a part of the largest sample of lesbians ever involved in research up until that time. Norm Thompson's doctoral dissertation and David Schwartz's master's thesis were explorations of the perceived child-rearing histories and personal adjustment of socially functioning gay men and lesbians in relation to their heterosexual counterparts. We found no differences between the homosexual and heterosexual samples in reported self-adjustment, and were pleasantly surprised to learn that lesbians were more self-confident and gay men less defensive than their counterparts. This in spite of the fact that I hadn't been at all certain that my lesbian friends, or I, for that matter, were models of mental health. Little or no research had been done, then or now, on the social development of gay men and lesbians. But we also found that the members of our homosexual sample reported themselves to have engaged in different patterns of childhood play than had the controls. As any dyke could have told us, adult lesbians were more likely to have played organized sports than were straight women. And, as every queen knows, gay men were not as likely to have played competitively.

Atlanta was a mecca for gay men and lesbians, although the term *lesbian* was never used and *dyke* was considered an expression of contempt. The big city of Atlanta offered large closets of opportunities for gays and lesbians from all over the South. It was not only the center of the civil rights movement, it was home to a homosexual population whose members never considered taking their concerns into the streets. I fell in love, dated, and became friends, usually in that order, with a large circle of lesbians. We remain close friends to this day.

This social group has been together and expanding for almost 40 years. A woman falls in love with someone new and, after a few months of bickering with her ex and the rest of us, rejoins us with her new lover. Well, perhaps *bickering* is not strong enough, especially given that one of our group shot out the windshield of another after that woman had run off with her long-term partner. Nonetheless, the weekly poker games and bowling tournaments continue, although we 50- and 60-year-olds are more likely to play golf than softball; 18 holes are a lot easier to get around than three bases. We are building our retirement homes close together, and when someone in the group becomes sick or ill, the women compete to take care of her. Because our social circle includes physicians and plumbers, we can usually attend to any contingency. When I visited Atlanta during the spring of 1996, I stayed with an old true love and her partner of more than a decade. Late one evening, after her partner had gone to bed, we sat comfortably, with me watching the news and her working on a crossword puzzle, like the old married couple we could have been. We still delighted in each other's company and talked about our past adventures, including the only time in Atlanta that I was accosted by the police. She and I had climbed Stone Mountain, young lovers happily on a picnic far away from the crowds. We spread out a blanket on a rock outcropping, sunbathing, confident of our privacy. Suddenly, two police officers in a helicopter descended on us like thunder. I don't who was more surprised. They averted their eyes, stumbled around, and finally chased us away, saying that we were out of bounds of the picnic area.

Living as a lesbian in the South in the 1960s, even in enlightened Atlanta, meant living in the closet and worrying about the police. Being on the faculty at Emory and serving as dean of women, I was especially careful about being known publicly as homosexual. Actually, this was true of most of my friends, whether they were schoolteachers, realtors, insurance agents, or whatever. Gay bars were raided regularly, and police keep records of gays and lesbians through automobile license plate numbers. Although I managed to avoid most encounters, my friends would tell me of being at parties in private homes and escaping through windows and down back alleys when the police arrived to arrest them simply for socializing with friends.

We restricted most of our activities to softball, basketball, poker, and occasional private parties. Many of my lesbian friends lived close together in the new apartment complexes that were being built in the suburbs of Atlanta, and we planned our own exclusive social and sports events. One friend, Sylvia, having access to tennis courts where she lived, held a HOTT (Homosexuals Only Tennis Tournament) complete with "official" ball girls, line judges, umpire, and photographer. Large lesbian audiences surrounded the courts, and winners were celebrated with a champagne party. When one of the group was picking up the T-shirts that had been ordered with the initials of the tournament imprinted on them, she was asked what HOTT stood for. She thought quickly and responded, "Hell of a Tennis Tournament." It was a hell of a tournament. My doubles partner and I won and moved into a new partnership of 18 years.

By this time, I had bought a home not far from Emory that became a center of subversive activity, not only for my lesbian and gay friends, but for clergy and student demonstrators involved in the civil rights movement. I never actually marched, but I would pick up the protesters at the ends of rallies in my Mustang convertible. We would retreat to the Quaker House, banners blowing in the wind, where I attended my first underground Mass, led by Philip Berrigan. I also met Dr. Martin Luther King, Jr., and eventually, sadly, helped arrange volunteers to assist with his funeral. With word of his assassination, Emory students, not known for their liberal proclivities, became instant members of the Southern Christian Leadership Conference. They staffed phone lines, baby-sat the King children, and draped large identifying placards on their expensive sports cars so they could drive through the streets of Atlanta and pick up visitors as they arrived at the airport and bus station.

The years at Emory were rich and rewarding. Although the administration never quite knew what to make of me, I will always be grateful that they hired a woman on the faculty and even asked me to be dean of women for a time. As dean, I delighted in those aspects of administration that not only allowed me to be a recreational director again but introduced me to women students across disciplines. For many I was their first and only female university administrator and/or professor. Some were lesbian, although we never discussed this aspect of their lives, or mine. Rather, we talked about their interests in careers and professional pursuits. Like my mentors, I sent a number off to graduate school whether they wanted to go or not. Many have become distinguished in their own right. I treasure our continued contact, and those who are lesbian and I sometimes review our closeted pasts and wish that we could have been more open. Bright young women, lesbian or straight, did not have an easy time growing up in the South in the 1960s, even though the conservative and parochial attitudes of Atlanta and Emory were bastions of liberalism in contrast to the intolerance of the rural Southeast. Recalling the last time the Yankees had some advice for the South, White southerners had built their barriers of bigotry against social change, refusing to accept integration and aghast at the thought of a women's movement. I chafed under the conservative bounds of Emory apathy; the terms *gay* and *lesbian* were unknown, and Emory students affirmed the war in Vietnam. Promotion and tenure had been difficult to come by for me; my woman partner, a high school basketball coach, had a salary almost equal to mine. In the early 1970s, I also spent a sabbatical leave in Hawaii, where my only continuing education was scuba diving. I began to wonder if there might be life beyond Emory and the South, although I really couldn't imagine leaving Atlanta and my friendship network.

On a job interview at the University of Massachusetts at Amherst in the spring of 1973, I pushed my way through the Student Union, surrounded by the aroma of drugs I had never smelled at Emory. Students in tie-dye staffed tables laden with flyers filled with information on almost every major or minor social movement. The community of Amherst had held a 9-year vigil against the war in Vietnam. The president of Amherst College had been to jail along with hundreds of student and faculty demonstrators who had shut down the five colleges. UMass was and is a "people's university," with most of the students, like me, first-generation college. I joined the Psychology Department, which already comprised more women and minority faculty than had ever been hired in the history of Emory.

My partner (from Alabama) had no intention of moving North until she visited me during the fall of my first semester. Seeing the beauty of New England (before the brutality of winter), she decided to join me in the Pioneer Valley. We were a faculty couple warmly welcomed by my colleagues and dean.

No doubt, being lesbian, female, and southern, I have been belittled and discriminated against at UMass. In fact, students walked out of the first classes that I taught when they heard my southern accent. Like most universities, UMass is plagued by institutional sexism, homophobia, and other prejudices. I prefer, however, to recall a charming incident of acceptance. The 5-year-old daughter of my next-door neighbors asked her mother, a social psychologist in my department, why I didn't have a "daddy" living with me. Ronnie carefully explained that my partner and I loved each other just like she loved the child's father. The youngster, having never seriously considered this possible arrangement before, frowned for a moment and then cheerfully announced that when she grew up, she would marry her best girlfriend (another faculty couple's 3-year-old daughter).

My partner and I settled into life in the Valley, a community rich with a history that began well before white Europeans settled these shores. I finally learned something about the first War of Independence. And I was delighted to discover that I lived close to the site where Daniel Shay led the only other armed rebellion against the government of the United States. I was even more intrigued to learn about the sites of the Underground Railroad and about Sojourner Truth, who joined a long line of strong women who to this day live in the Northampton area.

I also found a new family of friends and faculty that increasingly became a true blending of my public, professional, private, and personal lives. I began to teach courses in the psychology of women and to conduct research in women's health. For 5 years I served as department chair, which allowed me to be recreation director again. I planned department socials, only one of which was ever closed down by the police. We organized a sports program and proudly cheered our co-rec volleyball team to a university intramural championship. We also had a co-rec tag football team of some renown, because one of our male faculty had to be removed from the games regularly for fighting. Our women's intramural football team shared not one whit of this competitive spirit; we never won a game (our season average score was –2). We did, however, compete among each other; when one of our players sent our own linebacker to the infirmary with a concussion, I knew it was time for me to go back to softball.

I joined a team in a feminist league, where we spent more time deliberating the nature of politically correct competition than playing. Some of us secretly called ourselves the Politically Incorrect Girls (PIGs) because we wanted to keep score and liked to win. In spite of our competitive stance, however, we never came close to fighting even our archrivals the Hot Flashes. Rather, we held homecoming celebrations complete with lesbian queens and one majorette (with hair under her arms). As best I can recall, the state troopers were called only once, when a woman's team held a sit-in on second base while two men's teams played each other, thinking they had scheduled the field.

In the spring of 1992, I hitched a ride toward the Cape with some of my department colleagues who were attending an undergraduate curriculum meeting at another university. The director of our Under-graduate Studies Committee asked if I would consider teaching a new course on health psychology. Feeling rather generous of spirit, as I was on my way to Provincetown, I offered to teach lesbian psychology. You would have thought I had endowed a building. The members of the Undergraduate Studies Committee and the department chair, none of whom were gay or lesbian, jumped at the chance to have such a course offering. The secretaries helped type the syllabus, and the Provost's Office found funds for an additional teaching assistant and helped shepherd the course through the Faculty Senate (without dissenting vote). The Chancellor's Task Force on Gay, Lesbian, and Bisexual Issues was ecstatic, and the chancellor himself was quite pleased.

The first time I offered "The Psychology of Differences: The Lesbian Experience" (affectionately called Dyke Psych), I had thought that mostly lesbians would sign up for the course. In fact, I mentioned to the class that I had hoped to have all lesbians. The class members—lesbians, straight women, and three men—attacked as one. I apologized profusely and begged to start again, knowing immediately that I would have to redefine differences and reach new heights of sensitivity about straight people and sexual minorities.

We read about Greek goddesses, Boston marriages, and contemporary lesbian couples. Our guest lecturers were lesbian poets, writer, mothers, and transsexual performance artists. We found that every part of psychology had something to teach us, from human development through sexual differentiation to prejudice, social change, and our fears of the radical Right. We may have overemphasized interpersonal attraction and emotional intimacy in that we all talked openly and earnestly with each other about our social and sexual selves in a homophobic and sexist society. We discussed our differences, but talked more about our similarities. We shared our weaknesses, but more often celebrated our strengths.

Class members kept personal journals and worked on group projects of their own choosing. One group, mostly straight, having identified a new arena (for them) of social injustice, wanted to hold massive demonstrations on behalf of gays, lesbians, and transgendered persons. They may have secretly wished to close down the campus, but they sponsored a "Gay Awareness Day" instead. The day's events, held on the steps of the Student Union, were enormously successful, with speakers, lesbian music, tie-dye lavender T-shirts, and several hundred home-baked pink triangle cookies. The student newspaper headlined the happening with amazingly positive editorials and press coverage. Students of every sexual persuasion seemed to enjoy the idea of a new civil rights movement for social justice.

Several student groups, using class members, produced videos, including one on gay and straight women's reactions to lesbian music. Another video portrayed the story of a straight male who wakes up in a completely gay and lesbian world. Being in a heterosexual marriage, he can't get a job, rent an apartment, or enroll his children in school. Another group project was a replication of prior research showing that male, highly religious, politically conservative students, especially those who did not know a lesbian personally, were significantly more prejudiced toward lesbians than were students with other characteristics. Five undergraduates, all straight, presented these findings at a national psychology convention. Their poster, a serious collection of tables and statistics, was decorated with the multicolors of the gay flag. Dazzled by its brilliance, more than one conference participant remarked on the only psychedelic poster they had ever seen at a professional conference.

Each time I teach the class, we end with a dinner party at my home. We watch the class videos and, at one party, were entertained by a live lesbian band. At another party, which was held in December, the straight boys and butches first argued about and then helped each other put up the Christmas tree; students of every religious and sexual persuasion decorated it.

Having always been drawn to the water, my partner and I built a lakefront home 6 miles from UMass and another 6 miles to Northampton (Lesbianville, USA). We also have always had a home on the white, sandy beaches of the "forgotten" coast of Florida, close to my relatives and the swamps. A few years ago, we decided to separate, and she moved back to the redneck Riviera. She's family; I love her dearly and I try to visit often. Also, like my mother and most southerners, I love to entertain and have people come to visit and stay as long as they can. Once, in Atlanta, my "little sister" from college called and asked if she could come over to talk about some romantic problem. Jane arrived, with her dog, Ginger, and stayed for a year and a half.

Jane and I first met when I was 17 and she a year younger. We've always joked about her being my oldest and dearest living friend, but at age 58, she is dying of cancer. She lives in a suburban Atlanta neighborhood with at least four lesbian couples within two or three doors of her. Since she has been ill, she has been continually surrounded by her birth sisters and her extended lesbian family. Some months ago I went to Atlanta to see her. Known for her parties, Jane, as usual, arranged a gathering of old friends to visit while I was there. As she became tired and went to bed early, I climbed in with her, holding her until she fell asleep. None of us welcomes pain, and most of us fear death. But, like Jane, I rest comforted in my advancing years by the clear and constant care of an extended lesbian family. They have been with me as long as I have known how to love, and they will never leave me.

At this time in my life, I live happily in the beautiful Pioneer Valley. I still enjoy outdoor sports—hiking, biking, swimming, and sailing on the lake in the summer. During the winter, downhill ski slopes are close by and I keep my cross-country skis on my deck to use on the lake or on the wooded trails around my home. In fact, I've been taking breaks from working on this chapter to go cross-country skiing with my chocolate Labrador retriever, Murphy Brown. Somewhat impaired in winter sports, another consequence of being southern, I am further handicapped when Murphy romps happily through my carefully groomed tracks and tries to retrieve the skis, with me on them. I also enjoy soaking in my outdoor hot tub, a far cry from those no. 2 washtubs of my past filled with water heated on a wood stove. At night, Murphy and I curl up in bed together, joined by my three cats. The animals are comforting and cuddly, but I'd rather have a friendly human face on the pillow.

My social life is crowded and my Yankee friendship network wide. I've even started going to church again after 42 years of considering the term *Christian lesbian*, or vice versa, an oxymoron. I attend Congregational services (only an hour a week) and am always warmly welcomed by the lesbian minister as well as by a deacon who looks like the quintessential white-haired Yankee of a Norman Rockwell painting. He seems genuinely glad to have me in church along with other out lesbians from the community. His handshake shows no hint of sexual interest—nor does the preacher's, for that matter.

After three decades in academia, I have discovered what I do best: sabbatical. Once, my partner and I went around the world on standby. I have visited Thailand and Tibet and learned not to call people "heathen." On my last sabbatical I cruised the Mediterranean, shopped in Morocco, and rafted through the glowworm caves of New Zealand. This last winter break, I climbed temples in Burma, explored Angkor Wat in Cambodia, and hiked the rural highlands of North Vietnam. Occasionally I meet with psychologists and talk with women's groups, but I mostly enjoy the excitement of foreign adventures with enthusiastic traveling companions.

Having left the South and the closet, I still return as often as I can to Florida. Several lesbian friends originally from Atlanta also live in beach homes right next to mine. We feel accepted by and a part of our small community of 1,200 people. In fact, one of our straight friends warned the new Methodist preacher in town that she better be open to and affirming of the local lesbian and gay folks if she wanted to be successful in the church.

The last time I visited, my ex and I went next door to see our friend Sylvia, the same Sylvia who arranged the HOTT some 25 years ago. She bought my house when I left Atlanta and now lives retired and happy in another home she bought from me on the beach. As usual on a Saturday night, her home was filled with straight people from the community and lesbian friends from Atlanta. The same woman who had picked up the HOTT T-shirts so long ago strummed her guitar and, lesbian and straight alike, we sang old songs that bridged our growing-up years of the 1950s and 1960s. I thought about my cousins a few miles away, preachers and poachers, some just out of jail for fishing the bay for drugs instead of shrimp, others well-off folk who developed the Tupelo honey business in Florida. My Uncle Jennings is too frail to go oystering these days, but three generations of his children and grandchildren still take him fishing.

Having always wanted to be a southern gentleman, I still sometimes feel like a stranger in New England and occasionally envy my brother his storybook life. Named after my father with the initials of Robert E. Lee (from whom every southerner claims to be a direct descendant), my brother completed college on a full-time tennis scholarship and, with the help of military benefits, became a dentist and opened a practice in the South. He married a beautiful southern debutante, and they built an elegant home with swimming pool and lighted tennis court. Perhaps most important, they've raised two lovely daughters. My nieces were recently presented to society at their debutante cotillions. The South has become more enlightened, but they still "came out" as the gracious southern belles they are, not as lesbians.

Even though my brother has a lovely wife and the joy of daughters, is nationally ranked in Master's tennis, and seems to have recovered fully from the childhood physical abuse I perpetrated, I would not change my life for his. At one time, I might have welcomed the comfort and safety of society's acceptance in exchange for the feeling of being different. But I have learned, finally, that sometimes being strange is more of a blessing than a burden. My life as a lesbian is full and happy. I believe that I could live openly now almost anywhere. As a displaced southerner whose accent betrays me at my every word, however, I still feel torn between the North and the South. I think of those long, lazy southern seasons that shaped me, blurring boundaries and the sharp edges of sexuality. And I look at my Confederate flag and long for faraway family, friends, and old lovers. I wish we were all together.

4

Female, Lesbian, and Jewish
Complex and Invisible

SARI H. DWORKIN

Literature exploring research and theory about the difficulties of being a lesbian in a heterosexual dominant culture is abundant (Dworkin & Gutierrez, 1992a; Gonsiorek & Weinrich, 1991; Greene & Herek, 1994). Also prevalent are papers discussing the problems of being Jewish in a predominantly Christian society (Goldberg & Krausz, 1993; Gordis & Ben-Horin, 1991). Psychologists are just beginning to explore what is involved in the task of combining two marginal identities—being Jewish and lesbian—as well as the mental health problems that can result from the unsuccessful integration of these two identities. The literature in this area has been of a conceptual nature thus far. In this chapter I continue in that vein from a self psychology framework. It is my hope that empirical research will evolve from the conceptual exploration of these issues. My purposes in this chapter are to assist therapists working with women who are both lesbian and Jewish and to emphasize the importance of addressing these two, often invisible, identities within the therapeutic process.

It is important to consider briefly the psychological literature that theorizes about the development of the self, as we are dealing here with two self-identities. A comprehensive discussion of self psychology is beyond the scope of this chapter; however, some concepts of this framework are relevant to an understanding of the psychological difficulties inherent in developing a cohesive identity when two important aspects of the self are seen as marginal. Marginality results from a sense of differentness, which can lead to narcissistic injury and thereby result in loss of self-esteem and a fragmentation of the self. Gonsiorek and Rudolph (1991) provide a more detailed description of self psychology concepts applied to the coming-out process. According to self psychology, we all require mirroring self-objects during the course of development in order to regulate positive self-esteem (Baker, 1991). A *self-object* is defined as that part of something or someone else that is incorporated into the self. Lesbians may have difficulty developing the necessary mirroring self-objects in a society that is heterosexist and homophobic. Similarly, Jewish people may experience difficulty developing the necessary mirroring self-objects in a dominant Christian and anti-Semitic society. Difficult past and ongoing relationships can affect a woman's intrapsychic reality and damage her movement toward a cohesive sense of self. Psychological symptoms such as anxiety, depression, and rage may result. Another difficulty that may be experienced by a woman who is both a lesbian and a Jew is that of fulfilling idealizing self-object needs. Idealizing self-object needs help us to maintain a sense of connectedness and thereby help to regulate affect (Baker, 1991). Lesbians can usually find a lesbian community to meet lesbian idealizing self-object needs. Jewish women can find a Jewish community to meet Jewish idealizing self-object needs. Meeting idealizing self-object needs as a Jewish lesbian or lesbian Jew, however, may be difficult, in ways that this chapter will explore. It is important for the professional who examines the psychological needs of a woman who must combine these two identities to determine which identity is more prominent for her and why. It is also important that the professional determine which identity is the noun and which is the adjective. Wahba (1989) states, "I am a Jew and I have become a lesbian, and so I am a lesbian Jew" (p. 53). A lesbian's definition for herself can have important implications for therapy. Before a discussion of therapeutic considerations is possible, a basic understanding of the challenges involved in successfully integrating Jewish and lesbian identities is necessary.

Coming Out

The term *coming out* has implications for lesbians and for Jews, even though it is usually used only in connection with the development of a lesbian identity. De Monteflores and Schultz (1978) define coming out as a process whereby a lesbian adopts a nontraditional identity, restructures her self-concept, and reorganizes her personal history in order to fit that identity. The process of coming out as a lesbian encompasses four general stages: awareness, testing and exploration, identity acceptance, and identity integration (Sophie, 1985-1986). Briefly, awareness involves the woman's recognition that there is a category of persons called lesbians and that she may belong to that category. The stage of testing and exploration involves the woman's beginning to seek out other lesbians and coming out to some people. Identity acceptance involves the woman's acceptance of herself as a lesbian, and, finally, identity integration involves the woman's integration of her sexual orientation with the other aspects of her identity. For a Jewish lesbian, coming out as a Jew within the lesbian community can involve the same general stages. First, awareness occurs when Judaism begins to assume the importance for the woman that lesbian identity has assumed. Testing and exploration may be observed when a Jewish lesbian tests the lesbian community's acceptance of non-Jewish identity. Identity acceptance involves the woman's realization that her identity is that of a Jewish lesbian. Identity integration is the stage in which the Jewish lesbian develops pride about this consolidated identity (Dworkin, 1990).

A part of the coming-out process is the alteration of relationships with other people and with society as a whole. For a lesbian in a heterosexual society, one that continuously presumes the heterosexuality of most persons, there are always situations in which she will be required to make a decision about whether or not to come out as a lesbian. For a Jew in a Christian culture, the situation is much the same. Each time a Jewish woman makes a conscious decision not to remain invisible as a Jew, she comes out as a Jew (Wahba, 1989). Claiming a lesbian identity, a Jewish identity, or both identities carries costs and benefits. Claiming both identities means, among other things, grappling with persuading the heterosexual community that a lesbian identity is more complicated than sexual behavior and simultaneously persuading the lesbian community that a Jewish identity is more complex than mere religious affiliation (Klepfisz, 1990). "Jewish invisibility is a symptom of anti-Semitism as surely as lesbian invisibility is a symptom of homophobia" (Beck, 1982b, p. xv). Invisibility offers some protection and security in a hostile, insecure world, and there are certainly historical reasons for remaining invisible as a lesbian and as a Jew.

History

Anti-Semitism has existed throughout the world and throughout history. Since the time of Hitler, every Jew has been affected by the Holocaust in some way, no matter when that Jew was born (Beck, 1990). Until the end of World War II, Jews in the United States faced overt discrimination in jobs, housing, college admissions, and other areas of life (Beck, 1990; Brown, 1990).

Jews now face less overt discrimination in the United States, but anti-Semitism is still pervasive. Newspaper articles continually report events that confirm the existence of anti-Semitism. The skinheads in Billings, Montana, and Portland, Oregon, paint swastikas on homes and synagogues ("Montana City Reacts," 1994). An aide to Louis Farrakhan described Jews as "blood suckers of the black nation and the black community" (Taylor, 1994, p. A18). Vladimir V. Zhirinovsky, a Russian ultranationalist, won an election in Russia on a platform that defines the Jew as foreigner and unwanted in Russia (Erlanger, 1994). The civil unrest, rise of Islamic fundamentalism, and political instability in what used to be the Soviet Union raise new fears for Jews in that area of the world as flagrant anti-Semitism increases (Erlanger, 1994). Revisionist historians maintain that the Holocaust never took place. Estimates from a 1993 poll suggest that 62% of people in the United States share this belief (Riding, 1993). Beck (1990) believes that "most Jews, even the most assimilated walk around with a subliminal fear of anti-Semitism the way most women walk around with a subliminal fear of rape" (p. 22).

In many ways the lesbian experience parallels the Jewish experience (Klepfisz, 1990; Rogow, 1989). Both lesbians and Jews struggle against prejudice and advocate and struggle for civil rights and for the right to be visible. They also grapple with the conflict between assimilating and passing or maintaining a separate identity to work against bigotry and ignorance (Wahba, 1989). Throughout history, both Jews and gay people have been considered dispensable; they have suffered physical, verbal, and emotional abuse and have been put to death solely because of who they are (Beck, 1989; Rogow, 1989; Rose & Balka, 1989; Wahba, 1989). Tens of thousands of gay and lesbian people were put to death along with the millions of Jews murdered by Hitler's regime (Rogow, 1989). At various times throughout history, Jews have been forced to convert to Christianity and gay/lesbian people have been forced to "convert" to heterosexuality or to remain invisible. During the Inquisition, Jews were forced to convert or flee (Rose & Balka, 1989). Many became *Conversos,* outwardly converting to Christianity but continuing to practice the Jewish religion secretly.

Jewish people and gay/lesbian people have a long history of culture and traditions, have to expend enormous amounts of energy on resistance and survival, practice some rituals that have lost their meanings, and have special colors associated with their cultures (blue and white for Jews, purple for gay/lesbian) (Beck, 1989). Gay/lesbian people and Jewish people have both lived between two cultures.

Learning to pass—as an assimilated Jew, a heterosexual, or both—has been the norm for Jewish lesbians (Rose & Balka, 1989). Jewish immigrants have changed their names in order to become more Americanized (Kantrowitz, 1992; Kaye, 1982). Jewish women have undergone nose jobs, straightened their hair, and sat on their hands to avoid gesturing and to fit into the dominant cultural stereotypes of "normal" females. In the 1960s, Jewish college students in New York City were often forced to take speech classes to learn how to speak without dentalizing consonants, a characteristic of speakers of Yiddish (Klepfisz, 1990). The early activists of the 1960s within the antiwar movement, the women's movement, and the lesbian movement denied the seriousness of anti-Semitism both in their midst and in the society by failing to acknowledge its existence. Once again, Jewish and lesbian women felt the need to pass to survive (Beck, 1982a; Klepfisz, 1982, 1990). Anti-Semitism has not been considered an important issue within the feminist movement (Klepfisz, 1982, 1990), and multicultural aspects of women's studies curricula rarely include the struggles of Jewish women (Beck, 1990). The message has been and continues to be, "If you are a Jew it doesn't pay to advertise" (Weinrach, 1990, p. 548).

Stereotypes

Much of the anti-Semitism throughout history has been based on negative depictions and stereotypes of the ethnic and cultural features of Jews. Nazis founded much of their ideology of Jewish inferiority on the size and shape of the heads and noses of Jews. Stereotyping has continued within the lesbian and feminist communities in the form of such images as the "Jewish American princess" (or JAP) and the suffocating "Jewish mother" (Rofes, 1989; Siegel, 1986). Negative stereotypes are reflected in the denigration of ethnic behavior characteristic of some Jewish women. This may be observed in the depiction of a passionate, loud style of relating as pushy and aggressive (Kantrowitz, 1992; Rich, 1989; Rofes, 1989; Siegel, 1986). It may also be observed in the blaming of the ancient Hebrews for the destruction of the matriarchy (Beck, 1982b; Daum, 1982; Hendricks, 1985; Heschel, 1990; Plaskow, 1982), as well as in the expression of anti-Israel sentiments and the practice of equating Zionism with racism (Beck, 1989). The stereotype of Jewish women as Jewish American princesses negatively stigmatizes and assaults both women and Jews. For Jews, this stereotype conveys the message that the American dream is not intended for them. It is as if upward mobility is allowed, encouraged, and even desired for members of other ethnic minority groups, but for Jews the same behavior is seen as greedy, avaricious, and unsavory (Beck, 1990). Even in lesbian communities the JAP stereotype persists, sending Jewish lesbians the message that they are not safe anywhere (Beck, 1990). Negative and all-too-familiar stereotypes of Jews as "pushy, loud, money grubbing, [and] exploitative," and, particularly, that "they are taking over again, in the schools, the art world, even the movement" remind them of the constant danger of potential discrimination and harm they confront (Kantrowitz, 1992, pp. 83-84).

Religion

Historically, especially during the Holocaust, there has been confusion about whether Jews constitute a separate race, a particular religious group, a particular ethnic/cultural group, or some combination of all of these things. Currently, some Jews and gentiles perceive Jews as white, whereas other Jews and some gentiles consider Jews to be persons of color. A lesbian client of mine who was a member of an ethnic minority group stated that one of the reasons she felt comfortable working with me was that she considered Jews to be part of people of color. As a Jew of Eastern European descent, I consider myself to be white, although I agree with Melanie Kaye Kantrowitz's (1992) contention that I am not, nor is my culture, Anglo-American. An examination of the worldwide community of Jews makes it clear that we come in all different races, colors, and cultures. The majority of Jews in the United States are Ashkenazim, with their origins in the former Soviet Union and Eastern Europe. Sephardic Jews have their origins in Spain and the Mediterranean countries. What all Jews have in common is that we are a historically oppressed minority group. This is an important commonality, and the one most often emphasized, but it is only one of many common links.

The response of many Jews to lesbianism is based in part on certain interpretations of Jewish religious beliefs. Therefore, it is important for therapists working with Jewish lesbian clients to have some basic understanding of Judaism and its evolution within the United States. There are primarily three Jewish religious movements: Orthodox, Conservative, and Reform. Some Jews include the Reconstructionist movement within the Reform movement; others separate the Reconstructionist into a distinct fourth movement. A detailed exploration of theological differences within Judaism is beyond the scope of this chapter; suffice it to say that, consistent with my focus on Judaism's impact on women who are Jewish and lesbian, I consider Reconstructionism a part of the Reform movement under the progressive rubric for the purposes of this aspect of my discussion.

Orthodox Judaism interprets the Talmud (the compendium of Jewish laws and lore) literally. In this interpretation, license to condemn homosexuality unilaterally is viewed as an immutable fact. Women are relegated to a role that is secondary to men, although there are feminist Orthodox women who would disagree with this. Women cannot be counted as a part of the minyan (the quorum necessary for community prayer), cannot be called to the Torah, cannot worship with men, cannot be ordained as rabbis, and are excused from time-limited commandments due to what is regarded as their primary role as mothers and the demands of child rearing. Conservative Judaism relaxes some of the adherence to Jewish laws in keeping with modern life; includes women in all aspects of the religious service, including ordination; and welcomes gay and lesbian members to the synagogue. Despite the fact they are welcome as synagogue members, openly gay and lesbian people are excluded from key roles, such as serving on synagogue boards of directors and acting as religious school teachers. Despite a relaxed interpretation of Jewish law, Conservative Judaism still considers homosexuality to be against Jewish law. Both Orthodox and Conservative Judaism support civil rights but not religious rights for gay/lesbian people (Kahn, 1989-1990). The progressive Reform movement interprets Jewish teachings in light of humanism and scientific research. The Hebrew Scriptures are seen as divinely inspired, but written by human beings (Kahn, 1989). Kahn (1989-1990) writes: "The progressive argument ultimately depends on an article of faith. God does not create in vain" (p. 69).

When taken literally, the Hebrew Scriptures only overtly prohibit male homosexuality; female homosexuality is added to the prohibition later (Kahn, 1989-1990). According to the Talmud, lesbianism is a lesser crime than male homosexuality. Maimonides, who codified Jewish law, stated that a woman sleeping with another woman was not forbidden to a Cohen (man of the priestly class) or to her own husband if she was married (Schneider, 1984). Acts of lesbianism are merely considered obscene. However, this is not the case for male homosexuality. When male homosexuality is considered, it is deemed an abomination and a capital crime (Kahn, 1989-1990). Male homosexuality spills seed (as does masturbation), and because sex is primarily for procreation, spilling seed is a serious offense.

Until very recently, homosexuality has not been discussed publicly within Judaism (Nugent & Gramick, 1989). There is a myth that because homosexuality is rarely discussed among Jews, it rarely happens. In fact, homosexuality is seen by some Jews as part of Western culture and a negative product of assimilation (Kahn, 1989-1990). Homosexuality has been condemned as being against creation, as precluding reproduction, and as denying the possibility of family (Ackelsberg, 1989; Kahn, 1989-1990). The denial of family is considered a threat to the survival of the Jewish people and is a prominent feature in the condemnation of homosexual behavior.

In spite of harsh prohibitions, the Jewish religious response has included the favoring of civil rights and legal protections for gay/lesbian people (Elwell, 1989; Kahn, 1989-1990). Jewish people have always been concerned about keeping religious doctrine out of civil law (Kahn, 1989-1990). Historically, when religious doctrine has been combined with civil law, Jews have suffered. Jewish people have also been concerned with maintaining a cohesive Jewish community. "Separate not from the community," a statement made by Rabbi Hillel and an important value of Judaism (Beck, 1989), may partially explain the religious response to homosexuality.

Women, Lesbians, and Judaism

Lesbians are welcomed as Jewish women within the Jewish religious community. They are estimated to make up 3% of the Jewish female population (Schneider, 1984). Lesbian Jews are welcome to worship and become members of traditional synagogues, but full legitimacy is denied (Elwell, 1989; Kahn, 1989-1990). Lesbian behavior is condemned, but the woman is not. The belief reiterated is that discrimination against lesbians should end, but at the same time the expectation within Jewish ritual and practice is for lesbians to remain in the closet.

Jewish lesbians wishing to participate in the rituals of the religion must do so as single heterosexual women. They are devalued as women and invisible as lesbians. Historically within Judaism the biological fact of childbearing has led to oppressive rules for women (Hendricks, 1985). Women have been seen as unclean, evil, and immoral, and they are alleged to seduce men (Heschel, 1991). The language and rules of the religion are male dominated. For example, women may not divorce their husbands; only men can divorce. This has caused a major problem for many women in Israel, where marriage and divorce can take place only religiously. Sometimes Jewish lesbians have more difficulty as women than as lesbians within the religion (Schneider, 1984).

One of the difficulties for lesbians is the bias toward heterosexual marriage within Judaism (Cooper, 1989-1990; Heschel, 1991; Yeskel, 1989). Jewish women learn to be personally responsible for the survival of the Jewish people (Klepfisz, 1990; Yeskel, 1989). Since the decimation caused by the Holocaust, every Jewish woman has been taught that she should have as many children as possible (Kantrowitz, 1992). A woman is considered a full adult within the Jewish community only when she has children. The belief that lesbians don't have children (Plaskow, 1989) is still prevalent; this, combined with the belief that having children is the surest way to ensure Jewish survival (Klepfisz, 1990), results in the marginalization and infantilization of lesbians within the Jewish religion. Either they pass as single heterosexual women subject to community pressures to get married, remaining invisible as lesbians, or they come out as lesbians and are tolerated but not fully accepted as Jews.

The only places where lesbian Jewish women have found acceptance are the gay/lesbian synagogues of the Union of American Hebrew Congregations, part of the Reform Jewish movement (Cooper, 1989-1990), and the Reconstructionist synagogues. Even if a lesbian has found a place within a gay/lesbian synagogue, she must constantly press for the valuation of women. For lesbians, the gay/lesbian synagogues connected with the Reform movement have sometimes been a mixed blessing. There they are accepted as lesbians and as Jews, but are often challenged by sexism and attempts to dominate them exhibited by gay men (Schneider, 1984). Outside of her religious community, the Jewish lesbian must also struggle with the anti-Semitism of the lesbian community (Klepfisz, 1982).

Lesbian and Jewish Legitimacy

"Separate not from the community" is a powerful message learned by most Jews early in life. But where is the Jewish lesbian community? Many Jewish lesbians (especially in smaller cities and rural areas) find support within lesbian communities where few of the other women are also Jewish. It becomes difficult for them to follow the advice of this message learned early in the family, that their social needs can and should be met by the Jewish community (Abramowitz, 1989). The Jewish lesbian, especially a woman whose core identity is her Jewish identity (Brown, 1990), experiences two struggles: one over how to be Jewish and female, and one over how to be a lesbian and a Jew (Abramowitz, 1989). Finding herself in a primarily gentile lesbian community (except in some major metropolitan areas where there are large Jewish lesbian communities) can elicit feelings that "to do anything christian [sic] is to sin, not against god but against Jewishness; to betray my people" (Kantrowitz, 1992, p. 77). As ethnic identity is often prioritized over sexual orientation identity (Gonsiorek & Rudolph, 1991; London & Hirshfeld, 1991), a woman's perception that she has chosen the lesbian community over the Jewish community may be experienced profoundly as a betrayal of the Jewish community.

Of course, many lesbian Jews (even in smaller cities) keep their feet in both communities and have always participated as single (passing as heterosexual) women in mainstream Jewish congregations. The civil rights movements of the 1960s and 1970s, especially the women's movement and the gay and lesbian liberation movement, provided impetus for many Jewish lesbians to proclaim publicly both lesbian and Jewish identity. The Metropolitan Community Church (a gay/lesbian church) was the first spiritual home for lesbian Jews (Cooper, 1989-1990). Beth Chayim Chadashim, in Los Angeles, became the first gay/lesbian outreach synagogue and applied for membership in the Union of American Hebrew Congregations of the Reform Jewish movement.

The Reform Jewish movement was the first to affirm homosexuality as a legitimate lifestyle for Jews and to accept gay/lesbian outreach synagogues as members of the movement (Cooper, 1989-1990; Kahn, 1989-1990). The position taken by progressives is that there is no fixed view of halakah (Jewish law); rather, it changes over time to fit the culture and the environment (Abramowitz, 1989). Another component of this view is that a person can be Jewish and lesbian or gay and fulfill the covenant (Kahn, 1989-1990). Sex is not viewed as exclusively for procreation, but is seen as an important aspect of love and companionship (Plaskow, 1989). Lesbians who do not have children can fulfill their Jewish obligation to nurture family by teaching youth or participating in other religious activities for youth.

As more gay/lesbian outreach synagogues formed throughout the world, the World Congress of Gay and Lesbian Jewish Organizations was founded in 1980 (Cooper, 1989-1990). Recognition of gay and lesbian Jews prompted some mainstream Jewish organizations, such as the American Jewish Congress, to speak out against all discrimination, including discrimination against gays and lesbians. The new policy among progressive Jews was to "promote the integration of Judaism and homosexuality as two central and natural aspects of personal identity" (Cooper, 1989-1990, p. 91). According to Rabbi Alexander Schindler of the Reform movement, homosexuality "is a struggle that includes, but also goes beyond, civil liberties. It is, when all is said and done, a struggle for the integrity of selfhood" (quoted in Elwell, 1989, p. 234).

In previous sections I have presented Jewish legitimacy as an important identification with the religious community. But what about the Jewish lesbian who is not religiously observant? Where does she find her community?

Prior to the Holocaust in Europe, and shortly after that time in the United States, there existed a thriving Yiddish culture that was atheist, anti-Zionist, and socialist; the people within this culture considered Yiddish to be the language of the Jewish people (Klepfisz, 1990). A small renewal of this movement, identified as secular Judaism, is taking place (and possibly growing) today. Secular Jews consider the Torah a historical and literary document and view Jewish holidays as celebrations of historical and political events. Klepfisz (1990) observes, "A true commitment to Jewish secularism inevitably means that we must make decisions—just like observant Jews—about how to struc-ture our lives and our relations with Jews and non-Jews, how to incorporate the past (through songs, literature, holidays—traditional, contemporary, political and historical)" (p. 201). Such a commitment also entails understanding how all of this affects interactions with others.

Secular Judaism is considered an illegitimate form of Jewish identity within the present larger Jewish community (where one may choose assimilation or religious observance) and is relatively unknown within the lesbian community (Klepfisz, 1990). The Jewish lesbian who con-siders herself a secular Jew faces an even greater struggle to affirm her identity and find a community.

Liturgy

Moving from organizing gay and lesbian outreach synagogues to the realization that the invisibility of women and especially lesbians is evident in the traditional liturgy and community of Judaism proved to be a short step. Feminist Jews began to change the liturgy and to create new rituals when the women's movement was at its height. Jewish feminists created rituals for first menstruation, menopause, naming, and other important female life events, and gay/lesbian outreach synagogues voiced a commitment to gender equality.

To meet the need for a liturgy that promotes visibility rather than the usual invisibility of lesbians, gay and lesbian outreach synagogues use both a traditional liturgy and newly created prayers and rituals (Beck, 1989; Kahn, 1989). This fits within the Reform belief that whatever the Jewish community accepts over time is "authentic Jewish prayer" (Kahn, 1989, p. 185). Therefore, the new liturgy includes prayers that acknowledge the loss of gay and lesbian lives during the Holocaust (Cooper, 1989-1990; Kahn, 1989), that acknowledge the loss of lives from AIDS, and that recognize the importance of gay/lesbian pride with a special Shabbat service and view every Shabbat as a time when lesbians and gays do not have to pass as heterosexual but can be accepted for all of who they are (Kahn, 1989).

New rituals celebrate the life cycles of lesbians and gays. Rituals have been developed to recognize the coming-out process, to celebrate the commitment of a relationship, and to mourn the loss of a domestic partner. The major thrust of the progressive liturgy is to help lesbians and gays move toward acceptance and integration of their Jewish and lesbian/gay identities.

Jewish Values and
Lesbian Feminist Activism

Coming out as a lesbian can be a stimulus to coming out as a Jew (Beck, 1982b; Smith, 1991), and identifying at the core as a Jew can be a stimulus for lesbian activism (Brown, 1990; Klepfisz, 1990). There is a shared consciousness within the two minority, marginal identities. A lesbian weighs the costs and benefits of visibility and invisibility, and so does a Jew (Smith, 1991). Passing (as heterosexual, as non-Jew, as either or both) can be a choice, can result from denial, can cause pain, and is often felt to be impossible (Kantrowitz, 1992). Jewish identity is a social identity, a sense of self in relation to others (London & Hirshfeld, 1991). The same can be said for lesbian identity. Both identities fit the definition of reference group identity as advanced by William Cross (as cited in London & Hirshfeld, 1991). *Reference group identity* refers to an individual's different reference groups—religious, occupational, values (and sexual orientation). Lang (1993) asks, "What are Jewish identity?" (p. 279; he purposely uses the plural) and goes on to explain that "they" consist of religion, culture, history, politics, psychology and morality, faith, and common sense. In this schema, Jewish identity are a function of the past and of the immediate present. The same could be said of lesbian identity. A Jew struggles with the Christian assumptions of society and a lesbian struggles with the heterosexual assumptions of society. Jews experience oppression at the hands of the dominant culture, and so do lesbians.

Some of the core values of the Jewish religion form the basis of attitudes and behaviors of the lesbian Jew. "Separate not from the community" means seeking out lesbian community and Jewish community wherever she lives. Jewish teachings stress the importance of social justice and the belief that the stranger is to be treated well (Brown, 1990; Klepfisz, 1990). Jews know oppression and sympathize with others who are oppressed (Klepfisz, 1990; Nugent & Gramick, 1989; Rose & Balka, 1989). The two identities offer sources for resistance. Jewish identity is represented by resistance to the pressure to assimilate into a Christian culture, and lesbian identity is resistance to acting and passing as heterosexual (Rose & Balka, 1989). Other core teachings of Judaism that lead to an activist mentality include admonitions to argue and question, never follow blindly, make choices, choose life, speak directly to God, and take responsibility for your relationship with God (Brown, 1990; Smith, 1991). Jews are taught that they should be individual thinkers and that there are many opinions and many truths. "To be a Jew is to live with contradictions and diversity" (Brown, 1990, p. 49).

Implications for Psychotherapy

Overview

For the professional, translating all of this into therapeutic intervention requires figuring out how to be empathically attuned to a client who is "doubly other . . . marginal in both Jewish and American culture" (Rose & Balka, 1989, p. 3). It demands understanding the theory of ethnic identity that flows from Cobbs's ethnotherapy model for identity problems of Blacks and how this can be used in therapeutic work with Jewish lesbians (Klein, 1989). It means understanding how assimilation into Christian society and passing as heterosexual is, for lesbian Jews, "the blurring or erasure of identity and culture" (Kantrowitz, 1992, p. 104). The conflicts among assimilation, passing, and identification for members of two despised minority groups (Jewish, lesbian)—or even three, if we add gender—can lead to self-hate and even dissociation (Klein, 1989). Studies have shown that clear ethnic group identification (as cited in Klein, 1989) and clear lesbian identification (Miranda & Storms, 1989) lead to higher self-esteem and positive self-concept. These are common, concrete therapeutic goals.

Self psychology is a theoretical framework that can be useful in helping lesbian Jews to have corrective emotional experiences regarding acceptance of their dual minority status. In a self-psychology paradigm, change occurs within a relationship where the therapist becomes an empathically attuned self-object that is internally transmuted and used by the client to sustain cohesiveness (Baker, 1991). The therapeutic relationship helps the client to work out a way of maintaining pride and self-esteem in spite of the narcissistic injury of differentness and marginality as a lesbian in a heterosexual society and a Jew in a Christian society (Baker, 1991; Gonsiorek & Rudolph, 1991).

Self psychology can be useful in individual therapy to mirror the client's grandiose-exhibitionistic needs as a lesbian and a Jew, and her needs for idealizing twinship as a lesbian and a Jew. For group therapy, Klein's (1989) ethnotherapy appears to be a powerful tool for Jews "to challenge ethnic group stereotypes and divest them of their magic" (p. 34). There is no reason to believe that this type of group therapy could not be adapted to include myths and stereotypes about lesbians as well.

Following are the phases of Klein's (1989) ethnotherapy, with my own adaptations for a group process that simultaneously explores lesbian identity:

1. Present a personal ethnic identity lifeline and a personal sexual orientation identity lifeline.
2. Examine anti-Semitic incidents and their corollary homophobic and heterosexist incidents.
3. Construct a personal relationship to Jewishness without repeating negative messages. Similarly, construct a personal relationship to lesbianism without repeating negative messages.
4. Integrate historical issues with personal and interpersonal issues.

A major task for the therapist of an ethnotherapy group is to link nonverbal and verbal behaviors to both ethnic and sexual orientation issues within social, psychological, and historical contexts.

Klein's research on ethnotherapy groups yielded positive effects in terms of group members' abilities to work out negative feelings and stereotypes about self and ethnicity, to see problems in a social-historical context, to reevaluate messages from the dominant culture, and to understand feelings about aligning with one's own ethnic group and empathizing with the problems of other ethnic groups. Further research is needed to assess whether an ethnotherapy group that includes sexual orientation issues will be helpful for lesbian Jews.

The Therapist

Regardless of the theoretical framework to which a therapist ascribes, it is crucial that he or she consider and address all important aspects of the client's identity. This is particularly true for therapists working with Jewish lesbian clients. Greene (1994) explores the potential for certain kinds of errors in treatment when therapists work with clients who are lesbian or gay. Therapists sometimes either overemphasize these clients' sexual orientations in treatment or ignore the impacts of homophobia and heterosexism on the clients' lives. Too often in therapy, the Jewish aspect of a client's identity is totally ignored as well. Mental health professionals have finally recognized that religion can be a focus of treatment and have added a V Code (V62.89), "Religious or Spiritual Problem," to the *DSM-IV* (American Psychiatric Association, 1994), legitimating this important part of people's lives. Although many lesbians who identify as Jewish are not religious, it is important to assess how Judaism has an impact on their lives and to understand that a Jewish identity can incorporate Jewish secularism (Klepfisz, 1990). Developing an affirming lesbian identity in a homophobic world is difficult. Similarly, regardless of how affirming a woman is about her Jewish identity (whether cultural or religious), having grown up in an anti-Semitic world is bound to have affected her. It is important for the therapist to find out what meaning Judaism has or has had in a woman's life. According to Weiner (1990), internalized representations of Jewishness are often equated intrapsychically with the bad self. How has the client dealt with the desire to be accepted versus the appropriate protective need to be invisible as a Jew? If she has denied her Jewish identity, has there been some examination of the effects of this denial on her life? The similarities between challenges to developing an affirmative Jewish identity and challenges to developing an affirmative lesbian identity are obvious.

Therapists will be unable to help Jewish lesbian clients explore issues about lesbianism and Judaism if the therapists have not explored their own feelings about these issues. Non-Jewish therapists must address the anti-Semitism that they have been taught or exposed to, and Jewish therapists must address their internalized anti-Semitism (Weiner, 1990). Similarly, non-gay/-lesbian therapists must address externalized homophobia and lesbian/gay therapists must address internalized homophobia (Dworkin & Gutierrez, 1989) before working with Jewish lesbian clients. Non-Jewish therapists often fail to understand the historical and cultural Jewish experience and how the pervasiveness of oppression affects self-image, thoughts, attitudes, and behaviors (Weiner, 1990). Non-Jewish therapists, perhaps even more than heterosexual therapists treating lesbian clients, need to understand the lack of trust Jewish lesbian clients might show, either overtly or covertly, toward their therapists. Many Jewish people are taught from an early age that Christians cannot be trusted. Non-lesbian/-gay therapists, who have not developed an awareness of what it is like to live as a homosexual in a heterosexual world, might also lack the sensitivity necessary for empathic attunement. Jewish lesbian therapists who have worked on their own internalized anti-Semitism and homophobia may provide powerful models for Jewish lesbian clients. This is not to negate the powerful impact that may be achieved through the acceptance of lesbian Jewish clients by non-Jewish heterosexual, non-Jewish gay/lesbian, or Jewish heterosexual therapists, provided they have done the requisite personal and professional work on these issues.

The Client

The Jewish lesbian client has learned that certain perceived Jewish characteristics are not acceptable within the non-Jewish community, and the lesbian community is no exception. Similarly, certain perceived lesbian characteristics are deemed unacceptable by the heterosexual community. Jews as a group are often perceived by non-Jews as loud and pushy. Lesbians are frequently stereotyped as aggressive and castrating. The Jewish lesbian client has to learn how to accept her personal characteristics, particularly if those characteristics match the negative stereotypes, and negotiate acceptance by the communities that are important to her. In self psychology parlance, this is seen as the need for the client to have her grandiose-exhibitionistic self mirrored.

An important question that arises in therapy with Jewish lesbians is the perceived need to determine which community is most important to the individual client (Dworkin, 1990). Many Jewish lesbians come out as lesbians before they discover the importance of their Jewish heritage. The strategies that such women have found useful in coming out as lesbians can be helpful to them in their struggle to come out as Jews (Beck, 1982b). Coming out as a Jew within the lesbian community, when the community is intolerant, can make the Jewish lesbian feel that she must, at least visibly, sacrifice her connection to the Jewish community. This may be more likely if she does not live in a major metropolitan area. This can mean choosing to alienate herself from necessary familial/religious supports, a difficult and often painful choice (Hendricks, 1985). Sometimes, a Jewish lesbian's feeling that she must choose between the lesbian community and the Jewish community is based on unrealistic fears. The therapist must assist the client with this problem by helping her to sort out real versus unrealistic fears as well as strategies for getting the support that she needs. If getting support from both communities means keeping one aspect of her identity invisible (Jewish in the lesbian community or lesbian in the Jewish community), such a client will require help maintaining pride in who she is despite the invisibility of one dimension of self deemed necessary for survival (the narcissistic injury). Often, even in the most remote geographic areas where there is a lesbian community, it is easier to be accepted as a Jewish lesbian in the lesbian community than as a lesbian in the Jewish community. "This may involve re-embracing ethnic characteristics such as a passionate, argumentative style as opposed to the more restrained interactive style of many non-Jews (Rofes, 1989), using Yiddish phrases in everyday speech, expressing a need to visit Jewish neighborhoods in metropolitan areas and eating in delicatessens" (Dworkin, 1990, p. 10). The therapist should be aware that the client may be at different stages in her coming-out process as a lesbian (Dworkin & Gutierrez, 1992b; Fassinger, 1991; Greene, 1994) and in her coming-out process as a lesbian Jew (Dworkin, 1990).

Family

The literature is replete with material that documents the prominence of family dynamics in the acceptance of lesbian identity (Dworkin & Gutierrez, 1992b). The importance of family in the identity development of ethnic gays and lesbians is also well documented (Beck, 1982a; Chan, 1989; Loiacano, 1989; Rose & Balka, 1989). For the Jewish lesbian, family mirrors her Jewish identity but not her lesbian identity. Jewish communities, like other ethnic groups, often view homosexuality as a product of U.S. culture, a negative aspect of assimilation. Marriage and procreation symbolize entrance into adulthood and the continuation of the ethnic group. The fact that lesbians have not been able to marry legally and the myth that lesbians don't have children and therefore cannot continue the survival of the people combine to perpetuate homophobia in Jewish communities. Another factor that predisposes Jews to have negative attitudes toward homosexuality is the religious proscription against it. As a result, homophobia in Jewish families may be intense. Therapists who work with Jewish lesbians need to address the sequelae of family rejection that these clients face. Although most therapists today are sensitive to the family rejection lesbians face, the added narcissistic injury to Jewish identity with the lesbian community for Jewish lesbians must also be addressed.

Couples

Issues that arise within lesbian couples include differences in stages of the coming-out process for both partners; managing the family of origin and the family of procreation, if applicable; financial management; interracial pairing; monogamy versus nonmonogamy; impact of the lack of societal legitimacy for the relationship; and development of friendship networks and support systems. Many other issues are also discussed within the current literature (Ariel & Stearns, 1992; Browning, Reynolds, & Dworkin, 1991; Murphy, 1989, 1992). Jewish lesbians in interracial and interreligious relationships have all the aforementioned issues to deal with plus, for many, the added complication of differences in religion. The small size of many lesbian communities makes it difficult for Jewish lesbians to confine themselves exclusively to Jewish partners.

Intermarriage—marriage between a Jew and a non-Jew—has been a strong taboo within Judaism for generations (Sheldon, 1990). For a Jewish lesbian in a relationship with a non-Jewish lesbian, this may be another ingredient in the couple's ostracism from the Jewish community and yet another reason to feel guilty about betraying her people.

Guilt is only one problem an "intermarried" lesbian couple faces. Because Jews are a minority, many non-Jews do not understand the Jewish religion or culture, or the rituals important to both. There is also often a lack of understanding on the part of the non-Jewish partner about the history and intensity of oppression of Jews and its effects. Further, as noted above in the context of a Jewish client working with a non-Jewish therapist, many Jews may have an underlying mistrust of non-Jews, and this can foster some covert hostility in such a relationship. These issues may be magnified if the couple is an interracial (e.g., African American and Jewish) as well as an "intermarried" couple. Lack of trust and insufficient understanding of historical and cultural issues may be evident on both sides. Any present conflicts between the two communities will also affect the couple. It is important that an "intermarried" and/or interracial couple develop a safe enough climate to explore these issues. An aware therapist can be very helpful in this process. A simple exploration of the impact of holidays, such as Christmas or Kwanzaa, or the need expressed by the Jewish partner to include Jews within the support network (which in small communities can mean including heterosexuals within the support network) can provide an opening for these important inquiries.

If the Jewish partner has children, or if the couple plan to have children together, religious observance can take on added significance. The impact of the Holocaust on Jews often turns the most nonobservant Jew into someone more observant of Jewish traditions when children are brought into the picture. Again, the perpetuation of the Jewish people and their heritage becomes a primary obligation, especially for women. This can become an obstacle for the "intermarried" couple, particularly if the non-Jewish partner does not understand the significance of this obligation or feels left out.

Not every Jewish lesbian is part of a couple, although probably most have that goal at some time in their lives. Jewish lesbians who live in communities where it is difficult to meet other Jewish lesbians may have conflicts about that situation. Whereas some may make the choice to move to larger metropolitan areas, many are not able or are unwilling to do so. It is important for therapists to explore with such clients how they will resolve this dilemma. An aware therapist can help a client to brainstorm ways to maintain her Jewish identity and pride within an "intermarried" relationship. If the client lives in a community with a Reform synagogue, the therapist may suggest she attend services there, because most Reform congregations have high numbers of intermarried couples as members. The Reform movement also disseminates books that deal with the problems of intermarriage and raising children in interfaith households. Although, to the best of my knowledge at this point, such books address only heterosexual couples, many of the problems faced by lesbian couples are similar.

Jewish lesbians, whether single or part of couples, do not operate in a vacuum; they live within the contexts of communities, and these contexts must be addressed.

Community

As previously observed, "Separate not from the community" is an important tenet of the Jewish religion. The community is a place where the Jewish lesbian can have her idealizing needs met most easily. Jewish lesbians who live in large metropolitan areas and to whom the Jewish community is as important as the lesbian community frequently have the luxury of a Jewish lesbian support network. If a woman identifies as a secular Jewish lesbian, however, she may have difficulty affirming her identity even in a large metropolitan area. The therapist may need to help her find resources and make social connections. I suggest Irena Klepfisz's book *Dreams of an Insomniac* (1990) as a good place to begin.

Of course, a woman in therapy may be struggling with either a lesbian or a Jewish identity or both of these identities, and the therapist needs to be sensitive to the complexity of her struggle and her stage in the coming-out process before referring her to the Jewish lesbian community. Even with the existence of a strong Jewish lesbian community, a woman who wishes to keep her connections to her family, and perhaps to her congregation from early childhood, may have internal conflicts to negotiate if she is unable to affirm her lesbian identity within that Jewish community.

When the luxury of support from a Jewish lesbian community does not exist, choices need to be made. It is likely that the lesbian community has been the important community for the Jewish lesbian, as support was probably essential to her maintenance of a cohesive lesbian identity while she was coming out as a lesbian. For Jewish lesbians, awareness of the prevalence of anti-Semitism in the lesbian community can be very painful, sometimes even more painful than the homophobia in the Jewish community. Homophobia within the Jewish community is expected, as it is a routine feature of heterosexual communities. Anti-Semitism within the lesbian community often is not expected. Lesbians, because they are members of an institutionally oppressed group, are often presumed to be more tolerant and understanding of differences and less tolerant of discrimination than their heterosexual counterparts. Although this expectation is not uncommon, it is unwarranted. Therapists must be willing to address Jewish lesbian clients' pain and feelings of betrayal.

"Hiding is very unhealthy for the soul" (Wahba, 1989, p. 55). It can be very difficult for a woman to be out and open in communities that may not accept one or another of her identities. This complex issue should be a clear focus of the therapist's attention.

Conclusion

In this chapter I have addressed the importance of professionals' considering both lesbian and Jewish aspects of identity when conducting therapy with Jewish lesbians. Similarly, I have explored the importance of raising cultural issues with such clients. Most therapists have some awareness of the importance of sexual orientation and of different ethnic identities in clients' lives. That awareness, however, does not always include Judaism as an important aspect of ethnic, religious, or cultural identity, or as a routine feature of psychotherapy inquiries. I have briefly considered here the issues inherent in coming out as a lesbian and as a Jew, some historical contexts, the impact of the Jewish religion on identity and attitudes, and some implications of all these elements for the therapeutic process. As I have noted elsewhere, it is important that therapists "facilitate the Jewish lesbian client's journey to be complete, as a woman, as a Jew, and as a lesbian" (Dworkin, 1990, p. 13).

References

Abramowitz, A. (1989). Growing up in Yeshiva. In C. Balka & A. Rose (Eds.), *Twice blessed: On being lesbian or gay and Jewish* (pp. 21-29). Boston: Beacon.

Ackelsberg, M. A. (1989). Redefining family: Models for the Jewish future. In C. Balka & A. Rose (Eds.), *Twice blessed: On being lesbian or gay and Jewish* (pp. 107-117). Boston: Beacon.

American Psychiatric Association. (1994). *Diagnostic and statistical manual of mental disorders* (4th ed.). Washington, DC: Author.

Ariel, J., & Stearns, S. M. (1992). Challenges facing gay and lesbian families. In S. H. Dworkin & F. J. Gutierrez (Eds.), *Counseling gay men and lesbians: Journey to the end of the rainbow* (pp. 95-112). Alexandria, VA: American Association for Counseling and Development.

Baker, H. S. (1991). Shorter-term psychotherapy: A self psychological approach. In P. Crits-Christoph & J. P. Barber (Eds.), *Handbook of short-term dynamic psychotherapy* (pp. 287-319). New York: Basic Books.

Beck, E. T. (Ed.). (1982a). *Nice Jewish girls: A lesbian anthology*. Watertown, MA: Persephone.

Beck, E. T. (1982b). Why is this book different from all other books? In E. T. Beck (Ed.), *Nice Jewish girls: A lesbian anthology* (pp. xiii-xxxiii). Watertown, MA: Persephone.

Beck, E. T. (1989). Naming is not a simple act: Jewish lesbian-feminist community in the 1980s. In C. Balka & A. Rose (Eds.), *Twice blessed: On being lesbian or gay and Jewish* (pp. 171-181). Boston: Beacon.

Beck, E. T. (1990). Therapy's double dilemma: Anti-Semitism and misogyny. *Women and Therapy, 10*(4), 19-30.

Brown, L. S. (1990). How is this feminist different from all the other feminists? Or, my journey from Pirke Avot to feminist therapy ethics. *Women and Therapy, 10*(4), 41-55.

Browning, C., Reynolds, A. L., & Dworkin, S. H. (1991). Affirmative psychotherapy for lesbian women. *Counseling Psychologist, 19*, 177-196.

Chan, C. S. (1989). Issues of identity development among Asian-American lesbians and gay men. *Journal of Counseling and Development, 68*, 16-20.

Cooper, A. (1989-1990). No longer invisible: Gay and lesbian Jews build a movement. *Journal of Homosexuality, 18*(3-4), 83-94.

Daum, A. (1982). Blaming Jews for the death of the goddess. In E. T. Beck (Ed.), *Nice Jewish girls: A lesbian anthology* (pp. 255-261). Watertown, MA: Persephone.

De Monteflores, C., & Schultz, S. (1978). Coming out: Similarities and differences for lesbians and gay men. *Journal of Social Issues, 34*, 59-72.

Dworkin, S. H. (1990, August). *Female, lesbian, and Jewish: Complex and invisible.* Paper presented at the annual meeting of the American Psychological Association, Boston.

Dworkin, S. H., & Gutierrez, F. J. (1989). Counselors be aware: Clients come in every size, shape, color, and sexual orientation. *Journal of Counseling and Development, 68*, 6-8.

Dworkin, S. H., & Gutierrez, F. J. (Eds.). (1992a). *Counseling gay men and lesbians: Journey to the end of the rainbow.* Alexandria, VA: American Association for Counseling and Development.

Dworkin, S. H., & Gutierrez, F. J. (1992b). Introduction: Opening the closet door. In S. H. Dworkin & F. J. Gutierrez (Eds.), *Counseling gay men and lesbians: Journey to the end of the rainbow* (pp. xvii-xxvii). Alexandria, VA: American Association for Counseling and Development.

Elwell, S. L. (1989). The lesbian and gay movement: Jewish community responses. In C. Balka & A. Rose (Eds.), *Twice blessed: On being lesbian or gay and Jewish* (pp. 228-235). Boston: Beacon.

Erlanger, S. (1994, February 6). In Russia, Jews find new fears. *New York Times*, p. 4.

Fassinger, R. E. (1991). The hidden minority: Issues and challenges in working with lesbian women and gay men. *Counseling Psychologist, 19*, 157-176.

Goldberg, D. T., & Krausz, M. (1993). *Jewish identity*. Philadelphia: Temple University Press.

Gonsiorek, J. C., & Rudolph, J. R. (1991). Homosexual identity: Coming out and other developmental events. In J. C. Gonsiorek & J. D. Weinrich (Eds.), *Homosexuality: Research implications for public policy* (pp. 161-176). Newbury Park, CA: Sage.

Gonsiorek, J. C., & Weinrich, J. D. (Eds.). (1991). *Homosexuality: Research implications for public policy*. Newbury Park, CA: Sage.

Gordis, D. M., & Ben-Horin, Y. (Eds.). (1991). *Jewish Identity in America*. Los Angeles: Wilstein Institute of Jewish Policy Studies.

Greene, B. (1994). Lesbian and gay sexual orientations: Implications for clinical training, practice, and research. In B. Greene & G. M. Herek (Eds.), *Lesbian and gay psychology: Theory, research, and clinical applications* (pp. 1-24). Thousand Oaks, CA: Sage.

Greene, B., & Herek, G. M. (Eds.). (1994). *Lesbian and gay psychology: Theory, research, and clinical applications*. Thousand Oaks, CA: Sage.

Hendricks, M. C. (1985). Feminist spirituality in Jewish and Christian traditions. In L. L. B. Rosewater & L. E. A. Walker (Eds.), *Handbook of feminist therapy: Women's issues in psychotherapy* (pp. 135-146). New York: Springer.

Heschel, S. (1990). Anti-Judaism in Christian feminist theology. *Tikkun, 5*(3), 25-28, 95-97.

Heschel, S. (1991). Jewish feminism and women's identity. *Women and Therapy, 10*(4), 31-40.

Kahn, Y. H. (1989). The liturgy of gay and lesbian Jews. In C. Balka & A. Rose (Eds.), *Twice blessed: On being lesbian or gay and Jewish* (pp. 182-197). Boston: Beacon.

Kahn, Y. H. (1989-1990). Judaism and homosexuality: The traditionalist/progressive debate. *Journal of Homosexuality, 18*(3-4), 47-82.

Kantrowitz, M. K. (1992). *The issue is power: Essays on women, Jews, violence, and resistance*. San Francisco: Aunt Lute.

Kaye, M. (1982). Some notes on Jewish lesbian identity. In E. T. Beck (Ed.), *Nice Jewish girls: A lesbian anthology* (pp. 27-44). Watertown, MA: Persephone.

Klein, J. W. (1989). *Jewish identity and self-esteem: Healing wounds through ethnotherapy*. New York: American Jewish Committee.

Klepfisz, I. (1982). Anti-Semitism in the lesbian/feminist movement. In E. T. Beck (Ed.), *Nice Jewish girls: A lesbian anthology* (pp. 45-51). Watertown, MA: Persephone.

Klepfisz, I. (1990). *Dreams of an insomniac: Jewish feminist essays, speeches, and diatribes*. Portland, OR: Eighth Mountain.

Lang, B. (1993). The phenomenal-noumenal Jew: Three antinomies of Jewish identity. In D. T. Goldberg & M. Krausz (Eds.), *Jewish identity* (pp. 279-290). Philadelphia: Temple University Press.

Loiacano, D. K. (1989). Gay identity issues among Black Americans: Racism, homophobia, and the need for validation. *Journal of Counseling and Development, 68*, 21-25.

London, P., & Hirshfeld, A. (1991). The psychology of identity formation. In D. M. Gordis & Y. Ben-Horin (Eds.), *Jewish identity in America* (pp. 31-50). Los Angeles: Wilstein Institute of Jewish Policy Studies.

Miranda, J., & Storms, M. (1989). Psychological adjustment of lesbians and gay men. *Journal of Counseling and Development, 68*, 41-45.

Montana City reacts early to subdue racist organizations. (1994, February 20). *New York Times*, p. 11.

Murphy, B. C. (1989). Lesbian couples and their parents: The effects of perceived parental attitudes on the couple. *Journal of Counseling and Development, 68,* 46-51.

Murphy, B. C. (1992). Counseling lesbian couples: Sexism, heterosexism, and homophobia. In S. H. Dworkin & F. J. Gutierrez (Eds.), *Counseling gay men and lesbians: Journey to the end of the rainbow* (pp. 63-79). Alexandria, VA: American Association for Counseling and Development.

Nugent, R., & Gramick, J. (1989). Homosexuality: Protestant, Catholic, and Jewish issues: A fishbone tale. *Journal of Homosexuality, 18*(3-4), 7-46.

Plaskow, J. (1982). Blaming the Jews for the birth of patriarchy. In E. T. Beck (Ed.), *Nice Jewish girls: A lesbian anthology* (pp. 250-254). Watertown, MA: Persephone.

Plaskow, J. (1989). Toward a new theology of sexuality. In C. Balka & A. Rose (Eds.), *Twice blessed: On being lesbian or gay and Jewish* (pp. 141-151). Boston: Beacon.

Rich, A. (1989, December). The empowerment of Jewish women. *Matrix,* pp. 4-6.

Riding, A. (1993, December 5). A survey on Holocaust finds many in U.S. ignorant of it. *New York Times,* pp. 32, 142.

Rofes, E. E. (1989). Living as all of who I am: Being Jewish in the lesbian/gay community. In C. Balka & A. Rose (Eds.), *Twice blessed: On being lesbian or gay and Jewish* (pp. 198-204). Boston: Beacon.

Rogow, F. (1989). Speaking the unspeakable: Gays, Jews, and historical inequity. In C. Balka & A. Rose (Eds.), *Twice blessed: On being lesbian or gay and Jewish* (pp. 71-82). Boston: Beacon.

Rose, A., & Balka, C. (1989). Introduction. In C. Balka & A. Rose (Eds.), *Twice blessed: On being lesbian or gay and Jewish* (pp. 1-8). Boston: Beacon.

Schneider, S. W. (1984). *Jewish and female.* New York: Simon & Schuster.

Sheldon, A. (1990). A feminist perspective on intermarriage. *Women and Therapy, 10*(4), 79-89.

Siegel, R. J. (1986). Antisemitism and sexism in stereotypes of Jewish women. *Women and Therapy, 5*(2-3), 249-257.

Smith, A. J. (1991). Reflections of a Jewish lesbian-feminist activist-therapist; Or, first of all I am Jewish, the rest is commentary. *Women and Therapy, 10*(4), 57-64.

Sophie, J. (1985-1986). A critical examination of stage theories of lesbian identity development. *Journal of Homosexuality, 12*(2-3), 39-51.

Taylor, J. G. (1994, February 9). Black pastors condemn Farrakhan visit to Fresno. *Fresno Bee,* pp. A1, A18.

Wahba, R. (1989). Hiding is unhealthy for the soul. In C. Balka & A. Rose (Eds.), *Twice blessed: On being lesbian or gay and Jewish* (pp. 48-56). Boston: Beacon.

Weiner, K. (1990). Anti-Semitism in the therapy room. *Women and Therapy, 10*(4), 119-126.

Weinrach, S. G. (1990). Personally speaking: A psychosocial look at the Jewish dilemma. *Journal of Counseling and Development, 68,* 548-549.

Yeskel, F. (1989). You didn't talk about these things: Growing up Jewish, lesbian, and working class. In C. Balka & A. Rose (Eds.), *Twice blessed: On being lesbian or gay and Jewish* (pp. 40-47). Boston: Beacon.

5

From Apartheid to Mandela's Constitution
Black South African Lesbians in the Nineties

CHERYL POTGIETER

In documenting the trends and silences in psychology in South Africa between 1948 and 1988, Seedat (1988) highlights the manner in which "oppressive discourse historically informed and continues to inform the research agenda, practices and theoretical concerns of many South African psychologists" (p. xvi). Traditional areas within the discipline, such as psychometry, developmental psychology, social psychology, and educational psychology, have been prioritized as important research areas. Social issues, the psychology of women, the psychology of oppression, and human sexuality have received very little attention. The category that has received the least attention is, not surprisingly, human sexuality. Although Seedat does not distinguish between homosexuality and heterosexuality in South African psychological journals, my current review of the literature indicates that whereas sexuality has never been a focus of research per se, most researchers have not mentioned the issue of sexual orientation at all. The point of departure is always within a heterosexual framework.

Not only have researchers ignored the experiences of gay men and lesbians, the research that has been conducted has been focused primarily on the experiences of White males and, sometimes, White females. The Black majority, as usual, has been ignored. This is consistent with the core ideology of apartheid, an ideology that was interested only in creating a better life for White South Africans at the expense of the Black majority population.

In this chapter I examine the links among the South African state, the academic discipline and professional practice of psychology, and the political oppression of gay men and lesbians. What is highlighted is the differential response to White as opposed to Black lesbians and gay men. Another popular discourse within the Black South African context is the argument that gay and lesbian sexual orientations are un-African and represent a corrupt Western capitalist influence. In an attempt to dispel this myth, I provide a brief overview of lesbianism within non-Western contexts. Finally, I offer a rare glimpse into the lives of Black lesbians in present-day South Africa.

Position of Black Lesbians in South Africa

My research required many personal conversations and interviews with Black South African lesbians. In one of these conversations, a Black lesbian told me the following:

> To many in the South African society, people like me [Black lesbians] do not exist. It has been my experience that activists, both men and women, are beginning to recognize that lesbianism does exist, but it is seen as a White thing. It is seen as something that lefties are engaged in. It would have been easier if I was White. White families look down on you, but if you are not accepted you could very easily move out of the family house or even to another city. For Black people it is different. Families are very close to each other. . . . But you know what, my grandmother seems to understand . . . and an old lady that I know my whole life, although they think perhaps a *sangoma* [traditional healer] can help cure me. The White people who are like me [lesbian] do not like me because I am Black and have been in jail for politics.

This personal narrative suggests that Black lesbians in South Africa experience life very differently from White lesbians. The reader is reminded that just as there is no one uniform gay or lesbian experience, there is no singular Black gay or lesbian experience. Despite their heterogeneity, Black people, particularly Black women, in South Africa share a common oppression as a result of the apartheid regime. Thus Black lesbians similarly share many commonalities as a function of race, gender, and sexual orientation in an environment that is oppressive toward them on all of those levels. It is accepted that the majority of Black people in South Africa are working-class, and I would thus argue that Black lesbians share a common class experience as well.

Cornwell (1983) has observed that it would be difficult to imagine anyone more oppressed than the Black lesbian in America. I suggest that this holds true for Black South African lesbians as well. With regard to South Africa, it could be argued that Black lesbians will no longer experience racism as well as forms of antigay prejudice and discrimination as a result of the sexual orientation clause in the final South African Constitution. In addition, certain of the leaders of the African National Congress (ANC) have come out in support of lesbians' and gay men's rights. ANC chief whip Arnold Stofile is on record as saying: "We want people of South Africa to see that human interaction cannot be forced into narrow, religious, ceremonial relationships. There are other valid forms of partnership than the traditional, Christian, heterosexual marriage, and note needed to be taken of that. If we are talking about a rainbow nation, we must also accept a rainbow of norms." Another public example of a person in government who is supportive of gay rights is Jesse Duarte, Gauteng minister for safety and security, who opened the 1995 gay film festival with an impassioned plea for gay equality. Recently, Nobel Peace Prize winner Archbishop Desmond Tutu has also voiced support for gay and lesbian rights.

One may question whether or not these views represent only certain individuals in government, and whether they accurately reflect the views of the majority of South Africans, including most other political leaders, religious and educational institutions, and the media. In this respect it is important to note the discourse that was propagated by George Bizos, a leading human rights lawyer, in his defense of Winnie Mandela. Mandela was accused of murdering a youth activist. Her defense argued that she had in fact attempted to rescue the youth from his involvement with a Methodist minister and used homophobic rhetoric linking pedophilia to gay sexual orientation. A detailed discussion of the trial and its nuances is beyond the scope of this chapter, but interested readers are referred to Holmes (1994), who asserts that the discourse of public homosexuality used by the defense in this visible trial rested on the argument that gay or lesbian sexual orientation is not found in Black culture per se, and Blacks who are lesbian and gay have become so as a result of their being tainted by homosexuality in White culture. Hence, despite public tolerance, other less enlightened attitudes prevail. Given such a confusing state of affairs and the need to deny Black lesbians' existence, it is crucial that the experiences of lesbians, and especially Black lesbians, be documented and publicly acknowledged. In the following pages I examine the lives of gay men and lesbians, with a specific focus on Black lesbians, from the days of apartheid to life with Mandela and the new South African Constitution in the 1990s.

Legal Discourses of Homosexuality in South Africa

Gay men and lesbians have historically been the victims of discriminatory laws and prejudices. The Roman Dutch law, which, because of Dutch imperialism, has had an influence on the South African legal system since the 1800s, criminalized a range of sexual relations between adults. Under Roman Dutch law, all sexual acts, whether homosexual or heterosexual, were crimes if they did not lead to procreation (De Vos, 1995). All forms of unnatural lust "which was contrary to the order of nature" were classified as offenses. Unnatural acts were punished because they did not lead to the procreation of offspring, but for further reasons as well. In *Rex v. Gough & Narroway* (1926), they are characterized in the following manner: "These offenses were regarded as so abhorrent to all ideas of decency that they ought to be punished" (p. 162).

Unnatural offenses or crimes against nature included male-female sodomy, sexual relations with animals, and sex between males (Cameron, 1994). Sex between women did not escape being labeled a crime against nature in this framework of behavior and morality. According to the Criminal Ordinance of the Emperor Charles V, "If human being behaves unchastely with an animal, or male with male, or woman with woman, they have forfeited their lives, and they shall, according to the usual custom, be condemned to be burned to death" (*Rex v. Gough & Narroway*, 1926, p. 162). Masturbation (solitary) was also a crime under this law. Although these sexual offenses were cited as law, since the beginning of the 20th century most of them, when occurring between consenting humans, were no longer implemented or enforced by law (Cameron, 1994). Male-male sexual acts remained criminal offenses on the statute books.

De Vos (1995) speculates that sodomy and other sexual acts between males were not decriminalized for the following reasons: Legal, medical, and psychological discourse no longer outlawed all sexual activity that fell outside the boundaries of legal (marital) heterosexual sexual activity and that did not lead to the production of offspring, but now began to control or police the "inverts." Court documents described same-sex conduct as indecent, immoral, and disgusting (*Rex v. Gough & Narroway*, 1926). The courts branded homosexuals as a specialized and extraordinary class. Being branded different, special, and extraordinary usually translated into being legally, socially, and economically discriminated against in the South African apartheid state that existed after 1948.

Under South African law, being different and extraordinary meant being perceived as someone who required psychiatric intervention. Members of the legal profession who argued from the "in need of psychiatry" approach usually assumed that this was a more enlightened and liberal approach than the punishment course of action. Liberal judgments imposed fines instead of prison sentences, pointed out that gay culture (in terms of clubs) was common, and even went so far as to discuss whether in fact sodomy actually constituted a crime. However, the discourse that homosexuality represented abnormal, inappropriate, and shameful behavior was still entrenched and sanctioned. The reader is referred to *Van Rooyen v. Van Rooyen* (1994) and South African Parliament (1969) for examples of similar attitudes.

The control of sexuality and the stigmatization process were not limited to the courts. South Africa under Nationalist Party rule did not have an independent judiciary. In 1957 the government adopted the Immorality Act, later amended to the Sexual Offenses Act, the aim of which was to eliminate immoral behavior. Immoral behavior included sex between members of different "races" as created by the apartheid state, prostitution, cruising, and immoral or indecent acts committed by men older than 19 with men younger than 19. Initially, sexual acts between women were not constituted as crimes. However, in 1988 the act was extended to outlaw "immoral or indecent" acts between women and girls under 19. The media contributed to legitimating and entrenching the homophobic scare in its coverage of the first case under the extended legislation with headlines such as "Women Who Prey on Little Girls" (1989).

Cameron (1994) points out that the underage prohibition is discriminatory, as the age of consent for heterosexual sexual acts is 16. He further points out that the heterosexual age restriction is applicable only to acts "involving intercourse and to soliciting or enticing an under-age boy or girl to the commission of an immoral act." The law pertaining to homosexuality, however, includes any immoral or indecent act. Translated into practice, this means that committing or intending/attempting to commit a heterosexual sexual act without intercourse with a "child" is deemed a crime only when there is soliciting or enticement.

The links among the control of sexuality, "White" civilization, and the apartheid state are highlighted by the passing of Section 20A of the Sexual Offenses Act of 1957, which forbade "any male person from committing with another male person at a party any act which is calculated to stimulate sexual passion or to give sexual gratification." The definition of a party is "any occasion where more than two persons are present."

The incident described below led to the legislation's being passed. A house was raided in Forest Town in Johannesburg in January 1966, where the police discovered

> a party in progress, the like of which has never been seen in the Republic of South Africa. There were approximately 300 male persons present who were all obviously homosexual. . . . Males were dancing with males to the strains of music, kissing and cuddling each other in the most vulgar fashion imaginable. They also paired off and continued their love-making in the garden of the residence and in motor cars in the streets, engaging in the most indecent acts imaginable with each other. (description quoted in Cameron, 1994)

This discovery led to the "party" law cited above as well as the formation of a select committee of Parliament, convened at the minister of justice's request, to investigate the matter further. The minister of justice felt very strongly that homosexuality could not remain unchecked, as it would lead to the demise of the South African nation. We can assume that he meant the White nation, because the Black nation was not formally recognized as such and certainly was of no concern to an apartheid regime. The House of Assembly debates indicate that this view was not challenged by the so-called liberal parties in Parliament (South African Parliament, 1969). As Retief (1994) observes, "They were either silent or simply missing" (p. 102).

The debates in the House of Assembly further indicated the committee's division. On the one hand, conservatives believed that adults were abusing teenagers and that this led to increases in homosexuality; on the other hand, liberals argued that homosexuality was a psychological disorder requiring medical attention to eliminate it. Despite their differences, both camps agreed that homosexuality had to be outlawed. The investigation resulted in the banning of sexual acts between men at parties, an increase in the age of consent, and a ban on the manufacture of any aid used in "unnatural" sexual acts.

A noticeable characteristic of the report is that the term *homosexual* is used to refer to White males. Lesbians, both Black and White, and Black gay men are mentioned only in passing. Lesbians were assumed to be more the exception than the rule. In the minds of House members, lesbians existed in much smaller numbers than gay males, and were constructed as evil women because they did not produce children. It is interesting to note that sexual activity between two women has never been outlawed in South African law. According to De Vos (1995), the courts have never had to decide whether sexual acts between women should be punishable by law. This may further represent the marginalization of women as well as what I would describe as the ideology of disbelief. This ideology may be understood as the inability to believe that women do not need men, sexually and on other levels. I would further suggest that perhaps lesbians were not, in terms of the law and the Nationalist Party, important enough to warrant sufficient attention for officials to create laws governing their behavior. The House of Assembly's observation that "there was no evidence that lesbianism is being practised in such a way that it in itself justifies criminal sanctions" (South African Parliament, 1969, col. 4803) renders lesbians almost a figment of the imagination. I would speculate that there was a belief, among Whites, that lesbians were most likely confined to Black women, and the state already had laws to deal with them. This practice of turning a blind eye to what was deemed homosexual activity among Blacks was clearly the case regarding the activity in the mines (Dunbar, Ndatshe, & Sibuyi, 1988), but more stringent laws and a special commission were deemed necessary after the infamous raid on the White male party in Johannesburg. According to De Vos (1995), the word *lesbian* has been mentioned in only two reported cases in South African courts. In one of those cases, it was ruled that referring to a woman as a lesbian was derogatory.

The extension to girls of laws originally referring to immoral or indecent acts between boys and men under 19 marked the first time that lesbian "behavior" was recognized by the South African Parliament. However, lesbians have been marginalized and stigmatized in South Africa. A recent example of this is the legal decision in *Van Rooyen v. Van Rooyen* (1994), a case in which the court had to decide on a lesbian mother's access to her children, who were in the care of their father. Access was granted on condition that the woman and her partner sleep in separate beds when the children visited over weekends—when the children visited for longer periods, her partner was not permitted to sleep in the house. It goes without saying that such a judgment would not have been passed (with these conditions) had the couple been heterosexual. The court constructed homosexuality as "abnormal," "damaging to children," and "wrong." The judge expressed his views as follows:

> What the experts say is to me self evident that, even without them, I believe that any right thinking person would say that it is important that the children stay away from the confusing signals as to how the sexuality of the male and of the female should develop. . . . the issue simply comes down to the fact of the style of living, the attitude towards living, the activities, the behaviour or whatever else is involved in living from minute to minute, all that in the context of the lesbianism. (p. 325)

The "experts" in this case included psychologists who were not concerned that the applicant's partner spent the night on the premises. Rather, their concern focused on what they deemed the need to protect the children from confusing signals regarding presumably appropriate (heterosexual) sexuality, given the mother's lesbian sexual orientation.

If we examine the evidence provided by psychologists and psychiatrists and the great value attached to that evidence by the courts, it is clear that both disciplines and their members played a significant role in justifying the construction of homosexuality as behavior that should be deemed illegal. The following excerpt from a House of Assembly debate highlights this point: "It must be noted that the evidence [regarding homosexuality] was submitted by the most eminent authorities in this field in South Africa including professors from the well known universities and the Government departments" (South African Parliament, 1969, p. 9, col. 4804). Various police officers also looked to the psychological profession for assistance. The South African psychological study conducted by Liddicoat (1956) has the esteemed status in South Africa that the work of Kinsey and his colleagues occupies in the United States (Kinsey, Pomeroy, & Martin, 1948; Kinsey, Pomeroy, Martin, & Gebhard, 1953). The conclusion reached by the courts is that homosexuality is usually the result of a personality or genetic abnormality, however, it represents behavior that cannot be excused or go unpunished. In this scheme it is assumed that with the necessary psychological intervention, spiritual guidance, and banning of the sale of certain sexual objects, this "social evil" can be eradicated. Mental health professionals expressed the opinion that even the "most hard-baked" homosexual would give anything to live a normal, presumably heterosexual, life. With the assumption that such help was available, Assembly members felt "that the existing statutory sanctions should remain" (South African Parliament, 1969, p. 9, col. 4804).

It should be clear that South African law regarding sexual conduct and identities has been intrinsically linked to race, class, and gender, or, put simply, to the entrenchment of the apartheid ideology. The courts definitely have taken into account the races and ages of parties when making decisions regarding sentencing. The legal system has also dealt differently with female and male same-sex activity. De Vos (1995) correctly concludes that from the early years of the 20th century, the South African legal system has "treated the group of homosexuals differently and has been an important source of stigmatisation of both gay men and lesbians" (p. 20). He further cautions that these attitudes are still held by certain judges even in postapartheid South Africa.

Where Black women and men were concerned, the apartheid state had many laws at its disposal to harass them, and therefore it could be argued that the state did not need specific laws to use against Black lesbians. For example, as early as 1957, the Nationalist Party adopted the Immorality Act (later renamed the Sexual Offenses Act) in an attempt to stamp out what it deemed to be immorality. As mentioned previously, this act contained prohibitions against interracial sex, prostitution, cruising, and immoral or indecent acts committed by men older than 19 with men younger than 19. It can be concluded that in South Africa, it has never technically been illegal to be a lesbian, but the legal consequences of choosing to live an openly gay lifestyle have been sufficient to make gay men and lesbians think of themselves as criminals just for being who they are.

The Interim and Final
Constitution and Homosexuality

From the discussion so far, it is clear that prior to the interim constitution, homosexual behavior constituted the basis of a range of criminal offenses in the eyes of South African law. Although lesbian sexual acts and activity were not given the same attention or criminal status as male homosexual activity, since 1988 women have been criminally liable if they participate in sexual activities with women under the age of 19. It has also been ruled defamatory to refer to a woman as lesbian (*Vermaak v. Van der Merwe*, 1981). The argument used to support this ruling was that to be called a lesbian constitutes an insult that diminishes a woman's name and reputation in the "eyes of right-thinking persons."

Despite this history, South Africa is the first and only country in the world to include explicit protection on the grounds of sexual orientation in its constitution. Both the transitional and final constitution contain "equality clauses" that guarantee to every person the right to equality before the law and to equal protection of the law. The final constitution contains a nondiscrimination clause that states, "No person shall be unfairly discriminated against, directly or indirectly, and, without derogating from the generality of the provision, on one or more of the following grounds in particular: race, gender, sex, ethnic or social origin, colour, sexual orientation, age, disability, religion, conscience, belief, culture or language."

Cameron (1994) argues that adequate constitutional protection is necessary for people discriminated against because of sexual orientation, as it would at the least achieve decriminalization and would eradicate the "unnatural" sexual offense and the common law crime of sodomy. It would also remove Section 20A of the Sexual Offenses

Act of 1957 (the "at a party act") from the statute books, and the age of sexual consent would have to be made the same for both hetero- and homosexual acts. Legislative enforcement of nondiscrimination would be directed at places of employment, provision of public resources, and insurance eligibility (Cameron, 1994). Rights of free speech, association, and conduct would include the right to disseminate information and views, as well as equal rights of commercial association. The right to dress in drag would have to be included as well (Cameron, 1994). The establishment of permanent domestic partnerships would be another important measure. Cameron (1994) argues that nondiscrimination on the grounds of sexual orientation would have to include official recognition of permanent domestic partnerships, resulting in partner benefits that include pension, medical aid, and insurance. No further discrimination should be permitted regarding foster care and adoption. I would argue also that maternity leave should be granted to lesbian couples who choose to adopt or to bear children in the same way that it is for heterosexual women.

The inclusion of the sexual orientation clause in the constitution is another important step. There is a definite indication that there is a commitment to protect the constitutional rights of all citizens in South Africa. However, the question that can be asked is whether constitutional rights are enough. I would argue that we should not underestimate, nor should we overestimate, the role that constitutional protection can play. De Vos (1995) states that the inclusion of sexual orientation in the interim constitution was a major victory for gay men, lesbians, and bisexuals in South Africa. He cautions, however, that it poses novel questions regarding their relationship to the law and the strategies that should be employed to use the law to the benefit of the population it is intended to protect. Discussion of the latter issue is beyond the focus of this chapter and is best left to legal scholars to debate. However, the following statement made by a Black drag queen during a 1994 gay pride march in Johannesburg captures the potential liberating effect of constitutional protection: "Darling, it means sweet motherfuck-all. You can rape me, rob me—what am I going to do when you attack me? Wave the constitution in your face? I'm just a nobody Black queen. . . . But you know what? Ever since I heard about the Constitution, I feel free inside" (quoted in Visser, 1995).

The Denial of Lesbian and Gay
Sexual Orientations in African Culture:
A Default of Apartheid?

It is clear that lesbians and gay men may be found among Black persons, and that indeed lesbians and gay men may be found in all historical periods and across ethnic groups. Many individuals and groups who have histories of resisting racial and ethnic oppression, but who stop short of endorsing the same civil rights for lesbians and gay men, argue that lesbian and gay sexual orientations are not African. They attribute nontraditional sexual orientations to the corrupting influence of Western societies. I view such beliefs as unsupported and contradicted by historical evidence. In the late 1990s it should not be necessary to illustrate that both lesbians and gay men have been part of all societies throughout many periods. Despite my personal conviction on this matter, I recognize that if we are to educate people and thus counter such arguments, it is important to discuss this issue openly and disseminate the evidence. As has been indicated by a number of scholars, male homosexuality has received very little attention, but female homosexuality has been even more marginalized—rendered virtually invisible. Given these realities and this chapter's focus on Black South African lesbians, I will provide a brief overview of female homosexuality in African and other non-Western societies, prior to their colonization and domination by Western imperialists.

This should be viewed as a brief and not exhaustive discussion, in part due to space limitations. It must also be viewed as limited as a function of the suppression of historical documentation of female same-sex affiliations in these societies. What we see in historical accounts is often as much a function of what is there to be seen as it is a function of the willingness of the observer to see and document what is there. Another difficulty rests in the use of language and terminology that describes and assigns meaning to sexual behavior. There are conceptual differences across cultures in defining connections among gender, sexual behavior, and their meaning. Same-gender sexual behavior among persons who do not label themselves as lesbian, gay, or bisexual is still commonplace, and has been observed in my research sample. Another difficulty in examining this issue is that the label, and thus what some would argue is the social construction of "the homosexual," is not only culture bound, but can be traced to the recent as opposed to the distant past.

For convenience, I attempt to organize the history of same-sex female unions into the following sections: Native American cultures, African cultures, and Asian cultures.

Native American Cultures

Although there are very few sources that provide reports of same-sex behavior in Native American cultures, accounts by Katz (1992), Devereux and Whitehead (1937), Williams (1986), and Tafoya (Chapter 1, this volume) have proved helpful. A number of these accounts describe the same-sex unions typical of the *berdache* custom among Native Americans. The Native American *berdache* is a male or female who departs from his or her socially constructed gender role, thus acquiring certain of the traits and obligations of the other sex. According to Callender and Kochems (1985), the *berdache* does not cross gender lines so much as mix them. Many Native American cultures have even considered *berdaches* to constitute a third sex. Interestingly, in traditional cultures, *berdaches* have married individuals of the same sex and these marriages have been recognized by Native American laws. Williams (1986), for example, observes that *berdaches* have been condoned and valued as part of the cultures of a majority of Native American communities.

Although most academic attention has focused on male *berdaches*, female *berdaches* have constituted an equally important institution in these communities. Similar to the gender role crossing of the male *berdache*, the female *berdache* assumes many of the tasks traditionally performed by males, including hunting and heading a household. A female *berdache's* marital partner would be another woman (Williams, 1986). Blackwood's (1984) in-depth study indicates that female *berdaches* and female marriages were essential to women's status in most Native American societies. Native American beliefs about sexuality are reflected in the marriage system. Theorists such as Rubin (1975) have implicated marriage as one of the mechanisms that enforce and define women's sexuality. According to Rubin, the division of labor may be viewed as a taboo against sexual arrangements except those containing at least one man and one woman, thus supporting and perhaps privileging heterosexual marriage. Homosexual behavior occurred in contexts within which neither individual was cross-gendered, nor were such individuals seen as expressing cross-gender behavior. Furthermore, through the cross-gender role, women could marry one another. Native American ideology disassociated sexual behavior from the concepts of male and female gender roles and was not concerned with the identity of the sexual partner (Tafoya discusses this phenomenon in greater detail in Chapter 1 of this volume). The status of the cross-gender female's partner is telling in this respect: She was always a traditional female—that is, two cross-gender females did not marry. Thus a woman could follow the traditional female gender role yet marry and have a sexual relationship with another woman without being stigmatized for doing so (Blackwood, 1984). Blackwood, like other scholars, does not claim that Native American communities never dictated subordinate roles and positions to women at all; rather, scholars point out that the option to enter same-sex marriages as relationships with a formal, legitimate status increased the range of options available to all women in the tribes.

African Cultures

Scholars who have investigated homosexuality in various African societies have tended to focus on men. Anthropologist Evans-Pritchard (1970) has documented, for example, the institution of "boy wives" for military men among the Azande (Sudan). Parallel institutions or customs between women have not been similarly emphasized. Judith Gay's (1985) study of "mummy-baby" games among Basotho girls in Lesotho is an exception. According to Gay, these games start when young girls are still at primary (grade) school. In a mummy-baby relationship, an older girl, acting as "mummy," develops an intimate association with a younger girl (the baby). Generally, the mummy presents gifts to the baby, who reciprocates by obeying and respecting the mummy. The two share both emotional and informational exchanges. Although Gay's (1985) is the more in-depth study of this phenomenon, recently Kendall (1995) has reported on evidence of similar female-female relationships in Lesotho.

A form of same-sex union that may be peculiar to African cultures is the institution of "female husbands" or "woman marriage." The institution was not paid much attention until it was publicized in a work by Krige (1974), who describes woman marriage as the institution by which a woman may give bridewealth for, and marry, another woman. The woman who marries in such arrangements has full control of her "wife's" offspring (the duties of procreation are delegated to a male). Another example of same-sex female relationships in African society is found in the story of Ifeyinwa Olinke, who lived in the 19th century (Amadiume, 1987). Olinke was an industrious woman in a community where most of the entrepreneurial opportunities were seized by women, who thereby came to control much of the Igbo tribe's wealth. Ifeyinwa socially overshadowed her less prosperous male husband. As a sign of her prosperity and social standing, Ifeyinwa herself became a female husband to other women. Her epithet "Olinke" referred to the fact that she had nine wives.

Recently in South Africa there have been accounts confirming that homosexuality is an integral part of Black South African cultures (Louw, 1995; McClean & Ngoobo, 1994). McClean and Ngoobo (1994) illustrate how embedded, yet invisible, homosexual life is in the townships. The participants in their study, 20 men from the South African Black townships, are lovers of straight men, or *injongas*, who collude in the masquerade that their sexual partners are "women." The men in the study reported that their parents are aware of their homosexuality. Chan-Sam (1994) presents a collection of narratives of five Black South African lesbian lives, among them the Lovedu rain queen in the Northern Transvaal who apparently keeps up to 40 wives. This, in addition to my own study of more than 30 narratives of Black South African lesbians, makes the notion that female homosexuality is not part of Africa quite questionable. Chan-Sam (1994) interviewed a *sangoma* (traditional healer), and two of my respondents were *sangomas* as well. As Gevisser and Cameron (1994) note, the apparent tradition of lesbian *sangomas* in history is another area that warrants more research.

Asian Cultures

I will provide here a brief description of same-sex unions in China; Chan discusses Asian lesbians and traditions in greater depth in Chapter 11 of this volume. A tradition similar to the *berdache* tradition in Native American cultures, companionate same-sex marriage, and the transgenerational tradition of boy wives have been documented in Asian societies (Hinsch, 1990; Murray, 1992). As in other cultures, documentation has focused mainly on male same-sex relationships.

Literary sources from the Zhou Dynasty (1122-256 B.C.) contain examples of public affection between men. According to official histories, 10 of China's Han emperors (206 B.C. to 220 A.D.) enjoyed male lovers, pursuing open same-sex liaisons similar to those enjoyed by their contemporary Roman counterparts (Hinsch, 1990). These emperors married women to bear them heirs and also had one or more male lovers.

Hinsch (1990) is of the opinion that the Han society's tolerance of same-sex male relationships, the custom of male pair bonding and its celebration in poetry and other literature, and men's incorporation of their male concubines into their households are indicators of the genesis of same-sex marriages.

A review of Hinsch's work makes it clear that much less information is available on female same-sex unions in previous centuries. Hinsch does acknowledge, however, the existence of woman-woman unions, which he considers to have been marriages, formed during the Quing Dynasty. The first well-documented unions were those associated with the "marriage resistance movement" (Topley, 1975) in 19th- and early-20th-century southern China. The development of China's international silk industry during this period helped many women to attain economic independence. After acquiring this newfound freedom, thousands of women renounced marriage and became *sou hei*. When a woman decided to become *sou hei*, she took a formal ceremonial vow to remain unwed for a period, moved out of her parents' house, and built a "spinster house" with other *sou hei*. These women formed "sisterhoods," or small groups of women who would bond together for mutual support and affection. Hinsch (1990) observes that these relationships shared many of the characteristics of a "marriage" and that physical as well as emotional bonds often developed among the women:

> Within the group, a lesbian couple could choose to undergo a marriage ceremony in which one partner was designated as "husband" and the other "wife." After an exchange of ritual gifts, the foundation of the Chinese marriage ceremony, a feast attended by female companions served to witness the marriage. These married lesbian couples could even adopt female

children, who in turn could inherit family property from the couple's parents. (pp. 177-178)

The preceding examples of homosexuality and the existence of formally sanctioned same-sex relationships in the "ancient" world negate the idea that homosexuality is a modern Western "evil" as well as the idea that it is "un-African." In my own research, excerpts from interviews and focus groups that I have conducted also confirm that Black lesbians are as present in the new South Africa as they are elsewhere in the world.

South African Psychology and Homosexuality

Many authors have emphatically asserted that "the specific societal context has a very significant influence upon social scientists" (Chesler, 1976, p. 60; see also Billig, 1976; Essed, 1987). Thus it is important that I provide an overview of the societal context in which psychology developed in South Africa so that readers may comprehend fully the scarcity or complete absence of research in South African psychology journals on both male and female homosexuality.

The earlier discussion of the legal construction of homosexuality illustrates the links among the South African state, psychologists, and the law. Psychologists who have testified as expert witnesses in court cases regarding homosexuality have argued that homosexuality is a sickness and a sin. Although they have argued that it is a sickness, they have held the individuals who have that sickness responsible for their behavior. It has been asserted that homosexuals could be "cured" with spiritual as well as psychological intervention. Although the argument is not logical, this assertion has also been used to argue for the criminalization of homosexuality and prosecution of homosexuals. Psychologists have not publicly, or in any other way, questioned such criminalization.

The absence of any kind of opposition to the criminalization of homosexuality by psychologists is not surprising if one notes Seedat's (1988) statement that "in the case of South Africa, psychology's roots, development, form and practices are all informed by the dominant legacy of apartheid" (p. 50). Seedat shows that racist and oppressive political ideology and practices influenced and continue to frame the "thinking, practice and roles" of a large number of South African psychologists.

The architect of apartheid, H. F. Verwoerd, was a psychologist. In the first half of the 20th century, psychologists were involved in various studies and tests that justified the superiority of White South Africans. The reader is referred to Seedat (1988) for a detailed discussion of the role of psychologists in the entrenchment of apartheid. To determine where the majority of South African psychologists stood regarding the question of apartheid, one need only look toward the South African psychological organizations.

The first South African Psychological Association (SAPA) was formed in 1948—the same year in which the Nationalist Party, which officially created apartheid, came into power. For the first 9 years, until 1957, SAPA had only White members, although the group's constitution did not explicitly exclude Blacks. In 1957 a Black woman, the first Black woman psychologist in South Africa, applied for membership, but the majority of SAPA members were not prepared to accept her. Only 5 years later, in 1962, were Blacks admitted into this organization. At that point, however, a large number of members resigned from SAPA to form a psychological organization open only to Whites, the Psychological Institute of the Republic of South Africa (PIRSA). In 1976 the new organization had 500 members and the old organization had 338. PIRSA thus had approximately 48% more members than SAPA. This is a glaring example of psychologists' position regarding apartheid (Bisheuvel, 1976: Cooper, Nicholas, Seedat, & Statman, 1990).

The discussion earlier in this chapter of the legal construction of homosexuality illustrates the role that psychologists and psychiatrists played in the South African state's criminalization of homosexuality. The question that logically follows is, What did psychologists' academic discourse have to say about homosexuality? This question is particularly relevant given the role of psychologists in supporting the doctrine of "keeping the races separate" and thus supporting the apartheid regime. As far as I have been able to determine, not a single article addressing homosexuality has ever been published by any South African academic journal for psychologists. Whether this can be attributed to a complete absence of manuscripts on the topic or the unwillingness of journals and other publications to publish such submissions is unclear.

I do not wish to succumb to what Kitzinger (1987) describes as the "up the mountain saga," albeit not necessarily for the same reasons as Kitzinger. This is the name Kitzinger applies to a situation in which research is viewed over a long span of time and all past work is deemed unscientific, whereas new theories are quickly embraced as progressive. My review of the research conducted in South Africa on homosexuality will focus on how the research, in the context of international research trends, has presented the homosexual as sick, in need of help, and committing a sin, and particularly on how this research historically has failed to include the experiences of the majority Black population in South Africa.

It is interesting to note that from the early 1950s, psychology scholars primarily at the Afrikaans universities have completed theses and dissertations addressing homosexuality. As early as 1951, Loedolff drew attention to the possible dangers of homosexuality and recommended treatment intervention that would lead to homosexuals' being cured. Loedolff stressed that treatment was necessary for lesbians and gay men, because he erroneously believed that homosexuals were sexually attracted to children and were therefore dangerous to society.

In 1956, Liddicoat completed a dissertation that Blyth (1989) commends as presenting a balanced view of homosexuality. However, both Loedolff (1951) and Liddicoat (1956) ignored the experiences of Black people. It is also significant that both these research reports were used as evidence before the Select Committee in the House of Assembly debates regarding homosexuality. Botha (1975) has argued for a compassionate and patient attitude toward homosexuals. He recommends the treatment of homosexuality based on Christian beliefs; however, once again, his sample consisted of only White men. One wonders if his argument would have been similar had he focused on or even included Black gay men. Given the attitudes of the psychological profession and the South African state toward Black people (e.g., money should not be spent on them, as they cannot be helped), one could speculate that these arguments for compassion and patience represent a kind of faith only in the redemption of Whites. This is wholly consistent with the established views of the state—that the homosexual was deemed sick and a threat to South African Christian society, that faulty personality factors led to homosexuals' having this sickness, and so on. Despite arguments that homosexuality should be criminalized, most officials were not in favor of imposing heavy prison sentences on gay men. At the same time, Black people who were considered a threat to Christian society and who, according to the architects of apartheid, suffered from genetic and personality flaws (like those homosexuals were believed to have) were being given the heaviest prison sentences possible.

Researchers such as Jacobs (1975), Kotze (1974), and Prinsloo (1973), all working from the homosexuality as pathology or deviance model, all focused on gaining insight into the "phenomenon" and eventually curing the White gay South African male. Once cured, the White South African male would, in keeping with the logic and rationale of the time, take his rightful role in building a South African nation that reflected the principles and aims of the apartheid regime.

From the 1950s to the 1980s, there was very little research on lesbians or addressing lesbianism. Redlinghuys (1978) and Cronje (1979) both made comparisons between lesbians and heterosexual women. Once again, Black women's experiences were overlooked, and both studies suggested that "disturbed" roles within the family and generally problematic family relationships were factors contributing to female homosexuality.

Since the mid-1980s, more liberal, gay-affirmative research has been completed at historically White liberal universities. Some of this research has included a focus on lesbians and their children, and has challenged court decisions that have deemed lesbians unsuitable mothers (Tucker, 1986). Blyth (1989) explored the identities presented by gay women, and Knight (1989) contributed to gay-affirmative research with a focus on female couples. These two research projects were completed at the University of Cape Town and the University of Witwatersrand, respectively, the country's foremost historically White liberal institutions. Although this research can only make a positive contribution to building a gay rights culture in South Africa, once again the experiences of Black women were not part of these studies. Blyth recommends that the experiences of Black lesbians be researched and documented to create a more accurate context for understanding sexual orientation.

Another recent focus of academic psychology theses is found in the attempt to determine to what extent the homophobia of South African society is present in clinical interventions, and at what levels. Tarrant

(1992) examined 15 psychologists' attitudes toward homosexuality and approaches to therapy with gay clients. She found that the majority of the psychologists did not view homosexuality per se as being pathological. However, they evidenced a general lack of familiarity with the more recent literature and findings prevalent in the field. Although these psychologists did not condone discrimination against gay men and women in any way, they did not advocate an active role for combating heterosexism. The move toward gay-affirmative models of psychotherapy that has occurred in other parts of the world was not reflected among Tarrant's group of South African psychologists. Tarrant does not indicate the numbers of male versus female therapists interviewed, nor the numbers of White versus Black psychologists in the sample.

The attempt to create a unified South African nation at all levels has resulted in some scholars' arguing against the collection of data that reflect racial categories. This may be the reason for the conspicuous absence of race information in Tarrant's (1992) study. However, I agree with the ANC's position on this issue: If we are serious about addressing past inequalities, we must acknowledge racial and gender categories as part of a political empowerment strategy. Tarrant's research does not refer to, or demonstrate, an awareness of the race, gender, and class differences among gay and lesbian South Africans and their diverse experiences. These issues cannot be overlooked if we are serious about addressing the issue of heterosexist bias within therapy as well as in university curricula that are used in the training of future psychologists.

In conclusion, it is fair to say that issues pertinent to gay and lesbian South Africans, particularly Black South Africans, are not popular within the corridors of South African academia. Although discussions of lesbian and gay issues have been published in alternative South African journals (e.g., *Agenda*), such issues are certainly not even whispered about in the mainstream psychology journals. Organized psychology in South Africa launched a new, postapartheid psychological organization in January 1994. The new society has discussed the launch of a women's section in the organization, but at this stage a gay and lesbian section has not even been hinted at (Potgieter & De la Rey, in press).

The Voices

Over the past 3 years I have, with a research assistant, interviewed more than 30 Black lesbians from all over South Africa. The sample includes lesbians from both urban and rural settings, as well as from all classes and educational backgrounds. A large number of these women are not "out," and three of the women interviewed by my research assistant had never previously spoken to another lesbian. One of them said, "I thought I and [my partner] were the only women in the whole world that loved other women."

The women interviewed were accessed through individual contacts, organizations, and requests printed in various magazines. A number of the women who were not out were contacted through my research assistant, who lives in Khayelitsha, a large squatter camp (informal settlement) on the outskirts of Cape Town. She is active in gay and lesbian organizations and is known in the township to be a gay and lesbian rights activist. Thus she knew the *shebeens* (taverns) and bars, houses, washing areas, and so on where women who loved women could be found. Data from this study have been analyzed qualitatively, using discourse analysis, and extremely interesting issues have come to light. The following subsections reflect some of the discourses that have emerged from these interviews to date.

Lesbian Mothers

A number of the women spoke about the need, and at times pressure, to have a child. As one woman reflected: "In African culture you are only a woman, a real woman, once you have had a child. I have been a lesbian for a long time but decided to sleep with a man on two occasions to have a baby. I now have a child 3 years of age." A number of women echoed this sentiment. One observed: "Now that I have a child they [men] and others in the community do not ask so many questions about me [not having a man]. Now I can have a good relationship with [my female partner]. I do not mind having a child, in fact it was what I wanted, but I do not want the man. He is not around anyway; you know, these men disappear even when women want them."

What is interesting is the woman's accurate perception that having a child would allow her, in her words, to "get on with my life," while fulfilling and meeting an important social demand of her culture. A number of the women who had children had made conscious decisions to have them while in a lesbian relationship. Given their class background, decisions about artificial insemination versus heterosexual sex or other forms of insemination and the role of potential father were not major issues. Their class and race position dictated the route they had to follow in order to conceive a child. Usually, heterosexual sexual relations were the most readily available and least costly of their choices. In South Africa, White academics have alleged that Black women have not fought a feminist struggle. One need only listen to the narratives of these women to know how inaccurate such assumptions are. I would suggest that the route these women have chosen—using men for the strategic purpose of conceiving children, while planning to raise those children with female partners—is a conspicuous example of women exercising some control over their destiny under often difficult circumstances. I would further suggest that such behavior certainly represents Black lesbian feminism in an African context. This raises the issue of the need to broaden our concept of what constitutes feminism in lower-class, Third World contexts among people of color.

Black and Gay: The Difficulties

Many of the women interviewed spoke about how they had to move out of the Black community for fear of not being able to "love a woman." These women had grown up at the height of apartheid, when the Group Areas Act and other discriminatory laws were still in force. One of my interviewees explained a dilemma common to many women like her:

> I couldn't live in the township because of me loving a woman, and I could not live in town because of my skin color. I did find a place in town but had to leave for work early in the morning and stay in at night. I lived with a woman (White woman) who was a lesbian and she said it is hard to be a lesbian, but she said Blacks must understand apartheid. She was nice to me because I was a lesbian and I cleaned the flat for her, but I did not really like her because she did not like all Black people.

This woman, like a number of others, then moved back to the township "to be with people that were fighting apartheid." A number of the women spoke about White lesbians understanding the societal pressures and discrimination that are a result of their being lesbians but failing to display similar understanding of the corrosive effects of apartheid on South African Blacks, even to the point of openly supporting the apartheid regime.

Homophobia and the Black Community

Participants in this study spoke about the need to move out of their communities because they could not afford to "be seen with their girlfriends." It is interesting that most of the women were concerned about being seen going about publicly with a girlfriend in the township as opposed to being observed to be living with a girlfriend. As township houses, tents, and shacks in these areas of South Africa are generally overcrowded, where one shares a bed or living or sleeping quarters, and with whom, is not an issue. Space constraints dictate flexibility in these arrangements. However, being seen with a woman partner in public space poses a problem. Interestingly, however, many women said that when they spoke to their families about their being lesbians, the families' initial response was to get them healed, and they were taken to traditional healers. The discourse of the family seems to be that the homosexual person is sick and in need of healing. Another interesting observation is that a number of women said that their families did not evict them from the family home. One woman offered that her mother said that she would look after her just as she would look after any sick person. It is accepted in African communities that the immediate family looks after members in need of care; the latter are not sent to institutions. With respect to women who have been abused, for example, it has been found that shelters may not be an appropriate solution, as when women who leave shelters later go home, their families are not as supportive as might be expected. Family members feel that it is their responsibility and role to care for and protect other family members. This is a responsibility that families take seriously, whether they approve of the "sick" relative's conduct or not. When a family member goes to someone outside the family for help, others in the family may feel disrespected and may not be receptive to the individual when he or she is no longer in need of help.

Gay-affirmative research formally rejects the notion that gay people should be deemed sick—a position with which I wholeheartedly agree.

Yet, given the information gained from these interviews, one may ask, What would be strategically helpful to Black lesbians and gay men, in the short term, in African communities? For example, if they are not deemed sick by their families, on what basis would they receive family support? Would families feel they have no responsibility to support their gay or lesbian members? Or worse, would families view gay or lesbian members as bad people and reject them from the family fold? The problematic assumption of the sickness of homosexuality, in the Black South African context, ironically leads to a mandate for families to maintain contact with and support lesbian or gay family members rather than reject them. I believe that education and conscientizing are important, and that no behavior can be condoned if it opposes a human rights ethic. We need, however, to be strategic regarding political interventions across cultures with differing norms and expectations from family members.

Of the few women interviewed who were "out" to their families, many noted that the female members of their families were more understanding than were the males. These women also said that homosexuality was not spoken about, which accounts in part for the assumption that it does not exist. When members of the community have been "educated," they have been viewed as being more understanding than has generally been expected. In light of what these women report, one wonders if the Black South African community is as homophobic as some researchers suggest. At this stage, no research has been undertaken on the attitudes of South African Black heterosexuals toward homosexuality. Results of the focus groups I have conducted may yield more information on this issue when all the data have been analyzed.

Lesbianism and AIDS

It is extremely interesting that the Black lesbians I interviewed spoke about how they "cannot get this new disease," AIDS, because they do not sleep with men who do not like condoms. What is significant is that these women are aware of the dangers of AIDS. The popular discourse among some of the women is that only men can give you the disease. Strebel (1994) has noted that Black women, when discussing the risk of AIDS, do not call for a return to traditional family values in the form of the nuclear family, monogamy, and heterosexuality. Although the women interviewed did discuss AIDS in terms of discourses of sexual stigma and promiscuity, this did not encompass homophobic ideas. Strebel makes the point that in a society where homosexuality is not acceptable and is mostly invisible, issues and concerns regarding homosexuality may not be aired in public. Another factor is that in South Africa the AIDS pandemic among Blacks has affected primarily heterosexuals.

One can obviously speculate widely about these issues. While not agreeing with the notion that AIDS is a homosexual disease, one can concede the possibility that many individuals who are defining themselves, or are being defined by the medical profession, as heterosexual are in fact bisexual or gay, or at least engaging in more than heterosexual sexual activity. We may also assume that given the taboo against homosexuality, many people might not necessarily disclose this information or be honest with their doctors about their sexual practices. Neither sexual activity nor identity is static. South African medical professionals may perhaps have a vested interest in claiming that the disease primarily affects heterosexuals, as this would be consistent with the well-accepted myth that we do not have homosexuals in Africa. These are issues warranting further exploration.

Conclusion

The final South African Constitution, consistent with the interim constitution, contains a nondiscrimination clause regarding sexual orientation. It is hoped that psychology as an academic and professional discipline will begin to address issues that are pertinent to the lives of gay and lesbian South Africans from more affirmative perspectives. In doing so, practitioners and researchers need to take cognizance of race, class, and gender differences.

The struggle for gay and lesbian rights in South Africa was initially a White struggle. However, since the late 1980s Black people have been drawn into the fray in increasing numbers. Organizations have been founded, such as the National Gay and Lesbian Coalition, to lobby for gay and lesbian rights. The first gay and lesbian studies academic colloquium ever held in South Africa took place in October 1995. It is my hope that such meetings will become regular events, and in the future Black gay men and lesbians will assume a heightened level of visibility, as both conference attendees and presenters, and that the members of these marginalized groups' lives will assume greater prominence and be a focus of progressive academic inquiries.

References

Amadiume, I. (1987). *Male daughters, female husbands: Gender and sex in an African society.* London: Zed.

Billig, M. (1976). *Social psychology and intergroup relations.* London: Academic Press.

Bisheuvel, S. (1976). South Africa. In V. Sexton & H. Misiak (Eds.), *Psychology around the world.* Lincoln: University of Nebraska Press.

Blackwood, E. (1984). Sexuality and gender in certain Native American tribes: The case of cross-gender females. *Signs, 10,* 27-42.

Blyth, S. (1989). *An exploration of accounts of lesbian identities.* Unpublished master's thesis, University of Capetown, South Africa.

Botha, A. H. (1975). *Pastorale sorg aan die homosexuele mens.* Unpublished doctoral dissertation, University of Pretoria, South Africa.

Callender, C., & Kochems, L. (1985). Men and not-men: Male gender mixing statuses and homosexuality. *Journal of Homosexuality, 11*(3-4), 165-178.

Cameron, E. (1994). Unapprehended felons: Gays and lesbians and the law in South Africa. In M. Gevisser & E. Cameron (Eds.), *Defiant desire.* Johannesburg: Ravan.

Chan-Sam, T. (1994). Profiles of Black lesbian life on the Reef. In M. Gevisser & E. Cameron (Eds.), *Defiant desire.* Johannesburg: Ravan.

Chesler, M. A. (1976). Contemporary sociological theories of racism. In P. A. Katz & D. Taylor (Eds.), *Towards the elimination of racism.* Elmsford, NY: Pergamon.

Cooper, S., Nicholas, L. J., Seedat, M., & Statman, J. (1990). Psychology and apartheid: Struggle for psychology in South Africa. In L. J. Nicholas & S. Cooper (Eds.), *Psychology and apartheid: Essays on the struggle for psychology and the mind of South Africa.* Johannesburg: Madiba/Vision.

Cornwell, A. (1983). *Black lesbian in White America.* Tallahassee, FL: Naiad.

Cronje, C. J. (1979). *Lesbianisme: Etiologie in psigodinamika.* Unpublished master's thesis, Rand Afrikaans University, Pretoria, South Africa.

Devereux, G., & Whitehead, H. (1937). Institutionalized homosexuality of the Mohaive Indians. *Human Biology, 9,* 498-527.

De Vos, P. (1995). *On the legal construction of gay and lesbian identity in South Africa.* Paper presented at Gay and Lesbian Colloquium, Cape Town, South Africa.

Dunbar, M., Ndatshe, V., & Sibuyi, V. (1988). Migrancy and male sexuality in the South African gold mines. *Journal of South African Studies, 8,* 228-256.

Essed, P. (1987). *The Dutch as everyday problem.* Amsterdam: Cres.

Evans-Pritchard, E. E. (1970). Sexual inversion among the Azande. *American Anthropologist, 72,* 1428-1432.

Gay, J. (1985). Mummies and babies and friends and lovers in Lesotho. *Journal of Homosexuality, 12*(3-4), 97-116.

Gevisser, M., & Cameron, E. (Eds.). (1994). *Defiant desire.* Johannesburg: Ravan.

Hinsch, B. (1990). *Passions of the cut sleeve: The male homosexual tradition in China.* Berkeley: University of California Press.

Holmes, R. (1994). White rapists made coloureds and homosexuals: The Winnie Mandela trial and the politics of race and sexuality. In M. Gevisser & E. Cameron (Eds.), *Defiant desire.* Johannesburg: Ravan.

Jacobs, M. (1975). *Conditioned aversion applied to the treatment of homosexuality and compulsive ruminations.* Unpublished master's thesis, University of Witwatersrand, Johannesburg.

Katz, J. (1992). *Gay American history: Lesbians and gay men in the USA.* New York: Cromwell.

Kendall, K. (1995). *Looking for lesbians in Lesotho.* Paper presented at the Gay and Lesbian Colloquium, Cape Town, South Africa.

Kinsey, A. C., Pomeroy, W. B., & Martin, C. E. (1948). *Sexual behavior in the human male.* Philadelphia: W. B. Saunders.

Kinsey, A. C., Pomeroy, W. B., Martin, C. E., & Gebhard, P. (1953). *Sexual behavior in the human female.* Philadelphia: W. B. Saunders.

Kitzinger, C. (1987). *The social construction of lesbianism.* London: Sage.

Knight, S. (1989). *Towards an understanding of an invisible minority.* Unpublished master's thesis, University of the Witwatersrand, Johannesburg.

Kotze, C. G. (1974). *'n Diepteigologiese ondersoek na die verskynsel van homosexuele gedrag.* Unpublished doctoral dissertation, University of Pretoria, South Africa.

Krige, E. J. (1974). Women-marriage with special reference to the lovedu: Its significance for the definition of marriage. *Africa, 44,* 11ff.

Liddicoat, R. (1956). *Homosexuality: Results of a survey related to various theories.* Unpublished doctoral dissertation, University of Witwatersrand, Johannesburg.

Loedolff, J. J. (1951). *Homosexualiteit: 'n Sosiologiese studie.* Unpublished master's thesis, University of Pretoria, South Africa.

Louw, R. (1995). *The emergence of a Black gay identity in Durban.* Paper presented at the Gay and Lesbian Colloquium, Cape Town, South Africa.

McClean, H., & Ngoobo, L. (1994). Abangibh amayo balthi ngimnandi: Gay sexuality in Reef townships. In M. Gevisser & E. Cameron (Eds.), *Defiant desire.* Johannesburg: Ravan.

Murray, S. (1992). *Oceanic homosexualities: Describing gender defined homosexuality in Asian oceanic cultures.* New York: Garland.

Potgieter, C. & De la Rey, C. (in press). Gender and race: Whereto psychology in South Africa. *Feminism and Psychology.*

Prinsloo, S. W. (1973). *'n Vergelykende persoonlikeheidstudie tussen 'n groep passiewe homoseksualiteit en 'n kontrole groep.* Unpublished master's thesis, University of Pretoria, South Africa.

Redlinghuys, J. L. (1978). *'n Psignodinamiese ondersoek na die verskynsel van lesbinisme binne 'n gesinstruktuur.* Unpublished master's thesis, University of Pretoria, South Africa.

Retief, G. (1994). Keeping Sodom out of the laager: State repression of homosexuality in apartheid South Africa. In M. Gevisser & E. Cameron (Eds.), *Defiant desire.* Johannesburg: Ravan.

Rex v. Gough & Narroway. (1926). *Cape Division Law Report in South Africa, 159,* 162.

Rubin, G. (1975). The traffic of women: Notes on the political economy of sex. In R. Reiter (Ed.), *Toward an anthropology of women* (pp. 157-210). New York: Monthly Review Press.

Seedat, M. A. (1988). *Topics, trends, and silences in South African psychology, 1948-1988.* Unpublished doctoral thesis, University of the Western Cape, Cape Town, South Africa.

Sexual Offenses Act 23 of 1957 (Act of South African Parliament).

South African Parliament. (1969). House of Assembly debates.

Strebel, A. (1994). *Women and AIDS: A study of issues in the prevention of HIV infection.* Unpublished doctoral dissertation, University of Cape Town, South Africa.

Tarrant, S. (1992). *Psychotherapy with gay clients: Therapeutic approaches of clinical psychologists in Durban.* Unpublished master's thesis, University of Durban Westville, Durban, South Africa.

Topley, M. (1975). Marriage resistance in rural Kwangtung. In M. Woolf & R. Witke (Eds.), *Women in Chinese society.* Stanford, CA: Stanford University Press.

Tucker, C. (1986). *A medico-legal examination of homosexual women and their children: Ethical considerations and the role of the clinical psychologist.* Unpublished master's thesis, University of Cape Town, South Africa.

Van Rooyen v. Van Rooyen. (1994). *South African Law Reports, 2,* 325, Witersrand Local Division.

Vermaak v. Van der Merwe. (1981). *South African Law Reports, 3,* 78.

Visser, M. (1995, July). Cry freedom. *Attitude.*

Williams, W. L. (1986). *The spirit and the flesh: Sexual diversity in American Indian culture.* Boston: Beacon.

Women who prey on little girls (shady world exposed as house mother admits new sex charge). (1989, November 19). *Sunday Times,* p. 15.

6

Symbol of Privilege, Object of Derision
Dissonance and Contradictions

ARMAND R. CERBONE

If all black folk and yellow folk and red folk and brown folk disappeared tomorrow from America, America would still be multicultural but there wouldn't be a debate about multiculturalism. There's something called whiteness that was constructed, that hides and conceals a very rich multiculturalism among brothers and sisters of European descent in America.

Cornel West, *The Radical Democratic Tradition*, 1995

I am a white, Eurocentric, middle-class, professional male. To many people of color, I not only represent the dominant culture, I am the patriarchy as well. They see *me* as a part of their problem. Many of them believe I have no authority to speak about prejudice or oppression, much less to speak about it to them. For some time, I believed this to be true as well. On the face of things, I have enjoyed privileges and prerogatives others have been denied because of gender, race, or culture. I know that to be true. There have been much younger moments when I whispered to myself that I am glad I was born white and male. But I am also a *gay* Italian white male, stripped of the not inconsiderable privileges accorded heterosexuals as well as Anglo-Saxons. The pain that I as a gay man share with other gays does not equate with the pain that women and people of color suffer, even though our separate pains are inflicted by the same bigots. When I suggest that my sexual orientation has brought me pain, it may seem that I am denying or trivializing the pain women and people of color have felt, especially when felt at the hands of people very much like me. The suggestion that my experience of bias is at all like that of black, red, yellow, or brown persons, or that my experience may illuminate the experiences of these people, can seem egregious.

Nonetheless, I have experienced prejudice, and not only as a gay man. Although being gay is perhaps the most central experience of my life, being an Italian American is also part of my history. I was born just a few months before the United States declared war on Japan and the Axis powers. One of those European enemies was Fascist Italy. I grew up in the 1940s and 1950s in an Irish neighborhood in Boston, where Italians occupied a lower rung on the social ladder than the Irish, who arrived here just before us. It was during the Irish ascendancy in politics and business that we Italians were trying to establish our own foothold. Many contemporary Americans are too young to remember, and others may choose to forget, that Italians were objects of considerable scorn and derision. My first awareness of prejudice was hearing my kind referred to as "guineas" and "wops." One particularly noxious slur referred to Italians as "niggers turned inside out." This taught me more about prejudice than the KKK lynchings I read about or saw acted out in the movies I grew up on. Much later came "fairy," "faggot," and "cocksucker." The prejudice toward Italians may have been more subtle and attenuated than that reserved for blacks or Jews or homosexuals. When all was said and done, I was still white in a country that made larger distinctions between black and white than among whites. Still, the intense contempt reserved for my kind felt pernicious, toxic, and painful to me.

The intersection of that dual experience, of being Italian and gay in midcentury America, is the focus of this chapter. It is in this duality, I believe, that I can speak to another, albeit less visible, aspect of the diversity among lesbians, gay men, and bisexual men and women. This discussion demands some disclosure of personal experience. This is about *my* life. More particularly, it is about my psychosexual and psychosocial development. My task here is to make what is intensely individual serve to illuminate the lives of others who are admittedly often very different from me, but also often very similar. The difficulty here is not so much that I am shy. It is more that I seek to avoid a confessional narcissism on the one hand and the making of meaning-less generalizations on the other. How much of a claim does *my* life, or anyone's, legitimately have on the attention of others, no matter who they are? It is this dilemma and the conviction that I had no authority to speak that kept me silent for a long time and contributed to my avoidance of committing to this endeavor at all.

Two notions changed my mind. The first was voiced by Cornel West, whose words are quoted at the beginning of this chapter. Those words acknowledge the diversity that exists among white ethnic groups. This spoke directly to my experience of growing up first-generation Italian in a predominantly Irish neighborhood of Boston. I do not think I would have been so convinced by these words if the argument had not been expressed by an African American. West also implies that there are indeed prejudices and competition among groups of white persons as well as between blacks and whites. The fact that these words come from an African American legitimated for me what I always felt but would hesitate to voice out loud: that whites experience real oppression from other whites. Whiteness is a fiction, a social construct used to unite very different peoples against others who are different in color. Whiteness is but another construct created to make and keep others utterly *other*. Ignatiev (1995) observes that when white ethnic groups came to the United States, they found themselves in a land where skin color was a most important factor in determining social position. This construct of whiteness connected many people with conflicting back-grounds, who often hated one another, together against an "other" under the superficial rubric of "whiteness" and against anyone who was not white. Telling my story might help me find those bonds with others whose experiences on the surface *seem* very different.

The second notion that changed my mind about contributing to this volume is my absolute belief in the healing power of personal stories and narratives. When dealing with my homosexuality, nothing rouses me to anger or laughter or tears more than coming-out stories. It is the same with my Italian heritage. The issues are universal, each story a variation and permutation on common themes. Coming-out stories are our folktales. When shared, they normalize our experiences and reduce the devastating isolation homophobia enforces. They give us a place in the center of a time and a culture, and mitigate the marginality and irrelevance homophobia imposes. I proceed with a belief in this healing power of narrative in the lives of individuals and its capacity to illuminate the shared nature of struggle in lives of many who are different from one another.

Dissonance and Damage

Although being gay may be the most salient fact of my life, that salience is based in the recognition that it is the most salient feature of my person for others. Every attempt to normalize my sexuality has set me further apart from others or overly identified me with others with whom I share only my sexual orientation. In so many ways, it seems this dissonance resonates in one form or another throughout my life. There has been a confluence of contradictory messages and forces about who I am, about what I am for myself and others, and about how people perceive me and what they want from me.

When, for example, I told my mother that the man I lived with was my lover, her first words were, "Don't you think I knew? But I'm shocked!" I understood two things by that. The first reaction was for me: She was my mother; she knew her son. The second was for herself and others important in her world. It told me her worst fear had come true and that she felt shame before others. Two very different messages, two very different relationships implied. In her first response I was part of her and her world, her son, like her; in the second, I was utterly other, unlike her and her kind. Which one would prevail? How could I put those together?

Despite the double messages I received on this occasion and too many others to mention here, I enjoyed a very close and warm relationship with my mother. Not so with my father—it seems he disappeared about the time I was 4 years old. After that time, I remember very little interest from him. I always thought his alcoholism was the reason. Certainly, his disease wreaked the usual kinds of havoc in the family. His alcoholism disguised for many years his disappointment in a son who preferred books and cooking and acting to fixing cars and broken pipes. It also gave me a mask for my own disappointment and anger with him for abandoning me. It further provided a morally unassailable focus for my criticism of him and the smoldering rage I felt toward him.

In contrast, my father and my younger brother were friends. The family explanation for this was that I was my mother's son and he was my father's son. I felt special and not special, owned and disowned. Why this was so was never articulated beyond the observation that my father and brother were "men's men." What was I, then? "A gentleman," I was told over and over. "You have class." It was like being told my testicles were too small for me to be considered a real man. Women might like me, but I would never be the man's man my father or my brother was. As recently as a month ago, my mother reflected on this and acknowledged that I was not the macho son he wanted. The result was more dissonance. Admired by women but shunned by men. My mother reassured me often that my father loved me. I did believe it, but wondered why it was so hard for him to show it and why it hurt so much. The result was still more dissonance; I was loved but avoided. My father's behavior rarely matched the sentiments my mother reported he felt.

Being Italian meant being earthy and lusty. Italian men were Latin lovers, dark and suave romancers of women. They were stallions, direct, even out of control in their passionate pursuit of women. I grew up on the films of De Sica, Fellini, Magnani, Loren, and Mastroiani. Italians were large figures in these films, sometimes comic and bombastic, sometimes volatile and volcanic, but always intense about life and love. I loved these people. I was happy, and still am, to be Italian. While stirring my aspirations for a successfully heterosexual adjustment, these films were so *ultra*heterosexual they also served to underscore my anxieties about sex. I ended up feeling like an unsuccessful Italian as well as a failing Catholic.

Being Italian meant having a very proud history, if one regarded Italy's contributions to food and fashion, music, art, and architecture. Who in the Western world were our peers? Further back in time, our forefathers conquered and ruled the Western world for centuries. Even the papacy had been Italian for most of its existence. Very few peoples could boast of such accomplishments. I felt this pride intensely. I identified with anything and everything Italian or Latin. When I was 4 or 5 years old, my father took me to a boat show. As we waited in line for some free banana fritters, I am told I asked in a squeaky little voice, "Are these Italian bananas?"

Yet my contemporaries saw Italians as overly dramatic buffoons, puppets of Germany in World War II, hopelessly divided among ourselves thereafter, unable to govern or manage daily life, buried in bureaucracies that do not function, pompous and preposterous clowns, in love with life but ultimately inept and unsuccessful. This was certainly the impression I got from my Irish neighbors and friends at school. I am uncertain if I exaggerate here for the sake of emphasis or if I am just being Italian in doing so. Nonetheless, though it was often cloaked in humor, the derision was real, and it hurt. Today ethnic jokes are told about Poles, Mexicans, and other groups. In Boston in the 1940s and 1950s, the butt of every ethnic joke was an Italian. When I moved to the Midwest for graduate school and then settled there, I heard the very same jokes I had heard told about Italians in my childhood, only now they were told about the Polish and Mexicans. They were no funnier then than they were when I first heard them.

In my Italian family, we saw ourselves as better than our Irish neighbors, not to mention Protestants, Jews, and blacks. I grew up thinking the worst thing you could call someone was a black Protestant bastard. We believed that we were cleaner, more industrious, smarter, and better looking. It was customary for us to joke about the habits, dress, and appearance of anyone who was not Italian. We believed their criticisms of us were evidence of their envy. We were clannish and spent Sundays and holidays with family, doing Italian things. Our homes were filled with the sounds and smells of cooking and eating Italian foods, women in the kitchen arguing over whose tomato sauce was more like mama's, and men smoking and drinking in the parlors. After eating, in good weather there was boccie, Italian lawn bowling, and in bad weather there was *scopa*, an Italian card game. We even had our own language, a familial hybrid composed of sentences with English structure but peppered liberally with Italian argot. Above everything was the family, *la familia*, and pride in family. The movie *Moonstruck* captures the ethic and customs of my family very succinctly. More dissonance: How does one put together this state of being both top and bottom rung on the ladder simultaneously?

Embedded in my mother's comment that I had "class" was yet another layer of conflicting messages. There were tensions between second-generation Italian Americans and newly immigrated Italians. My mother was second generation and very Americanized. Her father was a successful businessman, an immigrant grocer, who made it big in the United States. He owned a number of properties and blocks of stores in the neighborhood where I grew up. His success was based on selling Italian meats and specialties to an Irish clientele, and his name commanded considerable respect. He was always referred to as *Mister*

Farnese (I'm using a fictitious name here to protect my family's privacy). In that neighborhood I was known by mother's and not my father's surname. I was instructed by grandparents, uncles and aunts, even by my mother on occasion, to use their last name to let people know who I was. The result was special treatment from merchants and greater regard within the parish environs. My father's family, on the other had, was fresh from Naples. In the eyes of my mother's Americanized family, they were good people, the salt of the earth, but ignorant and uncultured. Less educated and wedded to old ways, they still spoke only Italian at home and were shy and uncomfortable outside of family circles. They were judged crude, without good manners. Epithets that had been used to demean the Irish were used in the family about these lesser Italians in the same way. Comments such as "At least they aren't Sicilian" articulated yet another layer of within-group discrimination, implying that mainland Italians are superior to those from the island of Sicily. Having "class" meant that I was well mannered, polished, and refined. As a Farnese, I was a better breed of Italian. Evidently, even Italians thought there were good Italians and bad Italians. I was both. More dissonance.

Being Italian also meant being Catholic—not much help there. Once, when I was in the sixth grade, preadolescent interest in sexuality raised its head in class. A classmate had purchased a risqué get-well card for a fellow classmate who was in the hospital. When the nun who taught us shamed us boys for having laughed at it, she singled me out for particular scorn. I was studying to be an altar boy, months earlier than ordinarily permitted. An exception to the rules regarding age requirements had been made for me. "You are a whitened sepulcher," she accused. "All whitewash on the outside and rotting filth on the inside." A singular honor turned to abject humiliation. I can still see my tears falling onto my shoes and the floor and feel my cheeks hot with shame. I remember it still, but now with sadness for that misguided nun and with anger for that normal little kid.

It must be understood that in the Boston of the 1940s and 1950s, when the church spoke, through its priests or its lesser agents, the nuns, all heads bowed. Dissent was unheard of. Grumble one might, but privately. The city itself was divided as much into parishes as it was into geographic areas. Within 5 minutes of meeting someone, you had determined which parish he or she came from. The parish was a social, political, economic, and psychological entity as much as a spiritual and religious one. The church and the parish school were centers that encompassed all areas of life, from birth to death. Social position was determined by which parish one belonged to and what position one held in the parish church. The closer one was to the clergy, the higher one's station. I remember very well the significant summer evening my mother prepared linguine with white clam sauce, something she had never cooked before, for the monsignor's visit to our home. I wondered uncomfortably in my seat at the dining room table how and why we had merited this attention. Having the pastor to dinner was a singular honor that drew the awe and envy of one's neighbors. It further attested to the loftiness of our position in the community.

"We love the sinner, not the sin," the church preached about gays. "And you, my son, are a sinner. . . . But God loves you *anyway*." How does one make sense of that? How can the sin be punished but not the sinner? My sin is in me; I *am* this sin. I behave as a homosexual because I am homosexual. Would the church send my sin to hell without me? Everyone has original sin, they say. It is seen as a natural consequence of being a child of Adam and Eve. But, I reasoned, I am homosexual and surely a sin against nature itself. What is original sin compared to homosexuality? Were there ten commandments but only two important ones, the ones dealing with sexuality? What was a child to think? How could God's infinite love embrace a fetid sore on the Mystical Body of His Church? I felt regarded as if I were not even human like other humans, not even a child of God like other children, but, once again, apart and reviled. Once again I was left with more dissonance and confusion.

That God and his church forbade sex outside of marriage provided a cover for the anxiety I felt at the prospect of being sexual with women. My distaste for the pleasures of the flesh became witness to my sinlessness. That I was driven to distraction by desire for men I regarded as a divine crucible in which my mettle would be tested and my character forged. Ironically, that has been true, but not as I or the church would have imagined it. By avoiding the near occasions of sin, and even the distant ones, I could avoid my anxieties and be admired as pure and saintly. This was perhaps the most insidious damage done by the dissonance: that I worked the mixed messages to a self-defeating advantage. What power I could muster, what place I could claim in this world was in allying with what was morally correct and upright. I wrapped myself in rectitude. It was a natural evolution, then, that I would seek the priesthood.

I know now this was a Pyrrhic victory of sorts. At that time, I believed deeply that pursuing a career in religion blessed my struggle with transcendent meaning. The regimen of a religious life provided a structure for my life, the many rules gave me an order and stability I could not find anywhere else. The seminary removed me from an emotionally confused and volatile family life at the same time it gave me an honored place within it. Italians revere their priests. Celibacy exempted me from sexuality. The cassock and collar provided a ready explanation for my abstention from affairs of the flesh. While it made a virtue of being different and set apart, it made an enemy of my body and my need for emotional and physical intimacy.

Clinically, I was depressed and repressed and growing more deeply so each year. When, as a seminarian, I manifested very clear signs of depression, I was told my pain was spiritual aridity, God's way of calling me closer to him. Though I was admired for my conduct and values, I was alone and alien, very otherworldly. Internally I had become deeply divided and unsure. Being Catholic simply intensified, no, *sealed*, the repression and deepened my anxiety and depression. I didn't stand a chance.

Consonance and Resolution—of Sorts

Admitting and accepting my homosexuality marked the beginning of my healing the dissonance. It meant I could face my worst fear about myself and survive. It meant no more conflicting internal messages. *Embracing* my homosexuality was the river crossing that secured for me a coherent and worthy sense of self. My first experience of consonance occurred with my first visit to West Hollywood, California, in 1979. My days there changed my life. I spent an entire week dining out morning and evening, spending time on the beach, partying, being entertained in the homes of many men and women, and meeting luminaries of the lesbian and gay movement. By the end of the week I had met only two straight people—both were waitresses. I had lived fully for an entire week totally immersed in a gay subculture. Not once did I have to explain myself or dissemble or worry about how I would be perceived. Further, I felt *valued* for being gay. I felt free and rich and excited about the future. But when my host, who had provided all the introductions, housed me, and mentored me, leaned over to kiss me goodbye at the airport, I turned away. Sitting in the plane on the runway, waiting to return to Chicago, I realized the sin I had committed against my friend. I was red with shame and anger. In that moment I saw all the censoring of self, all the work of calculating what I could say or couldn't, what I could reveal or couldn't. And I saw my unwitting collusion with a world that insisted on denying the truth of my existence and the existence of others like me. To me, *that* was sin, not the sex I had or the love I felt. I vowed at that moment never to deny myself or my affections again. Later, at home in bed, my lover said to me, "You've changed!" "Yes, I have," I responded, "and I hope you like it, because I am not going back."

I think this event marked the beginning of the end for us. Years later, again in bed one night, he opined that he did not think homosexuality is in harmony with the universe. What, then, was he doing in our bed? It was a nail in the coffin of our relationship. A year or two later, he entertained a coworker in our home. Before she arrived he hid, in one closet or another, everything that might say I lived there. The closet metaphor was not lost on me. When I returned home and saw what he had done, I was startled and frightened. He had denied me and our relationship, though he meant only to deny his own homosexuality. It was all but the last nail in the coffin. That came when his therapist asked us in joint session why we were together. In unison we replied, "Because we love each other." "But what good is it?" he responded. In that moment his common sense took the floor from under me. Love is not always enough. I turned to my lover and said, "I guess I'll have to be the one to say it. It's over." I ended my 9-year relationship there. I learned that to have a successful relationship, both I and my lover would have to be equally comfortable with our homosexuality.

Gains and Losses

The healing with my mother began when I accepted that I might have to forfeit my relationship with her as well. Just as she may have known me and my true character intuitively, and privately feared that

I was gay, I knew her, too. I had seen her stand by others in our family who had violated some familial or social code, and I had seen her abandon some, too. When I came out to her, I did not know which side of her I would meet: the discordant mother who rejects or the loving mother who embraces. I warned her that I expected her as my mother to stand by me. If she were to do less than support me, I would shut a door on our relationship. *She* would be other; I would make her so. When she said a day later, with obvious pain in her voice, "I wish it weren't so and I wish I didn't know," she unwittingly drew a battle line between us. Minutes later, she added, "I don't want you two to sleep together in my house and I don't want to see you hug or kiss."

I left the room, fuming silently. When she asked when I would return for another visit, I said I didn't know. When pressed for a date, Thanksgiving or Christmas, I told her I couldn't come back to a home where I couldn't hug my lover. The battle was joined. In the course of our raging storm she told me, "You are my son. I would love you if you were a murderer or rapist!" All I could do was crumble in a heap of tears. What good was that love to me? She rushed to me, held my head against her stomach, and asked, "What do you want of me?" More sobs from me. Wasn't it obvious? "This does not feel like love to me," I told her. "Then you don't know what love is," my mother told me. "This love hurts. It hurts too much. All I did was tell you who I am." My anger gathered around me like armor. "What's so hard about that? Am I supposed to lie to you so you can go on believing I'm straight? For what? Your *comfort?* So *you* don't have to face bigots?"

During the battle, my Irish stepfather stood silently in another room rattling the change in his pockets. I remember thinking even then it must be hard for him to see this wrangling—after all, he's not Italian. This is how we handle such things. A truce emerged when my parents left for a dinner engagement and I left for the airport. A dark storm obliged us with violent thunder and lightning. Very Italian.

It took 5 years before the battling settled into acceptance. On one occasion my mother asserted that I had brought shame on the family. I replied, "*This* family! We've got convicted drug dealers, thieves, adulterers, and pederasts in this family. And you're telling me *I* brought shame on the family! This shame is yours, not mine." There is nothing like the truth to shatter illusions, and there is nothing like the truth to empower. I vowed not to remain in a relationship with someone who was ashamed of me. If she were to lose me, she said, she would never be happy again in her life. "Then choose," I told her. To her credit, she chose to understand and accept the truth about me. She grieves that I will not give her grandchildren and worries that some homophobe will shoot me or that I will die of AIDS—more high drama. Nor can she boast of my achievements around her retirement pool, because most of those achievements are within the gay community. We can talk now, occasionally with great honesty and mutual compassion. She has to deal now with the homophobia of her friends and fight the shame that threatens to well up in her. I support where I can, but I also remind her that I am her child and need her to be my mother. I have no other.

The healing with my father never happened. He was murdered during a robbery where he worked long before I came to terms with my sexuality. His disappointment and neglect still hurt me and still affect my life, not surprisingly. Mostly their impact is felt on my intimate relationships, where fears of abandonment and devaluing are easily stirred. They also make it difficult for me to risk the criticism of my professional peers, who constitute yet another family. They have made writing this essay difficult. With years of therapy, however, I have learned to move past many of my fears and to take calculated risks in pursuit of the things I want. I do understand my father better. I know he was damaged by alcoholism. But more, he felt inferior to others for being an uneducated immigrant Italian. How could a man who felt ashamed of himself give much reassurance, let alone guidance, to a precocious gay son?

As for the Catholic Church, healing has been more difficult and convoluted. The church's ambivalence on all matters sexual is troubling and troublesome. Its equivocations on same-sex relationships are pernicious. They deny me the very dignity of person and soul the church preaches I enjoy as a Catholic child of God. The church insists that I accept a permanent cleaving between my self and my sexuality. That leaves me ruptured spiritually and psychologically. To heal the breach it creates, it suggests a logic so tortured it twists my mind into a pretzel. Nor have I been able to find the comfort others have in distinguishing between the institutional church and the spiritual church. For me, this is one more distinction without difference. The church speaks when its bishops and priests speak. When its priests condemn homosexuals, the church condemns homosexuals. There is no consonance possible.

What healing I have managed has been predicated on my dissent, in saying no to all of that. As a result, I have absented myself from the church and its cacophonous dicta. The abstention extends now to all things and institutions religious. Nonetheless, I remain deeply spiritual. I am as excited today as I was as a child about the person of Christ. Whether he was divine or not is not an important issue anymore. That the example of his life can guide me when I am in doubt or in need of inspiration is. I ask *myself* now, not the church, What would Christ do in this situation? That has been the healing for me. It has allowed me to be who and what I am and become just a bit more than I was. Isn't that after all what all religions are supposed to do for us?

A significant result of that healing is that I have won back the body that was lost with my renunciation of sexuality. I had feared my body and hated it. Now I *live* in this body. Once terrified of things physical, I delight in the feel of my body running, skiing, skating, or swimming. What once threatened to betray me with its desires is now a source of joy and self-expression. Each year I grow more comfortable with sex and sexuality. This in turn has helped me to understand others in situations both clinical and social. I have learned, in assessing the sexual behaviors and relationships of others, to look more for the success or failure of a set of behaviors in achieving desired intimacy than in approximating one moral code or another. I am less burdened and constricted, more trusting and resilient, in relationships these days.

There are still times when self-questioning and doubt grip me. I lose my internal compass, lock up in fear of being judged unworthy, irrelevant. Such fears have made writing this chapter difficult. Sometimes I find that I strike an apologetic or tentative tenor. Whether I suffer these moments because my father abandoned me, or because he abandoned me because I was gay, or because I was derided for being the son of Italian immigrants at a time when Italians were particularly marginalized in a city where they were particularly visible objects of derision—these are questions that at some point become too convoluted to sort out. Therapy has allowed me to wring some profit from these pains: I look for the truth in things, for the rock of reason to stand on, no matter how slight it seems at the time. Truth will ultimately take and hold the center. Searching and finding have made my days an adventure—arduous, of course, but far less threatened.

Discussion and Summary

Prejudice blankets us all with layers and layers of dissonant and conflicting messages at every turn. The double messages stun our psyches and short-circuit our brains. They create paralyzing self-doubt, depress us, and arouse deep anxieties. Whether coming from family, friends, or strangers, they create an environment in which betrayal and treachery are constant threats. The threats can come from others or self. When directed at critical elements of selfhood, such as sexual identity, race, and culture, these contradictory messages encourage dissociative processes and internal splitting. I can still recall the anxiety a standard psychoanalytic text (Fenichel, 1943) could arouse in me during my graduate school days in the 1960s. Then, such texts argued that homosexuality was to be found in the majority of paranoid schizophrenics.

Depending on the significance of the source, such discordant messages can deliver severe blows to an individual's sense of self. If the conflicting messages come from parents, for example, the damage will likely be great, for parents are the first shapers of a child's identity as a distinct individual. Children are likely to accept what their parents tell them as true. If the damage occurs early in life, as it often does with sexuality, race, and culture, it will complicate development throughout life. If, as Freud has suggested, the business of life is to work and to love, working and loving will become very convoluted indeed. Individuals who are compromised by self-rejection and hate are more likely to accept marginal places in a culture that sees them as evil made flesh. Further, the isolation they suffer as a result hampers their ability to mobilize and combat the forces arrayed against them.

It seems that the ruptures engendered by prejudice begin to heal when damaged individuals recognize that the ruptures are not inherent in themselves but reside in the culture. The dissonance they hear about self is really the echo of the ambivalence and anxiety in others around them. The deficiency is in the ignorance of others, not in anything they know about themselves. When they accept this, they can mobilize themselves internally to counter the effects of bigotry. Healing has begun to take place when they can see prejudice—racism, sexism, homophobia—as an obstacle to happiness, not a preclusion.

Moreover, it would seem that prejudice is a many-headed hydra. Lop off one head and another grows to take its place. Every group seems to value itself at the expense of another group. Even subcultures stigmatize differences among themselves. Being gay provides no safe haven among other gays if one is not white. Being black among other blacks provides no immunity from abuse if one is gay. Being Italian among other Italians is no guarantee of safety either—there are better and worse classes of Italians. It seems that humans are infinitely adept at finding distinctions that allow them to stigmatize others.

Cornell West said it best. Whiteness *is* a fiction, one created to keep others out and to justify pogroms against the different. If whiteness is a fiction, then so is heterosexuality, and so is maleness in the ways they are used arbitrarily to privilege some and disadvantage others. The development of a heightened sense of self—"I am black, I am female, I am this or that"—is important for an individual's coming to know and understand self, and I do not seek to minimize its importance. It is a child at 2 learning he is he and not another that is both liberating and frightening. It is the opening act in the drama of balancing between love of self and love of others, a drama that plays throughout life.

I do not think there is anything particularly unusual in this story—not if you are gay, or black, or bisexual, or brown or red or yellow and female, or recently come to these American shores from a Third World country. It is simply my story of coming to terms with the realities of the prejudice I have experienced and the prejudice of which I am guilty. Thus far, I have learned that everybody is somebody's other. Whether victims of homophobia or of racism, we all bleed. Everyone's blood is precious, no one's more than another's. Ultimately, healing between men and women, between one ethnic group or nation and another, between one sexual orientation and another, can and will come when we accept that there are natural limits to self-realization and expression. Those limits are implicit in the knowledge that we all eat from the same table that is this Earth. No one owns the pie, but each has an equal claim to it. Committing to fairness and simple justice alone can keep us from devolving into the dissonant discord that has made it necessary for me to write this chapter.

References

Fenichel, O. (1943). *The psychoanalytic theory of neurosis.* New York: W. W. Norton.

Ignatiev, N. (1995). *How the Irish became white.* New York: Routledge.

West, C. (Speaker). (1995). *The radical democratic tradition* (Transcript). Boulder, CO: Alternative Radio.

7

Exploring the Lives of Older
African American Gay Men

CLARENCE LANCELOT ADAMS, Jr.

DOUGLAS C. KIMMEL

There have been several studies of older gay men and lesbians reported in recent years (Adelman, 1990; Francher & Henkin, 1973; Friend, 1987; Gray & Dressel, 1985; Kelly, 1977; Kimmel, 1979; Lee, 1987; Pope & Schulz, 1990; Quam & Whitford, 1992), but essentially all of the respondents in those studies have been White. Likewise, only anecdotal information about middle-aged or older African American lesbians exists (Kimmel & Sang, 1995; Sang, Warshow, & Smith, 1991).

There is some information about African American gay men in the research literature, but no empirical studies specifically of older men have been published. Three studies from the Institute for Sex Research included African American gay male respondents and provide some data relevant to the present study (Bell & Weinberg, 1978; Bell, Weinberg, & Hammersmith, 1981; Weinberg & Williams, 1974). They suggest that African American gay men are similar to White gay men on many dimensions, but that subtle differences may be found in the areas of vulnerability in occupations, family relationships (especially with extended kin), religiosity, and attitudes toward sexual behavior.

AUTHORS' NOTE: The study discussed in this chapter was supported by a grant from the Society for the Psychological Study of Social Issues, Division 9 of the American Psychological Association.

African American gay men have been described in personal reports (Beam, 1986; Boykin, 1996), fictionalized observations (Baldwin, 1956; Boykin, 1956), and video explorations (e.g., Marlon Riggs's film *Tongues Untied*). Only two empirical studies, however, have focused on this population. The first was a questionnaire study of 60 African American gay men conducted for a dissertation (Johnson, 1981). It found evidence that some African American gay men identify predominantly with their ethnic group, whereas others identify primarily with gay men. However, in the study sample, neither group reported a high degree of involvement with the broader African American community.

The second empirical study was based on interviews with three African American gay men and three African American lesbians (Loiacano, 1989). Respondents in the study expressed central concerns about finding validation in both the lesbian/gay community and the African American community, and about integrating their identities across these two dimensions. For some, the emergence of organizations for African American gay men and/or lesbians was helpful. The study also noted that for these African American gay men, coming out was less valued than among White gay men, because it could jeopardize the support they need as members of a racial minority and because racial bias exists also in the general lesbian and gay male community.

Icard (1985; Icard & Traunstein, 1987) has reported impressions of African American gay men from a social work perspective. In addition to findings similar to those noted above, Icard has observed that being a gay man is often seen as a "White phenomenon" in the African American community, which is generally extremely antigay. As in the White community, some gay men within the African American community maintain relatively high status as entertainers or within their churches, and this status may provide some degree of social acceptance as long as they do not reveal their sexual orientation openly.

The theoretical perspective of our study is the emerging focus on the ecology of development and the importance of contextual variables for understanding life-span development. We take the view that both living as a gay man and being African American are highly significant contextual variables. Based on previous studies of older White gay men, we predicted that the varied influences on their adult development and aging would create a mosaic of diverse adaptations in this particular group of men.

Sample and Methods

The sample consisted of 20 African American gay men in New York City. We recruited some respondents through an organization called Gay Men of African Descent (GMAD); we presented a description of the study at a general meeting of the organization and also advertised in the GMAD newsletter. In addition, some men were contacted through personal networks, including those of respondents who referred others for the study. Obviously, the sample is not representative of the total population of African American gay men. However, it is a particular segment of the group that is the focus of this exploratory study.

The respondents ranged in age from 39 to 73 years; average age was 56. All but 1 of the 20 were born in the United States (10 in New York State, including 8 in New York City; 5 in the South; and 4 in the Midwest); the nonnative was born in Haiti.

As a group, the respondents were highly educated and represented a variety of occupations and current living arrangements. All of the men indicated primarily or exclusively same-gender sexual orientation. For purposes of comparison, the sample was divided in half by age to form a middle-aged group (ages 39-57) and an older group (ages 58-73). Although the members of the middle-aged group had achieved higher levels of education than those in the older group, the difference between the two groups was not significant by chi-square analysis. Likewise, there were no differences between the two groups in current living arrangements or sexual orientation. The sample also was diverse with regard to socioeconomic status of the family of origin, heterosexual experience, and number of siblings; there were no statistically significant differences between the two age groups on these variables (see Table 7.1).

A 41-item questionnaire based on the instrument used by Berger (1982) in a previous study of White gay men over age 40 was given to the respondents to be mailed back identified only by code number. Berger had taken the items on his questionnaire from an earlier study of older gay men by Weinberg and Williams (1974). Among the 41 items, 10 assessed self-acceptance, 5 assessed depression, 3 assessed concealment of sexual orientation, and 1 was a global measure of happiness. Respondents were given a token payment of $10 upon return of the questionnaire (many requested that their checks be sent

Table 7.1 Comparison of Middle-Aged (39-57) and Older (58-73)
Respondents

	Middle-Aged (n = 10)	Older (n = 10)	Total (n = 20)
Educational level			
Doctorate	4	1	5
Graduate study	4	3	7
College only	2	5	7
High school only	0	1	1
Current living arrangement			
Alone	8	4	12
With lover	2	2	4
With roommate	0	3	3
With wife	0	1	1
Sexual orientation[a]			
Primarily homosexual, but more than slightly heterosexual	1	1	2
Primarily homosexual, but only slightly heterosexual	1	3	4
Exclusively homosexual	7	3	10
Heterosexual experience			
Yes	8	8	16
No	2	2	4
Social background of family			
Middle-class	2	0	2
Lower-middle-class	3	2	5
Working-class	3	7	10
Poor	2	1	3
Siblings: number (SD)	2.2 (2.35)	3.2 (3.19)	2.7 (2.77)

NOTE: Statistical analyses indicated no significant differences.
a. $n = 16$

as a donation to GMAD). Of the 20 targeted respondents, 17 returned
the questionnaire.

Although neither the present study nor earlier studies of gay men
have been based on samples that are representative of the population,
the questionnaire data allow comparison with the Berger (1982) sample. These data are presented as benchmarks only. Strict statistical
comparisons are not warranted because the samples are not representative and differ in historical era and geographic location, as well
as by race. A comparison between respondents in the present study
and those in the Berger study ($n = 112$) found that the present sample

was slightly older, more highly educated, higher in occupational status, and had more heterosexual interest. The subjects in the Berger sample scored slightly lower than those in the present sample on questionnaire items assessing self-acceptance and happiness; they scored slightly higher on items related to concealment of sexual orientation and depression. These slight differences may reflect the higher level of education in the present sample as well as social changes toward greater acceptance of gay men since the time of the Berger study. Clearly, however, the members of this sample of older African American gay men are not more depressed or closeted about sexual orientation, nor lower in self-acceptance and happiness, than were Berger's White gay men.

An open-ended life-history interview similar to the second author's earlier study of older White gay men was the major source of information in this study (Kimmel, 1979). In addition to demographic information, questions concerned relationship with the family of origin, involvement in the African American community, involvement with the gay community, friendships, history of sexual identity development, romantic relationships, perceived effects of being a gay man in general and with regard to aging, effect of aging on sex life, effect of the HIV/AIDS epidemic, discrimination (based on sexual orientation, age, and race), perceived effects of aging, and psychological issues related to growing older.

Interviews were tape-recorded with verbal permission given following an informed consent statement. A typical interview lasted about 90 minutes. The first author conducted most of the interviews; the second author interviewed only three respondents. Each respondent was given the choice of having an African American (the first author) or a White interviewer (the second author); none expressed a preference.

Demographic data were coded from the interviews by each coauthor separately; disagreements were resolved by discussion. Qualitative interview data were analyzed by categories, using the open coding technique of grounded theory (Strauss & Corbin, 1990). Specifically, 13 global themes were identified (e.g., family of origin, involvement with the gay community, sexual development), each with several subtopics. Factual data, summary statements, and key quotations from the interview tapes and transcripts were entered on a summary document for each theme by the second author. The theme summaries were reviewed by both authors, and errors, questions, and ambiguities were resolved by discussion. The data presented in this chapter represent summaries of seven of these themes, illustrated with relevant quotations.

Results

Seven topics from the interview of particular interest to life-span development are reported here: relationship with the family of origin, development of sexual identity, romantic relationships, involvement with the African American and gay communities, midlife issues, historical effects, and discrimination. The impact of acquired immune deficiency syndrome (AIDS) is also noted in terms of relationships and midlife issues.

Relationship With Family of Origin

Respondents reported that their families of origin were predominantly working-class, and most had at least one sibling. At the time of the study, nearly all of the respondents maintained ties with their biological families. Most frequent contacts were with siblings or other extended relatives. All four respondents who knew they had children maintained contact with them. Four out of the six who had been married maintained contact with their ex-wives. Nearly all of the respondents reported that someone in their families knew they were gay; only one reported a strongly negative reaction. There were no differences between the middle-aged and older samples on extent of family contact.

A few respondents mentioned gay members of their biological families. One noted that he had an uncle who was also "in the life" and that he had been in his company and with his friends a lot. Another respondent reported that he had a gay cousin, one said that he had two gay brothers, and another said that his son is bisexual. In addition, a respondent commented that his aunt often had gay people around the house and held parties attended by men in drag when he was growing up.

Although most of the respondents said their families knew they were gay, many had never specifically discussed their sexual orientation with family members—the fact was simply understood. Family members had met respondents' lovers or the situation was simply assumed after several years. Some were open only to siblings, but not to their parents. Only two respondents felt that no one in their families of origin knew that they were gay men.

Respondents reported that when they first discussed their sexual orientation with family members it was often traumatic. However, one respondent, age 60, reported that when he was young he was effeminate, and his father took him out and introduced him to a gay bartender. He said: "My father made remarks on occasion about my not being a man, but he never came out and said I was gay, or I was queer, to me."

Of the 10 respondents who answered the question about the effect of their families' knowing that they were gay, 5 said it had no effect, 3 said the family was accepting, 1 said it made the relationship better, and 2 left home as a result. A typical response of the majority who said the knowledge had no effect was this one from a 62-year-old respondent:

> My youngest brother has known for a long time. My sister knows. My son knows and he is bisexual. His mother *may* know; she remarried and he was gay—he and I became very close; she knows he was. Now she is married again; I don't think he is gay. Today if the family has a question about business, they come to me.

In contrast, one respondent who left home as a result of a friend telling his mother that her son was a gay man had a much more strained relationship with his family. He was 72 at the time of the interview:

> My family has lived make-believe on many issues. We've had family discussions that were very upsetting to me. But my personal life is my personal life. I'm from that era that if you're gay, the only time I ever felt I was gay per se was when I was in bed with somebody. The rest of my life I could not afford to try to be a success in this life and let any of this show. So the games that we played I guess it takes a lot out of you. But it becomes a part of your gay life so you don't even think about it.

In summary, respondents' relationships with their families of origin were typically important. Many respondents were open with some family members about being gay, and the reactions of their families were generally not hostile. In many families it was a topic that was not openly discussed, but a few respondents had gay relatives to whom they were close. Age cohort did not matter as much in terms of family reactions as did individual family situations.

Sexual Development

Age at the time of first same-gender sexual experience for these men ranged from early childhood to 27 years; the average age was 17.8 and the modal age was 18-19. There was little difference between the middle-aged and older men in the sample (18.2 versus 17.6 years of age).

Race was a dimension in the discovery of sexual orientation for some respondents, who commented that they had sexual contact with White men only so that no one in the African American community would learn of their sexual orientation. For example, one 56-year-old respondent, whose father was a Pullman porter who wanted his sons "to have the best" and took them to museums, the symphony, and dance performances, had his first same-gender sexual experience when he worked as a bellhop in a hotel, with a White man who was a hotel guest. He later learned that two of his brothers also were gay men. Following his first sexual experience with a gay men, he avoided African American gay men:

> Everyone knew one another. There were people my family acknowledged was gay—not put down, but was effeminate. I never identified with them because I didn't want to be found out. To be exposed that way you were very vulnerable. My family was very respected. So I took all my role models from the White community. My brothers also started out in the White community. Whites had the best of both worlds and had money—took me to dinner and gave me things; never money.

Although more than half of the respondents recognized gay men in their neighborhoods, three out of four said they did not have role models, and many noted that the gay men they knew about were negative models, often the brunt of derisive comments and sometimes spoken about as models of what not to become. One 45-year-old who had been married for 8 years to a woman commented when asked if he had any gay role models:

> None I was happy with. All the women were in butch or femme roles and all the men were sissies; I didn't know any "real men." To be gay was

screaming faggots walking up and down Greenwich Avenue. If being gay meant being a screaming faggot, I didn't want to be gay. So I got married.

Only five respondents reported that they had had positive role models; there was no difference between the middle-aged and older groups. One had an uncle (mentioned above) with whom he still has a friendship. Two had positive White role models. In addition, four respondents also mentioned famous persons as role models, such as James Baldwin.

There was considerable variation in respondents' paths to discovery of their sexual orientation and identities. Five examples illustrate this range. One 53-year-old respondent felt that he had "always known—I was sexually attracted to my father at a very young age and attracted to very masculine men my father related to"; yet, unlike others in the study, he did not have sexual relations with a man until he was 21 or 22 and never had heterosexual relations.

A second man (age 69) had his first same-gender sex at age 12 with an older boy in the next building and later was paid for sex (by friends of his gay uncle) when he was 15-16. He said, "It was hard times; I'd get my nuts off and get $2.00."

In contrast to this early awareness, one 62-year-old reported that he had very early heterosexual experience and always had girlfriends; his first other-gender sex was at age 17 or 18. He did not discover that he was gay until he was 27, when a girlfriend took him to a party where he met a man to whom he became attracted; he and this man double-dated with women for a year before they began to have a relationship.

Another respondent (age 41) self-identified as bisexual until he was 39, although he had has first live-in relationship with a gay man when he was 21. He went to the health service at his college because "nobody wanted to be gay in 1967" and had both male and female partners until "the end of my drinking days." He began speaking openly about being a gay man only at age 40, in Alcoholics Anonymous.

A fifth respondent (age 51) reported that he had been sexually abused by an older stepbrother beginning when they were ages 5 and 9, respectively; the abuse went on "for years." In his early teens he wanted to become a Catholic priest and he became an altar boy. However, after a same-gender sexual experience, "I went to Father K. to confess and found out that he was gay himself; he 'hit' on me. Isn't that terrible! I was in a state of suicidal guilt. . . . I left the church completely." He reported that he had no subsequent experiences until he was 25, when he fell in love with his fiancée's brother, who was an openly gay man.

As in the second author's previous study of White older gay men (Kimmel, 1979), some respondents found same-gender sexual relations to be a way out of a miserable environment and an entrée into a different world. One 59-year-old man said:

> In the beginning it was very exciting. Also it took me away from my surroundings, which I found very depressing—poverty and heroin addiction in the neighborhood. It was an escape for me too. I met people and we did things together. I met some older gay men and we become good friends. We'd visit on weekends. We'd go to Boston. We had sex together, but also would go cruising together to find partners. Also I met a photographer who I saw on a regular basis; he introduced me to the glamour of theater and dance.

These reports are consistent with the findings of other studies of gay men; the discovery of sexual orientation often occurs early, but is not necessarily acted upon until much later because of social stigma, guilt, and moral doubts (see Bell et al., 1981). Likewise, open acknowledgment of being gay or bisexual may not come until after considerable personal struggle and, in some cases, heterosexual marriage. One 67-year-old respondent, who had been married to a woman for 18 years and had two adult daughters, noted:

> I recognized that my homosexual tendencies were so strong that I realized it was only fair to myself and to my wife that I would sit down and articulate my feelings and get her views. . . . She understood. We are still friends. She remarried. We became best friends.

Six of the respondents had been married, heterosexually, and at least four had children; two others thought they might have children, but were not certain. Sixteen reported heterosexual experience. Equal numbers of middle-aged and older respondents reported heterosexual experience.

One respondent was married and living with his wife of 37 years and adult child at the time of the interview. He commented: "I don't think there was any deciding [about sexual orientation]. I always felt feelings for men. I was always effeminate. Always had attraction for both boys and girls; had sex play with both at age 9." When he was in the armed forces at age 19-20, he had a male lover who was 15-16 years older; they finally separated when the friend was transferred. The friend was married and our respondent never contacted him when he returned home from the service. The respondent also married then: "I wanted the security of a family; I wanted children." He described himself as "bisexual, leaning more homosexual." This respondent's comments suggest that the path to bisexuality may differ from the paths of either gay or heterosexual men.

Same-Gender Romantic Relationships

Sixteen of the men reported that they had lived with a male lover at some time; three others said they once had a male lover, but never lived with him; only one said he never had a male lover. Seven reported current same-gender romantic relationships.

Most of the respondents, 12 out of 20, were living alone at the time of the interview. Four were currently living with a long-term lover, three were living in a nonsexual relationship with a roommate, and one was living with his wife. Although more middle-aged respondents than older respondents were living alone, equal numbers in each group were living with lovers, and there was no significant difference between the groups in their living arrangements (see Table 7.1).

The extent of diversity in patterns of romantic relationships was as great as in any other aspect of the study. One respondent described his odyssey of romantic relationships up to age 45 this way:

> When I came out in 1965 my wife and I broke up; I had to define myself as a gay person. Then there was an 8-year relationship with a man that broke up. That was very painful. I should have gotten out after 2 years, but thought I had better hang on to this. When I got out I knew what I wanted and just waited. Thank the Lord it came along. We've been together 8 years. He was very supportive when my father died of Alzheimer's; I was there for him when his dad died 6 months later. We did it our way. The point is we choose our family; we choose our friends. I'm happy with what I've got; there isn't much I've compromised about.

In contrast to this satisfied report, one 52-year-old respondent who was a professional reported one live-in lover 12 years earlier and two other previous lovers. All three were African American and low income; he played the "femme role" with each. Now he is with a companion only on weekends. He commented:

> I was so concerned about not being a faggot and spent so much of my life hiding that part of me, hiding my sensitivity, playing basketball for all the wrong reasons. . . . I'm very concerned about my appearance; I spend a lot of time in the gym and worrying about it, practically at the point of panic. I'm concerned about if something happens to my friend, I'm back out there with all this mess—guys who are attractive and professional and treat you in a shabby way. What am I going to do for a lover? Many people my age are dropping dead—not just from AIDS. Will I have any friends when I'm old? Will anyone be around?

A third example of the variation in romantic relationships comes from a 61-year-old respondent who has always lived alone but who spent a lot of time with a friend while in graduate school:

> I had two real love affairs. One in college: a returning veteran from World War II. We enjoyed a very beautiful relationship and were inseparable for four years (1949-1953). After I went into the army he had another relationship and then he got married. In the sixties I met a man who was married and we remained friends for 10 years; he remained married. The height of sexual and physical satisfaction happened in the fourth and fifth years. I never experienced such sexual satisfaction after.

One of the four respondents living with a lover had been living with his partner for 34 years and had known him for "40-some-odd" years. He was 66 at the time of the interview. He said:

> I've never been married any kind of way. This is one thing that I've never said: It's never been a "he" or "she" or mention of a marriage; he's always been "my friend." We've roomed together, we've lived together . . . we've been the greatest of friends. . . . We've had the advantages that many greatly married people have had, but we never did consider it a marriage, unless it's a marriage of the minds. He almost thinks what I'm going to say before I say it and vice versa.

This man also noted that he "helped raise every last one" of his sister's and sister-in-law's children.

Two respondents had lost long-term partners to AIDS, one at age 52 after a 10-year relationship; the respondent cared for his partner over a period of 5 years, until he eventually died at home. The other was bereaved at age 34 after a 4-year relationship. Another respondent (age 69) suffered the loss of a partner of 30 years to a heart attack at age 59; he described the funeral very poignantly:

> He was a person that was meticulous and had everything in order. . . . I made calls to all his family. He had a will. He had a twin brother. They all came. His sister read out the will. Everything was to go to me. They were beautiful: "if that's the way he wanted it." His sister made arrangements to have him buried as a veteran. Beautiful. His funeral was on Armistice Day, flags all around; they had the fly-by.

Involvement With the African American and Gay Communities

Of the 20 respondents, 9 were involved with gay social organizations. Middle-aged respondents were involved more often than were older respondents, however, the difference was not significant.

With only two exceptions (an AIDS program and a legal group), respondents' involvement was with organizations focused on African Americans or people of color. Respondents noted that African American lesbian and gay social groups have a long history. For example, one 41-year-old commented:

> Older Black gay men before were referred to as Queen Bees and organized social groups where people learned to be gay. Over time, with drugs and economics, it's more difficult to open up their homes to large groups. When I came onto the scene in the early seventies, I had a sense it was something that was previously more exclusive and also very prevalent in the Black community. Also when friends went from one city to another it was a way to meet friends and sexual partners.

Dynamics of interracial social relationships within the gay community were reported to be very complex. Some respondents stated that they preferred to avoid social life with Whites. One 53-year-old respondent commented: "I seek out Blacks who have a Black consciousness. I get very distressed when I deal with Black gay men who spend a lot of time with White gays. . . . I'm very judgmental about them." Some respondents also reported that they had sexual relations only with African Americans. Most preferred to limit integrated social contacts to job-related activities. One 55-year-old respondent said:

I feel a sense, being a Black person in a White setting of, "What are you doing here?"—that kind of attitude, unless you are with a White lover. And even the few friends of mine that have a White lover, they have that kind of problem—because the lovers, the White guy, would be discriminated against; [people] wouldn't want anything to do with a White guy walking around with a Black lover.

The subtle and pervasive effects of being an African American man in U.S. society also interact with the effects of being gay. In some settings one can hide one's sexual orientation, but not one's skin color. As one 60-year-old respondent noted:

> My experience with Black gays has not always been the best. . . . I still think that they're more concerned with protecting themselves than with being with the overall Black gay community . . . more so with the problem of being Black than gay.

Involvement within the general African American community also was not particularly high for this sample. For example, most were not involved with an organized church (three were extensively involved and four had minimal involvement). Although the church is widely thought to be a major social force in the African American community, it may be that the stigma the church places on gay men and lesbians reduces the interest for many men in our sample.

Likewise, 15 of the 20 respondents had no involvement in other nongay organizations in the African American community. Perhaps this lack of interest reflects a lack of comfort as a gay man in these groups. One 73-year-old respondent commented:

> Church is an important part of my life. I believe in prayer. I go every Sunday and other services. I like to dress up. But I never got too involved in fraternity, lodges, and neighborhood groups. Being Black, gay, and old is a heavy load.

Midlife Issues and AIDS

A common theme of middle age for gay men is thought to be the fear of aging. One 43-year-old respondent said:

> You dread getting older because you no longer fit anybody's fantasy—not even your own. You can't put yourself in the fantasy if you don't have the

physique. The term *gay* means young and in the bars and partying. It conjures up images of youth, frivolity, carousing.

But another respondent, age 53, had a different viewpoint on aging:

> Black professionals like myself have a real commitment to give back to the community because otherwise we are not going to be able to reproduce ourselves. I get more out of these community groups than I'm giving. I think it's extremely important for people like myself, particularly since I don't have a family. Without it I don't think I'd be a fulfilled person.

An aspect of middle age that is compelling for many persons, including gay men, is that it is a point at which one has lived half of one's life; the endpoint comes dimly into view, and one is more aware of one's mortality (Kimmel & Sang, 1995). With the AIDS crisis now in its second decade, most midlife gay men have been confronted with the premature deaths of men their same age or younger. Some, of course, are themselves infected with the virus associated with AIDS and are unusually aware of the finiteness of life. When asked if he thinks about death, one 43-year-old respondent commented:

> Oh yes. Is everything in line? Am I prepared? I've been thinking of it for the 3 years I've known I have the AIDS virus. Although I feel fine, it's not to be taken for granted. I don't want a lot of pain. Will I die at home? In a hospital? Suicide? I want to prepare for it.

Another, age 45, who did not want to be tested for the virus associated with AIDS, said:

> In the gay community, I feel "revered." Thirty-year-olds treat me like I'm their father. Perhaps it's the gay movement; perhaps it's AIDS—they want to hold on to someone who has lasted longer than they have. But also I feel somewhat invisible and ignored because I'm not a kid. Gay youth tend to be, like adolescents, very cliquish, clannish, rebellious. They're finding out who they are. Some days I'm daddy; some days I'm just ignored.

Historical Effects of the Lesbian and Gay Civil Rights Movement

All 10 of the middle-aged respondents (ages 39 to 57) felt that the lesbian and gay civil rights movement was a positive change—even if it did apply primarily to "White boys in jeans." Nonetheless, many other respondents felt a need for secrecy. One 55-year-old respondent commented:

> I feel sincerely that Black gay men don't want to come out of the closet. They feel very uncomfortable around other gay people. Gays who have not accepted their gayness do not want to be integrated with other gay males, or they are very defensive. I find that Black gay men are very defensive about their sexuality.

Members of the older segment of the sample were also positive about the gay civil rights movement, but tempered their enthusiasm. A 58-year-old said: "Terrific. I applaud them. But it has had no impact on me." A 69-year-old said: "I'm all for it. But it's going to take a long while before they accept a gay person. Had to wait a long while before I could sit in the front of a bus."

Discrimination

Nearly all respondents (16 out of 19) reported experiencing racial discrimination. In contrast, only a few respondents noted examples of age discrimination (4 of 19) or antigay discrimination (3 of 20), and all of those were in the middle-aged group. A 59-year-old respondent described racial discrimination:

> My junior high school was going to send me to a vocational high school. I've always been a very good student. My mother knew I wanted to go to college, but you can't go from a vocational high school. It was almost as if she had no rights. And then when I graduated from high school, my counselor didn't want me to take the entrance exam for City College. He told me I wasn't college material. I told him, "Are you crazy? I'm in the Honor Society, in the top 10% of my class." That's very blatant. When I graduated from college I got a job in an accounting firm. I had to go to Toms River, New Jersey, to do an audit. The man wouldn't rent a room to me, he wouldn't honor the reservation.

Another respondent (age 56) commented about his experience of racial discrimination: "Every day. I am very much in touch with that. It's almost making me so anxious and the inner rage becomes my problem. Stress will kill me, I'm aware of it."

Because the gay community is a part of the broader society, there is discrimination there also. One respondent noted that music popular among African American gay men is not played in predominantly White gay bars, and African Americans are prevented entry by a double standard of ID card requirements after a quota is reached inside the bar. When asked if there is discrimination in the gay community, another respondent (age 58) noted:

> Absolutely. When I attend a gay benefit I am the fly in a plate of milk. We need to get more "people of color" on the Board. . . . When did they invite a Black person to their home? I assume there is as much bias in the gay community as elsewhere.

One 56-year-old respondent who reported feeling discrimination because of age commented:

> I may feel the same, but physically I look older. Salesclerks, or in a shop or job setting, you're treated differently. It's assumed that because you're a certain age that you no longer have an identity. I get upset: "This is an old guy—an old guy and Black. He doesn't have the money to buy anything. What's he doing in here?"

Age discrimination was also reported within the gay community. One respondent said that he felt that when he walked into a gay bar, the people there were thinking, "What's that old man doing in here?" For most, however, age and antigay discrimination were far less important than racial discrimination in their lives.

Discussion

Skin color, ethnic and racial background, gender, age, socioeconomic status, and sexual orientation are major variables important to an understanding of older African American gay men. Each individual who took part in our study is different from White gay men in subtle and complex ways because of the interpretation of race and color within our society. African American gay men are seen by some in the African American community as traitors to their families and to their race, because gay sex does not lead to procreation. Being gay is seen as a threat to the endangered masculinity of African American males.

Homosexuality is condemned by the church. The relatively scarce numbers of eligible African American men available to marry African American women are also seen as further reduced by gay men. Stereotypes persist in the African American community that gay men are effeminate, are cross-dressers, and want to be women. The gay male role models who are present are often perceived as negative. Moreover, close ties with extended family and assuming family child-rearing responsibilities can increase the vulnerability of African American gay men to social pressures. These attitudes, stereotypes, and pressures foster a climate that encourages internalized homophobia, secrecy, and social stress among African American gay men.

In addition, the lesbian and gay community is often seen as a White establishment that offers little genuine acceptance to people of color and ignores their specific concerns. Thus African American gay men may feel isolated from both communities. Older gay men may be isolated also from younger gay men, both by cohort differences and by age discrimination.

Previous research on White gay male aging has emphasized diversity in patterns of aging in contrast to the stereotype of the lonely dysfunctional gay man (Friend, 1990; Kimmel, 1978). Likewise, the data produced by this study suggest some of the diversity within this population of older African American gay men and some of the successful adaptations that they have created within their developmental context.

One observation we can make from this study is that live-in romantic relationships among our African American respondents were less frequent than have been found in previous studies of White gay men. It may be that men in long-term relationships were less likely to be available for our research study because they were not attending meetings or social gatherings where they would have been recruited for the study. Nevertheless, interwoven social norms about relationships, family obligations, and social pressures on gay men and African American men in our society may make long-term romantic relationships problematic for some. For example, two of the respondents reported histories of alcohol or drug abuse that interfered with intimate relationships. Also, some mentioned family responsibilities, such as caring for a sibling's children, that took precedence over a long-term relationship with a lover. Others noted the stigma and secrecy of gay life that made it difficult to maintain long-term live-in relationships.

Obviously, this group of respondents is representative of a particular segment of older African American gay men in New York City. The characteristics of this sample do not necessarily generalize to the total population of older African American gay men.

Future research needs to examine the interrelations of the major themes in this exploratory study: relationship with family of origin, development of sexual identity, romantic relationships, involvement with the African American and gay communities, midlife development, effects of historical changes, and discrimination based on race, age, and sexual orientation.

Empirical studies are needed also on other ethnic and racial groups of middle-aged and older gay men and lesbians. In particular, longitudinal data sources and the use of contemporaneous information (e.g., diaries) should be explored to reduce the effects of retrospective reporting that inherently limit the significance of the data described here and in similar studies.

References

Adelman, M. (1990). Stigma, gay lifestyles, and adjustment to aging: A study of later-life gay men and lesbians. *Journal of Homosexuality, 20*(3-4), 7-32.

Baldwin, J. (1956). *Giovanni's room.* New York: Dell.

Beam, J. (Ed.). (1986). *In the life: A Black gay anthology.* Boston: Alyson.

Bell, A. P., & Weinberg, M. S. (1978). *Homosexualities: A study of diversity among men and women.* New York: Simon & Schuster.

Bell, A. P., Weinberg, M. S., & Hammersmith, S. K. (1981). *Sexual preference: Its development in men and women.* Bloomington: Indiana University Press.

Berger, R. M. (1982). *Gay and gray: The older homosexual man.* Urbana: University of Illinois Press.

Boykin, K. (1996). *One more river to cross: Black and gay in America.* New York: Doubleday.

Francher, J. S., & Henkin, J. (1973). The menopausal queen: Adjustment to aging and the male homosexual. *American Journal of Orthopsychiatry, 43,* 670-674.

Friend, R. A. (1987). The individual and social psychology of aging: Clinical implications for lesbians and gay men. *Journal of Homosexuality, 14*(1-2), 307-331.

Friend, R. A. (1990). Older lesbian and gay people: A theory of successful aging. *Journal of Homosexuality, 20*(3-4), 99-118.

Gray, H., & Dressel, P. (1985). Alternative interpretations of aging among gay males. *The Gerontologist, 25,* 83-87.

Icard, L. (1985). Black gay men and conflicting social identities: Sexual orientation versus racial identity. *Journal of Social Work and Human Sexuality, 4*(1-2), 83-93.

Icard, L., & Traunstein, D. M. (1987). Black, gay, alcoholic men: Their character and treatment. *Social Casework, 68,* 267-272.

Johnson, J. M. (1981). Influence of assimilation on the psychosocial adjustment of Black homosexual men (Doctoral dissertation). *Dissertation Abstracts International, 42,* 4620B. (Order No. DA8201500)

Kelly, J. (1977). The aging male homosexual: Myth and reality. *The Gerontologist, 17,* 328-332.

Kimmel, D. C. (1978). Adult development and aging: A gay perspective. *Journal of Social Issues, 34*(3), 113-130.

Kimmel, D. C. (1979). Gay people grow old too: Life history interviews of aging gay men. *International Journal of Aging and Human Development, 10,* 239-248.

Kimmel, D. C., & Sang, B. E. (1995). Lesbians and gay men in midlife. In A. R. D'Augelli & C. J. Patterson (Eds.), *Lesbian, gay, and bisexual identities across the lifespan: Psychological perspectives* (pp. 190-214). New York: Oxford University Press.

Lee, J. H. (1987). What can homosexual aging studies contribute to theories of aging? *Journal of Homosexuality, 13*(4), 43-71.

Loiacano, D. K. (1989). Gay identity issues among Black Americans: Racism, homophobia, and the need for validation. *Journal of Counseling and Development, 68,* 21-25.

Pope, M., & Schulz, R. (1990). Sexual attitudes and behavior in midlife and aging homosexual males. *Journal of Homosexuality, 20*(3-4), 169-177.

Quam, J. K., & Whitford, G. S. (1992). Adaptation and age-related expectations of older gay and lesbian adults. *The Gerontologist, 32,* 367-374.

Sang, B., Warshow, J., & Smith, A. (Eds.). (1991). *Lesbians at midlife: The creative transition.* San Francisco: Spinster.

Strauss, A., & Corbin, J. (1990). *Basics of qualitative research: Grounded theory procedures and techniques.* Newbury Park, CA: Sage.

Weinberg, M. S., & Williams. C. J. (1974). *Male homosexuals: Their problems and adaptations.* New York: Oxford University Press.

8

Greek American Lesbians
Identity Odysseys of Honorable Good Girls

LEAH M. FYGETAKIS

—*First you will come to the Sirens, who bewitch everyone who comes near them. . . . When you have got clear of them, there is a choice of two courses, and I will not lay down for you which to take; use your own judgment. One course will bring you to a pair of precipitous rocks. . . . The other course leads between two cliffs. . . . in the side of [one] cliff is a dark gloomy cave, just where you will steer your ship. There Scylla dwells and yelps in her dreadful way. . . . She is a horrible monster! . . . The other cliff is lower. . . . they are not far from one another; and Charybdis underneath swallows down the black water. . . . she is a terror—don't be there when she swallows! No one could save you from destruction. . . . flight is better than fight. . . . All night long I drifted, and by sunrise Scylla and dreadful Charybdis were before me. Charybdis swallowed up the salt water; but I had been carried high up, and caught the wild fig tree; and I stuck to it like a bat. . . . How I longed for them! and they came at last. . . . I spread out my hands and feet and let go . . . the gods brought me to the island of Ogygia. There dwells Calypso, that goddess so beautiful and so terrible . . . and she loved me and cared for me. But why go on with my story?*

Homer, *The Odyssey*

In 1984, while living in Rochester, New York, I attended a lecture by Evelyn Torton Beck, editor of *Nice Jewish Girls: A Lesbian Anthology* (1982). Afterward there was a reception, and being one of the first to exit the auditorium, I found myself standing very near to her. As others

152

continued to file in, it seemed that every Jewish lesbian entering the room went straight to Beck like a magnet, creating an ever-widening circle, as I stood there in its wake. One could just feel the sparks and electricity flying. There was a sense of some very special bonding going on among all those women. I felt myself wanting to move over, very much wanting to be a part of that energy, but I didn't. Soon, I realized that I didn't really belong in this group; rather, I was aware that what was missing for me was a sense of having my own Greek lesbian community, a community to which to belong, with which to share life's stories and celebrate life's experiences as a lesbian raised and steeped in Greek culture and traditions.

I was born and raised in the United States, speaking Greek as my first language, and my dominant language until I entered first grade (I then continued to speak it in the home and in all-Greek settings while communicating in English when at school), regularly attending Holy Services of the Greek Orthodox Church, receiving weekly instruction through "Greek school" classes in language and culture for 6 years, and socializing with other Greek children through the Greek Orthodox Youth Association (GOYA). With the exception of attending public school, *everything* in my life was oriented around being Greek. My experience was typical of most first- and second-generation Greek American youth living in the United States (Callinicos, 1990). After such immersion in living as a Greek American, how was it that I had come to no longer associate with a Greek community? I found myself speculating that my gradual disenfranchisement seemed to coincide with my coming-out process, and I wondered how other Greek lesbians handled it. I had no idea because, to my knowledge, I had never met another Greek lesbian. Why did it seem as if being Greek and being a lesbian were two mutually exclusive experiences?

Perhaps my experience may be related to what Callinicos (1990) has found in the process of continuing her original study of 111 Greek American women who ranged in age from their mid-30s to mid-70s (as a side note, the only mention of a Greek American lesbian in her book comes when she refers to her sister). She has continued her work by interviewing the daughters of her original subjects, Greek American women in their early 20s to mid-30s. Callinicos states that

the Greek world in America remains largely androcentric, and . . . many feel it is a world that they are not inclined to continue to inhabit or perpetuate.

Simply put, they leave. . . . In some scholarly and lay quarters of female Greek America, it has been suggested that "the leaving" is the only way to achieve autonomy and fulfillment as a human being unfettered by these constraints. Young Greek American women are saying that the Greek American world must cease to view its women as auxiliaries and assistants. Otherwise, the exodus continues. (p. 17)

Returning to my story, I continued to long for the opportunity to meet some other Greek lesbians, but where and how might I meet them? Although I wasn't sure about the lesbian part, I knew that the way one meets other Greek people in general is through the *kinotita*. Every *kinotita*, or Greek community, is almost always centered on a Greek Orthodox church. Some 98% of all Greeks identify Greek Orthodoxy as their religion (Clogg, 1992; Morgan, 1984). As Greeks immigrated to the United States, each community would build its church, which served as the center of its social life as well as its spiritual life (Clamar, 1980). As Kalogeras (1992) notes, in the immigrant experience, no matter what remote island or part of the mainland they came from, Greeks became, first and foremost, Greek Orthodox. The church was a symbol of national/ethnic identity and provided Greek immigrants with a way to distinguish themselves from millions of other immigrants, providing continuity and identity. As I will address in more detail later, Greek Orthodoxy maintains a very negative (versus tolerant or even affirming) view of homosexuality ("The Orthodox View," 1993). Thus for a Greek lesbian forced to decide between self-truth and church teachings, leaving the church carries with it the burden of being perceived as rejecting her community and as "denouncing her Greekness." However, to remain under such conditions may be equally painful. In spite of the minefields involved, I decided that to find other Greek lesbians, I should start attending more Greek events again, even though it meant attending them through a Greek Orthodox church.

It seemed that an easy way to start would be to go to a Grecian festival. Many Greek American church communities engage in this type of annual fund-raising event, which they open to the general "American" public ("Around the USA," 1994). Typically, the *kinotita* cooks, bakes, sells its art, and demonstrates its regional folk dances in traditional costume for all to enjoy. I attended such a festival along with two lesbian friends who are not Greek. The first thing that happened, after we paid the price of admission, was that we each had our hands stamped. When I looked at my hand, there was the stamp of a crucifix.

I was aware of my discomfort, and worried about how this might feel to my Jewish friends. We then spent our time eating and people-watching, trying to identify just who among the visitors might actually be lesbians, to no avail. If there were any there, they never gave a clue. I danced a few folk dances, and then we decided to go one block away from the festival site to a lesbian bar. The memory is still very vivid for me of a schism in my heart that there, in one night, I had to be in two different places in order somehow to be integrated and whole.

Not to be deterred, I put out a challenge to all of my friends: "Find me one Greek lesbian within a 50-mile radius from Rochester, New York, and you will make me a happy woman. I will drive in rain, sleet or snow. . . . I'll travel as far as Buffalo. . . . I just want to meet *one*. The first friend who finds me a Greek lesbian will win a prize for her efforts!" Sad, but at the same time humorous, is that a few of them in the process of asking various acquaintances and even newly met strangers if they knew any Greek lesbians, returned to tell me that yes, indeed they had gotten some affirmative responses. Each time, when they followed up and asked what the name of this Greek lesbian was, the reply was, "I think its, Leah-something. . . . Leah Fygetakis." It always came back full circle to me. Although this further increased my sense of aloneness, at the same time I took solace in the fact that at least some people recognized me as being Greek. It took another 2 years, until I moved to Boston, for me to meet others like myself. Images that will always stay with me are those from my first Boston Gay, Lesbian and Bisexual Pride Day, when a group of us known as the Ionian Society put on our own miniversion of a Grecian festival as a part of the evening's selection of dance celebrations attended by the gay community. We baked and created dance tapes for weeks in preparation for this event. We invited friends, gay and straight, and passed out invitations to onlookers during the parade held earlier that day. And in the finest tradition, our small group of 15 shared our joy with another hundred as we ate, toasted with ouzo and Metaxa cognac, and danced the night away. It was a real coming home.

Why do I begin with this personal story? Although I have now been able to meet and associate with a small handful of other Greek American lesbians, I remain convinced that there are many more who have not been able to do so, even in large urban areas such as Boston. Not only are we invisible within Greek American communities, but we also keep ourselves invisible to each other. Why is this? What factors are operating here? And how, within such invisibility, do Greek lesbians successfully integrate a positive Greek lesbian identity? To begin exploring these questions, I interviewed 10 Greek American lesbians about their families, their childhoods, and their coming-out processes. I presented my preliminary findings at the 1990 meeting of the American Psychological Association during a symposium on ethnic factors in the coming-out process of lesbians. At one point during my talk, I turned to my fellow panelists and noted that each of their presentations represented an ethnicity about which I had been able to find at least some psychological or autobiographical literature (African American lesbians, Chinese lesbians, Latina lesbians, and Jewish lesbians), and that this was not the case regarding Greek lesbians. Even today, we still know nothing about Greek lesbians except what we've read about Sappho. So, at my colleagues' consistent urgings since that panel, comes this chapter, which has dual purposes. One is to present and discuss some of the key cultural concepts and relevant historical factors that I believe may be converging as forces in the development of a Greek American lesbian identity and in the coming-out process. The second is to use the information gathered through my interviews with 10 Greek American lesbians to help support and illustrate my proposed conceptualization. The sample is small and taken from only one area of the country. Consequently, care should be taken in making generalizations. I write this chapter as a beginning, presenting findings for others to confirm, refute, alter, or integrate.

Methodology

The 10 participants in my study were identified through various means. Six had at one time or another been members of the Ionian Society (a small Boston-area Greek gay and lesbian organization that existed between 1985 to 1990) and were acquaintances of mine. The remaining four were identified through referrals from non-Greek gay and lesbian social networks by virtue of Greek surname recognition. Attempts to solicit participants by leafleting at gay/lesbian and women's bookstores and by placing an ad in a gay community newspaper brought no inquiries or responses. Thus all 10 participants were found by word of mouth.

With each participant I followed a structured interview protocol, with subjective allowance made to explore particular questions more thoroughly as seemed warranted. I developed the protocol by adapting relevant portions of two previously published questionnaires and incorporating some additional questions of my own choosing. The two questionnaires that contributed to the development of the interview protocol were from studies conducted by Espin (1987) and Chan (1989), who focused on Latina lesbians and Asian American lesbians and gay men, respectively. All of the interviews were conducted during the summer of 1990 and were audiotaped. For the purposes of this chapter, each participant has been assigned an alias.

A comment on my own "closeness" to the culture and my acquaintedness with some of the participants would seem to be in order here. From my development of the interview questions to my search for participants, to my interpretations and derivations of meaning from their responses, I have continually attempted simultaneously to justify and criticize this closeness much as an anthropologist might. On the one hand, Dubisch (1993) discusses how the type of information obtained during fieldwork is often dependent on whether the ethnographer is viewed as a "stranger" or "one of ours" by those being studied: "In any given situation, what is observed often depends upon the observer's status, since what is presented to an insider will differ from what an outsider is permitted to observe" (p. 274). On the other hand, Chock (1986) warns that it is very difficult to provide a cultural analysis of one's own culture: "Unlike the anthropologist writing ethnography of some radical Other, the native anthropologist's authority in ethnography is not great enough to assure a hearing for the diverse cultural voices she narrates in ethnography" (p. 94). One could surmise from this brief discussion that this research is both the richer and the poorer for having been conducted by another Greek American lesbian.

Demographics of the Sample

The ages of the participating women ranged from 26 to 46. Two were in their 20s, two were in their 40s, and the remaining six were in their 30s, with the median age being 34 years old. Two had graduate degrees and one was in graduate school at the time of the study. Four others had bachelor's degrees, and the remaining three each had 1-2 years of college study. Their occupations were varied: One worked in human resources and development, one managed a family business, one was a social worker, one was a secretary, one was a small business owner, one worked in photography and sales, one was an insurance broker, one was a physical therapist, and two were teachers. Culturally consistent with the Greek immigrant experience, as a whole the participants had reached a much higher educational level than had their parents. Of the 20 parents, 4 had only a grade school education, whereas another 7 had ended their education with the completion of high school.

All of the participants were of either first- or second-generation Greek lineage. Four had Greek fathers who had immigrated to the United States and married first-generation Greek American women, four were second-generation daughters resulting from marriages between two first-generation Greek Americans, and the remaining two were second-generation daughters of Greek American and Irish American background. In terms of self-identification, none referred to themselves simply as "American." Nine stated that they refer to themselves as "Greek American," and one identified as "Greek" even though she was born in the United States and is an American citizen. One of the participants noted:

> It used to drive me crazy when I was little and we would visit the relatives in Greece. They would always ask me, "Which are you? Are you Greek or are you an American?" Of course, if you didn't want to get lectured on the supreme importance of Greek civilization and our proud heritage in democracy, philosophy, theater, the Olympics, etc., you knew what you had better answer . . . except I always said, "Both!"

Thus it seems clear that the Greek American identity does not easily fade from one passing generation to the next. It seems to have a long half-life. There were other commonalities among the participants as well. Six had visited the *patrida*, or mother country, and three had made the journey multiple times. Seven had one or both grandparents living in their homes during their childhoods or adolescence, and four had aunts, uncles, and cousins who lived in the same double- or triple-decker home as the nuclear family. All of the participants had been exposed to Greek being spoken within the home; seven still speak and understand the language. Eight attended Greek school classes for a median number of 6 years. All frequently attended various Greek cultural events and dances as children, with such activity dropping by half once they became adults. It is significant that whereas all the participants were raised in and attended Greek Orthodox churches, currently only six continue to identify as Greek Orthodox and *none* practice it.

A Brief History

Greeks have inherited a legacy of learning to rely only on the in-group (family) and to distrust any outsiders. This has evolved from a long history of repeated invasions by outsiders, with resulting occupations and/or refugeeism, political infighting and civil wars, puppet governments and military dictatorships, all frequently bringing with them death, famine, and economic devastation. Even priests are often viewed as untrustworthy, because priests had historically sometimes been known to succumb to bribery and become informants for those who were in power (for further historical information, see Clogg, 1992; Mazower, 1993). As there has been a growing awareness in the recent events surrounding the former Yugoslavia and the Balkan states, it may provide some clarification to note that Greece borders these countries and has had its borders similarly threatened and affected in the past. At the same time, Greece has always had both European and Middle Eastern contact by virtue of its being a Mediterranean country. Thus Greece has had an unusual blend of identifying as European and accentuating the legacy of the classical Hellenic period (which the rest of Europe and Great Britain have always revered) while being greatly influenced by Asia Minor. This influence is rooted in Greece's 400-year Ottoman-Turkish reign until the 1820s as well as in the expulsion of more than 1.25 million Greeks from Turkey in the 1922 holocaust known as the "major catastrophe" (Clogg, 1992; Salamone, 1986). These people were Greeks who had lived in Turkey for nearly 2,500 years, since Alexander the Great had conquered the Middle East. Feeling the pressure to leave in the few years prior to the catastrophe (1900-1921), many of these Greeks fled to mainland Greece and to the United States. An interesting fact is that the seat of Orthodox Christianity, the ecumenical patriarch, remains in Istanbul (referred to as

Constantinople by Orthodox Christians). The next wave of Greek immigrants to the United States came in the years following World War II. It should also be noted that few countries in Europe lost a higher proportion of their Jewish population as part of Hitler's "final solution" than did Greece. It has been estimated that as much as 90% (about 70,000) of the Greek Jewish population was killed, and some of the oldest Jewish communities in Europe perished as a result (Handelei, 1991; Mazower, 1993). The latest wave of Greeks immigrated to the United States between the late 1960s and the mid-1970s with the passage of the Immigration Act of 1965 (Constantinou & Diamantides, 1985). In summary, Greek immigrants to the United States have brought with them various aspects of this historical legacy.

What about modern Greece today? Until the revision of Greece's Family Law section of the Civil Code, which occurred during 1982 and 1983, the husband held authority in all areas of common life and in decisions to be made (Dontopoulos, 1982a). Upon marriage, women were required to take their husbands' surnames. Officially, mothers had no rights over their children. By law, if parents had property, they were obliged to give a *prika* (dowry) to each daughter (Morgan, 1984). Also, until the legalization of civil marriages in 1982, the only marriages considered legal were those that were conducted by the Greek Orthodox Church. Adultery was considered a criminal offense and was punishable by up to a year in jail.

Although many women in Greek urban areas are employed outside the home, such employment is tempered by an honor code (the *philotimo*, to be described later in this chapter) that links women's economic activity negatively with the honor and reputation of the family (Cavounides, 1983). Men fear that if their wives work, they will be viewed as being unable to support their families. Thus family status is enhanced if women do not work. The pursuit of individual goals is viewed as temporary and secondary to fulfilling the proper female role through marriage, maintenance of the household, and the rearing of children (Myrsiades & Myrsiades, 1992).

In 1978, the Hellenic Homosexual Liberation Movement (AKOE) was founded in Athens. It was originally concerned with opposing the attempted passage of a law on venereal diseases that would have permitted the government to prosecute prostitutes and homosexuals (Dontopoulos, 1982b). Much as in such organizations in the United

States, a few years ago a division occurred due to political differences and the Greek Homosexual Community (EOK) was formed. As of this writing, the headquarters of these two organizations are situated literally right next to each other in a high-rise office building on a floor that houses only two suites. Various publications have emerged, such as *AMFI* (from the Greek word meaning "both," implying freedom for either sexual orientation) and *Labyris*. However, issues appear on an irregular basis contingent on the activists'/writers' ability to raise new funds, and distribution remains limited mostly to Athens. Athens has also instituted a gay hot line and has a clinic, the Hygienomiki Scholi Athinon, that is involved in the medical and social issues surrounding AIDS (J. Schippers, personal communication, September 14, 1989).

Greece is represented among the member nations of the International Lesbian and Gay Association (ILGA). During the 1994 meetings of the American Psychological Association, Harold Kooden, a psychologist actively involved in bringing about ILGA's recent acceptance into the United Nations as a nongovernmental organization, relayed that a Greek female ILGA newsletter editor was incarcerated in 1993 for refusing to print ads that were apparently submitted by heterosexual men who were soliciting lesbians for sexual encounters (personal communication, August 1994). Dr. M. Fakinos, an associate professor of psychology at the University of Laverne in Athens, disclosed a similar episode in which a male editor of *AMFI* was also incarcerated in 1993 because authorities deemed some of the photographs in the publication to be obscene (personal communication, August 1994). In juxtaposing these two incidents, it would appear that a double standard exists regarding what may or may not be printed in gay and lesbian publications as opposed to other publications, and that gay and lesbian Greeks who choose to move beyond invisibility and give voice to their experience may run the risk of harassment and incarceration. Outside of Athens, gay and lesbian issues have very little visibility in Greece.

It must again be noted that, in order to understand the experiences of a Greek American woman, heterosexual or lesbian, one needs first to determine the timing of her own or her family's immigration and to what degree the family has assimilated to American culture. The less assimilated, the greater the likelihood that she may be struggling with some of the issues discussed in this chapter.

Key Cultural Concepts

This section addresses some of the key cultural concepts that are critical to an understanding of the undercurrents that may be influencing the identity development and coming-out process of a Greek American lesbian. These concepts are sex role socialization, virginity and virtue, the *philotimo*, the socialization of family loyalty and distrust of "others" (xenophobia), and isolation and invisibility.

In order to understand the experience of a Greek lesbian's coming-out process, we first need to understand the socialization process of young Greek girls in general and the role of (heterosexual) women in Greek culture. As Nicholas Gage puts it in his book *A Place for Us: A Triumphant Coming of Age in America* (1989): "From birth, a Greek girl is groomed for her wedding ('How can I marry you like that?' a Greek mother will invariably shout at a female toddler who has soiled her clothes). Everything that happens after a Greek woman's wedding day is anticlimactic except the birth of her son" (p. 153).

Greek is a culture of rigidly maintained family and sex roles (Welts, 1982). The husband/father's authority is ultimate and unquestioned. Wives and daughters are expected to comply with this patriarchal authority. Young girls are socialized early to understand that their brothers are held in higher esteem and that their brothers' activities are more important than their own (Callinicos, 1990). The role of a daughter is to obey and to support the efforts of the male members of her family in preparation for the day she marries and has a husband of her own. The expression *Eisai kalo koritsi* (You're a good girl) is commonly repeated from childhood to adulthood to those who dutifully fulfill their role expectations, which include helping their mothers by learning to keep a clean house, how to cook and sew, and how to be good hostesses. Thus a young girl grows up associating her "goodness" with serving men and, in this way, honoring her family.

Children are expected to obey instruction and not to express their own needs, wishes, or opinions (Welts, 1982). A very poignant example of this kind of socialization is found in the case of Demetra, one of the Greek lesbians interviewed in the study. Demetra vividly recalled an incident when, while sitting among a group of adults, she tried to join in the conversation by stating her opinion on the topic being discussed. Her father, ignoring her, turned to the adults and said, "*Akouse teen. . . . Anthropos nomezie mas eginai tora,*" which roughly translates into "Listen to her ... she thinks she's become a person now!" The sting of this comment, along with the chuckles that followed, left Demetra with a lasting impression that her opinions did not count—and, perhaps, neither did she.

Whereas American culture views adolescence as a typically stressful time and as a time when the adolescent begins to individuate *from* family, Greeks view adolescence as simply a part of the natural evolution of development whereby individuation occurs *within* the context of family (Pappajohn, 1988). Paternal authority still is not challenged. Instead, children learn to emulate their parents, progressively taking on more sex role-appropriate responsibility within the family and, through this process, developing their sense of increased maturity. Welts (1982) offers the following observations:

> Since Greek parents discourage dialogue with children, adolescents rarely turn to their parents to discuss their thoughts, feelings, or changing life values. Contact remains loving and loyal but somewhat superficial and ritualized around meals, holidays, and family gatherings. (p. 278)

> Offspring will always remain "children" no matter what status or professional achievements they attain. They will be expected to honor advice given freely by the older generation. This attitude contrasts with cultures where children are better educated than their parents and parents acknowledge their achievement by accepting their grown children as peers. (p. 277)

> Greek Americans do not separate from their parents yet are perceived as mature and adult by their community. It is not at all unusual for Greek American parents to move many miles to live near one of their children. ... Greek parents view their children's homes as extensions of their own territory. If one parent is widowed, the children are expected to take in the surviving parent. Daughters are expected to take care of aging parents. (p. 278)

As noted previously, the family structures of the research participants in this study reflected the commonality of such living arrangements. Seven of the participants had had their grandmothers or grandfathers living with them for some portion of their childhoods.

To understand further how women have been viewed within Greek society, it is informative to examine some of the anthropological literature focusing on a feminist analysis of gender, such as the work of Ortner (1974), Dubisch (1986), and Seremetakis (1991), who all discuss the concept of women as "polluters." This is the notion that women have the capacity to be powerful polluters (and thereby "destroyers") of the environment and yet, as Dubisch notes, they are also capable of controlling that pollution. Basically, women are viewed as being closely associated to "nature" (because of their natural processes, such as menstruation and childbirth), whereas men are closely associated with "culture" (because they are the creators of social order). In this model, nature and culture are viewed to be in opposition. In many societies, culture serves to control or regulate nature; culture is valued over nature, and, by association, women's status is viewed as subordinate to that of men. Furthermore, in Greek culture, female expressions of sexuality (another natural process) outside the context of marriage also pose a threat to social order. A common Greek expression to describe an adulteress is to say that she is deceiving her husband in the street. The street is where dirt and trash exist. It represents the outside "wild," compared to the home, which should, by Greek standards, be the picture of cleanliness and order. In short, it is every woman's responsibility to exercise the modesty and shame necessary to control her sexuality, along with the strict control that male guardianship provides (Dubisch, 1986).

To illustrate the concept of women as polluters, we return to Demetra, who talked about how it felt to be an adolescent and to have the entire congregation of her church know when she was menstruating. One of the Greek Orthodox religious (mis)beliefs passed on from mother to daughter is that a woman cannot receive Holy Communion while menstruating because she is considered to be "unclean," implying that there is a certain degree of "unholiness" associated with being in this state. In actuality, a Boston-area Greek Orthodox priest told me that Greek Orthodoxy itself does not directly address this issue; rather, it is folklore that has been perpetuated over the generations. In any case, culturally, it is viewed as a highly disrespectful act for a woman to present herself before God the Father in this state. Greek men have no equivalent restrictions. The message thus learned is that sometimes women are not worthy of God's blessings simply because of who they are. Thus when Demetra had her period, she dutifully remained seated as others in the congregation approached the altar for Holy Communion. She felt embarrassed being what she described as a "marked woman." Clamar (1980) notes that usually only widowed, postmenopausal women are allowed to cross the threshold of the Holy

Altar in order to clean the altar and its gold artifacts, a necessary exception because scrubbing is viewed as women's work. Furthermore, these women are not typically paid for this privilege. Common belief holds that any other woman who crosses the Golden Gates of the Altar will be forever cursed for her sin of pride. And what, if anything, does the Greek Orthodox Church have to say about homosexuality?

There are currently an estimated 3 million Greeks living in the United States (Dabilis, 1990; Saloutos, 1980). The *Orthodox Observer* is a monthly newspaper published for the Greek Orthodox Archdiocese of North and South America and mailed to the homes of all dues-paying members. Its total circulation is approximately 140,000. In August 1993, the *Orthodox Observer* published a summary of Greek Orthodox Church views on homosexuality. The summary stated that the Bible and holy tradition are recognized as sources of faith, and that homosexuality is considered a "grave sin" ("The Orthodox View," 1993, p. 7). In this framework, it is believed that homosexuality "breeds promiscuity"; corrupts the morals of the young and innocent, with "devastating effects on their psychic structures"; and undermines the traditional nuclear family. The article goes on to declare that procreation is the only purpose of sex that is not derived from the "fallen nature of man." Hence sexual desire or behavior born of desire is deemed sinful. Despite a clear condemnation of homosexuality per se, the article acknowledges the homosexual person's right to the legal protections and basic human rights extended to other citizens, as long as homosexual behavior is not legally protected. It notes that activities and organizations, particularly those using public funds, that seek to encourage the acceptance of homosexuality as a lifestyle "result in a disservice to the homosexual and to society." Instead, the article encourages the use of mental health services designed to treat homosexuality as an illness, and the passage of legislation to discourage homosexual behavior.

Because of the nuances involved in church teaching and church law, and the possibility of misinterpretation, I originally wanted to reprint the full text of the *Orthodox Observer* article here, instead of presenting the distillation you have just read. However, on attempting to secure permission to reprint the material from the *Orthodox Observer*, I found myself in a quagmire. At first, based on the introduction to the *Orthodox Observer* piece, I believed that the newspaper article had been excerpted from a book titled *Moral and Social Concerns*, reportedly written by the Reverend Dr. Stanley Harakas. Hoping to go to the original source, I attempted to locate this book, but was unable to do so because it does not exist. I then contacted Dr. Harakas directly. He confirmed that he has addressed the topic of homosexuality in some of his writings, but he has never published a book titled *Moral and Social Concerns*, and the "excerpt" appearing in the *Orthodox Observer* is not from any of his works (personal communication, November 19, 1996). He had a hunch that the material in the article may have been taken from a pamphlet previously published by the Archdiocese, and he kindly offered to call the *Orthodox Observer* to assure them that the material was not his. Given that the *Orthodox Observer* is published for the Archdiocese, it appeared a release should be attainable.

However, despite my numerous conversations with the newspaper's representative, and apparently the paper's editorial staff's own deliberations with the Archdiocese, permission was ultimately not granted. The reason given was that the Archdiocese plans to revise the views stated in the article, as they have changed since the article was published. I was told that it is unknown when such revision might be complete, and that these things can take some time. I can understand that. Even so, my preference would have been to reprint the article here with a notation that, indeed, the views expressed are currently undergoing revision. After all, it has been only about 3½ years since these views were published in the *Orthodox Observer* under the heading "The Orthodox View." Given that this newspaper is distributed to thousands of Greek Orthodox households, the information is anything but secret.

Perhaps this experience is a reflection of the intense feelings aroused in some people (Greeks, religious Greeks) by a topic that they simultaneously deny. In this example we can see an element that contributes to the difficulty Greek lesbians, and I would think Greek gay men as well, face in establishing a cohesive personal identity. This incident represented a personally and spiritually painful moment for me, as I did and still do identify as Greek Orthodox. However, whether in the context of academic freedom for psychotheological discourse or in counseling, both secular and religious, silence can serve no useful purpose. My hope is that I have accurately represented the church's views. Readers who are interested in seeing the original article as it appeared in the *Orthodox Observer* may request it from the photoduplication service of the Library of Congress, Washington, D.C.; refer to microfilm number 05972.

Beyond the religious and sex role socialization factors that serve as the backdrop to understanding the Greek lesbian's coming-out process, there are two key cultural elements that are very much entwined and central to an understanding of this process: the concept of women's virtue and the extreme importance of the *philotimo* in a Greek person's life (Dubisch, 1986; Kennedy, 1986).

Philotimo literally means "love of (one's own) honor." The *philotimo* is to be guarded at all costs. The following passage from Nicolas Gage's book *A Place for Us* (1989) illustrates the meaning and importance of the *philotimo* in a Greek person's life. In a conversation between Gage and his father, his father says:

> "But before I die, I want to tell you that I'm proud of two things in life. The first is all you've done, and the second is that none of my daughters ever shamed me. For that matter, even my nieces—all the Gatzoyiannis women —they've all been virtuous and never once dishonored our family."
>
> ... I blew up at him. "What's so important about that?" I snapped. "Why is your pride and the family honor based on the virtue of its women?"
>
> "You don't think that honor is important?" he asked me in a tone that intimidated me despite my anger.
>
> "Yes, honor is important!" I replied. "But it should be based on what we each do as individuals, not on the sexual propriety of our women relatives. In most families some girl is going to step out of bounds. Does that mean the entire family has to lose its good name and respect?"
>
> "To me, my friends and my enemies—yes!" he thundered. "All the men I grew up with lived in fear that one of their women would shame them. You could wake up one morning and find out that everyone you knew looked at you differently because some girl in your family did something crazy. That's why I'm proud that none of my daughters, none of the women in the whole family that bears our name, brought shame on me. I can walk with my head high before any man I know."
>
> I decided to drop the argument ... but his words helped me understand both his thinking and the societies I encountered in Iran, Iraq, Pakistan and Turkey, where women were oppressed and carefully guarded by men but carried within themselves the knowledge that they had a weapon that could shatter their entire family in a moment. (p. 408)

Now, imagine what a Greek lesbian might feel within such a context. The burden of possessing such a powerful secret that could shatter her entire family is heavy indeed. There will be more than mere disappointment if her homosexuality is discovered; she runs the risk that the family will be shamed and dishonored beyond repair.

Greek girls are taught from an early age that they should never lose their virtue (i.e., their virginity), as it is directly tied to the family's *philotimo*. In the northern mountains of mainland Greece, there are a number of villages, such as Naoussa and Souli, that have statues or songs commemorating the courage of their women for "dancing to their graves." As folklore has it, these women threw their babies and their other children off the cliffs and then, one by one, danced themselves off the edge rather than fall prey to the Ottoman-Turks during the struggle for Greek independence (1821-1827), and face probable rape and slavery. The community norms are such that these mass suicides and martyrdom are cited to daughters by their mothers as examples of the importance of women's protecting their virtue and honor. The lesson is one of death before dishonor.

As Gage (1989) notes, "A willful daughter can ruin a man and his descendants for all eternity" (p. 86). As within many other cultures, physical force may be used in attempts to control women. A Greek father may believe that it is indeed his painful duty to strike his child in the service of good parenting (Welts, 1982). It is not at all unusual in Greece to hear of a father or brother who had exercised physical violence against a daughter or sister who had left home. In the patriarchal atmosphere of the Greek family, a young woman cannot leave home unless it is to marry. Over the years, pursuit of education has become an acceptable reason for a young woman to leave home, but only when there is no reasonable alternative university within commuting distance of home. For many, a woman attempting to live on her own is immediately suspected of having loose morals (Dontopoulos, 1982b). The threat this poses to the family's good reputation and *philotimo* may result in the daughter's being disowned and/or being subjected to violence in an effort to teach her that such behavior is not condoned. Then, if by chance outsiders come to know of the daughter's willful actions, they will at least see that an attempt has been made to reestablish family control and order and that the *philotimo* isn't being given up without a good fight. In extreme cases, daughters who have been "willful" and compromised their perceived virtue have been killed. In fact, this still occurs in some Middle Eastern cultures today (Olster, 1994).

Whether a Greek woman is lesbian or heterosexual, because the *philotimo* is so important she has learned at a very young age to make use of lies and deception to cover up any shortcomings or unacceptable behavior, because, after all, nobody is perfect. The Greek word for "lie," *psema*, does not have the overtones of moral failure found in English (du Bolay, 1976). Kennedy (1986) notes that Greeks see lying as more socially acceptable than telling the truth if the truth goes outside social norms. So what we have is a culture in which the individual "cares deeply about maintaining the *appearance* of honor" (Kennedy, 1986, p. 138). Dishonor comes not so much from breaking the rules as from being caught (Dubisch, 1986).

An illustration of such collusion between parents and lesbian daughters is found in the case of Sophia, a participant in my study. During the interview process, I asked those lesbians who weren't explicitly out to their parents if they thought that their parents knew or wondered about their sexual orientation. Sophia responded that she has left gay newspapers out on the coffee table and her mother has never asked about them, and that, although this same mother makes it her business when visiting the new home of a relative or friend for the first time to inspect every room, every corner, and even open the linen closets, she has yet to venture beyond the kitchen and living room of the one-bedroom apartment that Sophia has been sharing with her partner for 4 years. Sophia believes that her mother doesn't want to see how many beds there actually are. The few times Sophia has begun to broach the topic of her lifestyle, ever so tentatively and lightly, her mother, sensing that maybe something was up, responded with, "I don't need to know anything beyond that you are happy." Sophia's partner is included in all family events and is by all appearances accepted and welcomed as her close friend.

In contrast, another Greek lesbian I interviewed, Veroniki, has been out to her family for 5 years, and the only contact she has with them occurs only if she initiates it. Family members do not invite her—and certainly they do not invite her partner—to family gatherings anymore. To invite her would give the appearance that they approve of her lesbian sexual orientation.

The emphasis and value placed on maintaining the appearance of honor go a long way in explaining why Greek American lesbians are so invisible within the Greek community and unfortunately to one another as well. Further obstructing the Greek American lesbian's outreach toward other Greek lesbians is the historical/cultural legacy mentioned previously—that of being socialized into believing that only within the family can safety and trust truly be relied upon. Illustrative is a common Greek proverb: "Do not ever confide your secret to your friend; for he will tell it to another friend and then it will be your misfortune" (as cited in Bucuvalas, Lavrakas, & Stamatos, 1980, p. 43). Of the 10 Greek American lesbians I interviewed, a number of them had dated Greek men prior to coming out, but none had *ever* dated a Greek woman. Of those who are partnered, all are partnered with non-Greek women.

Coming Out to Self and Family

Considering that most Greek American lesbians are caught up in a type of "family force field" of maintaining traditional roles and values and mediating their behaviors through a *philotimo* filter, how does a Greek lesbian come out to herself under such circumstances? It is a struggle, because to be a lesbian means choosing not to orient one's energies toward a man. Because the Greek lesbian has had years of socialization teaching her that she is only as good as the man she serves or will serve, her self-esteem is not based on as solid a foundation of individual merit. This leaves the Greek lesbian floundering to define herself and find meaning in her life in perhaps a broader way. She is at a disadvantage in that if she was raised in a traditionally Greek household, she may have to discover her individual needs, desires, and worth while trying to integrate her lesbianism.

Further appreciation of this dilemma may be developed by a look at the experience of the Greek American lesbian's heterosexual sisters. Following the publication of her book *American Aphrodite* (1990), Callinicos (1991) wrote an article about what she has labeled "the modern picture bride." It is based on more than 300 interviews done with first-, second-, third-, and fourth-generation Greek American women representing 20 states, from New Hampshire to California, in both rural and urban areas. What she outlines is that not much has really changed from the days of arranged marriages and dowry expectations in Greece. One of the questions she asked the women she interviewed was, "What is the meaning of the word 'freedom' to you?" The most frequent response was "Freedom to marry whomever I choose. No arranged marriage for me." Callinicos (1991) comments: "For most non-Greek American women of our era, 'freedom to choose' denotes options about where to live, whether or not to marry, whether or not to bear children, what school to go to or not to go to. For contemporary Greek American women to define the phrase 'freedom to choose' as narrowly as they have done so to me in these interviews, signifies that we haven't moved at all" (p. 175).

As noted earlier, Greek American lesbians are invisible to each other, and that invisibility continues even in language. Margaret Mead (1953) found that the Greek women she studied seldom knew the word for genitals. I asked each of the 10 women I interviewed if they could tell me any Greek words that would describe their sexual orientation. None knew any at all. In my own experience, the words likely to be heard are derogatory and refer only to men (e.g., *poustee* [faggot], *kounisteis* [swisher], *tetios* [that kind (of man)]). Loizos and Papataxiarchis (1991) have made similar observations regarding the lack of words to describe women's experience of their sexuality in general and same-sex attraction specifically. In conversation, Greeks seldom even refer to the island of Lesbos (home to Sappho) by its name. They prefer instead to refer to the island by using the name of its main city, Mytelini. To Greek American lesbians, it is both laughable and tiresome when non-Greek acquaintances make the same old misconceived comments to the effect that "you all invented homosexuality, with Sappho and all . . . it would be great if society was as accepting here as they are in Greece." Such remarks are extremely common and clearly indicate a lack of cultural understanding. As many ethnographers of the Mediterranean have observed, an "exaggerated horror at homosexuality" is common (Loizos & Papataxiarchis, 1991). As a matter of record, the Greek words for homosexuality and lesbian are *omophilophilia* and *lesvia*, respectively.

How did the Greek American lesbians in my study handle their own coming-out processes? In answering the question, "What did your parents teach you about sex and sexuality?" five of the participants said, "Nothing!" and three more said, "Very little." The other two respondents, Sophia and Irene, gave slightly longer answers: Irene stated that although not much was discussed, her mother seemed to be able to express herself as a sensual being; Sophia said that her parents were openly affectionate with each other in front of the children. Common recollections included such experiences as being able to socialize with boys only in a mixed male-female group, often through the GOYA or by being chaperoned. Several were not permitted to date until age 16 or until after high school. Several were permitted to go out only with other Greek Americans. For the most part, "Don't come home pregnant" was the extent of any discussion on sexuality between the parents and their daughters. Demetra noted that as a young girl, what she always heard was, "*Na min mas endropiasis* [Don't shame us]. All they cared about was appearances, not what you feel in your heart. It made me crazy. Everything centered on approval and on *Ti tha pi o kosmos* [What will people say]?" Nine of the participants stated that homosexuality had never been a topic of even the most general of conversations. Again, none even knew how to say *gay* or *lesbian* in Greek. Finally, two of the women had married men even though they had already become aware of their sexual attraction to women. A third was married, but came out to herself only following her divorce. A fourth entered a convent at age 19 and remained there until she was 25.

An assessment of those interviewed revealed that the median age of coming out to self was 17. Eight of the women referred to their identities as lesbian and two identified as gay; none identified as bisexual. (As a reminder, the median age of the participants at the time of their interviews was 34.) Here are some of their stories:

> I had crushes on girls as a teen. I knew there were gay men, but I didn't know there were gay women. I ended up getting married, in a Greek Orthodox Church, of course. It lasted 13 months. After my divorce, I met a woman who became my roommate. She took me to a gay bar. It took me about a year to come out. Meanwhile, I became aware of the Ionian Society and I called the phone number that was listed. It took another year before I went to my first meeting. I was just too scared. (Sophia, age 31)

> I always knew I was different. I came out to myself when I was 17, but I knew it wasn't common practice so I negated it for a couple of years. But I came out because I needed to. It was essential for me. Pride is a big deal to Greeks. I think that being brought up with Greek pride may have given me the inner strength to pursue my inner goal of coming out. (Theodora, age 30)

I came out at 21. I fell in love with my college roommate and I spent the next 10 years with her. I thought I happened to fall in love with her as an individual and not that we were lesbians. (Demetra, age 40)

I was 22 years old. When I was 20, I went to a therapist, which hampered my process. I decided to travel and got as far away from home as possible. I roamed New Zealand all by myself. I tried men, but it wasn't for me. I think you should note this because it may be important—I have a gay cousin and we both were raised by our grandmothers; not the same one, but different ones. We've talked about this a lot. We both feel that our love for our grandmothers was so great that it may have some relationship to why we now love women and are lesbians. Because our grandmothers lived at home with us, they made our mothers remain as children. My mother didn't become an adult until after my grandmother died and I already felt grown-up. I think that since my grandmother was raising me, it made my mother's role much less prominent. (Irene, age 29)

At the time of the interviews, seven of the participants were out to at least one parent, with three being out only to their mothers and four being out to both parents. Of the seven who were out, only three had come out by their own volition and initiation. The median number of years from being out to self to coming out to at least one parent was 8 years (ranging from 6 months, when Katina's mother directly asked her, to 19 years, when Veroniki was forced into her disclosure by a sister). Of the three who came out by choice, the median number of years from being out to self to being out to at least one parent was also 8 years.

The ages of the three participants who were not out to either parent were 29, 31, and 38, with the "secret" being maintained for 7, 15, and 10 years, respectively, since coming out to self. All had siblings. Two were able to be out with at least one of their siblings, and the third felt unable to be out with anyone in her immediate as well as extended family. At the time of the interview she had been out to herself for 10 years. Here is what these three women had to say to the question, "Can you explain why you've chosen not to come out to them?":

It won't be positive in any way at all! The gap of understanding would be too big and I wouldn't be able to handle their reaction. My fantasy fears are that my mother would have a heart attack and my father would disown me. Realistically, they would actually disown me. It is morally wrong in a religious way. They would be horrified if I shared my lifestyle, like if I told

my aunt and uncle and didn't tell them. It would be some sort of stigmatization. Anyway, they don't want to know. There is a pattern of avoidance.
I'm 38, and I don't talk about men. They've met my partner and I've lived
two different places with her. We maintain a separateness in bedrooms
and appearance. She's always welcomed by my parents and sister. Maybe
they don't know how to ask. They don't want their thoughts confirmed.
(Anastasia, age 38)

Recalling the story recounted earlier about Sophia's mother not
wanting to know more about the gay newspapers on the coffee table
and the true arrangements of her one-bedroom apartment, Sophia (age
31) also added:

Religion is a big deal. You have to understand that my Irish father converted
to Greek Orthodoxy. Not only that, but he held various posts like being
church treasurer and president of the Greek legion. In my family, all who
marry non-Greeks still have weddings in the Greek church. Everyone
marries on Sunday [the Holy Day]. Out of 30 Greek grandchildren, all are
Greek Orthodox. My cousins' kids, which are one-quarter Greek, have all
still been baptized as Greek Orthodox and they all go to Greek school classes
and to the Greek church.

I've never felt a need to tell my father because we never talk much anyway.
But my mother, yes. I do feel a need to come out. There have been times
when I've tried to broach the topic and before I get too far at all she'll say,
"Oh, I'm getting a migraine." She's gotta know. I can't see how she doesn't.
. . . My brother found me in bed with a woman, but we never discussed it.
I had a 5-year relationship with a woman and lived with her. My mother
loved her the first time I brought her over. She adored her. She often said
that she wished my brother could bring home a girl like her and I would
think, "Oh mother, if you only knew." During this time, I would say that I
talked about us in actively subtle ways. But after about 6 months my mother
liked her less. I think she was frightened at the importance she played in
my life. (Irene, age 29)

As I mentioned previously, four of the women were "discovered"
and did not come out of their own choosing. In Christina's case, her
mother had found her journal and read it. Christina described her as
being furious. Reparation has been hampered in that her mother has
had a recurring mental illness since Christina was 10.

In Demetra's case, her mother found and read a love letter when
Demetra was 22. She reacted by being "hysterical" and, according to
Demetra, contemplated taking an overdose of pills. She felt guilty for

"encouraging it" by having sent Demetra to a women's college, intending to protect her from men. She still views Demetra (age 40) as being "oversexed." Demetra has accepted that her mother will not be able to accept her and is not angry with her anymore. Family contact and loyalty have remained. Her father has never been told. "He'd be violently negative. We're not close. We never have discussions anyway. He thinks I'm crazy just for going camping." Interestingly, Demetra has a 3½-year-old son who was conceived through alternative insemination. Demetra sought her pregnancy while single, and she continues to be a single parent. Demetra's mother and Demetra have chosen to allow Demetra's father to believe the child was "an accident." As it was, her father did not embrace her and her child at first, and Demetra believed it would be far worse to have him know that her son resulted from willful, premeditated action. Demetra believed that he would view this as dishonor heaped upon dishonor to the family.

Katina's mother asked her directly about her sexuality only 6 months after Katina had come out to herself; she had not been planning on making a disclosure. Finally, Veroniki, age 36, came out after her younger sister learned of her homosexuality and gave her an ultimatum to tell their parents or she would do it for her. Though not completely severed from her family, Veroniki has minimal contact with them, and this tends to take place only if she initiates it.

Four of the women were out to their fathers. No participant was out to her father without also being out to her mother. In the case of one participant, being out to her father has been very indirect. Margarita (age 38) stated that her father was not informed by her, but rather by her mother. He was told 13 years after Margarita had told her mother. The matter has never been brought up or discussed between father and daughter, even though it has been 4 years since the disclosure and there have been many visits and opportunities to acknowledge this fact. During the 13 years prior to her mother's disclosure, Margarita stated that "the secret was hers, not mine. . . . She requested that I not tell him because she gets blamed for everything. She was also trying to protect my inheritance. She not only requested that I not tell anyone Greek in Buffalo, New York [Margarita's hometown], out of fear that it would somehow get back to my father, but she also asked me to not come out to any Greek people in Boston either. She said it would kill my father and that if his friends knew, he'd be destroyed."

Veroniki's case has already been described. Christina (age 26) told her father shortly after her mother had confronted her over what she had read in Christina's journal. Her parents were in the middle of divorce proceedings, and Christina felt it would be unfair of her to not tell her father even though she had not voluntarily come out to her mother. His reaction was to blame Christina's girlfriend. He asked Christina if the woman had attacked her. At the time of the interview, Christina described her father as being "tolerant."

Katina, age 32, stated that, depending on whose frame of reference one uses, she ran away from home and/or was kicked out of the house by her father when she was 19 years old, and she wasn't sure if she was out to her father or not. Her father

> didn't like my lifestyle too much so we had a few brawls. . . . He used to hit me. He was a typical Greek and I wasn't a typical Greek daughter. Most of my Greek friends were already married with children. I drank and partied and would come back during the wee hours of the night. Sometimes, I would sneak girls up into the room. After he accused me of being a lesbian, my aunt took me in, but he still doesn't *really* know. We didn't talk for 5 years after that. It's been better these last 2 years. Our relationship would get even worse than what it was if I were to confirm his suspicions.

Finally, Theodora (age 30) was the only one of the 10 participants who purposefully initiated her own coming out to her parents at the same time. She did this by coming out over the phone immediately after having told her sister-in-law and brother. It has been 5 years since she came out. Her parents reacted by saying they love her, although her mother has remained feeling guilty and self-blaming. The only person outside of the family to whom Theodora's mother can talk about Theodora's sexual orientation is Theodora's godmother, and that's because the godmother initiates the conversation. Theodora describes her father as still not understanding it, but that at least he has actually told some of his relatives. At the time of the interview, Theodora had been living with her partner for the past 14 months. Her parents had never met her, and when her parents call, the parents and partner do not talk to each other beyond the conversation necessary to get Theodora to the phone. This situation exists within a context of Theodora describing her partner as her "soul mate."

In 1989, Tremble, Schneider, and Appathurai reported on a study of three lesbian and seven gay Canadian young people from Asian,

Portuguese, Greek, Italian, and Indo-Pakistani cultural backgrounds (the one Greek youth was male). Of some interest to the preceding discussion of coming out to parents are two points made by these researchers. First, parents often do not understand what it means to be lesbian or gay, and the idea of lesbianism is often especially difficult for them to understand. Some parents are unaware that lesbians even exist, and when faced with the concept, may believe that their lesbian daughter wants to be a man. Another common misconception is that the daughter's homosexuality has been caused by the dominant culture, which is viewed as decadent, and that she has been overpowered. Second, gay and lesbian youth

> will be most in conflict with their cultures when religious beliefs are orthodox, when there exists a strong expectation to reside with the family until marriage, and to get married and have children, and when gender role expectations are polarized and stereotypical. Paradoxically, these values also provide the pathway to reconciliation between homosexual children and parents. When the love of children and the value of family ties are strong, nothing, including homosexuality, will permanently split the family. (Tremble et al., 1989, p. 257)

Tremble et al. also note that although there may not be a complete understanding, and positive feelings may continue to be absent, the focus on sexual orientation will eventually lessen, as will the conflict between parents and their gay children. Often, the parent-child relationship will remain intact, bound by love.

In the case of Greek American families, I would submit that parent-child relationships often return to the level Welts (1982) describes as being loving and loyal but somewhat superficial, with parents discouraging deeper connection and children (whether adolescent or adult) colluding in the maintenance of such dynamics by not talking about their feelings or concerns. For these families, love and loyalty are the qualities most valued, and as several of the cases in this study illustrate, families often avoid discussions of homosexuality (both prior or subsequent to coming out) so as not to pit love and the family's *philotimo* directly against each other. Sometimes a daughter will use the smallest of lies to avoid reminding a parent of the shame she or he feels but keeps hidden. For example, Demetra said, "I protect my mother from remembering her shame over me and what I am by saying, 'I'm going to the Cape' instead of more specifically saying that 'I'm going to Provincetown,' where she had once visited and found disgusting because of the gays and AIDS that was there." However, for some, this type of relationship is not possible, as in the case of Veroniki. If we were to ask her parents why they do not welcome her back into the fold, they would likely say it is out of great love for her and would reject the notion of its being "punishment." Veroniki herself says that if her parents were to invite her back, they would believe that this implied their acceptance of her lesbian sexual orientation. Greek parents believe that it is their duty to teach their children what is "right" even if that means the lessons can be learned only through a process as painful as rejection. Other Greeks would view these parents as "paying the ultimate sacrifice" in order to teach their children properly, and as executing their parental duties with honor. It is important that I end this discussion of parent-child relationships with a reminder that not all Greek Americans behave according to Greek cultural scripts. Again, the degree to which a family has assimilated to the dominant "American" culture will likely play a significant role in how family members view and experience one member's coming-out process. With equal caution, I should note that it is important to remember that many Greek Americans strongly identify with their Greekness, even though they may be several generations removed from immigration.

Coming Out in the Community: Integration or Coexistence of Dichotomous Values?

Thus far, I have focused on Greek American lesbians in the context of coming out to self and to family. At this point, it may be beneficial to step back and review a couple of criticisms that have been raised about theoretical assumptions and coming-out models as they stand today. First, as Greene (1994) has noted, of all the clinical and empirical research on lesbians that has been published, most has been conducted with white, middle-class lesbians, and therefore lacks generalizability to lesbians of color. As Greene states, the literature does not "take into account the realistic social and psychological tasks and stressors that are a component of lesbian identity formation for women who are of a visible ethnic minority group" (p. 390). Factors such as racism and discrimination, and their effects on the well-being of lesbians of color, are much too significant to ignore. In addition, Greene notes that the cultural heritages of lesbian women of color may include vastly different views regarding women's roles and homosexuality from those of the dominant culture.

At this point, I would argue that another problem exists with the psychological literature as it relates to lesbians, and that this is, perhaps, a less obvious problem. Researchers in the United States seem to treat the white race as if it comprises simply one monolithic ethnic culture. It is falsely assumed that all white Americans espouse the values of the dominant white (Anglo-Saxon Protestant) culture. Just as we cannot generalize most of the existing research to lesbians of color, it would be inaccurate to assume that these findings are generalizable to all white lesbians. It is indeed a rare study that inquires into or reports the ethnic backgrounds of its white lesbian subjects. I suspect that most of the research has been conducted using a subject pool that consists of those who primarily belong to or identify with the dominant culture because these are the women most likely to be "out" and, therefore, identifiable and available to be studied. Less likely to be out and available for study would be white lesbians who also belong to cultures that are less tolerant of homosexuality, for example, Catholic Italian Americans such as those living in a concentrated Italian community in Boston called the North End; members of the Portuguese community of New Bedford, Massachusetts; lesbians living in the concentrated Armenian community of Watertown, Massachusetts; those who are Russian, Serbian, or Byzantine Orthodox; or those who are Jewish Orthodox. Greene (1994) states:

> An understanding of the meaning and the reality of being a woman of color who is a lesbian requires a careful exploration of . . . factors. These factors include the nature and importance of the culture's traditional gender role stereotypes and their relative fluidity or rigidity, the role and importance of the family and community, and the role of religion in the culture. (p. 392)

In my opinion, these same factors should be considered in any attempt to understand the meaning and reality of white lesbians whose self-identity is highly related to an ethnic culture that is viewed as "different" from the dominant one, and even more so when religion is strongly embedded in that culture. This is not to say that ethnically identified white lesbians don't live in, identify with, and even accept many of the dominant culture's values as their own. At the same time, however, they likely have not relinquished their ethnic identities and those identities' concomitant values. Perhaps the simplest way to understand this is to consider the difference between "assimilation" and "acculturation." Researchers and clinicians alike are mistaken when they blur the distinctions between race and ethnicity and treat them as one and the same.

We now turn our attention to coming out in the community. When asked about their social networks, nine of the study participants replied that they socialized mostly with non-Greek gays, lesbians, and bisexuals. When asked if they were out to any Greek people other than family, nine said they were, but four of these women were out only to other Greek gays (by virtue of attending Ionian Society events). A fifth was out only to a Greek Orthodox priest. The sixth was out to a couple of Greek clients she had met through her job. Finally, three were out to one or two childhood friends. One of these three regretted having come out to her friends, as it was a negative experience and had been a source of gossip ever since. Thus, beyond participation in the Ionian Society, these participants' presentation of themselves as both Greek and lesbian to other Greek people seemed to be limited to one or two people at most. In fielding the question, "Would you say you are out in the Greek community?" none answered affirmatively. Seven stated that they believed it is harder to come out to Greeks compared with non-Greeks, and the remaining three experienced coming out to both groups as equally difficult.

However, it is interesting that although these women remain relatively closeted within the Greek community, this does not seem to extend to the greater community. In fact, seven of the women were involved in gay and lesbian rights activism as self-defined by participation in gay pride marches, participating in the wedding ceremony held during the 1987 March on Washington, and attending statehouse rallies around such issues as advocating for gays' and lesbians' rights to be foster care providers and supporting the Massachusetts gay rights bill. Considering the degree of press and camera coverage such events often bring, this is far greater visibility than one might expect from Greek American lesbians. Many of the participants' immediate family members and other relatives lived locally. Regardless, several noted that although they worried over being "found out," either by a parent to whom they were not out or by a family acquaintance who might be watching the news and feel compelled to gossip, all felt it was important to follow through.

As Fassinger (1991) notes, most of the existing models of gay identity development, such as Cass's (1979) widely cited model, have a

> linear and prescriptive flavor implying that developmental maturity rests on an immutable homoerotic identification as well as a positive public (and often political) identity. The models are insensitive to diversity in terms of race/ethnicity. . . . The unfortunate implication is that nonpolitical acceptance of one's gay identity is seen as a form of developmental arrest. (Fassinger, 1991, p. 168)

Thus I would propose that it is indeed an interesting juxtaposition that occurs when one tries to apply Western/American models of coming out to beliefs surrounding the development of a positive Greek American lesbian identity. On the one hand, an argument could be made that as a group, the 10 lesbians in this study still possess a fair degree of internalized homophobia and shame, as some are not out to one or both of their parents, none are out in their Greek American communities, and most worried about being shunned or that their families would be exposed to hurtful gossip (damaging the *philotimo*, thereby shaming the family). Yet, by another measure, many appear to have gone beyond merely "accepting" themselves and are on the far end of the continuum of "outness, advocacy, and celebration," even by Western standards. As one participant said:

> I get so annoyed with people who think that you're unhealthy or somehow not proud of yourself if you haven't come out to your family. I'm out in lots of other ways. The last thing a Greek person wants to hear is that they aren't proud! It's such an insult. I'm plenty proud, but I also love my family and I see no reason to hurt them . . . at least not at this point in my life.

Finally, the women were asked to talk about both the positive and the negative or painful aspects of being both Greek and lesbian:

> The Ionian Society is a positive. Having a Greek gay group . . . the level of friendship, intimacy, caring and support is much greater than in any other gay groups I know. . . . What I find painful is that I can't be myself in my church and in my culture and that my community would not celebrate my relationship. . . . I had always been very active in the church, but I left for a

couple of years following my divorce and then my coming out. I felt nervous and guilty over both, but then I went back in '85 and joined the choir. After 6 months I left again because everyone kept trying to fix me up [with men]. My conflict around the church is painful. (Sophia)

I like that I can hook into a gay community and a Greek community no matter where I live, even though I don't hook into the Greek community very much besides going to a few festivals, that type of thing. But I like knowing that I can. Being Greek is cool. I like the loyalty to family and friends. Greek people are warm. Also, Greeks are very political, which is probably helpful in terms of being lesbian and standing up for myself. And I like the Ionian Society as compared to New Englanders' culture. We're not reserved and private. We get in there with each other . . . we're earthier. The negatives. . . . If I wanted to be a practicing Greek Orthodox, I couldn't do it. . . . There's a shortage in meeting Greek lesbians to date. It's my fantasy. I'd like to be able to speak Greek with my lover. I like the language and I wish I could use it. (Margarita)

I like being ethnically based in my relationship. My partner is from Puerto Rico and speaks Spanish, which is attractive to me. I would not be comfortable with someone who is a WASP, I know that. I like the rich heritage of being Greek. I'm proud to be Greek. Also, I'm proud to be a lesbian in spite of being Greek and not succumbing to marriage after marriage because I'm supposed to. It's a strength. I'm not doing it to spite my parents. What's painful is that for Greeks, being Greek and lesbian is polar opposites. There's no such animal. To admit it is to be scorned. The most painful part is having come out to the folks. (Veroniki)

Both Greeks and gays know how to have a good time! I wish it were easier to be out to all the relatives. They'd never understand. (Katina)

Greekness has always been important. I don't know why yet. But it's always been important to affirm. . . . I think the Greek work ethic and the push to always strive for success probably has served me well as a lesbian since I won't ever have a man taking care of me. . . . I feel anxious about going to the Greek church and other people's expectations. I wouldn't be accepted as a lesbian, and even though there's no direct discrimination, the subtle is still painful. . . . Oppression is painful. Connection with Greek gay friends becomes important. (Theodora)

There's a part of me that likes being different, unique and special. But what's difficult is to not fit in anywhere. Not as a Greek single parent or a lesbian single parent. Most lesbians who are moms are in couples. My sense of self is constantly from within. I don't get the benefit of either community. (Demetra)

I'm glad I have an ethnic heritage and that it's an accessible culture. Lots of people know and enjoy Greek food; lots of people have been to Greece. At least I'm not seen as odd or different because of being Greek. What I don't like is that the Greek community is closed-minded. I don't think that they're just being ethnocentric. I really think they are closed-minded. There is passive, automatic acceptance of anyone who is Greek or Greek oriented and an initial distrust of anyone who isn't. (Anastasia)

I'm proud of my heritage. I think about Sappho and Lesbos and I'm proud to be both lesbian and Greek. What's negative is that a homosexual marriage would not be acknowledged in the church and it's not respected in the community. To be in a lesbian relationship is breaking all traditional barriers and laws. Of all the things I could do, this tops them all, you know what I mean? It's like Greeks think it's the worst thing for a [Greek] woman not to marry a Greek, but being a lesbian really tops it all! (Christina)

I don't see any positive aspects of being both. People say, "What's wrong with her that she's not married?" How can I go to Greece with a lover and stay on my family's inherited property? But none of this would be an issue if I were with a man. I wish I could be out. I wish people could understand my recent breakup with my lover of 5 years. I wish I could have support by people who I love and who love me. (Irene)

I don't think of the two together; I think of myself as lesbian, but it's nice being Greek. I never felt negative over being Greek. I've always been proud of that. (Maria)

So, to what extent should the members of this small sample of Greek lesbians be viewed as having successfully integrated the duality of their experiences as Greek and as lesbians into one healthy and positive Greek lesbian identity? Those prone to respond from an Anglo-American dominant culture perspective would likely say that these women do not have an integrated positive Greek lesbian identity because they are living in dichotomy. Although they may be sharing themselves as lesbians and even as Greek lesbians in the gay community, they have truncated the sharing of themselves as lesbians with their families and lessened their participation in their Greek communities. In the dominant culture, dichotomy is viewed as antithetical to integration. However, it is important that we also consider the response through a Greek cultural lens. Within Greek culture, learning to live and solidify one's identity within dichotomy is a normal part of adult development.

For example, as I have noted above, for generations Greek women have warned their daughters that menstruation places them in a state of unholiness. Each month, Greek women are kept imprisoned for the sin of being women, prevented from seeking spiritual connection with God through Holy Communion. Yet, amazingly, even within such a context of shame, among my Greek childhood friends as well as for a number of the 10 study participants, menarche was a time of great *public* celebration. Immediately, extended family members were called, including transatlantic calls to Greece, to share the good news. As emerging adolescent girls, we would tease each other over whether our mothers had sent themselves into the kitchen yet to make *loukoumades* (puffed fried rice balls steeped in honey and cinnamon). This was our way of checking to see whether one of us had started her period yet. It was customary for mothers to make *loukoumades* in celebration and to honor their daughters' arrival to womanhood. Indeed, as letters would arrive from Greece in the weeks following such an event, we would learn of the aunts and grandmothers who also joined in connected celebration by cooking their own batches of *loukoumades* to share the news with their families and friends. Somehow, living in such a dichotomy was normal. Much as a fish doesn't know that it is wet, we didn't question the reason for celebration in such a context of shame. Menstruation brought both. It simply was the way it was.

Also, as I have noted, the Greek culture is a patriarchal one. Yet an interesting paradox exists that is illustrated by an old folk saying that goes something like this: "The man may be the head of the family, but the woman is the neck which controls the direction the head will turn!" (see Rouvelas, 1993). If folk sayings represent what a culture generally accepts as guiding wisdom, then what is the underlying message regarding authority and power, the public and the private? By dominant white Anglo-American cultural standards, it would appear that this saying is not particularly flattering to either sex. By Greek standards, it acknowledges that women do have (indirect) power and that men and women alike simply learn to live in a public/private dichotomy. It remains important to keep up appearances. Because Greek

American lesbians have been socialized within this type of family context, we would expect them to approach and balance the dichotomies of their reality by exercising behaviors similar to those modeled by their parents.

A Greek song called "Maria in Yellow" is another small illustration of the dichotomy within Greek culture. When I was a child, "the adults," my friends, and I would dance to this song at Greek picnics and festivals. The song still remains very popular at Greek festivals today. As I have noted, women's virtue is anything but a laughing matter in Greek culture, yet this song mocks virtuous behavior and seems to indicate that women would like nothing better than to "step upon" their husbands and commit adultery. Although the song pokes fun, it nonetheless contains a double message for behavior and an interesting puzzle for young girls. In English, the lyrics are as follows: "Maria in the yellow, who do you love better? Who do you love better, your husband or your neighbor?" Maria answers, "I love my husband, but I love the neighbor more. . . . May my husband turn to marble, and my neighbor into a rose, so that I may step upon the marble while I keep cutting from the rose."

Moving beyond illustrations from Greek popular culture, Welts (1982) has observed that many first-generation Greek American children have been thrust into parenting themselves while they are at the same time expected to act as though they are dependent upon their parents. This is particularly apparent in regard to education. As was the case with the members of this study's sample, most Greek immigrants have pushed their children to reach higher levels of education than they themselves had been able to achieve. Thus Greek immigrant parents may not be particularly able to understand what their children are learning or to help their children with their homework. Ultimately, the children may be left on their own to make such major decisions as choosing a college and a major program. Furthermore, some children may serve in the role of language and cultural interpreters for their mothers and grandmothers when they go shopping or to doctor's appointments (Callinicos, 1990). Thus, although children are generally expected not to have opinions and to obey parental instruction, they may also be forced by circumstances to assume adult responsibilities and decision-making tasks. As Welts (1982) notes, "Dutifully, they ignore the contradiction" (p. 277).

These illustrations provide a glimpse into the paradoxical cultural structure within which Greeks live. So why should Greek lesbians act any less Greek? Holden (1972) says, "Spirit and flesh, ideal and reality, triumph and despair—you name them and the Greeks suffer or enjoy them as the constant poles of their being, swinging repeatedly from one to the other and back again, often contriving to embrace both poles simultaneously, but above all never reconciled, never contented, never still" (p. 27). I would propose that Greek American lesbians are simply being culturally consistent when they stay closeted in Greek community yet visible and active otherwise. Greeks are used to living their lives in dichotomy. This is not to say that Greek American lesbians do not feel the effects of oppression or do not feel pain and regret over such dichotomy.

To flesh out the idea of living in dichotomy a little further, I would like to shift from my framework of writing this chapter for what I have assumed will be a mostly North American/possibly British audience and close by sharing a contextual transformation that occurred for me when I recently had the opportunity (and challenge) to address an international audience in Athens during the IV European Congress of Psychology. I was told that this would be only the second time that this Congress held a symposium on gay and lesbian psychology. I found myself wondering whether any Greek psychologists would actually attend. I speculated that it would be all too easy for many of them to skip this symposium because they likely viewed gay and lesbian people as something "other," far removed from their personal or professional experiences. For those who might come, I wished somehow to leave them with an appreciation of the Greek American lesbian experience in a personal, directly accessible, and memorable way.

I decided to make use of a familiar experience as an analogy, namely, immigration, and with it, a related Greek word, *xeniteia*, which viscerally speaks volumes. Large numbers of Greeks living in Greece either have themselves been immigrants at one time or another (seeking educational or work opportunities or refuge) or know members of their immediate or extended families who have. In fact, immigration is so common that descriptive poetry and songs abound in a style that might be seen as reflecting a type of "blues" tradition.

I believe that the essence of the Greek American lesbian's experience can be captured by the analogy drawn from the general Greek immigrant experience and applied to the "traveling between communities" and the duality of existence that the Greek American lesbians in this study described. My paper was titled *When Ethnicity and Sexual Orientation Identities Intersect: Overcoming the Feeling of* Xeniteia *in Greek American Lesbians* (Fygetakis, 1995).

The word *xeniteia* is derived from the root word *xeno*, or "foreign." As defined by Moskos (1989), *xeniteia* connotes the sense of sojourning in foreign parts. With it comes concomitant feelings that might best be described as deep yearning or homesickness for one's own people. This love for and nostalgia associated with one's culture is often transmitted from one generation to the next. It is my contention that Greek American lesbians undergo a process parallel to the immigrant experience of *xeniteia*. That is, Greek American lesbians must by necessity seek lesbian companionship and relationships within the larger dominant American culture because they see coming out within their Greek American communities as too difficult and risky. In much the same way as immigrants, Greek American lesbians, seeking to make life better for themselves and to be truer to their own spirits, leave for a new land, still loving those they leave behind. Ironically, although they leave to avoid expected disapproval and rejection, for many the resulting feeling is the same; one of being somewhat an exile, removed from their own people and yearning for the familiar comfort and joy of kinship that belonging to a Greek American community provides. In 1963, Theano Papazoglou Margaris won a Greek state prize for literature for her book of short stories *The Chronicle of Halsted Street* (1962). A refugee from the major catastrophe, Margaris settled in Chicago in the 1920s. Many of her stories deal with the emotional anguish of the immigrant caught between two worlds. In one story, titled "The Suspended Ones," Margaris captures the immigrant's quandary as to what is his *patrida* (homeland). Briefly, the 49-year-old protagonist of the story travels back and forth between Greece and the United States, trying to find the place where he feels most at home after having lived in the United States for many years. He seems never to be content, no matter where he is. Margaris evokes the dilemma by amending the adage "You can't go home again" with "and you can't really find a home where you are" (see Moskos, 1989, p. 99).

Clearly, the 10 women who took part in this study have all spoken of this same pain. Yet, although they may be searching for a place where they feel "one and at home," they have all expressed joy and great pride in the positive aspects of being Greek and of being lesbian.

Thus when those of us who hold the biases of the dominant culture are entrusted to hear about a Greek American lesbian's pain, we must learn to appreciate the duality of her self-identity and to help her reinforce the positive strengths of both. Those of us who have been schooled in gay/lesbian/bisexual-affirmative psychotherapy should be very careful not to view the Greek American lesbian as simply needing to work through her internalized homophobia and "acculturate" better to her lesbian identity and community. It is my hope that this chapter has contributed toward a better understanding of the complexities involved for women who identify as Greek American lesbians. If there is a main point to be made, it is that these women should not be discounted as simply not brave enough, not proud enough, or not having enough of a positive lesbian identity. On the contrary, they are on an odyssey, attempting to "embrace both poles simultaneously" with dignity and honor.[1]

Note

1. Information on gay and lesbian organizations, publications, meeting places, and legal issues in Greece can be found at the Web site http://www.geocities.com/WestHollywood/2225/index.html. Many of the postings are in English; some are in Greek. Additional software is required to make Greek entries readable.

References

Around the USA: Festival conference slated. (1994, February). *Orthodox Observer*, p. 17.

Beck, E. T. (Ed.). (1982). *Nice Jewish girls: A lesbian anthology*. Watertown, MA: Persephone.

Bucuvalas, E. G., Lavrakas, C. G., & Stamatos, P. G. (1980). *Treasured Greek proverbs: The Greeks have a saying for it . . . .* Ridgewood, NJ: Treasured Greek Proverbs.

Callinicos, C. (1990). *American Aphrodite: Becoming female in Greek America*. New York: Pella.

Callinicos, C. (1991). Arranged marriage in Greek America: The modern picture bride. In D. Georgakas & C. Moskos (Eds.), *New directions in Greek American studies* (pp. 161-179). New York: Pella.

Cass, V. C. (1979). Homosexual identity formation: A theoretical model. *Journal of Homosexuality, 4*(3), 219-235.

Cavounides, J. (1983). Capitalist development and women's work in Greece. *Journal of Modern Greek Studies, 1*, 321-338.

Chan, C. S. (1989). Issues of identity development among Asian-American lesbians and gay men. *Journal of Counseling and Development, 68*, 16-20.

Chock, P. P. (1986). Irony and ethnography: On cultural analysis of one's own culture. *Anthropological Quarterly, 59*(2), 87-96.

Clamar, A. (1980, August). *A changing Greek-American woman and the unchanging Greek Orthodox Church.* Paper presented at the 88th annual meeting of the American Psychological Association, in Montreal, Quebec, Canada.

Clogg, R. (1992). *A concise history of Greece.* Cambridge: Cambridge University Press.

Constantinou, S. T., & Diamantides, N. D. (1985). Modeling international migration: Determinants of emigration from Greece to the United States, 1820-1980. *Annals of the Association of American Geographers, 75,* 352-369.

Dabilis, A. (1990, July 28). A tale of two countries: Greek Americans call the U.S. home. *Boston Globe,* pp. 1, 6.

Dontopoulos, C. (1982a, October). The women's movement in Greece: Part I. *Off our backs,* pp. 6-7, 26.

Dontopoulos, C. (1982b, November). The women's movement in Greece: Part II. *Off our backs,* pp. 6-7, 28.

Dubisch, J. (1986). Culture enters through the kitchen: Women, food, and social boundaries in rural Greece. In J. Dubisch (Ed.), *Gender and power in rural Greece* (pp. 195-214). Princeton, NJ: Princeton University Press.

Dubisch, J. (1993). "Foreign chickens" and other outsiders: Gender and community in Greece. *American Ethnologist, 20,* 272-287.

du Bolay, J. (1976). Lies, mockery, and family integrity. In J. G. Peristiany (Ed.), *Mediterranean family structures* (pp. 389-406). Cambridge, UK: Cambridge University Press.

Espin, O. M. (1987). Issues of identity in the psychology of Latina lesbians. In Boston Lesbian Psychologies Collective (Ed.), *Lesbian psychologies: Explorations and challenges* (pp. 35-55). Urbana: University of Illinois Press.

Fassinger, R. E. (1991). The hidden minority: Issues and challenges in working with lesbian women and gay men. *Counseling Psychologist, 19,* 157-176.

Fygetakis, L. M. (1995, July). *When ethnicity and sexual orientation identities intersect: Overcoming the feeling of xeniteia in Greek American lesbians.* Paper presented at the IV European Congress of Psychology, Athens.

Gage, N. (1989). *A place for us: A triumphant coming of age in America.* New York: Simon & Schuster.

Greene, B. (1994). Lesbian women of color: Triple jeopardy. In L. Comas-Diaz & B. Greene (Eds.), *Women of color: Integrating ethnic and gender identities in psychotherapy* (pp. 389-427). New York: Guilford.

Handelei, J. (1991, November). [Untitled speech]. Presented at the Artzenu Yisrael Future Leadership Mission, Yad Vashem, Jerusalem.

Holden, D. (1972). *Greece without columns: The making of the modern Greeks.* Philadelphia: J. B. Lippincott.

Kalogeras, Y. D. (1992). Narrating an ethnic group. *Journal of the Hellenic Diaspora, 18*(2), 13-34.

Kennedy, R. (1986). Women's friendships on Crete: A psychological perspective. In J. Dubisch (Ed.), *Gender and power in rural Greece* (pp. 121-138). Princeton, NJ: Princeton University Press.

Loizos, P., & Papataxiarchis, E. (1991). Gender, sexuality, and the person in Greek culture. In P. Loizos & E. Papataxiarchis (Eds.), *Contested identities: Gender and kinship in modern Greece* (pp. 221-234). Princeton, NJ: Princeton University Press.

Margaris, T. P. (1962). *The chronicle of Halsted Street.* Athens: Fexis.

Mazower, M. (1993). *Inside Hitler's Greece: The experience of occupation 1941-44.* New Haven, CT: Yale University Press.

Mead, M. (Ed.). (1953). *Cultural patterns and technical change.* Paris: UNESCO.

Morgan, R. (1984). Greece. In R. Morgan (Ed.), *Sisterhood is global: The international women's movement anthology* (pp. 266-277). Garden City, NY: Anchor.

Moskos, C. C. (1989). *Greek Americans: Struggle and success.* New Brunswick, NJ: Transaction.

Myrsiades, L. S., & Myrsiades, K. (1992). *Karagiozis: Culture and comedy in Greek puppet theater.* Lexington: University Press of Kentucky.

Olster, M. (1994, February 4). Few Arabs will denounce "honor killings" of women. *San Diego Union-Tribune*, p. A-28.

The Orthodox view: Guidelines on homosexuality. (1993, August). *Orthodox Observer*, p. 7.

Ortner, S. B. (1974). Is female to male as nature is to culture? In M. Z. Rosaldo & L. Lamphere (Eds.), *Women, culture, and society* (pp. 67-87). Stanford, CA: Stanford University Press.

Pappajohn, J. (1988, October). *The evolution of intergenerational relations in the Greek American family.* Paper presented at the Fifth Annual Symposium of the Hellenic Scientists Association of Boston, "Hellenism in transition: Our families, our children, ourselves," Massachusetts Institute of Technology.

Rouvelas, M. (1993). *A guide to Greek traditions and customs in America.* Bethesda, MD: Attica.

Salamone, S. D. (1986). *In the shadow of the holy mountain: The genesis of a rural Greek community and its refugee heritage.* Boulder, CO: East European Monographs (distributed by Columbia University Press, New York).

Saloutos, T. (1980). Greeks. In S. Thernstrom (Ed.), *Harvard encyclopedia of American ethnic groups.* Cambridge, MA: Harvard University Press.

Seremetakis, C. N. (1991). *The last word: Women, death, and divination in inner Mani.* Chicago: University of Chicago Press.

Tremble, B., Schneider, M., & Appathurai, C. (1989). Growing up gay or lesbian in a multicultural context. *Journal of Homosexuality, 17*(3-4), 253-267.

Welts, E. P. (1982). Greek families. In M. McGoldrick, J. K. Pierce, & J. Giordano (Eds.), *Ethnicity and family therapy* (pp. 269-288). New York: Guilford.

9

Crossing Borders and Boundaries
The Life Narratives of Immigrant Lesbians

OLIVA M. ESPIN

When immigrants cross borders, they also cross emotional and behavioral boundaries. Becoming a member of a new society stretches the boundaries of what is possible in several ways. One's life and roles change, and with them, identities change as well. In the new culture, new societal expectations lead to transformations in identity. The identities expected and permitted in the home culture may no longer be those expected or permitted in the host society. Boundaries are crossed when new identities and roles are incorporated into life. Most immigrants who, either eagerly or reluctantly, cross geographic borders do not fully suspect how many emotional and behavioral boundaries they are about to cross.

For women, the crossing of borders and the subsequent crossing of boundaries take specific forms. Migration—and the acculturation process that follows—opens up different possibilities for women than for men, particularly with reference to gender roles and sexual behavior (Espin, 1984, 1987a, 1987b, 1990; Espin, Cavanaugh, Paydarfar, & Wood, 1990; Espin, Stewart, & Gomez, 1990; Goodenow & Espin, 1993).

AUTHOR'S NOTE: An earlier version of this chapter was delivered as the Presidential Address to the Society for the Psychological Study of Lesbian and Gay Issues, Division 44 of the APA, at the 102nd Annual Conference of the American Psychological Association, Los Angeles, August 1994.

Frequently, newly encountered sex role patterns, combined with greater access to paid employment for women, create possibilities for new lifestyles that previously may have been unavailable. One case in point is an openly lesbian life. For example, some women become employed outside the home for the first time in their lives after migration. Many of them encounter new opportunities for education. All of them are confronted with new alternative meanings of womanhood provided by the host society. The crossing of borders through migration may provide, for both heterosexual and lesbian women, the space and "permission" to cross boundaries and transform their sexuality and sex roles. For lesbians, an additional border/boundary crossing takes place that relates to the "coming-out" process. Coming out may have occurred in the home country. It may have occurred after the migration, as part of the acculturation process. Or, in some cases, it may have been the motivating force behind the migration. Indeed, in some cases, it is sexuality—trying to escape the constraints imposed by the home society on her lesbianism—that determines a woman's migration. In other cases, migration provides the space and permission for a woman to come out at a later date. In other words, a woman's awareness of her lesbianism or a lesbian identity may or may not have been present when the decision to migrate was made. In any case, for most women, issues of sexuality are usually not part of the conscious decision to migrate. Yet many lesbians have experienced discrimination because of their sexuality before their migration. Some also experience discrimination based on sexual orientation combined with ethnic discrimination after their migration.

Immigration, even when willingly chosen and eagerly sought, produces a variety of experiences with significant consequences for the individual. No matter how glad the immigrant might be to be in a new country, the transitions created by immigration often result in many different feelings: the loneliness that results from the absence of people with shared experiences; strain and fatigue from the effort to adapt to and cope with cognitive overload; feelings of rejection from the new society that affect self-esteem and may lead to alienation; confusion in terms of role expectations, values, and identity; "culture shock" resulting from differences between the old country and the new; and a sense of impotence resulting from an inability to function competently in the new culture. As I have discussed in my earlier writing:

The loss experienced by [an immigrant] encompasses not only the major and obvious losses of country, a way of life, and (perhaps) family. The pain of uprootedness is also activated in subtle forms by the everyday absence of familiar smells, familiar foods, familiar routines for doing the small tasks of daily life. It is the lack of . . . "the average expectable environment" . . . which can become a constant reminder of what is not there anymore. It is the loss of this "average expectable environment" that can be most disorienting and most disruptive of the person's previously established identity. (Espin, 1992, p. 13)

A significant consequence of this transition is a growing sensation of discontinuity of identity (Garza-Guerrero, 1974). The psychosocial context in which the individual's sense of identity was originally formed has been left behind. Consequently, the individual struggles with reorganizing and reintegrating identity within the new context. The dilemma for immigrant lesbians is how to integrate who they are culturally, racially, and religiously, as all immigrants must do, with their identity as lesbians. Because they are immigrants *and* lesbian, they have to be polycultural in the host society and among their own people (Espin, 1987a).

For those who are still adolescents or young adults, confronting the transition created by immigration presents yet another task. On the one hand, it is easier for them to adjust to the new way of life because their identities are not yet consolidated. On the other hand, adolescent or young adult immigrants have lost peers and other emotional "guideposts" that would have served in the development of identity in the context of a familiar culture. Frequently, parental disorientation in the new culture, coupled with the adolescents' greater skill at managing the new culture and language, increases their fear of being lost and not being able to count on parents for protection from perceived threats in the environment (e.g., Lieblich, 1993). As Erikson (1964) observes, "The danger of any period of large-scale uprooting and transmigration is that exterior crises will, in too many individuals and generations, upset the hierarchy of developmental crises and their built-in correctives; and [make them] lose those roots that must be planted firmly in meaningful life cycles" (p. 96). Life cycle development,

apart from the influence of ethnicity and immigration, [also includes] gender [as] a crucial factor in the development of identity. Not only is sexual maturity a major hallmark of the transition from childhood to adulthood, but sex roles have a pervasive influence on every aspect of adult life. . . . If sex roles are problematic for adolescent females in general, this is doubly true for immigrant females, particularly those from more traditional cultures. The immigrant adolescent [girl] is faced with having to adjust to two sex cultures. While there are undoubtedly both national and urban-rural differences in the strength of tradition in the area of sex roles, many cultures are far more heavily sex differentiated than [mainstream] American culture. Though all immigrants face the problem of acculturation, the pressures on males and females are different. . . . While [usually] males are encouraged to acculturate rather quickly, females are more frequently expected by their families to maintain traditional roles and virtues. (Goodenow & Espin, 1993, pp. 176-177)

Although understudied, the role of women in international migration has begun to draw attention from researchers, policymakers, and service providers. The experiences of immigrant and refugee women in Europe, the United States, Israel, and other parts of the world are being made the focus of studies that emphasize exclusively women's perspectives on the migration process (e.g., Andizian et al., 1983; Cole, Espin, & Rothblum, 1992; Gabaccia, 1992; Phizachlea, 1983). These studies, however, have been concerned primarily with women's struggles to adjust to new societies and, in a few cases, to deal with the loss of country and social networks. They have tended to address women's increased participation in public life (such as labor participation and education). Little is known still about the experiences of both heterosexual and lesbian immigrant women in private realms, such as sexuality. Yet, as we know, sexuality is not private (see, e.g., Brettell & Sargent, 1993; Foucault, 1981; Laqueur, 1990; Parker, Russo, Sommer, & Yaeger, 1992), which explains why so many cultures and countries try to control and legislate it. Indeed, as one historian has observed: "Sexual behavior (perhaps more than religion) is the most highly symbolic activity of any society. To penetrate the symbolic system implicit in any society's sexual behavior is therefore to come closest to the heart of its uniqueness" (Trumbach, 1977, p. 24; quoted in Necef, 1994). Referring specifically to women in the Middle East, the Lebanese author Evelyne Accad (1991) asserts:

Sexuality seems to have a revolutionary potential so strong that many political women and men are afraid of it. They prefer, therefore, to dismiss its importance by arguing that it is not as central as other factors, such as economic and political determination. . . . [However,] . . . sexuality is much more central to social and political problems . . . than previously thought, and . . . unless a sexual revolution is incorporated into political revolution, there will be no real transformation of social relations. (p. 237)

Sexuality is a universal component of human experience, yet how it is embodied and expressed is not. As anthropological, historical, and literary studies contend, "sexuality is culturally variable rather than a timeless, immutable essence" (Parker et al., 1992, p. 4). Even what is considered to be sexual is often strikingly different for people in different cultural environments.

The study of women's experiences reveals a varied representation of sexual/gender differences among cultures. These cultural constructs inextricably inform the expression of female sexuality. Cultural traditions, colonial and other forms of social oppression, national identity, and the vicissitudes of the historical process inform the development and perception of female sexuality. Worldwide, definitions of what constitutes appropriate sexual behavior are strongly influenced by male sexual pleasure. Even for lesbians, these definitions carry significant weight—if not altogether conscious. These definitions are justified in the name of prevalent values in a given society: nationalism, religion, morality, health, science, and so forth. Worldwide, women are enculturated and socialized to embody their sexual desire or lack thereof through their particular culture's ideals of virtue. The social group's expectations are inscribed in women's individual desires and expressed through their sexuality (Jaggar & Bordo, 1989). This is not to say that gay men's sexuality is not subjected to conscious and unconscious controls by society. However, the expectation of conformity to society's sexual norms exercises pressure on all women's sexuality, regardless of sexual orientation, in ways that do not burden most men. Women's reproductive capacities are frequently appropriated by the state to establish control over both citizens and territories. Historically, warriors have celebrated victories and assuaged the frustrations of defeat through the forceful possession of women's bodies; war and rape are deeply connected. The present situation in Bosnia and other war-torn regions of the world brings this reality to the forefront in a tragic and dramatic way.

We know that the sexual behavior of women serves a larger social function beyond the personal. It is used by enemies and friends alike as "proof" of the moral fiber or decay of social groups or nations. In most societies, women's sexual behavior and their conformity to traditional gender roles signify the family's value system. This is why struggles surrounding acculturation in immigrant and refugee families center frequently on issues of daughters' sexual behavior and women's sex roles in general. For parents and young women alike, acculturation and sexuality are closely connected (Espin, 1984, 1987a). Moreover, the self-appointed "guardians of morality and tradition" who are ever present among immigrant "communities" are deeply concerned with women's roles and sexual behavior. It is no secret that religious leaders are rather preoccupied with women's sexuality. All over the world, we are witnessing how "women, their role, and above all their control, have become central to the fundamentalist agenda" (Yuval-Davis, 1992, p. 278) of Protestants, Catholics, Muslims, and others. Considering that immigrant communities are more often than not besieged with rejection, racism, and scorn, these self-appointed "guardians" have always found fertile ground from which to control women's sexuality in the name of preserving "tradition." Women's subservience is advocated as a type of "steadying influence." Whereas young men are allowed and encouraged to develop new identities in the new country, girls and women are expected to continue living as if they were still in the old country. They are more often than not forced to embody cultural continuity amid cultural dislocation.

Groups that are transforming their ways of life through a vast and deep process of acculturation tend to focus on preserving "tradition" almost exclusively through the gender roles of women. Women's roles become the bastion of traditions:

> The "proper" behavior of women is used to signify the difference between those who belong to the collectivity and those who do not. Women are also seen as "cultural carriers" of the collectivity who transmit it to the future generation, and the "proper" control of women in terms of marriage and divorce ensures that children who are born to those women are not only biologically but also symbolically within the boundaries of the collectivity. (Yuval-Davis, 1992, p. 285)

Barbara Schreier (1994), the curator of a recent exhibition on immigrant women's clothing from 1880 to 1920 held at the Chicago Historical Society, studied the case of Jewish immigrants to the United States at the beginning of the 20th century. During a period of increased immigration and intense public preoccupation with young women's sexuality, a significant period when large numbers of young immigrant unmarried women living in North American cities were gainfully employed (Nathanson, 1991), "contemporary observers did not pay as much attention to male plumage; even when they did, their words lack the moralistic, beseeching, and condemnatory tones with which they addressed women" (Schreier, 1994, p. 9). According to Schreier, the Jewish press admonished young women at the time in lengthy editorials not to use their savings to buy frivolous items of clothing. Similarly, many a family conflict had its source in parental anger toward daughters whose meager wages bought coveted clothing rather than contributed further to the family's resources. Other authors who have written about the same historical period tell us that women resisted domination from both the larger society and their own communities through a variety of means. The new freedom ethnically diverse young immigrant women acquired as wage earners expressed itself through the clothes they wore and their refusal to accept chaperons and other forms of parental control over their sexuality (Ruiz, 1992). Immigrant women's identity conflicts and identity transformations continue to be expressed in our time through clothing and sexuality.

All pressures on immigrant women's sexuality, however, do not come from inside their own cultures. The host society also imposes its own burdens and desires through prejudices and racism. Women immigrants in the United States, particularly those who are not white, experience degrees of "gendered racism" (Essed, 1991, 1994). Even though racism may be expressed subtly, the immigrant woman finds herself between the racism of the dominant society and the sexist expectations of her own community. Paraphrasing Nigerian poet and Professor 'Molara Ogundipe-Leslie (1993), we could say that immigrant women have several mountains on their back, the two most obvious ones being "the heritage of tradition" and "the oppression from outside." The racism of the dominant society makes the retrenchment into tradition appear to be justifiable, whereas the rigidities of tradition appear to justify the racist/prejudicial treatment of the dominant society. Paradoxically, the two "mountains" reinforce and encourage each other. Moreover, the effect of racism and sexism is not only felt as pressure from "the outside," but it also becomes internalized, as are all forms of oppression. Women exposed to direct contact with the dominant society experience the contradictions more dramatically, although perhaps less consciously, than those who do not confront the dominant society on a regular basis (e.g. Essed, 1991, 1994). As Essed (1994) argues:

> From a macro point of view, the massive and systemic reproduction of belief systems which legitimate certain dominant group positions, predispose individuals to internalize these ideas, whether or not they themselves occupy these dominant positions. From a micro point of view, however, individuals do not necessarily and unthinkingly accept "dominant" ideologies. Moreover, the cognitive domain of individuals is a fundamental area where new and critical knowledge can generate change. . . . The study of individual motivation and sense-making in the process of resistance against confining race and gender boundaries is still, however, largely unexplored. (p. 101)

Immigrant women who are lesbian develop their identities against the backdrop of these contradictions. As expressed by Bhavnani and Haraway (1994) in a "conversation" that appears in a special issue on racism and identities of the journal *Feminism and Psychology*, "These young women, in their embodiment, are the points of collision of all these powerful forces, including forces of their own" (p. 33).

Thus we need to increase our knowledge and understanding of how the contradictions and interplays of sexuality/gender and racism in both the home and host cultures are experienced and "made sense of" by women immigrants. In the past year, I have been engaged in a study that seeks to increase knowledge and understanding of sexuality and gender-related issues among immigrant and refugee women. Through this study, I have explored the main issues and consequences entailed in crossing both geographic and psychological borders and boundaries. Specifically, my research explores how sexuality and identity in both lesbians and heterosexual women are affected by migration. I begin here by focusing on the crossing of borders and boundaries implied in the processes of immigration/acculturation and coming out. Both processes are central to the life experiences of lesbians who have migrated from their countries of origin. I then address two important aspects of these boundary and border crossings: the importance of geography and place, and the role of language in the experiences of immigrant lesbians.

This study is still in its preliminary stages. It focuses on the expression and experience of women's sexuality in different cultures as they are created by disparate social forces. In the following pages, I present some preliminary results of the study, make suggestions for the examination of unexplored aspects of these experiences, and offer some directions for future study.

I have collected narratives through individual interviews and/or focus groups. As defined by Basch (1987), "The focus group interview is a qualitative research technique used to obtain data about feelings and opinions of small groups of participants about a given problem, experience or other phenomenon" (p. 414). The narratives explore immigrant women's understanding of sexuality and their internalization of cultural norms. These open-ended narratives allow for the expression of thoughts and feelings while inviting participants to introduce their own themes and concerns. Such narratives constitute a particularly valuable research method when the concepts being explored are "new territory" for participants and/or the researcher (Mishler, 1986; Riessman, 1993). In addition to its value as a research tool (e.g., Denzin, 1989; Josselson & Lieblich, 1993; Riessman, 1993), retelling the life story has been shown to have a healing effect (Aron, 1992). This is particularly the case for subjects in my study whose migrations were motivated by some form of persecution. Focus groups provide opportunities for in-depth interviewing of a group concerning a particular topic. They provide the researcher with additional flexibility to probe unanticipated areas during the initial design of the discussion questions. This form of in-depth group interviewing is effective and economical in terms of both time and money, thus it is a pragmatic approach for any study done with limited funds and limited personnel (see, e.g., Krueger, 1994; Morgan, 1988, 1993; Stewart & Shamdasani, 1990).

The Role of Narrative Research in Psychology

Although other social sciences have used narratives to understand human life, there is a contradiction within psychology in relation to the use of narratives. On the one hand, there is a tradition of narrative use for research in psychology, particularly in the field of personality psychology (e.g., some classic works in the field, such as Murray's *Explorations in Personality*, 1938; Allport's *The Use of Personal Documents in Psychological Science*, 1942; and White's *Lives in Progress*, 1966). In addition, the whole field of psychotherapy, beginning with Freud, is based on the use of narrative. Psychotherapy is a reconstruction of the life story, the telling of one's story to a sympathetic listener. In the process of having one's story listened to and responded to in a different way, one's habitual modes of reaction take on reinterpreted meaning, and become assumed and incorporated in a different way. Diagnosis is nothing but a way of organizing a narrative and making sense of disparate symptoms and experiences.

On the other hand, psychological research has been dominated by formal research methods that isolate characteristics and behaviors for study with the use of experimental and statistical procedures. This perspective, which has dominated psychology since the 1950s, perceives the use of narrative for research as "soft," "unscientific," and lacking in validity. Even psychotherapy, in an effort to appear "scientific," has sought categories that would reify its processes. Freud himself developed categories such as id, ego, superego, transference, libido, and so on that reified the narratives and life stories on which he based his theories.

Recently, renewed interest in the use of narrative in psychology has emerged from several perspectives. Within psychology itself, several new currents are connected to this new interest in story/narrative. There is renewed interest in "the role of narrative in establishing personal identity" (Polkinghorne, 1988, p. 105), in the idea that "a self needs a story in order to be." Erikson (1975) has spoken about the need to reconstruct life through narrative so that life outcomes take on the appearance of having been planned. McAdams (1990) has studied the role of narrative in "binding together our lives in time" (p. 166). These authors and others emphasize how narratives transform the passing of life into a coherent self (Polkinghorne, 1988, p. 119).

As numerous theorists have recently argued, cultures provide specific plots for lives (Polkinghorne, 1988, p. 153). Rosenwald and Ochberg (1992) note that "social ideology [is] individually appropriated in the construction of life histories and selves" (p. 5). "When people tell life stories, they do so in accordance with models of intelligibility specific to the culture. . . . Not only acceptable behavior, but also acceptable accounts of behavior are socialized. . . . Accounts bind individuals to the arrangements of the society enforcing the models" (Rosenwald, 1992, p. 265). Stories/lives develop through compromises in which the individual desire and societal stabilizing power balance each other or push each other's limits. "The tales we tell each other (and ourselves) about who we are and might yet become are individual variations on the narrative templates our culture deems intelligible" (Ochberg, 1992, p. 214). These authors point to a process by which the culture speaks through the narrator and the culture provides the individual with the needed support to live, develop, and feel "normal." Indeed, even models of "craziness" have to meet standards that are culturally acceptable. Explanations of the etiology of psychological disturbance vary cross-culturally to include spirit possession, the chemicals in a person's brain, and critical events in an individual's past.

Other social sciences have sought explanations for human behavior in the cultural context, but for psychology this is almost a novelty. Although Erikson's influence and feminist and cultural psychologists have been very strong on the impact of cultural forces on the individual, psychology has persisted in using intrapsychic individual explanatory models.

Surely, we agree that culture and history are powerful forces in human development. What, then, happens to the individual life, sense of self, and life story when cultural narrative changes abruptly, as with migration? Although "the story about life is open to editing and revision" (Polkinghorne, 1988, p. 154), some editing and revision may require more work than others. "Re-writing one's story involves major life changes" (Polkinghorne, 1988, p. 182). What happens when events that are not "personal events" in the usual way "invade" the life story (e.g., traumatic historical events, historical dislocation, sociopolitical events)? Events that happen "out there" in the world are not only "social" but also "psychological" (e.g., revolutions, wars, migration, peace accords, earthquakes or other natural phenomena). Some of these events disrupt individual lives for days or weeks; others totally change the life course. These events transform the "plots" provided by the culture and social context. Either they transform the culture itself or, because the individual finds him- or herself in a new cultural context, they allow a different kind of story. Some classical studies of life history have their sources in such cataclysms (e.g., Thomas & Znaniecki, 1918-1920/1927; and innumerable studies of survivors of the Holocaust). Studies of women's life stories have been included in this genre in the past few years (e.g., Franz & Stewart, 1994).

I am interested in migration as a "historical event" that disrupts and detours the life course. I look at personal narratives as the stories created by individuals to recover the threads of their own lives after migration. In short, I explore how questions of national identity and sexual identity are determined and negotiated by immigrant and refugee women.

The Study

My study of the sexuality of women immigrants, like much research using life narratives, has two roles. One is descriptive and explanatory, the other is therapeutic (i.e., reconstruction of the life and reintegration of it and of the dislocation into the life). Obviously, the research itself is not therapy—rather, this research is intended as a fact-finding enterprise. However, it is my hope that it will also have a "side effect" as a therapeutic or "healing" process for those participants traumatized by historical events. I, along with research ethicists, believe it is the ethical responsibility of the researcher to ensure that any study protects participants against the potentially damaging effects of recapitulating traumatic experiences.

By the end of the study, I plan to conduct individual interviews and/or focus groups in several large cities in the United States (probably San Diego and San Francisco, California; Boston; Chicago; Miami, Florida; and Seattle, Washington) with both lesbian and heterosexual immigrant women. The choices of these cities have been determined by two factors. One is the relatively high probability of accessing a wide range of cultures/countries of origin and populations, because these cities have rich ethnic and racially mixed populations of immigrants/refugees. These sites also complement one another because they represent geographic and ethnic diversity within the United States that crosses national origins. The second reason I've chosen these cities is pragmatic: Personal plans and professional connections facilitate my travel and access to these cities. Immigrant women who are lesbian have been (or will be) recruited in the chosen cities through personal contacts and friendship pyramiding. They have been (or will be) asked to participate voluntarily in focus groups or in individual interviews. Both group and individual interviews last from 1 to 3 hours. The women recruited so far have ranged in age from early 20s to mid-70s, and all have been college educated. A few are still in the process of completing their higher education. These women were chosen on the basis of their ability to articulate their experiences with the research topic and their fluency in English (as well as their languages of origin). The interviews have focused in depth on the respondents' individual life stories and experiences.

The Focus Groups: Process

Topics discussed in the focus groups and in the individual interviews cover a wide range of concerns. These include coming out, lesbianism and bisexuality, conflicts of loyalty between home and host culture sexual norms, being lesbian in the United States and in the country of origin, sex education in the schools and at home, silences about sex in the respondents' families, menstruation, arranged marriages versus dating, sexual relationships outside one's ethnic group, sex and violence, sex and romance, and sexual behavior and heterosexual intercourse. The discussions have explored the "protective" behaviors of respondents' parents that silently express proscriptive sexual ideology for women. Generational differences among women that are usually associated with gender role differences and sexual behavior have also been discussed. Particularly, how does one's generation affect acculturation and differential access to the host culture? This clearly circumscribes or expands an individual's repertoire of sexual behaviors and gender roles.

Interviews and focus groups have been taped, transcribed, and analyzed following accepted techniques for the analysis of qualitative data (e.g., Silverman, 1993; Strauss, 1987). The study emphasizes the geographic and psychological borders and boundaries crossed by women in the process of migration. As stated earlier, the crossing of borders through migration may provide for women the space and "permission" to cross other boundaries and transform their sexuality and sex roles. The notion that "identity is not one thing for any individual; rather, each individual is both located in and opts for a number of differing and, at times, conflictual, identities, depending on the social, political, economic and ideological aspects of their situation" (Bhavnani & Phoenix, 1994, p. 9) is particularly significant for the study of the experiences of immigrants. For lesbian immigrants, it is a central component of their psychology, thus it is at the core of this exploration.

Immigration and Coming Out: The Narratives

Immigrants are as preoccupied with events in the life course as they are affected by the vicissitudes of place and geography. This phenomenon/preoccupation has two components. One is the preoccupation with the vicissitudes of the actual place (country of origin) that gives that place almost a sense of unreality in spite of its constant psychological presence in the life of the immigrant. The other is what I call a preoccupation with "what could have been" that translates into ruminations about what kind of life could have been lived and other "what ifs"—"what life could have been" if the immigrant had lived in the country of origin or in another country or if the immigration had taken place at this or that stage of life. The following two quotations exemplify these two aspects of the preoccupation with place characteristic of immigrant psychology:

> My trip made me realize that my memories had a geography. That what I remembered had actually happened in a definite physical space that continues to exist in reality and not only in my memory. That my country, in fact, exists beyond what I think or feel or remember about her. This realization, which may seem all too obvious, was the more powerful because before my return I never knew that I felt as if my country did not have a real existence beyond my memory. (Espin, 1990, p. 159)

> My trip put me in touch with childhood friends and made me reflect about the differences in our lives, about the choices to stay or leave that have dramatically influenced our life projects. None of us has any way of knowing what our lives would have been like without the historical dislocations that have marked them. The only known factor is that powerful historical events have transformed the life course of those of us who left and those of us who stayed. . . . Those who stayed, if not uprooted, have also been under the effects of dramatic historical transformations. It is impossible to know if our decisions have resulted in a better life project for any of us, although we each hope and believe to have made the best decision. (Espin, 1990, p. 159)

Bandura's (1982) discussion of the importance of chance encounters for the course of human development addresses the impact that chance may have as a determinant of life paths. For some people, chance encounters and other life events are additionally influenced by historical and political events far beyond their control. It is true that all human beings experience life transitions, but for people who have been subjected to historical dislocations, life crossroads feel, intrapsychically, more drastic and dramatic (Espin, 1990).

For immigrant lesbians, this preoccupation is tied to the process of "coming out." It is also inextricably linked to the process of developing a lesbian identity as well as the development of sexual orientation. Some lesbians are preoccupied with the relationship between childhood events and their having become lesbians. To this, the immigrant lesbian adds thoughts/concerns and general "what could have been" ideas concerning her lesbianism, concentrated in a basic question: Would I have become a lesbian if I had not emigrated? This preoccupation is of course connected with the process of acculturation that all immigrants experience in their adaptation to a new country and that all lesbians and gay men undergo in the process of coming out. The immigrant lesbian acculturates as an immigrant and sometimes as a lesbian at the same time. Even if she was a lesbian before the migration, she needs to learn to be a lesbian in her new cultural context. If she comes from a background other than European, she also has to acculturate as a so-called minority person.

> Identity development for persons of ethnic or racial minority groups (or immigrants) involves not only the acceptance of an external reality that can rarely be changed (e.g. being Black, Puerto Rican, Vietnamese, Jewish), but also an intrapsychic "embracing" of that reality as a positive component of one's self. By definition, in the context of a heterosexist and sexist society, the process of identity development for [immigrant lesbians] entails the embracing of "stigmatized" or "negative" identities. Coming out to self and others in the context of a sexist and heterosexist American society is compounded by coming out in the context of what is usually a sexist and heterosexist [culture of origin] immersed in racist society. (Espin, 1987a, p. 35)

This process is exemplified in an excerpt from an interview with a Cuban lesbian who participated in one of my previous studies:

> As a child my self-definition was not conscious, since there was no need for awareness of ethnic identity while I lived in Cuba. Coming to the United States instantly brought to my awareness at the age of 10 what being Latina meant in this country. I would say that the need to assert that identity was strengthened by the racism in the U.S. In my teens I passed through a period of acculturation in which to some extent I internalized society's views of

ethnic groups in a very subtle way. During college, I became active in political and community activities and went through a "militant" phase in which I came to understand the nature of racism and oppression more deeply. Presently, I consider myself to have a more universal or humanistic perspective and I am able to appreciate as well as critically analyze my cultural heritage. (quoted in Espin, 1987a, p. 45)

In addition to tracing identity formation, another important aspect of the focus groups has been to explore the vocabularies of sex in different languages—specifically, what it is permissible to say about sex in which languages. I am particularly interested, considering the importance of linguistic categories in narrative studies, in the language in which the narrative is told. I am specifically interested in discerning lesbians' comfort with descriptive terms about lesbianism in their first languages. The preference for using one language over another is deeply related to identity, but it is also related to other factors not yet studied (see, e.g., Espin, 1984, 1987b, 1994; Necef, 1994). As Torres (1991) argues, "The problem of identity emerges in discussions of language and how to give voice to a multiple heritage. The obvious and yet revolutionary answer is through the use of mixing of the codes that have shaped experience" (p. 279). Eva Hoffman's (1989) *Lost in Translation* is a fascinating autobiographical account of the impact of language on the life of the immigrant. According to Hoffman, only after narrating in therapy, in English, the events that happened to her in Polish, did she feel like an integrated person. As previously observed, psychotherapy constructs a meaningful story out of disjointed, painful events and contradictory fragments of the life story that are not integrated. For lesbian immigrants, the integration of two languages in addressing sexuality may be a step toward integrating both cultural backgrounds. Conversely, the exclusive preference of one language over another may result from an effort to compartmentalize the contradictions inherent in being a lesbian and an immigrant. In the interviews, I have explored variations that have emerged in the speakers' comfort and discomfort when addressing sexuality in their mother tongues or in English. Even among immigrants who are fluent in English, the first language often remains the language of emotions (Espin, 1987b, 1992). Thus speaking in a second language may "distance" the immigrant woman from important parts of herself. Conversely, a second language may provide a vehicle to express that which is inexpressible in the first language, either because the first language does not have the vocabulary or because the person censors herself from saying certain taboo things in the first language (Espin, 1984, 1987a, 1994; Necef, 1994). I contend that the language in which messages about sexuality are conveyed and encoded has an impact on the expression of sexual thoughts, feelings, and ideas and reveals important clues to an individual's identity process.

Among the participants in this study, two apparently contradictory patterns concerning language have emerged. In several cases, after the completion of an interview or group session conducted in English, participants have said that they could have expressed themselves and answered my questions more easily had they been able to do so in their first language. However, the same participants believed that although it would have been easier to use their first language in terms of vocabulary, it was easier to talk about these topics in English. They believed that feelings of shame would have prevented them from addressing these topics in the same depth had they used their first language.

Other participants, on the other hand, said that they could not have had such discussions in their first language because they actually did not know the vocabulary or were not used to talking about sexuality in their native language. These women had migrated at earlier ages, usually before or during early adolescence. They had developed their knowledge of sex and, obviously, had come out while immersed in English. The women who manifested this second pattern explained that they could not conceive of "making love in their first language," whereas those in the former scenario felt unable to "make love in English."

Is the immigrant lesbian's preference for English when discussing sexuality, as I have clinically observed and the participants in this study have expressed, motivated by characteristics of English as a language, or is it that a second language offers a vehicle to express thoughts and feelings that cannot be expressed in the first language? Or does the new cultural context, in which English is spoken, allow more expression of the woman's feelings? Acquired in English, these experiences and expressions may become inextricably associated with the language (as happens with professional terminology acquired in a second language). In any case, all the lesbians interviewed, even when other parts of the interview were in Spanish, resorted to English when describing their sexuality. Interestingly, this pattern has been observed among other populations, such as young heterosexual Turkish men and women in Germany and Denmark (Necef, 1994).

I will devote the remainder of this discussion to presenting vignettes excerpted from the participants' stories to illustrate current findings. All identifying information and names have been modified to protect the confidentiality of the participants. Only information directly relevant to the study has been preserved as reported. Several life stories, at once very similar yet quite different, illustrate lesbians' diverse adaptations to migration.

Maritza and Olga are both Cuban. Both migrated to the United States when they were 22 years of age, during the 1970s. Olga comes from a middle-class family, Maritza from a poor, working-class family. Maritza had come out as a lesbian in Cuba, when she was 14. She had (and still has) considerable artistic talent as a musician and a poet. From a very early age she identified her lesbianism as a consequence of her artistic talent. In Cuba and other Latin American countries there is a widespread association between artists and homosexuality that is more or less accepted. Maritza was rebellious as an adolescent, and more or less openly displayed her preference for girls. At the age of 22 she decided that staying in Cuba, considering the government's position on homosexuality, was impossible for her. Although she was completely in favor of the revolution, and precisely because of her connections to it, she masterminded an escape during a trip to Eastern Europe for young artists that was sponsored by the Cuban government. Her family continues to live in Cuba. Despite the passage of time, they strongly disagree with her decision to leave the country. In the United States, Maritza refuses to participate in anything having to do with gay/lesbian activism. She lives a very private life, although she makes no secret about her sexual orientation. She has continued to write poetry and compose music, but soon after her immigration she decided that "poems and songs were not going to feed her" and she actively began to pursue other professional endeavors. Writing in Spanish did not provide her with a significant audience in an English-speaking country, and writing creatively in English was next to impossible for her. These were not minor factors in her decision to enter another career. She is now a financial consultant and has a successful practice and a solid income. Her love relationships, with very few exceptions, have usually been with Spanish-speaking women. She is one of those who "cannot make love in English."

Olga left Cuba because of her disagreement with the revolution. She came to the United States with her family in one of the "freedom flights" instituted after 1968. Although she was aware of having had feelings for other girls during her childhood and adolescence, she did not acknowledge those feelings at that point, because lesbianism was "sinful" and she was devotedly Catholic. She came out as a lesbian 2 years after arriving in the United States, and for some years after her coming out, she remained tormented by feelings that what she was doing was sinful. However, she was very much in love with another Cuban woman she had met in Los Angeles, where she lived with her family. They both became involved in Dignity, a group of gay Catholics then newly constituted. Olga began her political activity in gay/ lesbian issues, through Dignity, mostly inside the lesbian community. She continues to be so involved. She is convinced that she would never have come out as a lesbian had she stayed in Cuba and believes that the process of acculturation to the United States made it possible for her to come out. She has a degree in social work and works for a government agency that serves a predominantly Latino population. She remains mostly closeted in the Latino community, concerned that the revelation of her lesbianism might have a negative impact on clients and colleagues alike.

The use of language of another interviewee, Lorena, is determined by deeply embedded cultural messages. She is an accountant and has been out as a lesbian for almost 20 years. She is more comfortable speaking about her sexual orientation in English and in the United States than discussing it in Spanish or in her native Puerto Rico. She attributes these preferences to the negative association she has to the many "dirty words" used in Spanish to describe lesbians, as well as to the fact that her family lives in Puerto Rico. She came to the United States at age 30 and came out a few months later. She believes that the stage at which her migration occurred made a difference. The shifts in identity necessitated by the coming-out process and the migration were additional factors in her already solid personal identity. Although she initially found it "foreign" to see herself as a lesbian, she did not have doubts about "who she was" as a professional, a Puerto Rican, or whatever.

Cindy, on the other hand, came to this country when she was 2 years old, so she does not remember much about her native Taiwan, nor did she ever learn of sex or sexual vocabulary in Chinese. In fact, her only knowledge of Chinese comes from her parents, who never spoke about sex and obviously were not going to teach her much about lesbianism. Her parents spoke to her always in Chinese, and she remembers being the target of a fair amount of teasing even from her Chinese American schoolmates whenever they heard her speak with her parents.

Cindy remembers being very affectionate with another girl during seventh grade and having other schoolmates refer to them as "homos." Because she had no idea what the term meant, she asked her brother, 2 years older than she, about the meaning of this word, which she intuited as pejorative in some way. Her brother, however, reassured her that the term referred to *Homo sapiens*. This meant human being, so she reasoned that it did not have any negative implications. Years later, after coming out, Cindy was rather amused at both her own and her brother's limited knowledge about English slang terms concerning sexuality at the time. For several years after high school, Cindy was sexually involved with a man she loved deeply. When the relationship ended, she was devastated and relied on her friendship with another woman who had been a college classmate to carry her over these bad times. Eventually, she and the woman became lovers, and she has lived as a lesbian since then. She believes becoming a lesbian was just one more thing she could not share with her rigidly traditional parents. As she could not talk to them about anything that really mattered to her, it was not difficult to keep the truth of her life as another secret. And as she spoke Chinese only with her parents, she never spoke about her sexuality in Chinese.

For these women, migration clearly offered certain freedoms that fostered the development of a lesbian life. Their political, religious, and social affiliations with the lesbian community vary greatly. Their shared experience is the link between migration and sexual self-expression.

All of the women interviewed describe experiencing a broader cultural openness regarding lesbianism in the United States than in their home countries. This has resulted in a conflict of loyalties between their host and home cultures. Their families and cultural traditions, while providing comfort and stability, frustrate and limit their lesbian lives.

Both Maritza and Olga are out to their families. Even though there is no particular conflict with their family members concerning their lesbianism, they know their parents and siblings would still prefer that they live heterosexual lives. Lorena and Cindy, who are not fully out to their families, find expression of their sexuality in the environment of their cultures of origin more conflictual. The developmental stages they were in at the time of their migration and coming out dramatically modified those experiences for these women. Those who migrated after adolescence appear to be less conflicted both about their lesbianism and about cultural issues. This may be because these women had formed identities that were already somewhat solid before they had to undertake the extra tasks involved in migration. Even when the coming-out process occurred after the migration, with its attendant identity changes, the process was less disruptive for those who migrated at later developmental stages. Regardless of their differences, these four women are in agreement about the difficulties of acculturating to U.S. society. They express experiencing feelings of alienation in the midst of a racist society. All four mention initial difficulties making friends and dealing with language differences. Simultaneously, they believe that living in the United States has opened economic opportunities for them and their families. And migration, they agree, has opened doors for them both as women and as lesbians.

Conclusion

Several behavioral patterns have emerged from the interviews. Most of the women immigrants interviewed have revised their social expectations; they have worked hard at negotiating gender roles and sexual orientation with their families and with the host culture alike. The younger women's experiences illustrate the simultaneous process of acculturation and identity formation. The language and cultural differences encountered have been compounded for some of them by the normally stressful tasks of adolescence and the coming-out process. In general, their adaptations have been successful, even though each has chosen a specific individual path.

Apparently language, both the native tongue and English, is used to provide relational safety. It serves as an instrument that either enhances intimacy or provides distance in relationships and self-definition. At this point in the study, I can hypothesize that the stronger the cognitive psychological identity development in the native language, the greater the comfort experienced when using it in intimate and sexual relationships and encounters. This may, however, be negated if the actual words in the first language are charged with negative connotations. Language choice may also be modulated by the salience of other factors in cultural identity—for example, if identification with race or class or cultural background is greater than with femaleness or lesbianism.

Talking to these women has been exciting and enlightening. At this point, I look forward to continuing this study. It will undoubtedly help me clarify important aspects of both lesbian and heterosexual immigrant women's lives.

Speaking of the power of the erotic in women's lives, the late poet Audre Lorde (1984), who was also an immigrant, said:

> Our erotic knowledge empowers us, becomes a lens through which we scrutinize all aspects of our existence, forcing us to evaluate those aspects honestly in terms of their relative meaning within our lives. And this is a grave responsibility, projected from within each of us, not to settle for the convenient, the shoddy, the conventionally expected, nor the merely safe. (p. 57)

Lorde warns us, "In order to perpetuate itself, every oppression must corrupt or distort those various sources within the culture of the oppressed that can provide energy for change" (p. 53). One such source is women's erotic energy. Lorde encourages all "women . . . to examine the ways in which our world can be truly different" and not to be afraid of "the power of the erotic" (p. 55). "Once we know the extent to which we are capable of feeling that sense of satisfaction and completion, we can then observe which of our various life endeavors bring us closest to that fullest" (p. 54). This is a necessary endeavor for immigrant women in the essential process of developing their identities and struggling against the racism they encounter.

References

Accad, E. (1991). Sexuality and sexual politics: Conflicts and contradictions for contemporary women in the Middle East. In C. T. Mohanty, A. Russo, & L. Torres (Eds.), *Third World women and the politics of feminism* (pp. 237-250). Bloomington: Indiana University Press.

Allport, G. (1942). *The use of personal documents in psychological science.* New York: Social Science Research Council.

Andizian, S., Catani, M., Cicourel, A., Dittmar, N., Harper, D., Kudat, A., Morokvasic, M., Oriol, M., Parris, R. G., Streiff, J., & Setland, C. (1983). *Vivir entre dos culturas.* Paris: Serbal/UNESCO.

Aron, A. (1992). Testimonio, a bridge between psychotherapy and sociotherapy. In E. Cole, O. M. Espin, & E. Rothblum (Eds.), *Refugee women and their mental health: Shattered societies, shattered lives* (pp. 173-189). New York: Haworth.

Bandura, A. (1982). The psychology of chance encounters and life paths. *American Psychologist, 37,* 747-755.

Basch, C. E. (1987). Focus group interview: An underutilized research technique for improving theory and practice in health education. *Health Education Quarterly, 14,* 411-448.

Bhavnani, K.-K., & Haraway, D. (1994). Shifting the subject: A conversation between Kum-Kum Bhavnani and Donna Haraway, 12 April, 1993, Santa Cruz, California. *Feminism and Psychology, 4*(1), 19-39.

Bhavnani, K.-K., & Phoenix, A. (1994). Editorial introduction: Shifting identities shifting racism. *Feminism and Psychology, 4*(1), 5-18.

Brettell, C. B., & Sargent, C. F. (Eds.). (1993). *Gender in cross-cultural perspective.* Englewood Cliffs, NJ: Prentice Hall.

Cole, E., Espin, O. M., & Rothblum, E. (Eds.). (1992). *Refugee women and their mental health: Shattered societies, shattered lives.* New York: Haworth.

Denzin, N. K. (1989). *Interpretive biography.* Newbury Park, CA: Sage.

Erikson, E. H. (1964). *Insight and responsibility.* New York: W. W. Norton.

Erikson, E. H. (1975). *Life history and the historical moment.* New York: W. W. Norton.

Espin, O. M. (1984). Cultural and historical influences on sexuality in Hispanic/Latin women. In C. Vance (Ed.), *Pleasure and danger: Exploring female sexuality.* London: Routledge & Kegan Paul.

Espin, O. M. (1987a). Issues of identity in the psychology of Latina lesbians. In Boston Lesbian Psychologies Collective (Ed.), *Lesbian psychologies: Explorations and challenges* (pp. 35-55). Urbana: University of Illinois Press.

Espin, O. M. (1987b). Psychological impact of migration on Latinas: Implications for psychotherapeutic practice. *Psychology of Women Quarterly, 11,* 489-503.

Espin, O. M. (1990, August). *Ethnic and cultural issues in the "coming out" process among Latina lesbians.* Paper presented at the 98th Annual Meeting of the American Psychological Association, Boston.

Espin, O. M. (1992). Roots uprooted: The psychological impact of historical/political dislocation. In E. Cole, O. M. Espin, & E. Rothblum (Eds.), *Refugee women and their mental health: Shattered societies, shattered lives* (pp. 9-20). New York: Haworth.

Espin, O. M. (1994, June). *Crossing borders and boundaries: The life narratives of immigrant women and the development of identity through place, sexuality, and language.* Paper presented at the conference "Immigration, Language Acquisition, and Patterns of Social Integration," Jerusalem.

Espin, O. M., Cavanaugh, A., Paydarfar, N., & Wood, R. (1990, March). *Mothers, daughters, and migration: A new look at the psychology of separation.* Paper presented at the annual meeting of the Association for Women in Psychology, Tempe, AZ.

Espin, O. M., Stewart, A. J., & Gomez, C. (1990). Letters from V.: Adolescent personality development in socio-historical context. *Journal of Personality, 58,* 347-364.

Essed, P. (1991). *Understanding everyday racism: An interdisciplinary theory.* Newbury Park, CA: Sage.

Essed, P. (1994). Contradictory positions, ambivalent perceptions: A case study of a Black woman entrepreneur. *Feminism and Psychology, 4*(1), 99-118.

Foucault, M. (1981). *The history of sexuality*. Harmondsworth: Penguin.

Franz, C. E., & Stewart, A. J. (Eds.). (1994). *Women creating lives: Identities, resilience, and resistance*. Boulder, CO: Westview.

Gabaccia, D. (Ed.). (1992). *Seeking common ground: Multidisciplinary studies of immigrant women in the United States*. Westport, CT: Praeger.

Garza-Guerrero, C. (1974). Culture shock: Its mourning and the vicissitudes of identity. *Journal of the American Psychoanalytic Association, 22,* 408-429.

Goodenow, C., & Espin, O. M. (1993). Identity choices in immigrant female adolescents. *Adolescence, 28,* 173-184.

Hoffman, E. (1989). *Lost in translation: A life in a new language*. New York: E. P. Dutton.

Jaggar, A., & Bordo, S. (Eds.). (1989). *Gender/body/knowledge*. New Brunswick, NJ: Rutgers University Press.

Josselson, R., & Lieblich, A. (Eds.). (1993). *The narrative study of lives*. Newbury Park, CA: Sage.

Krueger, R. A. (1994). *Focus groups: A practical guide for applied research* (2nd ed.). Thousand Oaks, CA: Sage.

Laqueur, T. (1990). *Making sex: Body and gender from the Greeks to Freud*. Cambridge, MA: Harvard University Press.

Lieblich, A. (1993). Looking at change. Natasha, 21: New immigrant from Russia to Israel. In R. Josselson & A. Lieblich (Eds.), *The narrative study of lives* (pp. 92-129). Newbury Park, CA: Sage.

Lorde, A. (1984). *Sister outsider: Essays and speeches*. Freedom, CA: Crossing.

McAdams, D. (1990). Unity and purpose in human lives: The emergence of identity as a life story. In A. Rabin, R. A. Zucker, R. A. Emmons, & S. Frank (Eds.), *Studying persons and lives* (pp. 148-200). New York: Springer.

Mishler, E. G. (1986). *Research interviewing: Context and narrative*. Cambridge, MA: Harvard University Press.

Morgan, D. L. (1988). *Focus groups as qualitative research*. Newbury Park, CA: Sage.

Morgan, D. L. (Ed.). (1993). *Successful focus groups*. Newbury Park, CA: Sage.

Murray, H. (1938). *Explorations in personality*. New York: Oxford University Press.

Nathanson, C. A. (1991). *Dangerous passage: The social control of sexuality in women's adolescence*. Philadelphia: Temple University Press.

Necef, M. U. (1994). The language of intimacy. In L. E. Andersen (Ed.), *Middle East studies in Denmark* (pp. 141-158). Odense, Denmark: Odense University Press.

Ochberg, R. L. (1992). Social insight and psychological liberation. In G. C. Rosenwald & R. L. Ochberg (Eds.), *Storied lives: The cultural politics of self-understanding* (pp. 214-230). New Haven, CT: Yale University Press.

Ogundipe-Leslie, 'M. (1993). African women, culture, and another development. In S. M. James & A. P. A. Busia (Eds.), *Theorizing Black feminisms* (pp. 102-117). London: Routledge.

Parker, A., Russo, M., Sommer, D., & Yaeger, P. S. (Eds.). (1992). *Nationalisms and sexualities*. New York: Routledge.

Phizachlea, A. (Ed.). (1983). *One way ticket: Migration and female labour*. London: Routledge & Kegan Paul.

Polkinghorne, D. E. (1988). *Narrative knowing and the human sciences*. Albany: State University of New York Press.

Riessman, C. K. (1993). *Narrative analysis*. Newbury Park, CA: Sage.

Rosenwald, G. C. (1992). Conclusion: Reflections on narrative self-understanding. In G. C. Rosenwald & R. L. Ochberg (Eds.), *Storied lives: The cultural politics of self-understanding* (pp. 265-289). New Haven, CT: Yale University Press.

Rosenwald, G. C., & Ochberg, R. L. (1992). Introduction. In G. C. Rosenwald & R. L. Ochberg (Eds.), *Storied lives: The cultural politics of self-understanding*. New Haven, CT: Yale University Press.

Ruiz, V. L. (1992). The flapper and the chaperon: Historical memory among Mexican-American women. In D. Gabaccia (Ed.), *Seeking common ground: Multidisciplinary studies of immigrant women in the United States* (pp. 141-157). Westport, CT: Praeger.

Schreier, B. A. (1994). *Becoming American women: Clothing and the Jewish immigrant experience, 1880-1920*. Chicago: Chicago Historical Society.

Silverman, D. (1993). *Interpreting qualitative data: Methods for analysing talk, text, and interaction*. London: Sage.

Stewart, D. W., & Shamdasani, P. N. (1990). *Focus groups: Theory and practice*. Newbury Park, CA: Sage.

Strauss, A. L. (1987). *Qualitative analysis for social scientists*. Cambridge, UK: Cambridge University Press.

Thomas, W. I., & Znaniecki, F. (1927). *The Polish peasant in Europe and America*. New York: Alfred A. Knopf. (Original work published 1918-1920)

Torres, L. (1991). The construction of the self in U.S. Latina autobiographies. In C. T. Mohanty, A. Russo, & L. Torres (Eds.), *Third World women and the politics of feminism* (pp. 271-287). Bloomington: Indiana University Press.

Trumbach, R. (1977). London's sodomites. *Journal of Social History, 11*.

White, R. (1966). *Lives in progress* (2nd ed.). New York: Holt, Rinehart & Winston.

Yuval-Davis, N. (1992). Fundamentalism, multiculturalism and women in Britain. In J. Donald & A. Rattansi (Eds.), *Race, culture, and difference* (pp. 278-291). London: Sage.

10

Ethnic Minority Lesbians and Gay Men
Mental Health and Treatment Issues

BEVERLY GREENE

The past decade has witnessed significant growth in the psychological literature that appropriately explores gay and lesbian sexual
orientations from affirmative perspectives. Similarly, there has been a
significant increase in the study of the role of culture and ethnicity in
psychological development and the process of psychological assessment and treatment. In both areas, relevant discussions are taking
place concerning the effect of membership in institutionally oppressed
and disparaged groups on the development of psychological resilience
and vulnerability. Although a rapidly expanding body of literature
reflects exploration of both areas from a wide range of perspectives,
scant attention has been paid to lesbians and gay men who are members of ethnic minority groups.

A preponderance of the empirical research on or with lesbians and
gay men has been conducted with overwhelmingly white, middle-
class respondents (Chan, 1989, 1992; Garnets & Kimmel, 1991; Gock,
1985; Greene, 1994, 1996; Greene & Boyd-Franklin, 1996; Mays &
Cochran, 1988; Morales, 1992). Similarly, research on members of eth-

AUTHOR'S NOTE: This chapter is a revised and expanded version of "Ethnic Minority
Lesbians and Gay Men: Mental Health and Treatment Issues," *Journal of Consulting and
Clinical Psychology, 62*, 243-251. Copyright © 1994 by the American Psychological Asso-
ciation. Adapted with permission.

nic minority groups rarely acknowledges differences in sexual orientation among group members. Hence there has been little exploration of the complex interaction between sexual orientation and ethnic identity development, nor have the realistic social tasks and stressors that are a component of gay and lesbian identity formation in conjunction with ethnic identity formation been taken into account. Discussion of the vicissitudes of racism and ethnic identity in intra- and interracial couples of the same gender and their effects on these couples' relationships has also been neglected in the narrow focus on heterosexual relationships found in the literature on ethnic minority clients. There has been an equally narrow focus on predominantly white couples in the gay and lesbian literature.

These biases are rarely stated in titles of papers or in statements explaining the limited generalizability of their findings, despite a clear injunction in psychological research to do so. Such narrow research perspectives leave us with a limited understanding of the diversity within these groups and leave practitioners ill equipped to address the clinical needs of the members of these groups in culturally sensitive and competent ways.

A range of factors should be considered in determining the impact of ethnic identity and its dynamic interaction with sexual orientation in any client's life. Heterocentric thinking leads to a range of inaccurate and unexamined but commonly held assumptions about gay men and lesbians. These assumptions are maintained in varying degrees by members of ethnic minority groups, as they are in the dominant culture. One of the most commonly accepted of these fallacious notions is that to be gay or lesbian is to want to be a member of the other gender, which is socially constructed as the opposite gender. In such a framework, men are expected to be sexually attracted to women only, and women to men only. Sexual attraction to the other gender is embedded in the definition of what it means to be a normal man or woman for cultural groups reviewed in this discussion. Support for this premise from traditional psychological perspectives facilitates a range of other interconnected but equally inaccurate assumptions. One is the presumption of psychological normalcy of heterosexual or reproductive sexuality. This leads to the assumption that women who are sexually attracted to other women wish to be men or are defective women, and that men who are sexually attracted to other men are similarly defective males. Another insidious assumption connected to these is that conformity to traditional gender stereotypes of roles and physical appearance, and its corollary, is a direct reflection of heterosexual orientation. The mistaken conclusions in this scheme are that men and women who do not conform to traditional gender role stereotypes must be gay or lesbian and that those who do conform to such stereotypes must be heterosexual. Hence an understanding of the meaning of being an ethnic minority gay man or lesbian requires a careful exploration of the importance of cultural gender roles and both the nature and relative fluidity or rigidity of the culture's traditional gender stereotypes. For members of some oppressed groups, specifically African and Native Americans, reproductive sexuality is viewed as the means of continuing the groups' presence in the world. Hence birth control and expressions of sexuality that are not reproductive may be viewed by group members as instruments of genocide.

The extent to which parents or families of origin may control or influence adult family members and the importance of the family as a tangible and emotional source of support warrants understanding. Other factors to consider include the importance of procreation and the continuation of the family line; the nature, degree, and intensity of religious values; the importance of ties to the ethnic community; the degree of acculturation or assimilation of the individual or family into the dominant culture; and the history of discrimination or oppression the particular group has experienced from members of the dominant culture. Examination of the history of discrimination of the ethnic group should include group members' understandings of their oppression and their strategies for coping.

Another important dimension is that of sexuality. Sexuality and its meaning are contextual, therefore what it means to be a gay man or a lesbian will be related to the meaning assigned to sexuality in the culture. It is important to explore the range of sexual behavior that is sanctioned, in what forms it may be expressed and by whom, and the consequences of compliance or failure to comply. An exploration of the role of ethnic stereotypes in the creation of ethnosexual mythologies about ethnic group members is another important part of this inquiry.

Despite similarities in the histories of members of ethnic minority groups, generalized descriptions of cultural practices may never be applied with uniformity to all members of any ethnic group. Just as there are many ways in which ethnic group cultures are different from the dominant culture, there is great diversity within ethnic groups. Practitioners need to explore all clients' cultural heritages from those persons' own unique experiences of their upbringing. This chapter serves as a framework or outline from which to begin examining clinical work with ethnic minority gay men and lesbians from more diverse perspectives.

Latino Americans

Latino American cultures embrace a wide range of persons with different languages and cultural norms, coming from many different places in the world. The comments offered here apply broadly to features observed across many different groups of people who would consider themselves Hispanic or Latino American. The reader is warned that these groups may differ from one another as much as they differ from the dominant Anglo-American culture. They include, among others, Puerto Ricans, Mexican Americans, Latino Americans, and people of many Spanish-origin Caribbean islands.

In Latino American cultures, family is regarded as the primary social unit and source of support, with well-established gender roles (Amaro, 1978; Espin, 1984, 1987; Hidalgo, 1984; Morales, 1992; Vasquez, 1979). Women are expected to be overtly submissive, virtuous, respectful of elders, and willing to defer to men, and may be expected to reside with their parents until they are married. Men are expected to provide for, protect, and defend the family with great loyalty (Morales, 1992). Language may carry deep affective meaning, is imbued with cultural values, and may express emotions that do not freely translate from Spanish to English (Espin, 1984). Espin has observed that one may find few or no words for "lesbian" or "gay man" within the Spanish language that are not negative (see Chapter 9, this volume). There is a strong sense of interdependence among Latino family members that the naive Anglo therapist may incorrectly view as undifferentiated. As Latino Americans are often overrepresented among lower socioeconomic groups, economic realities and concerns must also be taken into account (Morales, 1992). Espin (1987) also notes that the time of and reasons for immigration, issues related to separation from the homeland, and the process required to mourn such losses are also important factors for practitioners to consider in treating many Latino gay men and Latina lesbians.

Women in Latino cultures are encouraged to maintain emotional and physical closeness with other women, and such behavior is not presumed to be lesbian (Amaro, 1978; Espin, 1984, 1987; Hidalgo, 1984). Closeness with female friends during adolescence may provide the means of protecting the virginity of young women, by diminishing their contact with males. The open discussion of sex and sexuality between women is not culturally sanctioned. Women are expected to be naive and ignorant about sexual matters, whereas males are expected to be experienced and knowledgeable (Espin, 1984). Further, it is not uncommon for Latino men to engage in same-gender sexual behavior without acquiring a gay identity. The more active, masculine role, referred to as the *buggaron*, holds higher status than the role of the passive recipient, who is presumed to be more female identified (Carballo-Dieguez, 1989; L. Comas-Diaz, personal communication, January 1993; Espin, 1984; Vasquez, 1979).

Rather than behavior, it is the overt acknowledgment and disclosure of a gay or lesbian identity that is likely to meet with intense disapproval in Latino American communities (Espin, 1984, 1987; Hidalgo, 1984; Morales, 1992). This phenomenon has been found to be consistent to varying degrees across the ethnic groups reviewed in this chapter and has been observed by Smith in her work with African American clients as well (see Chapter 14, this volume). This disapproval may have many origins. Espin (1987) contends that in labeling themselves lesbian, Latinas force a culture that denies the sexuality of women to confront it. Lillian Comas-Diaz (personal communication, January 1993) explains this as a function of the cultural importance of saving face as a key component of maintaining dignity and commanding respect. Hence being indirect is the culturally prescribed way of managing conflict, as participants do not lose face. Labeling oneself gay or lesbian implies not only consciously participating in behavior that is condemned, but actively confronting others with one's choice to do so, violating the injunction to be indirect. This phenomenon has been observed in Asian cultures as well.

According to Trujillo (1991), the majority of Chicano heterosexuals view Chicana lesbians as a threat to the established order of male dominance in Chicano communities, as their existence has the potential of raising the consciousness of Chicanas, causing them to question their situation or to see possibilities for their independence. Another variable in the origins of such attitudes is that of the influence of Catholicism in many Latino communities.

Espin (1984), Hidalgo (1984), and Morales (1992) suggest that Latino disapproval of homosexuality is more intense than the homophobia found in the dominant Anglo community. They further suggest that a powerful form of heterosexist oppression takes place within Hispanic cultures, leaving many gay and lesbian members feeling pressure to remain closeted in those communities to avoid the ridicule and outcast status that would result from open acknowledgment of their identity. The pressure to remain closeted within one's ethnic community and the experience of that community as more homophobic than the dominant culture appears to be consistent across ethnic groups. It should be noted, however, that there have been no empirical studies assessing attitudes toward homosexuality among specific ethnic minority groups. The degree to which this perception conforms to reality remains to be explored more thoroughly.

For a Latino, declaring a gay or lesbian sexual orientation may be experienced as an act of treason against the culture and the family. Espin (1984, 1987) and Hidalgo (1984) note that a gay or lesbian family member may maintain a place in the family and be quietly tolerated, but this does not constitute acceptance of a gay or lesbian sexual orientation. Rather, it frequently constitutes a form of denial. This observation is consistent with the behavior observed in families in other ethnic minority groups, with responses to disclosure being as diverse as families themselves.

Despite the anti-gay/-lesbian sentiment of Hispanic communities and families, Espin (1987) and Hidalgo (1984) have found a deep attachment among Hispanic lesbians and gay men to their ethnic communities and a frame of reference that most frequently claims ethnic identity and community as primary concerns. The fear of being an outcast from a community of such importance and the energy and behaviors required to balance this with a lesbian or gay identity can make life very difficult. This reality for Latino American gay men and lesbians is shared by their counterparts in other ethnic groups and has important mental health implications. Specific issues relevant to treatment will be discussed in a later section.

Asian Americans

The term *Asian* refers to many different groups of persons with different cultural values originating in many different geographic regions. For the purposes of this discussion, the term *Asian Americans* is used to refer specifically to Americans of Japanese or Chinese ancestry, because it is with these groups that most research has been done.

The most salient features of traditional Asian American families are the expectation of obedience to parents, parents' demand for conformity consistent with the respect accorded to elders, and the hierarchical delineation of both gender roles and generational lines (Bradshaw, 1990; Chan, 1992; Garnets & Kimmel, 1991; Gock, 1985; Pamela H., 1989). Men are expected to continue the family lineage and name by marrying and having children (Chan, 1989; Tremble, Schneider, & Appathurai, 1989). Women are expected to recognize their importance and derive satisfaction from the roles of dutiful daughter and, ultimately, wife and mother (Chan, 1992; Pamela H., 1989). The development of a sexual identity may be difficult, as sex is deemed a taboo topic, to be avoided, and shameful if discussed openly (Chan, 1992; Pamela H., 1989). Connie Chan (personal communication, February 1992) notes that sex is presumed to be unimportant to women, who are deemed to be of lesser importance than men. Hence sexual relationships between women may occur but are not taken seriously unless they are accompanied by an acknowledgment of a lesbian sexual orientation. Chan also notes that although many men have sexual relations with other men, those relationships are not necessarily seen as gay.

Among Asian Americans, open disclosure that one is gay or lesbian is seen as a threat to the continuation of the family line and a rejection of one's appropriate roles within the culture as well (Chan, 1992; Garnets & Kimmel, 1991; Wooden, Kawasaki, & Mayeda, 1983). The maintenance of outward roles and conformity is an important and distinctive cultural expectation. Gay or lesbian offspring may be experienced as a source of shame, particularly to mothers, who are considered responsible for preventing such occurrences (Chan, 1992; Pamela H., 1989).

Gay men and lesbians who are members of ethnic minority groups frequently report feeling pressure to choose between the two communities and subsequently determine which aspect of their identity is primary. In her 1989 study of Asian American gay men and lesbians, Chan found that most respondents identified primarily as gay men or lesbians rather than as Asian Americans. She also found, however, that the primacy of sexual orientation and ethnicity shifts during development, depending on which stages of ethnic identity development and sexual orientation identity formation the individual fits at that time. Identification may also vary depending on the need at the time. Unlike gay and lesbian members of other ethnic groups who report feeling discriminated against more because of race than sexual orientation, members of Chan's Asian gay male sample reported experiencing more discrimination because they were gay than because they were Asian. This finding underscores the importance of exploring subtle cultural differences in experiences that are common across broad parameters.

Pamela H. (1989) writes that the persistent invisibility of Asian American gay men and lesbians within Asian ethnic communities is slowly changing with the development of lesbian and gay support and social groups within those communities. Such groups have developed in part in reaction to experiences of invisibility and racial discrimination in the broader gay and lesbian communities, which are predominantly white and often offer little contact with other gay and lesbian Asian Americans.

Chan discusses homosexual identity formation among Asian Americans in greater detail in Chapter 11 of this volume.

African Americans

African Americans are a diverse group of persons whose cultural origins, with some American Indian and European racial admixture, are in the tribes of Western Africa. Their ancestors were unwilling participants in their immigration as the primary objects of the North American slave trade (Greene, 1986, 1996; Greene & Boyd-Franklin, 1996). Their cultural derivatives include strong family ties that encompass nuclear and extended family members in complex networks of obligation and support (Greene, 1986, 1996; Greene & Boyd-Franklin, 1996; Icard, 1986). In African American families, gender roles have been somewhat more flexible than they have been in white families and in many of their ethnic minority counterparts. This flexibility is explained in part as a derivative of the value of interdependence and somewhat more egalitarian nature of some precolonial African cultures. It is also a function of the need to adapt to racism in the United States, which made it difficult for African American men to find work and thus fit the ideal of the Western male provider. Hence rigid gender role stratification was somewhat impractical. This does not mean, however, that sexism is not a part of contemporary African American communities. Nonetheless, the African American family and community have functioned as a necessary protective barrier and survival tool against the racism of the dominant culture.

The sexual objectification of African Americans during slavery and the subsequent manipulation of popular images of African Americans have fueled stereotypes of sexual promiscuity and moral looseness (Clarke, 1983; Collins, 1990; Greene, 1986, 1990, 1996; Greene & Boyd-Franklin, 1996; Icard, 1986). Such images are relevant to the way that African American men and women are viewed and certainly to the way many view themselves. The legacy of sexual racism plays a role in the response of many African Americans to gay or lesbian family members or others in their community. The African American community is also viewed by many of its gay and lesbian members as extremely homophobic and rejecting of gay and lesbian persons, generating pressure for them to remain closeted (Clarke, 1983; Gomez & Smith, 1990; Greene, 1996; Greene & Boyd-Franklin, 1996; Icard, 1986; Mays & Cochran, 1988; Poussaint, 1990; Smith, 1982). As their counterparts in other ethnic minority groups have also found, the strength of African American family ties often mitigate against outright rejection of gay and lesbian family members despite clear rejection of gay and lesbian sexual orientations. Smith describes some of the diverse methods African American families use in managing their conflicts about lesbian and gay members in Chapter 14 of this volume.

Homophobia among African Americans can be viewed as multiply determined. One determinant is the presence of Christian religiosity, which is often a part of the strong religious and spiritual orientation of African American cultures. In this context, selective interpretations of scripture are used to reinforce homophobic attitudes (Claybourne, 1978; Greene, 1996; Icard, 1986). Clarke (1983) and Smith (1982) cite heterosexual privilege as another determinant of homophobia, particularly among African American women. Because of the rampant sexism in both the dominant culture and African American culture, and the racism of the dominant culture, African American women often find themselves on the bottom of the racial and gender hierarchical heap. Hence being heterosexual gives them slightly higher status than being lesbian.

Sexuality represents an emotionally charged issue for African Americans, intensified by pejorative sexual myths and stereotypes. Internalized racism may be seen as another determinant of homophobia among African Americans, particularly for those who have internalized racist stereotypes of sexuality. Such persons may harbor an exaggerated need to demonstrate their "normalcy" (Clarke, 1993; De Monteflores, 1986; Gomez, 1983; Greene, 1986; Greene & Boyd-Franklin, 1996; Poussaint, 1990). Hence gay men or lesbians may be experienced as embarrassments by African Americans who perceive themselves as inferior (Poussaint, 1990). Dyne (1980) suggests that homophobia may also represent a reaction to the perceived shortage of marriageable males in African American communities and the perceived importance of continued propagation of the race.

The studies of Bell and Weinberg (1978), Bass-Hass (1968), and Mays and Cochran (1988) are among the few that have included all or significant numbers of African American gay and lesbian respondents. Some of their findings are as follows. African American lesbians have been found to be more likely than white lesbians to maintain strong involvements with their families, to have children, and to depend to a greater extent on family members or other (African American) lesbians for support. They have also been observed to have continued contact with men and with heterosexual peers to a greater extent than their white counterparts. African American men have been noted to derive less benefit from the white gay and lesbian communities than have their white counterparts. African American gay men and lesbians have also been observed to be more likely than white gay men and lesbians to experience tension and loneliness, but are less likely to seek professional help. These findings suggest that African American gay men and lesbians may be more vulnerable than their white counterparts to negative psychological outcomes.

Despite the acknowledged homophobia in the African American community, African American gay men and lesbians claim a strong attachment to their cultural heritage and to their communities and cite their identity as African Americans as primary (Acosta, 1979; Mays, Cochran, & Rhue, 1993). They also cite a sense of conflicting loyalties between the African American community and the gay and lesbian community when confronted with homophobia in the African American community. Their concerns about rejection by the community if their gay or lesbian sexual orientation is known may be realistic (Dyne, 1980; Greene, 1996; Icard, 1986; Mays & Cochran, 1988).

Native Americans

Like other ethnic groups united under one name, American Indians represent hundreds of different tribal groups, cultures, and languages. Common to many tribes is the importance of spirituality, family support, and the continued existence of the tribe (V. Sears, personal communication, 1992). Motherhood is an important role for Native American women, as children are seen as the future of the tribe. Despite this, there is no great pressure to marry, and many lesbians have children (V. Sears, personal communication, 1992). Any understanding of sexuality among American Indians must take their colonization and the influence of Western religion into account, as it often had the result of suppressing and altering traditional cultures and obstructing their transmission (Weinrich & Williams, 1991). Still, in the Native American context, sex was not discussed openly but was accepted as a natural part of the world and a gynocentric culture (Allen, 1984; V. Sears, personal communication, 1992).

Allen (1986) and Williams (1986) both note that in precolonial Indian tribes, physical anatomy was not inextricably linked to gender roles, and that mixed-gender or alternative gender roles were accepted. Men who might be considered androgynous by today's standards were highly valued; they were viewed as people who combined aspects of masculine and feminine styles spiritually as well as in personality traits and behaviors (Weinrich & Williams, 1991). Similarly, women who preferred engaging in activities that were usually performed by men were accepted.

Contemporary American Indians, particularly on reservations, are less accepting than their ancestors, in part as a function of internalized oppression and loss of contact with traditional values (V. Sears, personal communication, 1992; Williams, 1986). Hence Indian gay men and lesbians may experience more pressure to be closeted if they live on reservations than not, prompting many to move to more urban areas (V. Sears, personal communication, 1992; Williams, 1986). The move away from the reservation, however, may result in the experience of loss of culture and support from family and other Indians, and can precipitate feelings of isolation (V. Sears, personal communication, 1992).

The degree of acceptance among Native Americans of a gay or lesbian sexual orientation may also be a function of the views of the religious group that was involved in colonizing a particular tribe (V. Sears, personal communication, 1992). For more information on Native American lesbians and gay men, see Chapter 1 in this volume, by Terry Tafoya.

Gay and Lesbian People of Color

Gay men and lesbians may be found among many other ethnic groups whose members may be considered persons of color. However, they remain even more invisible than those discussed above. Gay men and lesbians who identify with the cultures of India and Pakistan, for instance, find themselves confronted with many psychological tasks similar to those faced by other visibly ethnic gay men and lesbians. However, members of this group are markedly heterogeneous and do not necessarily identify with members of other ethnic minority groups in the United States, nor do all view themselves as persons of color. Vaid has observed that many Indians see Britain as their mother country and see themselves as white (see Meera, 1993). Therapists who treat members of this group must consider the psychological demands made of persons who are viewed as persons of color, literally because of the color of their skin, but who do not experience themselves as members of ethnic minority groups who are socialized in the United States.

As in Asian cultures, gender roles are clearly delineated within Indian families, and obedience to parents is expected. Sexuality is not discussed openly, and anything that departs from heterosexuality may not be discussed at all (Chasin, 1991; Jayakar, 1994). Marriages are frequently arranged by parents based on assumptions about what is good for the families, rather than with consideration of the individuals involved. According to Jayakar (1994), a woman is expected to conform to her surroundings as a fluid conforms to the shape of the vessel that contains it, and to derive her power in the family from being the mother of a son. Lesbians and gay men within the Indian culture, however, are virtually absent from the psychological literature; much of what is available on this population is found only in the form of independent films and popular literature (e.g., Parmar, 1992; Ratti, 1993).

Treatment Implications

Countertransference Dilemmas

Gay and lesbian sexual orientations, racial differences, and the social conflicts that surround these matters are issues about which most people have intense feelings, and clinicians are no exception. The sensitive treatment of ethnic minority gay or lesbian clients brings these provocative issues together in a profound way and raises a range of challenges for even the most experienced psychotherapists.

Initially, therapists must be culturally literate—they must have broad familiarity with the general characteristics of their clients' cultures as well as with the special needs and vulnerabilities of gay and lesbian clients. Most graduate training programs do not routinely offer training in either of these areas, so therapists must be willing to seek such training elsewhere. For instance, they may combine attendance in special workshops or classes with individual or group supervision with clinicians who have training in both these areas. The failure of therapists to seek out such training can result in less-than-adequate treatment for ethnic minority lesbian and gay clients. Furthermore, therapists must be able to apply their cultural literacy to the development of a wide range of practical skills for addressing such matters in practice.

The interaction between culture and sexual orientation is dynamic and encompasses two major dimensions around which people organize their assumptions about who they are in the world. For most people, culture and sexual orientation interact with other salient components of their identities as well. In therapy, separating issues of culture, sexual orientation, other aspects of identity and their interactive results, and mechanisms developed to adapt to life stressors is complex. Therapists who have not taken the time to explore fully the manifestations of these dilemmas will find it difficult if not impossible to unravel them successfully. This exploration should include the therapists' personal examination of their own personal feelings and responses to ethnic minority clients and to gay men and lesbians, and of course examination of their own sexual orientations and ethnicities. Therapists must also be aware of the stereotypes and beliefs about ethnic minority and gay and lesbian persons that they have internalized without question. These variables may, if unexamined, predispose therapists to make a range of inaccurate assumptions about clients and their experiences.

Heterosexual therapists who are insecure in their own feelings about sexual orientation or who expect gay and lesbian clients to be preoccupied with sexual matters may be predisposed to have greater expectations of eroticized transferences from clients of the same gender. If therapists have personal needs to see such transference, they may tend to overlook or minimize issues that are of greater importance to their clients. Insecure heterosexual therapists may find such transference reactions frightening, and may perceive them as threats to their own sexual orientation. If therapists fear that such transference reactions will occur, they may tend to overlook them or may avoid appropriate explorations of material that might expose such feelings in their clients as well as the clients' direct expressions of such material. Heterosexual therapists who lack a sense of security about their sexual orientation may also find themselves "leaking" personal information to clients, particularly in the midst of eroticized transference reactions, presumably to let the clients know that they, the therapists, are not gay or lesbian, whereas with heterosexual clients they are generally neutral about such matters.

Most therapists struggle with the delicate balance involved in urging ethnic minority gay or lesbian clients to assume greater personal responsibility, when appropriate, without seeming insensitive to the realistic barriers of the multiple levels of real, not fantasized, discrimination. Therapists err, however, if their feeling sorry for clients, or admiring clients (romanticizing clients' struggles), leads them to avoid setting appropriate limits in treatment or calling clients' attention to their own roles in their dilemmas. Such therapists may feel uncomfortable when more than support and validation for the clients' struggles with discrimination are warranted.

Therapists who are white and heterosexual may inadvertently find themselves bending over backward to accommodate ethnic minority gay or lesbian clients, failing to set appropriate limits or behaving in ways they would not with other clients. Such behavior may be evoked in therapists if clients make them feel guilty, angry, uncomfortable, or incompetent. In such situations, therapists may feel a need to compensate clients in some way for the therapists' feelings of inadequacy. White, heterosexual therapists may also feel guilty about their membership in two dominant and oppressive groups and may seek to compensate by indulging ethnic minority gay and lesbian clients. Of course this indulgence, motivated by the therapists' guilt rather than by their genuine concern for the clients' welfare, is never helpful to clients.

J. White (personal communication, January 1993) has observed that sex, like any other behavior, may be seen as a vehicle for communicating feelings and, as such, warrants exploration in therapy. It is not unusual for gay or lesbian clients to refuse or to express reluctance to explore this area with heterosexual therapists. Such reluctance is understandable, as many gay and lesbian clients have accurately experienced such inquiries as voyeuristic on the part of homophobic therapists. It is important for therapists to be sensitive to clients' feelings about making such disclosures, but that does not mean that the material should go unexplored. It is the therapists' responsibility to earn their clients' trust and to help their clients to understand the importance of such inquiries. It may be useful for therapists to help their clients to understand who they feel sexually excited by and why. Heterosexual therapists, however, may respond to clients' reluctance to explore this area by avoiding any further discussion of the material. Although they may view this as respecting their clients' feelings, therapists must consider whether this is really in their clients' interests or if it serves another purpose—such as the therapists' need to avoid what the material may elicit in themselves, or the therapists' need to avoid challenging any of their clients' assumptions or perceptions. This may arise out of some irrational fear of what clients may do in response to such questions or the therapists' guilt about not gratifying their clients. For example, a therapist may fear that if a client is confronted and subsequently leaves therapy, this may reflect badly on the therapist. Hence therapists' insecurities about treating ethnic minority gay and lesbian clients and the anxiety that they may terminate treatment can cripple therapists' ability to challenge and explore these clients' feelings appropriately.

White, heterosexual therapists may have difficulty understanding and accepting the realistic barriers imposed by racism and homophobia in their ethnic minority gay and lesbian clients' lives. They may respond to this difficulty by attempting to move too quickly past such communications by avoiding or dismissing them, or by minimizing their importance. Although clients may use problems associated with race and sexual orientation to avoid exploration of more painful material, the realistic magnitude of life stressors associated with these dimensions cannot be underestimated; they warrant the same respectful attention in therapy as do intrapsychic explorations.

The gay or lesbian therapist who is also a person of color may be predisposed to certain countertransference dilemmas. The most obvious is observed in the therapist who is overidentified with the client and as a result tends to overlook or minimize psychopathology. The therapist may attribute all of the client's problems to the barriers that result from ethnicity and sexual orientation, rather than explore other significant aspects of the client's personal life.

The ethnic minority gay or lesbian therapist may face additional issues related to the maintenance of therapeutic boundaries. Most therapists are faced with the challenge of maintaining appropriate distance without seeming aloof and disinterested in the client's well-being. Clients from diverse cultural backgrounds, however, may have different interpretations of the therapist's interpersonal distance. This is complicated by the tendency for some ethnic minority gay and lesbian clients to harbor idealized expectations of therapists who are similar to them. There may be a tendency among such clients to presume that these therapists "know" exactly how they feel because they are the "same" and will not need to ask questions or explore issues related to ethnicity or sexual orientation. Although such assumptions may seem initially flattering, therapists must be careful not to reinforce such beliefs. Blind acceptance of these assumptions can cut off exploration rather than facilitate it and may reflect a therapist's need to substitute "social" discussions for therapeutic inquiries. Therapists should incorporate discussion of social context and issues to understand better how these affect their clients' lives, the realistic tasks and challenges they bring, and what kinds of feelings they evoke. Exploration of such matters should not become the basis for intellectual discussion as a substitute for therapeutic inquiry.

Gay and lesbian clients who are members of ethnic minority groups may be vulnerable to isolation and estrangement. Therapists who are members of these groups are vulnerable to these conditions as well. For this reason, ethnic minority gay and lesbian therapists must be sure that they have developed networks of supportive peers and colleagues and adequate social and emotional interests and supports in their own lives. If they have not, they may be vulnerable to the tendency to seek to gratify these needs inadvertently through their client counterparts. In this scenario it can become tempting for therapists to view clients as social acquaintances or potential friends or lovers. This is particularly true when therapist and client share important attributes or life experiences, and when they are members of minority groups in the midst of hostile environments, where there are few other people who share those important attributes. However, when therapists succumb to this temptation they engage in unethical practice, abdicating their primary role and their responsibility to their clients as therapists in favor of gratifying their own personal needs. Furthermore, clients' requests for such contacts or relationships do not relieve therapists of the responsibility for the negative effects of such behavior on clients. The failure to maintain appropriate boundaries in this area can effectively undermine clients' treatment.

Mental Health Issues

Ethnic minority gay men and lesbians exist as minorities within minorities, with the multiple levels of oppression and discrimination that accompany such status. They bear the additional task of integrating two major aspects of their identities when both are conspicuously devalued; their sexual orientation may be devalued by those closest to them. Most are socialized in their respective ethnic communities, with strong ties to families of origin as well as extended family, before becoming aware of a gay or lesbian sexual orientation, in complex networks of interdependence and support. Members of ethnic minority groups receive positive cultural mirroring during development, usually but not exclusively through their families. This helps to buffer the demeaning messages of the dominant culture. Ethnic minority gay men and lesbians also learn a range of negative stereotypes about gay and lesbian sexual orientations long before they know that they are gay or lesbian themselves. The subsequent internalization of these negative attitudes, gleaned from loved and trusted figures who may have challenged similar stereotypes about their ethnic group, complicates the process of gay or lesbian identity development and self-acceptance.

Regardless of the specific ethnic groups to which they belong, ethnic minority lesbians and gay men must manage the dominant culture's racism, sexism, and heterosexism. They must also manage the sexism, heterosexism, and internalized racism of their own ethnic groups. For most gay and lesbian members of ethnic minority groups, their ties to their ethnic communities are of great practical and emotional significance. Their communities may be important havens against racism as well as crucial sources of support. The homophobia in these communities makes gay and lesbian members more vulnerable and perhaps more inclined to remain closeted within their ethnic communities and hence invisible to them (Chan, 1992; Espin, 1984; Greene, 1996; Greene & Boyd-Franklin, 1996; Mays & Cochran, 1988; Morales, 1992). How important these ties may be to individual clients varies depending on the degree of attachment to cultural roots and degree of acculturation (Falco, 1991). The appropriate, intense ties many ethnic minority gay men and lesbians have to their ethnic communities may complicate the coming-out process for them in ways not experienced by their white counterparts. Decisions about coming out to family members are fraught with anxiety for most gay men and lesbians, but for ethnic minority lesbians and gay men, there is additional risk—they cannot presume acceptance by the broader gay and lesbian community.

Just as sexual orientation oppression creates greater stressors for lesbians compared with heterosexual women, the combined effects of racism, heterosexism, and, for lesbians, sexism create intense stressors for ethnic minority gay men and lesbians (Morgan & Eliason, 1992). Gonsiorek (1982) discusses the anxiety-provoking nature of the coming-out process and the tendency for such anxiety levels to result in the expression of behaviors or feelings that may resemble symptoms of severe psychopathology. He cautions therapists against misinterpreting these symptoms and suggests that they may be indicative of the acute stress of coming out, rather than signs of underlying psychiatric disorder. The same advice holds true for minority clients. Whereas we may assume that the stress of coming out is intense for members of minority groups because they must manage multiple oppressions, we must also assume that individuals bring unique resources and vulnerabilities to this task. Ethnic minority group members, unlike their white counterparts, have often been forced to learn useful coping mechanisms against racism and discrimination. When confronted with managing other devalued aspects of their identities, they may call on the mechanisms used against racism to assist them. Problems occur when previously learned coping mechanisms are maladaptive or self-destructive, hence clients in this category are perhaps more vulnerable to the development of serious pathology. Other variables include not simply the mere presence of other stressors, but their intensity and the amount of foreground as opposed to background attention they warrant.

There are no empirical data available based on significant numbers of ethnic minority gay men and lesbians to justify more than clinical speculations in this area; however, it might be safe to say that it is somewhat easier for white gay men and lesbians to be out than it is for their ethnic minority counterparts. Smith, in Chapter 14 of this volume, discusses a range of issues that may make the process of coming out for members of ethnic minority groups very different from the process experienced by their white counterparts. Further research is needed.

The quiet toleration of gay and lesbian family members observed in many ethnic minority families is frequently marked by denial and the need to view gay and lesbian sexual orientation as something that exists outside the culture or something that is acquired through too much assimilation into the dominant culture. The concept of gay and lesbian sexual orientations as diseases acquired from whites or postures that are culturally dystonic is common among ethnic minority group members. Potgieter (Chapter 5, this volume) encountered such beliefs in her research with Black South African lesbians, despite evidence to the contrary. Tremble et al. (1989) suggest that attributing gay or lesbian sexual orientation to some outside source may in fact enable some families to accept a family member while removing themselves or that family member from any perceived sense of responsibility. Members of ethnic minority communities often view identity as if it were a singular entity. Identification with one's ethnic group is often perceived as if it were dichotomous or as if it mutually excludes other aspects of identity. Hence a person's being gay or lesbian is often viewed as a volitional repudiation of his or her ethnicity.

Ethnic minority gay men and lesbians find themselves confronted with racial stereotypes and discrimination in the broader gay and lesbian community. With the exception of those in big cities, most minority communities are not large enough to maintain a distinct gay and lesbian subculture of their own (Tremble et al., 1989). Hence interactions with members of the dominant gay and lesbian community become important outlets for social support and for meeting others. However, ethnic minority members commonly report discriminatory treatment in gay and lesbian bars, clubs, and other social gatherings within the gay and lesbian community (Chan, 1992; Dyne, 1980; Garnets & Kimmel, 1991; Greene, 1996; Greene & Boyd-Franklin, 1996; Gutierrez & Dworkin, 1992; Mays & Cochran, 1988; Morales, 1992). Many report feeling an intense sense of conflicting loyalties to two communities; they are marginalized in each community and are required to conceal important aspects of their identities to survive in each.

Ethnic minority gay men and lesbians frequently experience a sense of never being part of any group completely, leaving them at risk for feelings of isolation and estrangement and thus increased psychological vulnerability. When in the midst of groups of others like themselves, they may tend to idealize the group members. What follows is the expectation of a level of similarity, acceptance, being liked, and being understood in ways that never quite live up to the fantasy. Hence they may experience an awful sense of aloneness or disappointment or a heightened sense of not fitting in anywhere when these environments fail to meet all of their unrealistic expectations. Although the variance within ethnic groups may be as wide as the variance outside them, differences may be concealed by surface similarities that are very important.

Some clients with more serious preexisting psychopathology may tend to idealize people who are like them and devalue people who are not like them, rather than make judgments on a person-by-person basis. In some clients this may reflect a particular stage of gay/lesbian ethnic minority identity development. However, it may also represent their own deeply rooted sense of self-hate. In any case, such a stance increases clients' difficulty in getting support from the outside world by restricting the range of people from whom it may be obtained, and often fuels a self-fulfilling fear of being unable to get support. In more seriously disturbed clients this phenomenon of idealization and devaluation may rapidly alternate. Clients will idealize and then rapidly devalue the same part of themselves and, if known, that same part of their therapists. Ethnicity and sexual orientation are overdetermined characteristics for idealizing and devaluing stances, and such behavior may be most acute during the coming-out period or at other times of crisis.

Conclusion

Elements of the dominant culture have the potential to have negative effects on the health and psychological well-being of gay men and lesbians who are members of ethnic minority groups. Further, research on predominantly white, middle-class gay men and lesbians may obscure many of the issues relevant to ethnic minority group members. It is important for mental health practitioners to be aware of the unique combinations of stressors and psychological demands impinging on members of these and other ethnic groups, particularly the potential for isolation, anger, and frustration. Aside from being culturally literate, practitioners must develop a sense of the unique experiences of these clients with respect to the importance of their ethnic identities and sexual orientation, and the need to establish priorities in an often confusing maze of loyalties and estrangements.

References

Acosta, E. (1979, October). Affinity for Black heritage: Seeking lifestyle within a community. *Blade* (Washington, DC), pp. A-1, A-25.

Allen, P. G. (1984). Beloved women: The lesbian in American Indian culture. In T. Darty & S. Potter (Eds.), *Women identified women* (pp. 83-96). Palo Alto, CA: Mayfield.

Amaro, H. (1978). *Coming out: Hispanic lesbians, their families and communities.* Paper presented at the National Coalition of Hispanic Mental Health and Human Services Organization, Austin, TX.

Bass-Hass, R. (1968). The lesbian dyad: Basic issues and value systems. *Journal of Sex Research, 4,* 126.

Bell, A. P., & Weinberg, M. S. (1978). *Homosexualities: A study of diversity among men and women.* New York: Simon & Schuster.

Bradshaw, C. (1990). A Japanese view of dependency: What can Amae psychology contribute to feminist theory and therapy? *Women and Therapy, 9*(1-2), 67-86.

Carballo-Dieguez, A. (1989). Hispanic culture, gay male culture, and AIDS: Counseling implications. *Journal of Counseling and Development, 68,* 26-30.

Chan, C. S. (1987). Asian lesbians: Psychological issues in the "coming out" process. *Asian American Psychological Association Journal, 12*, 16-18.

Chan, C. S. (1989). Issues of identity development among Asian-American lesbians and gay men. *Journal of Counseling and Development, 68*, 16-20.

Chan, C. S. (1992). Cultural considerations in counseling Asian American lesbians and gay men. In S. H. Dworkin & F. J. Gutierrez (Eds.), *Counseling gay men and lesbians: Journey to the end of the rainbow* (pp. 115-124). Alexandria, VA: American Association for Counseling and Development.

Chasin, S. T. (1991, September/October). [Interview with Urvashi Vaid, executive director of the National Gay and Lesbian Task Force]. *Visibilities*, pp. 4-9.

Clarke, C. (1983). The failure to transform: Homophobia in the Black community. In B. Smith (Ed.), *Home girls: A Black feminist anthology* (pp. 197-208). New York: Kitchen Table.

Claybourne, J. (1978). Blacks and gay liberation. In K. Jay & A. Young (Eds.), *Lavender culture* (pp. 458-465). New York: Jove/Harcourt Brace Jovanovich.

Collins, P. H. (1990). Homophobia and Black lesbians. In P. H. Collins, *Black feminist thought: Knowledge, consciousness, and the politics of empowerment* (pp. 192-196). New York: Routledge, Chapman & Hall.

De Monteflores, C. (1986). Notes on the management of difference. In T. Stein & C. Cohen (Eds.), *Contemporary perspectives on psychotherapy with lesbians and gay men* (pp. 73-101). New York: Plenum.

Dyne, L. (1980, September). Is D.C. becoming the gay capital of America? *Washingtonian*, pp. 96-101, 133-141.

Espin, O. (1984). Cultural and historical influences on sexuality in Hispanic/Latina women: Implications for psychotherapy. In C. Vance (Ed.), *Pleasure and danger: Exploring female sexuality* (pp. 149-163). London: Routledge & Kegan Paul.

Espin, O. M. (1987). Issues of identity in the psychology of Latina lesbians. In Boston Lesbian Psychologies Collective (Ed.), *Lesbian psychologies: Explorations and challenges* (pp. 35-55). Urbana: University of Illinois Press.

Falco, K. L. (1991). *Psychotherapy with lesbian clients*. New York: Brunner/Mazel.

Garnets, L. D., & Kimmel, D. C. (1991). Lesbian and gay male dimensions in the psychological study of human diversity. In J. Goodchilds (Ed.), *Psychological perspectives on human diversity in America* (pp. 137-192). Washington, DC: American Psychological Association Press.

Gock, T. S. (1985, August). *Psychotherapy with Asian Pacific gay men: Psychological issues, treatment approach, and therapeutic guidelines*. Paper presented at the meeting of the Asian American Psychological Association, Los Angeles.

Gomez, J. (1983). A cultural legacy denied and discovered: Black lesbians in fiction by women. In B. Smith (Ed.), *Home girls: A Black feminist anthology* (pp. 120-121). New York: Kitchen Table.

Gomez, J., & Smith, B. (1990). Taking the home out of homophobia: Black lesbian health. In E. C. White (Ed.), *The Black women's health book: Speaking for ourselves* (pp. 198-213). Seattle, WA: Seal.

Gonsiorek, J. C. (1982). The use of diagnostic concepts in working with gay and lesbian populations. In J. C. Gonsiorek (Ed.), *Homosexuality and psychotherapy: A practitioners handbook of affirmative models* (pp. 9-20). Beverly Hills, CA: Sage.

Greene, B. (1986). When the therapist is white and the patient is Black: Considerations for psychotherapy in the feminist heterosexual and lesbian communities. *Women and Therapy, 5*(2-3), 41-66.

Greene, B. (1990, December). African American lesbians: The role of family, culture and racism. *BG Magazine*, pp. 6, 26.

Greene, B. (1994). Lesbian women of color: Triple jeopardy. In L. Comas-Diaz & B. Greene (Eds.), *Women of color: Integrating ethnic and gender identities in psychotherapy* (pp. 389-427). New York: Guilford.

Greene, B. (1996). The legacy of ethnosexual mythology in heterosexism. In E. Rothblum & L. Bond (Eds.), *Preventing heterosexism and homophobia* (pp. 59-70). Thousand Oaks, CA: Sage.

Greene, B., & Boyd-Franklin, N. (1996). African American lesbians: Issues in couples therapy. In J. Laird & R. J. Green (Eds.), *Lesbian and gay couples and families: A handbook for therapists* (pp. 251-271). San Francisco: Jossey-Bass.

Gutierrez, F. J., & Dworkin, S. H. (1992). Gay, lesbian, and African American: Managing the integration of identities. In S. H. Dworkin & F. J. Gutierrez (Eds.), *Counseling gay men and lesbians: Journey to the end of the rainbow* (pp. 141-156). Alexandria, VA: American Association for Counseling and Development.

Hidalgo, H. (1984). The Puerto Rican lesbian in the United States. In T. Darty & S. Potter (Eds.), *Women identified women* (pp. 105-150). Palo Alto, CA: Mayfield.

Icard, L. (1986). Black gay men and conflicting social identities: Sexual orientation versus racial identity. *Journal of Social Work and Human Sexuality, 4*(1-2), 83-93.

Jayakar, K. (1994). Women of the Indian subcontinent. In L. Comas-Diaz & B. Greene (Eds.), *Women of color: Integrating ethnic and gender identities in psychotherapy* (pp. 161-181). New York: Guilford.

Mays, V. M., & Cochran, S. D. (1988). The Black Women's Relationship Project: A national survey of Black lesbians. In M. Shernoff & W. A. Scott (Eds.), *A sourcebook of lesbian/gay health care* (2nd ed., pp. 54-62). Washington, DC: National Lesbian and Gay Health Foundation.

Mays, V. M., Cochran, S. D., & Rhue, S. (1993). The impact of perceived discrimination on the intimate relationships of Black lesbians. *Journal of Homosexuality, 25*(4), 1-14.

Meera (1993). Working together: An interview with Urvashi Vaid. In R. Ratti (Ed.), *A lotus of another color: An unfolding of the South Asian gay and lesbian experience* (pp. 103-112). Boston: Alyson.

Morales, E. (1992). Latino gays and Latina lesbians. In S. H. Dworkin & F. J. Gutierrez (Eds.), *Counseling gay men and lesbians: Journey to the end of the rainbow* (pp. 125-139). Alexandria, VA: American Association for Counseling and Development.

Morgan, K., & Eliason, M. (1992). The role of psychotherapy in Caucasian lesbians' lives. *Women and Therapy, 13*(4), 27-52.

Pamela H. (1989). Asian American lesbians: An emerging voice in the Asian American community. In Asian Women United of California (Ed.), *Making waves: An anthology of writings by and about Asian American women* (pp. 282-290). Boston: Beacon.

Parmar, P. (1992, June 14). *Flesh and paper: An interview* [S. Namjoshi, interviewee] (N. M. Kabir, Producer; P. Parmar, Director). New York: WNET.

Poussaint, A. (1990, September). An honest look at Black gays and lesbians. *Ebony*, pp. 124, 126, 130-131.

Ratti, R. (Ed.). (1993). *A lotus of another color: An unfolding of the South Asian gay and lesbian experience*. Boston: Alyson.

Smith, B. (1982). Toward a Black feminist criticism. In G. Hull, P. Scott, & B. Smith (Eds.), *All the women are white, all the Blacks are men, but some of us are brave* (pp. 157-175). Old Westbury, NY: Feminist Press.

Tremble, B., Schneider, M., & Appathurai, C. (1989). Growing up gay or lesbian in a multicultural context. *Journal of Homosexuality, 17*(3-4), 253-267.

Trujillo, C. (Ed.). (1991). *Chicana lesbians: The girls our mothers warned us about.* Berkeley, CA: Third Woman.

Vasquez, E. (1979). Homosexuality in the context of the Mexican American culture. In D. Kukel (Ed.), *Sexual issues in social work: Emerging concerns in education and practice* (pp. 131-147). Honolulu: University of Hawaii, School of Social Work.

Weinrich, J., & Williams, W. L. (1991). Strange customs, familiar lives: Homosexuality in other cultures. In J. C. Gonsiorek & J. D. Weinrich (Eds.), *Homosexuality: Research implications for public policy* (pp. 44-59). Newbury Park, CA: Sage.

Williams, W. L. (1986). *The spirit and the flesh: Sexual diversity in American Indian culture.* Boston: Beacon.

Wooden, W. S., Kawasaki, H., & Mayeda, R. (1983). Lifestyles and identity maintenance among gay Japanese-American males. *Alternative Lifestyles, 5,* 236-243.

11

Don't Ask, Don't Tell, Don't Know

The Formation of a Homosexual Identity and
Sexual Expression Among Asian American Lesbians

CONNIE S. CHAN

Although identity is a fluid concept in psychological and sociological terms, we tend to speak of identities in fixed terms. In particular, those aspects of identity that characterize observable physical characteristics, such as race or gender, are perceived as unchanging ascribed identities. Examples of these would include identifications such as *Chinese woman*, or *Korean American woman*, or even broader terms such as *woman of color*, which are ways of grouping together individuals who are not of the hegemonic "white" race in the United States. We base these constructions of identity upon physical appearance and an individual's declaration of identity. However, even these seemingly clear distinctions are not definitive. For example, I, as a woman of Asian racial background, may declare myself a woman of color because I see myself as belonging to a group of ethnic/racial minorities. However, my (biological) sister could insist that she is not a woman of color because she does not feel an affiliation with our

AUTHOR'S NOTE: This chapter is reprinted, by permission, from Connie S. Chan, "Don't Ask, Don't Tell, Don't Know: Sexual Identity and Expression Among East Asian-American Lesbians," in *The New Lesbian Studies: Into the Twenty-First Century*, edited by Bonnie Zimmerman and Toni A. H. McNaron (New York: The Feminist Press at The City University of New York, 1996), pp. 91-97.

group goals, even though she is a person of Chinese ancestry. Does her nonaffiliation take her out of the group of people of color? Or does she remain in regardless of her own self-identification because of her obvious physical characteristics? Generally, in the context of identities based upon racial and physical characteristics, ascribed identities will, rightly or wrongly, continue to be attributed to individuals by others. It is left up to individuals themselves to assert their identities and demonstrate to others that they are or are *not* what they might appear to be upon first notice.

The issue of *sexual* identity is more ambiguous still, whether taken as a concept by itself or in context with cultural, racial, ethnic, or gendered identities. With sexual identity, even more so than with other aspects of identity, it is generally those individuals who would be considered "sexual minorities," such as lesbians, gay men, and bisexuals, who define and declare their sexual identities. Unless there is a specific focus upon sexual orientation, few in the "majority" would identify as heterosexuals.

Given the assumption of heterosexuality as the norm, it is an inherent political statement to acknowledge a sexual identity. Even if it is one identity among several, and one is not prioritizing it over racial, ethnic, gendered, and professional identities, individuals who declare a sexual identity may become identified primarily in terms of their sexual identity. Perhaps it is because of this "primacy effect" of transgressive sexual identity that lesbians of color may be reluctant to take on a label of a sexual identity. When they do, it can overshadow their racial/ethnic identity, which affords a sense of social belonging and group cohesion. Research on Latina lesbians (Espin, 1987) and Asian American lesbians and gay men (Chan, 1989) has found that most respondents preferred to be validated for both their ethnic and lesbian/gay identities. Instead, their experience was that they were perceived as being primarily lesbian/gay once their sexual identities were known, negating their ethnic/racial identities as Latina or Asian American, or even their gendered identities as women.

Cultural background may also play a major role in determining how individuals include sexuality in their sense of identity. Non-Western cultures, such as East Asian cultures, may not have concepts of sexual identity comparable to the concept found in Western cultures. Western models of sexual identity development and paradigms of identity for the individual self may not be applicable to individuals who have non-Western cultural backgrounds. Although it is impossible to generalize about the characteristics of "people of color" as an inclusive group, or to group non-Western cultures together, some of the issues of sexual identity addressed in this chapter are applicable to other ethnic minority groups beyond the specificity of bicultural issues as they relate to East Asian Americans.

Because sexuality is contextual, what it means for a woman to have a sexual identity is related to the meaning given to sexuality for females in a particular culture. Thus the range of sexual behaviors considered acceptable—the forms of expression, the existence of a sexual identity, who may express which forms of sexuality—as well as what behaviors are perceived to be deviations from these norms are all cultural factors that must be considered in understanding the formation of sexual identity.

As a social movement, defining and declaring one's homosexual identity has been likened to the discovery of a map to be used in exploring "a new country" (D'Emilio, 1983). In the beginning of the lesbian/gay rights movement, by choosing an "out of the norm" sexual identity, such as identifying as a lesbian or as a gay man, individuals declared a separateness and individuality in sexuality that identified them as members of a self-defined sexual minority group. These declarations of identity were both individual and internal in a psychological sense, but also external and group based in a political and social sense. These identifications created an "identity politics" that was crucial in the making of a gay/lesbian movement as well as a civil rights movement.

Much as ethnic minority people of color defined themselves in terms of racial minorities in the 1960s and 1970s, homosexual men and women, by identifying and declaring a sexual minority status, chose to define themselves in a new category as a means of empowerment and group cohesion. To achieve this empowerment, both sexual minorities and racial minorities chose to accentuate, to draw attention to, aspects of their being that previously were viewed as negative and stigmatized (race or homosexuality), and to express pride, not shame, at their minority status.

It has been widely accepted in psychology that individuals who affirm previously stigmatized identities generally pass through several stages of development en route to embracing their new identities. Vivienne Cass's (1979) model of homosexual identity formation has frequently been cited as describing the process through which an individual develops an integrated identity as a homosexual person. Cass's six stages begin with the premise that an individual starts with an initial self-awareness that some of his or her feelings and behaviors can be defined as homosexual, which creates conflict about a sexual (and perhaps social) identity that had previously been defined as heterosexual. From this basic premise of self-awareness, the individual goes through stages in which she or he accepts, has pride in, and finally integrates a lesbian/gay identity with other aspects of self.

This model, although generally perceived as universally applicable, does not exist within a vacuum, and it presupposes that there are favorable social conditions that must be present to allow for the affiliation and identification described to occur. In Stages 4 and 5, for instance, individuals seeking identity acceptance have increased contact with other homosexuals and immerse themselves in homosexual culture and community. A lesbian/gay presence in some urban areas in some countries allows this to occur far more readily than in places where no homosexual culture exists.

Moreover, a sexual identity is not merely a naming of how one perceives one's own sexuality or sexual expression; it is also a political identity. There are individuals who do not consider themselves lesbian or gay who engage in sexual activity with same-sex partners; there are also individuals who consider themselves lesbian or gay who do not have sexual contact with same-sex partners. What was once known as a homosexual identity developed into a lesbian/gay identity as sexual orientation became a strategy for group formation and cohesion, and as a way to address discrimination. In the context of identity politics, a lesbian or gay identity developed into a form of resistance against conformity and restriction. The trend toward a queer theory and culture takes this resistance one step further in its refusal to fit into the fixed categories of heterosexual, homosexual, or bisexual, by creating a greater flexibility in sexual politics and naming sexual identity.

The significance of the naming is crucial, however, to the construction of a sexual identity. If, as Foucault has noted, without the name, there is only the "half life of an amorphous sense of self," is this the situation, now, at the end of the 20th century, where Asian American lesbians and gay men find themselves? In their Asian cultures of origin, Asian Americans do not have the categories of lesbian, gay man, and bisexual as identities by which to define themselves. Thus it is not only the lack of categories but also a fundamental difference in the construction of sexuality, sexual expression, and sexual identity, as well as identity itself, that has resulted in a limited concept or no concept of sexual identity as we know it in the Western sense.

A crucial distinction between traditional East Asian culture and Western culture is the concept of sexuality and sexual expression as a private matter. Any direct and open discussion of sexuality is unusual in East Asian cultures, as sexuality is considered to be a very sensitive subject. Even among one's closest friends, a discussion about sexuality is considered to be awkward and highly embarrassing at best, and at worst, strictly taboo (Tsui, 1985). This extreme discomfort with open and direct discussion of sexuality is sometimes misread and misconstrued by Westerners as *asexuality* or as an extreme repression of sexual interest on the part of Asian Americans. Both perceptions, though common, are incorrect. However, what is presented publicly is very different from what is tolerated and expressed in private with sexual intimates.

The distinction between private and public selves is an important concept in East Asian culture. The public self is that which conforms to gendered and familial role expectations and seeks to avoid actions that would bring shame not only upon oneself but also upon one's family. Within the Asian part of an Asian American's culture, there is little support for an *individual* public identity of any kind beyond the role one is expected to play within the family. As a psychological concept of self-definition, an individual's identity, forged against a backdrop of societal forces, may be perceived as universal, but it is in fact a Western concept. In East Asian cultures such as Chinese, Japanese, and Thai, the concept of individual identity, whether by self-definition or ascribed, may not exist. Instead there is only group identification and identity as a family member, a social role that is related to an assignment of one's place in society.

Much as there is no identity outside of the family role, there is no concept of a sexual identity or of external sexual expression in the Asian part of the culture beyond the familial expectation of procreation. Sexuality would rarely be expressed in the context of the public self; it is usually expressed only within the private self. Especially for women, the private self is never seen by anyone other than an individual's most intimate family and friends (in some cases, women may choose never to reveal their private selves to anyone). The dichotomous nature of the public self and the private self is far more distinct than in Western cultures, where there is more fluidity between the two. The relevance of this public/private split within Asian cultures is that not only is there very little public expression of sexuality, but private expressions of sexuality may take on different forms for Asian Americans than would be the norm in Western cultures. One example of this would be in erotic behavior, which may be expressed only privately and in far more indirect ways than are generally found among Westerners. Many such behaviors might be misperceived as nonerotic in nature by Westerners, who are unaccustomed to very subtle nuances, such as a change in the register of the voices of two women having a conversation; minimal physical contact, such as the brush of a hand against another person; language patterns that might reflect affection but are indiscernible to the casual observer; and quick glances, perhaps holding a gaze just a second longer than might be expected. With private sexual expression, what outsiders see is not necessarily what is being conveyed; one must be familiar with the cultural nuances to understand.

Popular and erotic images of Asians contribute to the myth of asexuality or passivity in sexual expression among Asians, particularly Asian females. For Asian American women, the historical visual sexual images in film have been two basic types: the Lotus Blossom Baby (a.k.a. China Doll, Geisha Girl, shy Polynesian beauty) and the Dragon Lady (prostitute, devious madam). Asian women in film are, for the most part, passive figures who exist to serve men (Tajima, cited in Fung, 1991). Because Asian women are supposedly passive and compliant, both sexually and in relation to men, they have been "fetishized in dominant representation," in stereotypical roles that certainly limit the range of sexuality depicted. Moreover, in the absence of a body of lesbian pornography, whether in film or magazines, images of Asian lesbians are rarer still in widely distributed markets. Even Chinese American women novelists such as Maxine Hong Kingston, Amy Tan, and Gish Jen, although they explore bicultural issues, do not represent Asian American women strongly as sexual beings of *any* orientation.

Two notable exceptions are the short documentary *Women of Gold*, which profiles Asian lesbian athletes at the 1990 Gay Games, and poetry, essays, and stories written by Asian American lesbian writers Kitty Tsui, Willyce Kim, and Merlo Woo. In one of Kitty Tsui's (1983) poems, she describes her attempts to integrate both aspects of her total identity, her lesbian self with her Chinese American self, while at a dinner banquet with her extended family. There is slightly more inclusion of Asian American lesbian and gay representation in lesbian/gay literature, but without accessible representations of Asian lesbian women that are erotic and politically viable, media images provide little support for a lesbian or bisexual identity among Asian Americans that is not a hegemonic, Western cultural identity.

Thus it appears that the paradigms of sexual identity formation and sexuality to which we in the West are accustomed must be adapted if we are to understand the "Asian" cultural influence upon sexual expression in Asian American lesbians. Only if sexuality and homosexuality can be expressed without disrupting the integrity of an individual's prescribed role within the family can it be tolerated. With only a sketchy identity as a person distinct from the identity as a member of a family, having a sexual identity or identifying an "alternative lifestyle" may be literally inconceivable except to those who are relatively highly acculturated into a Western identity. As a result, there is a common perception that proportionately fewer lesbian, gay, and bisexual Asian Americans are "out" compared with non-Asians. If that perception is numerically accurate, it can be explained by cultural prohibitions against public expression of sexual orientation.

In the case of Asian Americans who identify as being openly lesbian, it is likely that they are relatively acculturated into and have been influenced by American or Western culture. A study of lesbian/gay Asian Americans supports this concept, indicating that Asian American lesbians and gay men, although preferring to be affirmed for both sexual and ethnic aspects of their identities, if forced to choose between affiliations, identified more closely with the lesbian/gay, as well as American cultural, aspects of their selves (Chan, 1989). This study's sample population of self-identified Asian American lesbians and gay men was already skewed toward a population that might be considered to be more assimilated and Westernized, because the subjects considered themselves to be lesbian or gay. Even so, some of the results give us an indication that Asian American lesbians and gay men respond to pressures from both their cultures, Asian and American. Respondents were more likely to come out to non-Asians than to other Asians, reflecting the pressure to maintain privacy within the Asian culture. Many others had not disclosed their sexual identity to their parents, even though they had been out a mean of 6.2 years. Responding to American expectations, some did report wanting to belong and feel part of a gay and lesbian community, and even sought out dates with white lesbians/gay men to feel more comfortable with the hegemonic "lesbian/gay scene."

Summary

In conclusion, sexual identity is not an essential fixed given for any individual, nor is it developed within a vacuum. Lesbian and gay identities have evolved over a 200-year span in the West, heavily influenced by social and political conditions, including the initial sexual categorization by sexologists, the formation of male homosexual identity, the construction of the "New Woman" stereotype in the early 20th century, and the politicization of lesbian, gay, bisexual, and queer identities in the past two decades.

But these modern homosexual identities are still Western constructs. There are no comparable sexual identities in East Asian culture. Even for a Chinese woman in Beijing to have a lesbian identity, and well she might, she has to define herself through Western cultural concepts. An Asian American who is defining a sexual identity must also adapt Western models of sexuality and sexual expression to meet her own needs. At the same time, Asian American lesbians have to respond to East Asian cultural influences that require a different set of demands on family responsibilities, privacy, and the forms of sexual expression that are considered to be acceptable for females. Balancing the Western pressure to come out and be openly lesbian against the Asian cultural demand for privacy requires juggling contradicting forces. Whereas some women may never openly admit or act upon their homosexuality, others will embrace the Western model enthusiastically; still others will be openly lesbian only in safe, generally non-Asian, environments.

However, the East Asian cultural restrictions upon open expression of sexuality may actually create less of a dichotomization of heterosexual versus homosexual behavior. Instead, given the importance of the concept of having only private expression of sexuality, there could actually be more allowance for fluidity within a sexual behavioral continuum. The cultural prohibition against defining or declaring sexual orientation/identity may ironically result in a broader range of acceptable behaviors even as public identities are more rigidly defined.

Lesbian studies and women's studies have tended to focus upon the evolution of people whose primary political and "ethnic" identification is gay, and who have been able to organize a multidimensional way of life on the basis of their homosexuality. But we need to focus upon other forms of homosexuality, other ways in which homosexual relations have been organized, understood, named, and left deliberately unnamed (Chauncey, 1989). We need to be careful not to view the evolution of a homosexual identity only through a Western lens, expecting, perhaps, that non-Western cultures, with modernization, will eventually follow the same course in achieving greater openness concerning homosexual behavior. Cultural differences in the construction of identity and in the expression of sexuality have to be taken into account. We are just beginning to know which questions to ask.

References

Cass, V. C. (1979). Homosexual identity formation: A theoretical model. *Journal of Homosexuality, 4*(3), 219-235.

Chan, C. S. (1989). Issues of identity development among Asian-American lesbians and gay men. *Journal of Counseling and Development, 68*, 16-20.

Chauncey, G., Jr. (1989). Christian brotherhood or sexual perversion? Homosexual identities and the construction of sexual boundaries in the World War I era. In M. Duberman, M. Vicinus, & G. Chauncey, Jr. (Eds.), *Hidden from history: Reclaiming the gay and lesbian past* (pp. 294-317). New York: New American Library.

D'Emilio, J. (1983). *Sexual politics, sexual communities. The making of a homosexual minority in the United States 1940-76*. Chicago: University of Chicago Press.

Espin, O. M. (1987). Issues of identity in the psychology of Latina lesbians. In Boston Lesbian Psychologies Collective (Ed.), *Lesbian psychologies: Explorations and challenges* (pp. 35-55). Urbana: University of Illinois Press.

Fung, R. (1991). Looking for my penis: The eroticized Asian in gay video porn. In Bad Object Choices (Ed.), *How do I look? Queer film and video* (pp. 145-160). Seattle: Bay.

Tsui, A. (1985). Psychotherapeutic considerations in sexual counseling for Asian immigrants. *Psychotherapy, 22*, 357-362.

Tsui, K. (1983). *The words of a woman who breathes fire*. San Francisco: Spinsters Ink.

12

The Relationships Among Self-Esteem, Acculturation, and Lesbian Identity Formation in Latina Lesbians

MARTA A. ALQUIJAY

The exploratory research described in this chapter investigated the relationships among self-esteem, acculturation, homosexual identity formation, and socioeconomic status and other demographic factors in Latina lesbians. The relationship between self-esteem and group membership, particularly in groups that do not hold high status in North American culture, is not well understood. There are varying opinions as to the importance of the relationship between these constructs. In early studies, Rosenberg (1965) found no support for the assumption that self-acceptance (high self-esteem) in ethnic minority-status individuals is related to the prestige held by their group. More recently, some researchers have suggested a relationship between self-esteem and group identification (Bohon, Singer, & Santos, 1993). Still others suggest that specific factors, such as conscious choice about one's ethnic identification and active interest in learning about one's cultural heritage, influence the relationship between self-esteem and group membership (Marcia, 1966; Phinney & Alipuria, 1990).

One of the underlying assumptions of this study was that the process of acculturation and the process of lesbian identity formation are two ways in which an individual claims group membership. It was further assumed that self-esteem is related to group membership in a group of subjects who self-identified as Latina lesbians. In particular, it was conceptualized that high self-esteem would afford the individual tools that would facilitate the process of moving from one to another master identity (i.e., heterosexual to homosexual identity and acculturation). Additionally, it seemed likely that skills learned in the process of acculturating by Latinas could be generalized onto the process of lesbian identity formation. This would in turn give the individual who is familiar with the process of acculturation a greater skill level when confronted with the prospect of developing a homosexual identity.

Thus the central question of this study was, Does higher self-esteem enable a woman to develop more fully a concept of herself as a Latina and as a lesbian, given the fact that these are stigmatized identities in North American society? In an effort to answer this question, three hypotheses were proposed. First, it was predicted that socioeconomic status (SES) would be significantly correlated with homosexual identity development. That is, the higher the subject's SES, the more comfortable she would be with her homosexual identity. Second, it was expected that after SES was controlled for, self-esteem would predict homosexual identity group membership. More specifically, it was expected that the higher the subject's self-esteem, the more comfortable she would feel about her homosexual identity. Finally, it was expected that after SES was controlled for, cultural typology (as measured by the Cultural Life Style Inventory; Mendoza, 1989) would predict homosexual identity group membership in such a way that those individuals who scored in the Cultural Incorporation typology were expected to be more comfortable than other subjects about their homosexual identity.

Subjects

The subjects in this study were 92 self-identified Latina lesbians living in Southern California. As this population is not one that is easily accessible, the sample was nonrandom. Subjects were contacted through friendship pyramiding and snowball methods (Nemeyer, 1980; Oberstone & Sukoneck, 1976); through lesbian organizations, including support groups and political and cultural organizations; and through friendship networks. The majority of the participants (*n* = 40) were born in the United States; the second-largest group consisted of subjects who were born in Mexico (*n* = 25). Of the remainder, 16 were born in Central American countries, 6 in Caribbean countries, and 5 in South American countries. Within the group of 52 immigrants, the mean number of years living in the United States was 16.70, with a standard deviation of 11.56 years. Their ages ranged from 19 to 62 years, with a mean of 32.92 years and a standard deviation of 8.98 years. The average age at migration was 17.20 years, with a standard deviation of 9.32 years. Their annual household incomes ranged from below $15,000 to more than $60,000. It is interesting to note that 33% had income levels below $15,000 per year, and only 13% had annual incomes above $60,000, despite the fact that 44.6% had some college education and 41.3% had earned college degrees. These income statistics may reflect the cumulative effects of wage inequities for women, people of color, and homosexuals. The subjects' endorsements of homosexual identity using Cass's six stages was collapsed into three groups: 12% of the subjects ($n = 11$) endorsed Group 1 (Stages 1 and 2), 42% of the subjects ($n = 39$) endorsed Group 2 (Stages 3 and 4), and 46% ($n = 42$) endorsed Group 3 (Stages 5 and 6), reflecting greater commitment to a lesbian identity.

The instrument used to measure self-esteem was the Coopersmith Self-Esteem Inventory, adult, short version (Coopersmith, 1990). Reliability for this instrument has been estimated using Spanish-surnamed, Black, and Anglo children, adolescents, and young adults. It is a self-report questionnaire consisting of 25 questions. The raw score is multiplied by 4 to obtain a full score. Subjects scoring within the upper quartile are considered to have high self-esteem, and scores falling within the lower quartile are considered to reflect low self-esteem.

Acculturation was measured using the Cultural Life Style Inventory (Mendoza, 1989), a 29-item, self-report instrument. This instrument can produce three different typologies of acculturation: The *Cultural Resistance* typology reflects an individual who either actively or passively refuses to acquire the cultural norms of the host culture, maintaining those of the native culture; an individual who substitutes the norms of the host culture for those of the native culture would be expected to endorse items in the *Cultural Shift* typology; finally, the *Cultural Incorporation* typology reflects an individual who adapts customs from both the native and the host cultures. The Cultural Life Style Inventory is designed to determine whether each of these typologies is a dominant or nondominant style for the individual. The *Cultural Non-dominance* typology reflects an individual who does not endorse any of the above typologies as a dominant lifestyle, and who may have all of them present to some degree in one of the five dimensions measured by the instrument. These dimensions include intrafamilial language use, extrafamilial language use, social affiliations and activities, cultural familiarity and activities, and cultural identification and pride. With the permission of the author of the inventory (R. H. Mendoza, personal communication, December 1992), the items in the instrument were modified to reflect more accurately the population being studied. Reliability for this instrument has been measured through examination of its internal consistency, temporal stability, and equivalence for the Spanish and English versions using Mexican American and Anglo-American populations.

Homosexual identity development was measured using Cass's (1979) Homosexual Stage Allocation Measure. Cass describes profiles that represent the stages of homosexual identity development. The instrument lists seven paragraphs describing different types of people. The first paragraph is a baseline reflecting a heterosexual individual, and the following paragraphs describe incrementally progressive endorsements of a homosexual identity, reflecting the six stages postulated by Cass: Identity Confusion, Identity Comparison, Identity Tolerance, Identity Acceptance, Identity Pride, and Identity Synthesis. For this study, these stages were collapsed into three groups: Group 1 was made up of Stages 1 and 2, Group 2 consisted of Stages 3 and 4, and Group 3 comprised the last two stages. Endorsement of the initial stages on the scale indicates a minimally developed homosexual identity, whereas endorsement of the latter stages reflects a highly developed homosexual identity. Although Cass's instrument has not been the subject of thorough statistical analysis, it has been used in a number of unpublished studies (Cohen-Ross, 1984; Gellman, 1985; Rhoads, 1982; Sommers, 1982). Cohen-Ross (1984) found that individuals whose sexual attraction, behavior, and fantasy are exclusively homosexual, as measured by the Kinsey Scale of Sexuality (Kinsey, Pomeroy, Martin, & Gebhard, 1953), and who had high self-esteem endorsed the more evolved stages of homosexual identity development in Cass's measure.

A demographic questionnaire was developed specifically for this study. It is a 24-item instrument that includes questions regarding age, socioeconomic status, education, and relationship status as well as the Kinsey Scale of Sexuality. Subject's level of education, household annual income, and occupation were combined to measure socioeconomic status. All instruments were made available in both English and Spanish. All were self-administered in groups of three to eight subjects, and required approximately 20 to 30 minutes to complete.

Results

Hypothesis 1 predicted that socioeconomic status would significantly correlate with homosexual identity development, such that the higher the SES, the more comfortable the subject would feel with her lesbian identity. SES was made up of three factors that were analyzed separately: occupation, income, and educational level. The hypothesis was only partially supported. Occupation was found to have a significant positive correlation with homosexual identity group membership ($r = .34, p = .002$). Therefore, subjects with occupations rated highly on Hollingshead and Redlich's (1958) scale of values for different occupational groups were more likely to endorse Stage 5 or 6 of Cass's measure than were those who had lower-rated occupations. Neither income nor education level was found to have a significant correlation with homosexual identity development.

Hypothesis 2 predicted that after SES was controlled for, level of self-esteem would significantly predict level of homosexual identity development. It was expected that the higher the self-esteem, the more comfortable the individual would be with her homosexual identity. Self-esteem was not found to be significant in predicting homosexual identity group membership. Here it is worth mentioning that the scores obtained by the subjects in this study on the self-esteem measure were significantly different from what might have been expected. Whereas Coopersmith (1990) has generally found the mean score to fall within a range of 70-80, with a standard deviation of 11-13, the mean score in this study was 40.86, with a standard deviation of 12.90.

Hypothesis 3 predicted that after SES was controlled for, cultural typology would significantly predict level of homosexual identity. That is, it was expected that individuals who scored dominantly in the Cultural Incorporation typology would be more comfortable with their homosexual identity. Unfortunately, an insufficient number of subjects scored within the Cultural Incorporation typology ($n = 5$) to include this group in the analysis. Therefore, the hypothesis was not supported. The remaining three classifications—Cultural Resistance, Cultural Shift, and Cultural Non-dominance—were analyzed. Cultural Resistance was found to be significant in predicting membership in Group 1 of homosexual identity ($\overline{\chi}$ = .73). Group 1 was made up of the first two stages of homosexual identity development, Identity Confusion and Identity Comparison. Cultural Shift and Cultural Non-dominance were not found to be significant in predicting membership in a homosexual identity group ($\overline{\chi}$ = .31 and $\overline{\chi}$ = .36). Predictor variables accounted for 14.4% of the total variance in homosexual identity group membership.

Supplementary analyses were carried out after a discriminant function analysis revealed that the predictor variables (SES and Cultural Typology) are best at differentiating between Group 1 (Stages 1 and 2) and the remaining two groups of homosexual identity combined (Stages 3-6). Thus the latter four stages were further collapsed into one group and compared with the two earlier stages. This procedure yielded a significant relationship among education and Cultural Resistance typology as predictors of homosexual identity group membership ($\overline{\chi}$ = 13.92, df = 6, p = .03). Specifically, it was found that Latina lesbians in Stages 3 through 6 of Cass's measure are more likely to have higher levels of education ($\overline{\chi}$ = 2.54) than are those in Stages 1 and 2 ($\overline{\chi}$ = 1.82; $F[1, 90]$ = 6.70, p = .01). Conversely, those in Stages 1 and 2 of the Homosexual Stage Allocation Measure are more likely to score in the Cultural Resistance typology ($\overline{\chi}$ = .73) than are those in Stages 3-6 ($\overline{\chi}$ = .33, $F[1, 90]$ = 6.70, p = .01).

The remaining analyses addressed questions asked in the demographic questionnaire and their relationship to homosexual identity. In these analyses, homosexual identity groups were not collapsed. It was found that subjects' self-ratings on the Kinsey Scale of Sexuality correlated significantly with their self-ratings on the Homosexual Stage Allocation Measure. Specifically, those subjects who endorsed the more exclusively homosexual range of Kinsey's scale were also more likely to endorse the more evolved stages of homosexual identity development on Cass's scale. Subjects were also asked about their intent to have sex with a male in the future. Those women who reported that they planned to have sex with a male in the future (72.7%) also endorsed the earlier stages (Identity Confusion and Identity Comparison) of Cass's measure. Only 7.7% of subjects in Group 2 (Identity Tolerance and Identity Acceptance) and 2% of those in Group 3 (Identity Pride and Identity Synthesis) reported plans to have sex with a male in the future. Thus for this group of lesbians, intention to have sex with a male in the future is significantly related to homosexual identity stage.

Information was also collected with regard to subjects' participation in the lesbian and gay community. It was found that 71.4% of those women who identified in the latter stages of homosexual identity development (Stages 5 and 6) belonged to some form of support, political, or social group in the lesbian and gay community. Only 38.5% of those endorsing Stages 3 and 4, and 36.4% of those endorsing Stages 1 and 2, of homosexual identity development belonged to any such group. Finally, subjects were asked whether they attributed their homosexuality to their being "born that way" or to their "choosing" to be homosexual. Responses to this question were not significantly related to level of homosexual identity development. Within the total subject pool, there was a tendency to attribute homosexuality to being "born that way": 66% of the subjects responded that they were born homosexual, 23% responded that they chose to be homosexual, and 11% gave "other" answers. Among those who gave other reasons, answers ranged from "I don't know" to "It doesn't matter, I'm just glad that I am."

Discussion

The focus of the study was the investigation of the relationships among self-esteem, cultural typology, and homosexual identity in Latina lesbians. Additionally, variables such as socioeconomic status, subject's self-rating on the Kinsey Scale of Sexuality, intent regarding future sexual activity with a male, participation in the lesbian and gay community, and the way in which a subject explained her homosexuality were explored in relation to homosexual identity development.

Socioeconomic Status and Homosexual Identity

With regard to SES, three variables were studied: income, education, and occupation. In the original analysis, occupation significantly correlated with homosexual identity group membership: The higher the occupational rating, the stronger the lesbian identification. In a sup-

plementary analysis, education was also found to correlate with homosexual identity. Subjects with higher educational levels were more
likely to rate themselves in Stages 3 through 6 of Cass's measure.
Income was not found to correlate significantly with homosexual
identity.

These findings reflect an interesting relationship between income
and education as well as occupational levels. As stated earlier, despite
relatively high percentages in the sample of women with some college
education and even college degrees, a disproportionately small number of the subjects earned annual incomes of $45,000 to $60,000 or
above. It is commonly accepted that women still earn 70 to 80 cents for
each dollar earned by men. Furthermore, people of color tend to be
underpaid for work equivalent to that done by their white counterparts. Similar discrimination in employment and pay is faced by
lesbians and gay men. Latina lesbians in this study seem to be faced
with cumulative discrimination resulting from membership in three
"minority" status groups, making the discrepancy between their level
of education and occupational status and the amount of money earned
more pronounced. This may explain the finding that although occupational and educational levels significantly correlated with homosexual
identity, income did not. It may be that for Latina lesbians, a higher-
status job, which has been linked with higher job satisfaction, may
provide psychological, social, and material resources that facilitate
homosexual identity development. Higher occupational status seems
to denote more power than income for Latinas (Bohon et al., 1993).
Such power may translate into self-confidence to define oneself and
integrate all aspects of the identity regardless of society's judgment of
any of those aspects. The subjects in this study expressed their clarity
with regard to self-definition and integration by endorsing the more
evolved stages of the Homosexual Stage Allocation Measure. They
were more likely to identify as lesbians, despite the fact that this is a
stigmatized identity within North American culture.

Although Latina lesbians in this study may be facing greater obstacles in terms of their earning power, they seemed to have developed
coping strategies based on factors other than income. This may reflect
a greater adherence to traditional Latina/o values, which do not place
as great an emphasis on material wealth as does the North American,
Anglo culture. It may also be that the subjects in this study are aware
that their incomes are not a fair representation of their professional

worth, and this awareness may make income a less salient factor for them in terms of self-confidence. This assumption may be further supported by the finding that subjects in this study had higher levels of education than the population at large. Higher levels of education have been linked with greater awareness about sociological issues (e.g., racism, sexism, and heterosexism) and their impacts upon individuals' lives. Higher educational levels have also been linked with increased ability to manage finances.

Educational level was found to be more significant in making a gross differentiation between the first two stages of homosexual identity development and the final four stages. This finding may suggest that although education is significantly related to homosexual identity development, this relationship may have an impact only at a particularly crucial time in the development, and then level off. Here it may be helpful to note that one of the hallmarks of the first two stages of identity development, as postulated by Cass, is confusion. Level of education may play an important role in providing the tools necessary for an individual to progress from the confusion of the first two stages on to later development. However, once an individual has accepted the concept of homosexuality as one that has personal relevance, it is likely that positive support and facilitative resources are more useful for helping the individual continue her development along the continuum of homosexual identity. This assumption is supported by the finding that those women who were more involved in the lesbian and gay community were more likely to endorse more evolved levels in Cass's measure.

The fact that it was necessary to collapse the six stages first into three and then into two distinct groups may suggest that the process of homosexual identity development involves fewer stages than Cass has postulated. Models of homosexual identity development involving fewer stages have been suggested by Troiden (1979) and Bourne (1990). The failure of the variable of education to differentiate between the latter stages may also be taken as support for a shorter model of identity development. However, education's impact on the process of homosexual identity development in this study may also be mitigated by the area in which the subjects live. It may be that living in Southern California, specifically Los Angeles, as the majority of the subjects did, may provide the tools that formal education provides in otherwise more restricted environments. Here I am referring to the relatively wide range of services and resources available and the large size and visibility of the lesbian and gay community in the Los Angeles area. The relatively "progressive" attitude toward homosexuality found in urban areas may also have a facilitative effect on homosexual identity development. Thus in a less progressive, more rural area where the lesbian and gay community is not readily accessible, education may play a greater role in homosexual identity development than it does in an area such as Los Angeles, where its impact may be diminished.

Self-Esteem and Homosexual Identity

Global self-esteem, as measured by the Coopersmith Self-Esteem Inventory, adult, short version, was not found to be a significant predictor of level of homosexual identity development. In this study the mean score obtained by the subjects was lower and the range of scores wider than have been reported in other studies. The lack of significant results may support Rosenberg's (1979) assertion that there is no connection between the status of an individual's group within the larger culture and that person's self-esteem. In light of more recent findings, it is more likely that global self-esteem is not linearly related to the status held by the group with which one identifies. Bohon et al. (1993) found that using the long form of the Coopersmith question-naire and analyzing it using five different factors (global self-esteem, social-power self-esteem, family relations self-esteem, significance to others self-esteem, and decision-making self-esteem) resulted in a significant difference between the self-esteem of Anglo- and Mexican Americans. The findings in the present study may also suggest that the manner in which self-esteem is conceptualized does not reflect univer-sal values. Varying cultural norms may prescribe that self-esteem be expressed in ways other than what present instruments measure. The concept itself may take on different meanings in relation to different cultures or within the context of otherwise diverse groups. For exam-ple, current mainstream definitions of self and, by implication, self-esteem focus on individuality and independence. In cultures where interdependence is valued, the concepts of self and self-esteem may take on different meanings. The Latina/o culture as well as the more woman-identified lesbian culture may adhere to values of interde-pendence and cooperation that would necessitate a different approach to measuring self-esteem within these communities.

The lower scores obtained by the subjects may also be interpreted as reflecting the impacts of multiple stigmatizations upon identity. Latina lesbians, who are likely to be subject to prejudice based on ethnicity, gender, and sexual orientation, must deal with a number of stressors simultaneously. This may overburden their ability to cope and may reduce self-esteem levels. However, although the subjects did obtain relatively low self-esteem scores, they simultaneously endorsed more evolved stages of homosexual identity, a finding that has been correlated with healthier overall adjustment (Cohen-Ross, 1984; Gellman, 1985; Rhoads, 1982). It is likely, then, that their scores on the self-esteem measure are more reflective of the inappropriateness of the measure for this population than of actual self-esteem levels.

Cultural Lifestyle Typology and Homosexual Identity

Subjects in this study were categorized into three groups reflecting the Cultural Resistance, Cultural Shift, and Cultural Non-dominance typologies. The number of subjects scoring within the Cultural Incorporation typology ($n = 5$) was too small for statistical analysis. Only the Cultural Resistance typology was significant in predicting homosexual identity development. A high percentage of subjects scoring within the Cultural Resistance typology also scored in Group 1 of homosexual identity development (Stages 1 and 2). No significant number of subjects scoring within the Cultural Resistance typology endorsed the more evolved stages of homosexual identity development (Stages 3-6). This finding must be evaluated carefully, as the number of subjects involved in the analysis was small ($n = 11$).

This finding suggests that those individuals who are less acculturated may be more traditional in terms of their attitudes toward homosexuality and therefore less evolved in that aspect of their identities. It is generally assumed that individuals who are less acculturated into U.S. mainstream society have more negative views toward homosexuality. However, this assumption is not fully supported by the findings of researchers who have looked at attitudes toward homosexuality in communities of color. For example, Morales (1990) asserts that Mexicans have more homophobic attitudes than do other groups, but Bonilla and Porter (1990) report that the relationship between ethnicity and attitudes toward homosexuality is a complex one. Bonilla and

Porter found that Latinas/os were more tolerant than African Americans, and just as tolerant as whites, on the moral dimension of attitudes toward homosexuality. Conversely, on the civil rights dimension of attitudes toward homosexuality, less acculturated Latinas/os were less tolerant than were members of the other two groups. Thus the impact of acculturation on attitudes toward homosexuality cannot fully account for the finding. Looking at what is involved in the earlier phases of both processes may give us a better idea of what the relationship reflects.

As mentioned earlier, the first two stages of homosexual identity development as postulated by Cass are characterized by crisis regarding personal identity, social alienation, confusion, and turmoil, among other things. Similarly, the first stages of acculturation may include feelings of inefficiency within the host culture (Alva, 1985). It may be that individuals scoring within the Cultural Resistance typology of the Cultural Life Style Inventory have not acquired a sense of efficiency that would facilitate their ability to manage the mainstream culture. This same sense of inefficiency may prevent their further progress into the latter stages of homosexual identity development. Mendoza (1989) has also noted that positive experiences within the host culture have been negatively correlated with Cultural Resistance. This would imply that individuals scoring within the Cultural Resistance typology may not have had positive or supportive experiences within the host culture. This may reflect a diminished support system. A lack of sources of support and connection to the lesbian and gay community may also keep an individual from evolving into the latter stages of homosexual identity development. This is suggested by findings in this study that individuals in the earlier phase of homosexual identity development participated up to 50% less often within the lesbian and gay community than those endorsing the more evolved stages. It is likely, then, that there are other factors at work creating the significant relationship between less evolved homosexual identity and Cultural Resistance typology. It is possible that these individuals are feeling a lack of a sense of efficacy, which prevents them from furthering both their homosexual identity development and their process of acculturation. This situation may be exacerbated by a lack of support systems.

Neither Cultural Shift nor Cultural Non-dominance was found to be significant in predicting stage of homosexual identity. It may be that although both homosexual identity development and acculturation are affected by similar factors initially, their progression may be dependent on different processes. Alternatively, it may be that our ability to measure these processes is not sophisticated enough to measure any significant relationship that exists.

An interesting finding in this study was that a significant number of subjects scored in the Cultural Non-dominance direction. R. H. Mendoza (personal communication, February 1993) has noted that this is a current trend. This trend may be reflective of possible changes in the process of acculturation, or it may reflect the increased complexity of the dynamics of acculturation within the context of a multicultural environment such as Los Angeles. It has been noted that the metropolitan Los Angeles area contains the greatest number of diverse ethnicities represented within the United States; 92 different languages are spoken within the Los Angeles school system alone. It is not unusual for a person living in Los Angeles to eat a typical "American" breakfast, have Central American food for lunch, and then have Thai food for dinner. Thus the behaviors that have traditionally been thought of as defining cultural allegiance may not be applicable within this context. An individual scoring in the Cultural Non-dominance typology, then, may not be one who is marginalized in terms of her or his cultural identity; rather, she or he may be expressing multiculturalness in ways that the current scoring system does not recognize.

Supplementary Analysis

As stated earlier, subjects who rated their experiences as being predominantly to exclusively homosexual also endorsed the later stages of homosexual identity development. Likewise, those who reported no intention to engage in sexual activity with men in the future also endorsed Stages 3 through 6 of the Homosexual Stage Allocation Measure. These findings lend support to the construct validity of Cass's scale and to the appropriateness of these instruments for use with Latina lesbians. The result may also reflect a decreased level of confusion and increased clarity about one's object of sexual and romantic attraction. Subjects who found themselves in Stages 5 and 6 of the Homosexual Stage Allocation Measure also were more likely to be involved in social, political, or support groups within the lesbian and gay community. Thus this type of participation may be an important facilitative factor in the development of a more evolved homosexual identity. Exposure to the lesbian and gay community may provide greater possibilities for the development of awareness and development of a support system as well as create greater demands on the individual to commit to a lesbian identity.

Limitations

The nature of the subject selection process used for this study limits the study's generalizability/external validity. The need to use nonrandom strategies is a common problem faced by researchers who are attempting to access subjects in communities that are not readily available. Subjects in this study do not seem representative of all Latina lesbians; rather, they represent those who live in Los Angeles and have higher levels of education, higher-status occupations, and greater commitment to a lesbian identity than most. The instruments used pose an additional limitation. None of the instruments used in the present research has been designed specifically for or normed on Latina lesbians. This is a common problem faced by researchers interested in cross-cultural studies, and it has become urgently important that we develop such instruments.

Specifically, with regard to the Cultural Life Style Inventory, the present results support Mendoza's assertion that the instrument is in need of revision. The scoring criteria may need to be altered, and an item analysis may be helpful for choosing items that more accurately measure cultural typologies. The assessment of self-esteem within ethnically or otherwise diverse groups continues to be problematic. The construct validity may be questionable for this study's population. Studying self-esteem in terms of various factors, as suggested by Bohon et al. (1993), may yield more useful data than looking at it from a global perspective.

A final limitation arises from the use of self-report questionnaires. The validity of data collected in this manner has been questioned. Accuracy depends on a range of factors, including subjects' capacity for insight and honesty in responding. The use of self-report instruments is widespread, however. Such instruments are useful for comparisons of results from various studies using the same or similar instruments, and they tap into individuals' beliefs and feelings regarding issues related to themselves.

Implications for Clinical
Intervention and Assessment

This study's findings suggest that clinicians working with Latina lesbians must be prepared to address psychosocial issues related to ethnicity, gender, and sexual orientation, in addition to issues presented by the clients. In an effort to help a client clarify her sexual orientation, it may be helpful for a therapist to aid her in exploring the extent of her sexual and romantic behaviors, attractions, and fantasies, as well as her plans regarding future sexual contact with males. Clients who are in the initial stages of homosexual identity development may benefit greatly from education regarding homosexuality. This education may take the form of cognitive interventions, bibliotherapy, referrals to educational films and television programs, and referrals to lesbian and gay community organizations that provide educational resources and activities. The findings of this study also suggest that those clients who are in the more evolved stages of homosexual identity development may benefit from participation within the lesbian and gay community, such as in social, political, and support groups. Clinicians who work with lesbian or gay clients need to be familiar with such resources in order to refer their clients appropriately. Clinicians also need to be aware of the triple levels of discrimination faced by Latina lesbians and their impact on these women's daily lives. Mere awareness of all the obstacles they face may help Latina lesbians to develop alternative coping strategies. Clinicians also need to be aware that Latina lesbians may define and express self-esteem in ways that differ from those of other clients.

The results of this study also suggest that Cass's Homosexual Stage Allocation Measure is a valuable tool when used with Latina lesbians who are U.S.-born as well as with those who are immigrants from various Latin American countries. (It is important to note again that the subjects in this study had relatively high educational levels and occupational status and were relatively highly evolved in terms of their homosexual identity.) Further, the results suggest that the measure may be most effective for distinguishing gross divisions between the first two of Cass's stages and the latter four.

References

Alva, S. A. (1985). The political acculturation of Mexican American adolescents. *Hispanic Journal of Behavioral Sciences, 7,* 345-364.

Bohon, L. M., Singer, R. D., & Santos, S. J. (1993). The effects of real-world status and manipulated status on the self-esteem and social competition of Anglo-Americans and Mexican-Americans. *Hispanic Journal of Behavioral Sciences, 15,* 63-79.

Bonilla, L., & Porter, J. (1990). A comparison of Latino, Black, and Non-Hispanic white attitudes toward homosexuality. *Hispanic Journal of Behavioral Sciences, 12,* 437-452.

Bourne, K. A. (1990). *By the self defined: Creating a lesbian identity.* Unpublished doctoral dissertation, University of Southern California.

Cass, V. C. (1979). Homosexual identity formation: A theoretical model. *Journal of Homosexuality, 4*(3), 219-235.

Cohen-Ross, J. (1984). *An exploratory study of the retrospective role of significant others in homosexual identity development.* Unpublished doctoral dissertation, California School of Professional Psychology, Los Angeles.

Coopersmith, S. (1990). *Coopersmith Self-Esteem Inventory: Manual* (8th ed.). Palo Alto, CA: Consulting Psychologists Press.

Gellman, B. (1985). *Sexual function and dysfunction in homosexual males.* Unpublished doctoral dissertation, California School of Professional Psychology, Los Angeles.

Hollingshead, A. B., & Redlich, E. C. (1958). *Social class and mental illness.* New York: John Wiley.

Kinsey, A. C., Pomeroy, W. B., Martin, C. E., & Gebhard, P. (1953). *Sexual behavior in the human female.* Philadelphia: W. B. Saunders.

Marcia, J. (1966). Development and validation of ego-identity status. *Journal of Personality and Social Psychology, 3,* 551-558.

Mendoza, R. H. (1989). An empirical scale to measure type and degree of acculturation in Mexican American adolescents and adults. *Journal of Cross-Cultural Psychology, 20,* 372-385.

Morales, E. S. (1990). Ethnic minority families and minority gays and lesbians. In F. W. Bozett & M. Sussman (Eds.), *Homosexuality and family relations* (pp. 217-239). New York: Harrington Park.

Nemeyer, L. (1980). Coming out: Identity congruence and the attainment of adult female sexuality. *Dissertation Abstracts International, 36,* 6394B. (University Microfilms No. 80-24138)

Oberstone, A., & Sukoneck, H. (1976). Psychological adjustment and lifestyle of single lesbians and single heterosexual women. *Psychology of Women Quarterly, 1,* 172-188.

Phinney, J. S., & Alipuria, L. (1990). Ethnic identity in college students from four ethnic groups. *Journal of Adolescence, 13,* 171-183.

Rhoads, A. (1982). *Personality characteristics of single and coupled male homosexuals.* Unpublished doctoral dissertation, California School of Professional Psychology, Los Angeles.

Rosenberg, M. (1965). *Society and the adolescent self-image.* Princeton, NJ: Princeton University Press.

Rosenberg, M. (1979). *Conceiving the self.* New York: Basic Books.

Sommers, M. (1982). *The relationship between present social support networks and current levels of interpersonal congruency of gay identity.* Unpublished doctoral dissertation, California School of Professional Psychology, Los Angeles.

Troiden, R. R. (1979). Becoming homosexual: A model of gay identity acquisition. *Psychiatry, 42,* 362-373.

13

Sexual Identity and the Discontents of Difference

CARLA M. TRUJILLO

I often think of our sexual identities and wonder what factors might influence how we develop them. Many scientists currently devote a great deal of time, energy, and money to exploring the merits of theories of social construction (Weinrich, 1987), genetic predisposition (Hamer, Hu, Magnuson, Hu, & Pattatucci, 1993), and small hypothalamus (LeVay, 1991). (For an excellent analysis of these issues, see Byne, 1995.) The detailed discussion that these complex theories warrant is beyond the scope of this chapter, however, the reader is referred to other sources below. It was Sigmund Freud (1905/1961) who originally postulated that we are all born inherently bisexual. Perhaps, to a certain extent, many of us are. With that in mind, I raise the following question: How much of our sexual or romantic attractions, our sexual orientations, are contrived or housed in an arena of only culturally acceptable or constructed thoughts and behaviors, influenced by many powerful factors?

Inculcating Models

With relatively few exceptions, many of our inculcating models for sexual identity are largely heterosexual. For many it is our parents and some additional combination of our schools, news and entertainment media, peers, and religion. Researchers exploring the origins of sexual

266

orientation have asked gay men and lesbians when they first felt they were attracted to others of the same sex. Many have reported that it was early in life, whereas for others it was much later (Boxer & Herdt, 1993, p. 5; Wishik, 1995). Generally speaking, the largest number of gay men and lesbians in the United States come out in their early 20s (Wishik, 1995). Sexual identity, and the concomitant practice of it, even for heterosexuals, seems to be formed earlier, but tends to solidify around this age (Boxer & Herdt, 1993, p. 8). Because our models while we are growing up are largely heterosexual, we lesbians, gay men, and, to a certain extent, bisexuals have to begin the process of disengaging the identity-forming influence of heterosexuality before we can confront ourselves and come out (Pierce, 1995). A lesbian or a gay man must disengage her or his rationalization system of heterosexual modeling both socially and physically. I am not equating desire with modeling. Rather, I am simply stating that we have to open ourselves up to consider other models of identity. We must contend with *what* we are attracted to in very conscious ways, whereas most heterosexuals can follow the predetermined dominant cultural script. It seems this must be a conscious act even if the process of rationalization goes against it. For example, in a support group for lesbians for which I acted as facilitator, one participant stated that neither she nor her woman partner of 5 years had ever referred to themselves as lesbians. When I asked how they did identify themselves, they simply remarked that they were two women who happened to be together. Obviously, one of them came to some kind of clarity, otherwise she would never have come to a support group explicitly designated for lesbians.

Many people possess extensive denial systems that are amazing in their power to influence behavior. It can be extremely difficult for some people to disengage themselves from the models through which we are socialized. In this regard, many institutions seek to keep us from confronting ourselves by imposing guilt, disgust, shame, and self-hatred on us before, during, and even after we engage in that confrontive process. Negative judgment of any sexuality is a remarkably difficult parameter to navigate around, and obviously it is much more difficult for those who are not heterosexual. How we behave sexually is part of our core identity (Boxer & Herdt, 1993, p. 179). We can amass positive, mixed, or negative concepts of our cultures or ethnicities. We can choose, and as people of color we often do, to participate in multiple identities—outwardly, inwardly, emotionally, and intellectually—

regarding these self-concepts. However, the process of sex and its relation to attraction and love are entities that are deeply entrenched in the deepest aspects of our being. These entities of sex and love are aspects of self that we are continually attempting to negotiate. We can deny their existence, but we usually do not do well when we attempt to circumvent our authentic desires (Penelope, 1992, p. 43).

Sexual Options

The insidious effects of racism, sexism, classism, and homophobia also extend into our senses of identity and sexuality. We have seen and heard much about how these factors influence who we are and how others regard us (Pierce, 1995). Each serves to undermine our sense of character, its development and potential, in ways that we are probably not even conscious of. Who we are—that is, how we form our identities —could be influenced by the choices we make among the options available to us. In living our lives we are given options for defining or fulfilling ourselves. Sexually, we are also given options, some more limiting than others.

I am fully aware that I have greater opportunities to fulfill myself in my sexuality than others who have been in my position. I am Chicana. I grew up poor, and my parents did not possess any formal education. I was attracted to women as early as I can remember. The attraction continued. As a child I was consciously aware of my attraction to girls, but I did not think I had any options other than to marry a man or to remain unmarried. By becoming economically self-sufficient and (with extreme difficulty) rejecting familial expectations, I expanded my options. Somehow in this process I disengaged heterosexual modeling and incorporated as much positive relearning as I could. I am still confronted with societal negation of my lifestyle and am often besieged by the negative repercussions of homophobia and discrimination. Despite having to cope with discrimination, I know that I have greater opportunities for positive sexual identity than do many people in the United States and throughout the world.

In Laura Esquivel's *Like Water for Chocolate* (1994), which is set in Mexico, a young Mexican girl born last in her family is not allowed by family tradition ever to marry. Instead, she is obliged to live with and take care of her mother until she dies. This brings to mind the multitudes of gay men and lesbians who have had to and must continue to conform to familial and/or societal traditions of marriage. I make no claims as a historian, but evidence in many forms indicates that there have always been men and women born attracted to the same sex (see, e.g., Boswell, 1980; Duberman, Vicinus, & Chauncey, 1989; Faderman, 1992; Katz, 1976; Watanabe & Jun'ichi, 1989). Given limitations in options vis-à-vis the aforementioned constructs of class, economics, and patriarchy, many lesbians and gay men probably married, denied or downplayed their desires, partook in them surreptitiously, or entered the church in an attempt to suppress sexuality altogether in celibacy.

If we look at sexuality and the practice of it from a global perspective, we can see how many people remain limited in fulfilling their true desires. Many people in certain countries cannot publicly acknowledge same-sex attractions for fear of retribution. Some lesbians and gay men have suffered death as a penalty for their sexual orientation or sexual behavior in countries such as Peru. In such countries, lesbians and gay men live in dread of being found out (Chauvin, 1991). When gays or lesbians in Peru seek to get together with others in their country, or to organize themselves, they must adhere to clandestine methodologies much akin to underground group survival tactics and the old social survival tactics of lesbians and gay men in the United States. Human rights organizations have reported that sexual minorities in Mexico have repeatedly been subject to murder, allegedly by death squads and with implicit government approval (International Gay and Lesbian Human Rights Commission, 1993). It has been indicated that the police either have been directly involved or have simply looked the other way. In Brazil, between 1980 and 1985, unidentified groups murdered more than 1,500 persons who were members of sexual minorities ("Solidariedade," 1995). In Ecuador, more than 100 gay men have been assassinated since 1987 by unidentified assailants ("Ecuador Murders," 1992). In the United States, hate crimes against gays and lesbians have increased, from 697 reported incidents in 1988 to 1,898 reported in 1992 (National Gay and Lesbian Task Force, 1992, p. 12). These figures do not include, of course, unreported crimes or attacks, nor do they reflect the increasing numbers of voter initiatives against gay rights. Recall in the 1980s how Cuba decided to rid itself of its "undesirables." Purges of Cuban gays and lesbians were commonplace. A gay man or lesbian in Cuba often had to sneak around at great length just to sleep with his or her partner. Those who were caught were jailed. Hence when they found opportunities to go to the United States, many did so (personal communication with "Maria Elena," September 14, 1982).

Most Asian languages do not have a word meaning "lesbian" (Pamela H., 1989). This may or may not be related to the common belief that Asian lesbians do not exist at all. When my edited volume *Chicana Lesbians: The Girls Our Mothers Warned Us About* was first published in 1991, many Chicanos remarked to me that they had not thought Chicana lesbians even existed. I responded that there were at least 26 of us right there in the volume who they could ponder over. Other countries are known for openly discriminating against lesbians and gay men as well. Russia and other nations that were part of the former Soviet Union arrest and imprison men suspected of being gay (Gessen, 1994). This is taking place although change is slowly occurring as gay and lesbian groups become more visible. Another basic consensus of many in the former Soviet Union is that lesbians do not exist there either. In many American Indian tribes, lesbians and gay men were once referred to as "two-spirit" people, accepted and treated with respect (Whitehead, 1993). Due to the pervasive homophobic attitudes of the United States and other conquering nations, most Native American lesbians and gay men are no longer accorded this kind of reverence and acceptance. If anything, many are ridiculed and discriminated against (Gould, 1994). (Tafoya discusses Native American gay and lesbian issues more extensively in Chapter 1 of this volume.)

From a global perspective, homophobia and its consequences result in countless people having limited options from which to choose in living their lives as gay or lesbian people, if they live them at all. Controlling human bodies and minds and engaging in the ideology of the presumed superiority of heterosexuality, many countries (including the United States) institute laws based in social mores and ideologies that subsequently control the sexualities of their people. This also occurs, of course, for heterosexual women. This social control extends into the realm of personal fulfillment and satisfaction for many women, lesbians, and gay men. Homophobia, with its roots in sexism, imposes itself in insidious forms of domination throughout Western and non-Western consciousness.

Sexuality, then, in accordance with its tie with identity, can be regarded as a privilege. The fact that I can be an out lesbian and not formally persecuted by the U.S. government is a privilege. Concomitantly, my identity, which is affected by the options or limitations afforded me, is influenced by how much I can practice and be fulfilled in my sexuality. It would indeed be liberating if I, or any lesbian, were allowed to love another woman and be supported in that love without having to feel that my or her identity is intrinsically connected to it. But because of social scripts, their confines, and the discriminatory practices of U.S. society, there is no recourse for an out lesbian but to have sexual orientation constantly integrated into her collective and daily consciousness. This occurs to such an extent that it can become a focal point—as it has for me and many others—in defining who we are as persons. It seems that when an individual is consistently negated, she or he must consistently "negate the negation" (N. Alarcon, Mujeres Activas en Letras y Cambio Social, Summer Research Institute, personal communication, August 1990). This can often take an emotional toll. Although the energy used to remain in the closet is far greater than that used in being out, I maintain that the energy required simply to *be* a lesbian or gay man exceeds the energy needed to be heterosexual.

Hence not only are sexuality and its practice regarded as privileged constructs, so is identity, especially when it is connected to sexuality. In the case of gay men, lesbians, and transgendered people, this relationship is painfully apparent. The amount of privilege I am given to practice my sexuality coincides with the effect of that privilege on my identity's potential. Identity politics, then, is created as a strategy for change and empowerment because it becomes a necessity for personal fulfillment (Perez, 1994). W. E. B. Du Bois's term "dual consciousness" (1897) and Michael Omi and Howard Winant's (1986) theorizing on race relations apply to gay men's and lesbians' need to contend with what I view as a form of "triple consciousness." First, we must contend with what society thinks of us. This is Omi and Winant's conceptualization of a "macro identity" (pp. 66-67). As illustrated, the various forms of discrimination, bias, and acceptance that society metes out to us control and affect the development of identity. They impose a direct, often physically overt, connection. Second, we must also contend with how we think of ourselves, regardless of what society thinks of us. Here we attempt to develop our potential in response to our true inner selves, the inner desires of love, attraction, and sex. This is the inner self I alluded to earlier in this chapter. Third, we have to contend with the dissonance of how we think of ourselves in response to what society thinks of us. If society contends that we as gay men or lesbians are "sexually deviant" and "pathological"—historically the definition of homosexuality as a mental disorder defined by the American Psychiatric Association (1974) and perpetuated by other societal, familial, religious, and criminal justice systems—then we must formulate a defense or reaction to these contentions. This results in varying degrees of self-love/hate, denial, and acceptance. This is where "gay positive" movements originate and create strategies for social change. These three levels of consciousness affect us simultaneously and to varying degrees. They act as agents in defining, encouraging, allowing, and constraining our ability to integrate our "true selves" fully with all the other elements that form our identities. Hence the necessity arises for me, as Gayatri Chakravorty Spivak (1990) has noted, of essentializing myself as a woman, a Chicana, and a working-class lesbian as a strategy for politicking. Ideally, I do not want my race, class, gender, or sexuality to be an issue, or a basis for mistreatment, special treatment, or disregard. My preference is to have people look at me as a *human being*. Realistically, however, in most cases this does not happen. Out of fear and ignorance, people either seek the lowest common denominator, stereotype, or render me invisible, both of which produce similar results. When this occurs, and it does occur, I find myself struggling for air in an effort to regain my humanity or protect my injured heart. Therefore, I must participate in a contradiction—the contradiction of essentializing the very aspects of my difference. This is to keep myself from disappearing. This is a tool necessary for my survival.

New Movements

There is a contemporary view that we are on the brink of great change. During the 1980s, a large amount of activism took place, resulting primarily from the AIDS crisis. This activism, propelled by groups such as ACT-UP and gay and nongay supporters, made us much more difficult to disregard. Even more, the major Democratic Party candidates in the 1992 election declared their support for gays and lesbians, and activists took it upon themselves to make our presence more public, using savvy, image-conscious techniques in an attempt to change Americans' attitudes. David B. Mixner, the primary strategist in bringing the gay and lesbian community together with the Clinton administration, was quoted in the *Los Angeles Times* as saying, "We are more than just a political entity, more than just a special interest group. . . . We are a civil-rights movement" (Rothman, 1995, p. M3). Sexual identity is now beginning to be connected with pride and strength. It is interesting to see how the United States is slowly coming to grips with the concept that gay and lesbian people are human beings. Yet the military still insists that gay men will be committing sodomy in bunkers. Realistically, it seems highly unlikely that anyone would be thinking of sodomy if missiles were going off around him. What do you suppose lesbians would be thinking about in bunkers? As usual, no one ever wants to speak about us or ask what we might be thinking about in bunkers, even though lesbians constitute an estimated 25% of the military (Shilts, 1993). One lesbian who had served in the military, when interviewed on CNN (April 24, 1993), put it this way: "Well gosh, if they got rid of all us gays and lesbians they'd have to start a draft."

It seems, however, that the real point for many gay men and lesbians who are involved in this issue is an attempt, through acceptance in the military, to prove our "normalcy." Because many of us so dearly wish to be regarded as "normal human beings," we fail to engage in any critical analysis of what we are doing in our efforts to be considered "normal." Being "normal" can mean anything from "I am gay and I am a Republican" to "I am gay and I am an accountant." With the latter point of identity as referent, many of us hope that Americans will see something to which they too can relate. This, as a comparative example, was why many African American novelists in the 19th century incorporated such main characters as the stereotypical tragic mulatto, in the hope that they could display some aspect of "humanity" (read: whiteness) in Black folks that white folks could relate to (Christian, 1985). A similar problem exists today for many gay men and lesbians who fail to analyze what they are saying and doing about the military's policy. For example, Mixner has observed that he never thought that he would support the presence of gay men and lesbians in the military. Historically, he has been opposed to the military. However, because he believes that serving in the military is a human right, he feels compelled to advocate for that right for lesbians and gay men who wish to serve, despite his personal opposition to the institution on principle (Golden, 1993). Others have pointed out to me that the military is a crucial barrier to integration. Some gay political analysts believe that admittance to the military is the first step toward acceptance in society and point specifically to the example of African Americans (Thompson, 1993). This is an extremely complex argument that should be examined closely. However, one thing is sure. Regardless of the course members of the gay and lesbian community pursue in their battle to serve openly, we must continue to question the motives and actions of the military and to maintain a critical perspective in examining our own efforts to become a part of it.

Though we have seen some positive trends, the fight for equality is obviously anything but over. It is only now really beginning. People usually fail to acknowledge how often gay, lesbian, bisexual, and transgendered people have been at the vanguard of new thoughts and ideas, nor do they recognize how many of us have been active agents in other civil rights movements. Many women of color have argued previously about the instrumental role women of color have played in fighting for recognition and validation of differences between human beings. Many others have contended that as women of color, as lesbians of color, we cannot and should not be forced to choose between our racial identities and our sexuality. Both encompass unique and integral aspects of ourselves. Close examination of the works of Cherríe Moraga, Gloria Anzaldúa, and the late Audre Lorde reveals that they never separated themselves or their concerns from their communities, nor have they denied their sexuality in the process. To be either cast out by our ethnic communities for being gay or negated by our gay communities for being persons of color reflects retrograde ideology. These struggles have not been resolved, yet, thankfully, there are increasing numbers of gay, lesbian, bisexual, and transgendered people of color who have become cognizant of their differing "marginalities" and are unwilling to separate them. Many gay and lesbian people of European descent are also beginning to recognize that the voices of people of color *do* matter, and that they can no longer disregard our input or downplay our differences.

Perhaps due somewhat to the widening of the recognition of difference and lessening feelings of the need for conformity, identity seems to be becoming more fluid in the gay and lesbian community. When I came out 15 years ago, the lesbian communities I lived in worked intensely to try to convince me to act, look, and think within certain modalities. This was part of the costume, part of the philosophy, part of other lesbians' being able to recognize who you were when you were seen in public. Even how we were supposed to have sex was dictated by strict guidelines. Although I can now publicly admit that I never did as I was told, I certainly would not acknowledge it back then. Instead, I quietly contended with the limitations of lesbian feminist dogmatism while seeking and usually finding other women who felt, albeit quietly, as I did.

While I served as editor for the now-defunct magazine *Out/Look*, I was often confronted with transgressive personalities/identities in the gay and lesbian community. I met lesbians who identified as lesbians and slept with women exclusively, women who slept with women and with men on occasion, women who slept with gay men only, and women who slept with no one.

Sexual behavior no longer seems confined exclusively by identity criteria. With regard to how I wish to carry myself in the lesbian world, I can be a butch, a femme, neither, or both. Actually, I could not be a butch, at least not according to the spell checker on my computer. It failed to recognize *butch* as the proper word to use in this chapter. Rather, it recommended four other options: *bitch, batch, botch,* or *beach.* I then asked for its preference, and it said *botch.* So I could be a botch or a femme, neither or both. I can shave, not shave, pierce, have long or no hair, wear makeup, dresses or pants, boots or high heels. I can join practically any kind of social support or interest group and find gay or lesbian people whose interests match my own. No longer will I find lesbians only in dark, unmarked bars owned by mafiosi. In fact, many of those bars no longer exist, perhaps because of wider recognition of who we are, assisted by the many people who have come out of the closet and by those who have joined the AA movement. I can be many things and still consider myself a lesbian. I can be a separatist, or have many men friends, have children any way I want, and even some heterosexuals will stand up for my rights. The fluidity of our lesbian/gay identities is apparently no longer hampered by rigid ideologies and behaviors.

Unfortunately, this still does not mean that we are accepted or free from persecution. As I noted earlier, the mere existence of sexual identity confines us. I can be fired from my job, beaten, or killed for being a lesbian. In almost every aspect of daily living, from work, marriage, and adoption even to the right to be considered a family member for purposes of visiting my partner in a hospital, I am still discriminated against. I am continuously dehumanized, disregarded, and marginalized. And because I am a lesbian of color, I am still largely ignored, as are most women of color, whether they are heterosexual or lesbian.

I am invalidated by my family and stereotyped in the minds of many. I am charged by the mainstream with personalizing too much, suspected by my own communities for "succeeding" in the white heterosexual world. I am granted conditional acceptance by some and receive minimal toleration by others. I am desperately attempting to live, amid all this prejudice and negation, a life as positive and fully self-actualizing as I can.

However, I speak up when people tell me I should not. I question my own as well as everyone else's motivations. I fight for my integrity when others tell me to give up. I believe that I will still learn, change, and grow. Finally, I continue to hope that, with enough people around me who are finally seeking to confront their homophobia, their racism, and sexism, ultimately I and others like me will not always feel the need to speak up against my negation. I might actually be able to settle back and relax. I could use a rest.

References

American Psychiatric Association. (1974). *Diagnostic and statistical manual of mental disorders* (2nd ed.). Washington, DC: Author.

Boswell, J. (1980). *Christianity, social tolerance, and homosexuality: Gay people in Western Europe from the beginning of the Christian era to the fourteenth century.* Chicago: University of Chicago Press.

Boxer, A., & Herdt, G. (1993). *Children of horizons.* Boston: Beacon Press, pp. 6, 8, 179.

Byne, W. (1995). Science and belief: Psychobiological research on sexual orientation. In J. P. De Cecco & D. A. Parker (Eds.), *Sex cells and same-sex desire: The biology of sexual preference* (pp. 303-344). New York: Haworth.

Chauvin, L. (1991, March 18-24). Struggling in Peru. *Boston Gay Community News,* p. 8.

Christian, B. (1985). *Black feminist criticism: Perspectives on Black women writers.* Elmsford, NY: Pergamon.

Duberman, M. B., Vicinus, M., & Chauncey, G., Jr. (Eds). (1989). *Hidden from history: Reclaiming the gay and lesbian past.* New York: New American Library.

Du Bois, W. E. B. (1897, August). Strivings of the Negro people. *Atlantic Monthly, 80,* 194-198.

Ecuador murders part of a campaign of harassment. (1992, April). *Gay Times,* p. 20.

Esquivel, L. (1994). *Like water for chocolate.* Garden City, NY: Doubleday.

Faderman, L. (1992). *Odd girls and twilight lovers: A history of lesbian life in twentieth-century America.* New York: Penguin.

Freud, S. (1961). Three essays on the theory of sexuality. In J. Strachey (Ed. & Trans.), *The standard edition of the complete psychological works of Sigmund Freud* (Vol. 7). London: Hogarth. (Original work published 1905)

Gessen, M. (1994). *The rights of lesbians and gay men in the Russian Federation.* San Francisco: International Gay and Lesbian Human Rights Commission.

Golden, D. (1993, June 6). Mixner's moment. *Boston Globe Magazine,* pp. 14-15, 30-44.

Gould, J. (1994). Disobedience (in language) in texts by lesbian Native Americans. *Ariel: A Review of International English Literature, 25*(1), 32-43.

Hamer, D. H., Hu, S., Magnuson, V. L., Hu, N., & Pattatucci, A. M. L. (1993). A linkage between DNA markers on the X chromosome and male sexual orientation. *Science, 261,* 321-327.

International Gay and Lesbian Human Rights Commission. (1993, February 17). *Anti-gay violence continues in Mexico: Gay leader assassinated* (Press release). San Francisco: Author.

Katz, J. N. (1976). *Gay American history: Lesbians and gay men in the U.S.A.* New York: Crowell.

LeVay, S. (1991). A difference in hypothalamic structure between heterosexual and homosexual men. *Science, 253,* 1034-1037.

National Gay and Lesbian Task Force. (1992). *Anti-gay violence, victimization, and defamation in 1992.* Washington, DC: Author.

Omi, M., & Winant, H. (1986). *Racial formation in the United States.* New York: Routledge & Kegan Paul.

Pamela H. (1989). Asian American lesbians: An emerging voice in the Asian American community. In Asian Women United of California (Ed.), *Making waves: An anthology of writings by and about Asian American women* (pp. 282-290). Boston: Beacon.

Penelope, J. (1992). *Call me lesbian: Lesbian lives, lesbian theory.* Freedom, CA: Crossing.

Perez, E. (1994). Irigaray's female symbolic in the making of Chicana lesbian *sitios y lenguas* (sites and discourses). In L. Doan (Ed.), *The lesbian postmodern* (pp. 104-117). New York: Columbia University Press.

Pierce, C. (1995). Rejecting, denying, tolerating. In H. Wishik & C. Pierce (Eds.), *Sexual orientation and identity* (pp. 47-75). Laconia, NH: New Dynamics.

Rothman, C. (1995, September 3). David Mixner: Will the gay vote turn out for Clinton in 1996? *Los Angeles Times,* p. M3.

Shilts, R. (1993, April 16). A groundbreaking look at gays in the military. *Larry King Live,* CNN.

Solidariedade entre gays e punks. (1995, June 17). *Jornado de Brasil,* p. 17.

Spivak, G. C. (1990). Practical politics of the open end: Interview with Sara Harasym. In S. Harasym (Ed.), *The post-colonial critic: Interviews, strategies, dialogues* (pp. 95-112). New York: Routledge.

Thompson, D. (1993, December 17). Appellate judges question military's gay policy. *Sacramento Bee,* p. A3.

Trujillo, C. M. (Ed.). (1991). *Chicana lesbians: The girls our mothers warned us about.* Berkeley, CA: Third Woman.

Watanabe, T., & Jun'ichi, I. (1989). *The love of the samurai: A thousand years of Japanese homosexuality*. London: GMP.

Weinrich, J. D. (1987). *Sexual landscapes: Why we are what we are; why we love whom we love*. New York: Scribner's.

Whitehead, H. (1993). The bow and the burden strap: A new look at institutionalized homosexuality in Native North America. In H. Abelove, M. Barale, & D. Halperin (Eds.), *The lesbian and gay studies reader* (pp. 498-527). New York: Routledge.

Wishik, H. (1995). Appendix D: Childhood experiences. In H. Wishik & C. Pierce (Eds.), *Sexual orientation and identity* (pp. 191-207). Laconia, NH: New Dynamics.

14

Cultural Diversity and the Coming-Out Process
Implications for Clinical Practice

ALTHEA SMITH

The coming-out process is defined as the experience of acknowledging a gay, lesbian, or bisexual sexual orientation to oneself and others. In this paradigm, coming out is characterized by a person's development and acceptance of her or his homosexuality and homosexual identity (Hopcke, 1992). In many cases, coming out has surfaced in the psychological literature as an individual's sexual development related to self-acceptance and self-esteem.

In the social discourse about coming out, there are many common assumptions that may be of questionable validity but often go unchallenged. One assumption is that the process of coming out is a singular constellation and is dichotomous. That is, a person is either out or not. It is also presumed that acknowledging a gay/lesbian or bisexual sexual orientation, especially to heterosexuals, can reduce the level of homophobia, as it provides others with positive role models of non-stereotypical gay, lesbian, and bisexual people. Disclosing one's sexual orientation is also thought to be a ubiquitously positive experience that creates self-acceptance and confidence through repeated practice. In fact, for gay men and lesbians, not making public pronouncements about their sexual orientation is presumed to be negative and less than healthy psychologically and is characterized by negative terms, such as *hiding, being in the closet,* and *being closeted.* Hiding or being closeted is presumed to indicate shame, denial, and self-hatred. In various

forms, these assumptions have found their way into the conceptuali-
zations of research on coming out, clinical work with clients, and
treatment considerations. Most of these assumptions, however, are
based on clinical and empirical studies conducted with White lesbians
and gay men. Lesbians and gay men of color have received scant
attention in the psychological literature. In this chapter I explore some
issues and raise some questions about coming out as a process that is
always embedded in a cultural context that can profoundly shape the
experience of that process for individuals. Further, I discuss the importance of cultural context in psychotherapy with lesbian, gay, and
bisexual clients.

Coming Out: Research

In recent years there has been much research and expanding interest
in the process of coming out for lesbian and gay people. The research
on coming out currently available in the psychological literature defines it as the outcome of a successful process of gay, lesbian, and
bisexual identity development. An important distinction here is that I
view coming out to be as much a process as an outcome. Dempsey
(1994) describes a stepwise linear model that includes four stages of
coming out: sensitization, identity confusion, identity assumption,
and identity commitment. It is presumed that being stuck in one of the
first three of these stages can contribute to a person's remaining in the
closet. An implicit assumption in the goal of encouraging an individual
to come out is that coming out is a positive, monolithic, linear, stagelike
process that happens once in a person's lifetime. According to another
model, the coming-out process occurs in six specific stages: feeling
different, acknowledging one's homosexuality, disclosure to others,
acceptance of homosexual identity, exploration and experimentation,
and intimacy (Martin, 1991).

Others have described the process of coming out as a time of
reckoning with losses. Thompson (1992) notes that such losses include
the loss of a heterosexual lifestyle, loss of the rituals of marriage and
divorce, loss of societal acceptance of one's relationships, and loss of
the esteem of family and community. Still other researchers have
focused on the factors associated with being out, such as income,
occupation, where one lives, and the nature of one's friends. These

issues are often discussed with the assumption that being out is a desired state in and of itself (Harry, 1993). Conversely, in the psychological literature coming out has also been identified as a source of anxiety and stress, a cause of suicide, and a sign of arrested sexual identity development.

Many assumptions about coming out have been developed through research involving predominantly White or White-identified lesbians, gay men, and bisexuals, for whom individualism, independent identity, and separation from family of origin are important parts of growing up. There has been little discussion of cultural differences in the meaning, process, or role of coming out, particularly but not exclusively for people who are not White and middle-class. In the discussion below, I raise for consideration several assumptions about the coming-out process that may vary across cultures. I explore some of the cultural aspects of coming out and discuss their implications for therapy with individuals, couples, and families of color.

Clinical Issues

The influence of cultural differences on the process of coming out has important clinical implications for (a) the meaning and process of coming out for clients, (b) transference issues for clients in the therapeutic relationship, and (c) countertransference issues based on therapist's sexual orientation and ethnicity, whether the therapist is similar to or different from the client.

The process of coming out can raise challenging clinical issues for clients who seek help as well as for the clinicians who work with them. Some of the common themes and feelings clients may bring to therapy regarding coming out include guilt about sexual attraction to members of the same sex; self-hatred, expressed in depressive affect or suicidal ideation; rejection from the family and its sequelae as a result of the clients' disclosure of their sexual orientation; alienation from the lesbian, gay, and bisexual community; and difficulty in interpersonal relationships because of mistrust and suspicion, and the realistic need to be careful about what is disclosed to whom. The last of these issues can be a function of an individual's having to conceal so much that is relevant about him- or herself that it interferes with the spontaneity needed in authentic relationships.

White gay male, lesbian, and bisexual clients may raise issues regarding the loyalty or trustworthiness of their gay or lesbian partners or friends of color if those persons are not out. Being out has become a kind of litmus test for determining whether or not an individual will be supportive in the battle against heterosexism. Clients of color may often feel pressured, pigeonholed, or not understood by White friends and lovers. White clients may report feeling abandoned by their Black, Asian, or Latino partners or counterparts to fight homophobia alone.

In interactions with gay or lesbian clients, therapists of color may be stereotyped by clients and others as homophobic because of assumptions the clients may make about the therapists' religious beliefs. Issues of countertransference should be kept in mind by lesbian, gay, and bisexual therapists who work with lesbian, gay, and bisexual clients in interracial couples, and by therapists of color when they work with White gay clients. To work effectively with clients, therapists need to understand the cultural complexities involved in coming out, what coming out means for each client, and why some people choose to come out and others do not.

There are many reasons individuals from different cultural groups do not come out in particular ways. Successful therapy outcomes may rest on clinicians' understanding of some of these reasons. In the psychological literature on coming out, there is little mention of cultural diversity and how it might affect this process differently for members of different groups. For instance, coming out is presumed to emerge from a linear sequence of development and is seen as a singular and dichotomous event despite a lack of inquiry about what being out means to different people. If a client says that she or he is out to her or his family, what does that tell a therapist about who actually knows and how they found out? Does it mean that the individual's parents know? Does "the family" include grandparents, aunts, or uncles? If the client's siblings know but the client has never told her or his parents, is she or he really out? What if the client did not tell the parents directly but told a sibling who then told the parents, and the parents have never mentioned the issue to the client? Is the client out to her or his parents? Do persons have to disclose their sexual orientations to someone in their biological families to be out? How is this regarded if an individual does not have close contact or a close relationship with family members? Does it still count and for how much? Does a client have to disclose to someone "significant" in the family or his or her life in order to be out? If so, who would qualify? Furthermore, does the client him- or herself need to speak the words?

Is being out related to the risk of rejection an individual takes in telling someone? Is a person more out if the negative consequences he or she incurs are great? Do these consequences have to be real or can they be only perceived? What if close friends know but the family does not—is the person considered out? Is a person considered out if his or her gay friends know, but not the person's best heterosexual friend from high school or old boy-/girlfriends? What if no one at work knows?

Coming out is complex, and understanding what it means, what the process is like, and what criteria a person uses for deciding who he or she needs to tell in order to be "really" out has important implications for clinical work and research. When a research questionnaire asks participants if they are out without asking more detailed questions about what this means to them, it can have important effects on responses and on accurate interpretation of the data collected.

Culture and Coming Out

There is little available in the psychological literature on cultural differences and the process of coming out. However, based on other research paradigms in psychology and cross-cultural psychology, some relevant cultural factors can be identified. For instance, a researcher or clinician might explore cultural attitudes and beliefs about sexuality, including reproduction, and attitudes toward homosexual behaviors. Kanuha (1990) refers to fears of extinction as a basis for anti-lesbian attitudes and behaviors among some members of ethnic minority groups. Similarly, cultural values and beliefs about gender and gender role expectations are tied to culture and have implications for reactions to coming out. The importance of traditional gender role stereotypes and the degree of flexibility or rigidity of gender roles should be explored as well (Chan, 1987; Espin, 1984; Greene, 1994). This cultural view would emphasize clients' cognition and beliefs about homosexuality in some context and therefore pinpoint the ways the process of coming out is made more or less difficult for them. Espin (1984) notes that in most cultures a range of sexual behaviors is tolerated, and that the range varies from culture to culture.

Another way to approach coming out and cultural diversity would be to focus on coming out and cultural identity as individual processes that a person moves through in his or her development. That is, the two would be treated as separate developmental processes, with sexual orientation apart from who a person is as a cultural being. Whereas coming out is characterized as the development and acceptance of a homosexual identity, the development of cultural identity—whether racial/ethnic identity development, acculturation, or assimilation—may be seen as a separate, unrelated process. Cultural identity and sexual orientation are treated as separate and distinctive in the literature, and they are rarely integrated in work describing the ways clinicians treat clients coping with sexual identity issues. Espin (1987) specifies variables such as time and reason for immigration, language, acculturation, and assimilation as some of the relevant cultural factors in the lives of immigrant lesbians (see also Amaro, 1978; Espin, 1984, and Chapter 9, this volume). These approaches suggest that many cultural variables affect the lives of lesbian, gay, and bisexual people of color. In addition, the diversity of the gay, lesbian, and bisexual community and our growing understanding of the impact of cultural diversity creates a need to rethink the coming-out process, taking these cultural factors into account. Many researchers have pointed out the importance of the family as a primary social unit within communities of color, and in particular among African Americans (Boyd-Franklin, 1990; Hidalgo, 1984; Morales, 1989), and many others have addressed cultural issues in the coming-out process (Amaro, 1978; Chan, 1987; Greene, 1994; Mays & Cochran, 1988; Morales, 1989; Wooden, Kawasaki, & Mayeda, 1983). They have also suggested the importance of considering the multidimensionality and nonlinear complexity of the coming-out process. Researchers and clinicians need a new language to emphasize the psychological meaning and role of coming out in a cultural context.

Cultural Diversity and Coming Out

Psychology is currently reflecting a growing awareness that individuals do not exist in a vacuum, that they are affected in interactive ways by their environments. Clinical theory and empirical research have begun to take culture into account more actively in the diagnostic and treatment process. Family therapists are incorporating race and ethnicity into their understanding of therapy techniques (Boyd-Franklin, 1990; McGoldrick, Pearce, & Giordano, 1982). Although necessary steps are being taken toward recognizing the importance of culture in psychological functioning, too often culture is considered only in an additive way. This has left researchers and clinicians with the task of figuring out how cultural considerations should be integrated technically on a case-by-case basis. Recently, researchers have described the importance of noticing that an individual is embedded in a family as well as in a cultural context at the same time. This is reflected in Szapocznik and Kurtines's (1993) definition of *contextualism* as the knowledge that a person's psychology is a function of the individual within a family within a culturally diverse context. Contextualism is one paradigm that may be used for exploring the complexity of cultural diversity and the coming-out process.

The contextualist approach suggests that an individual's process of coming out might best be understood through consideration of the individual as part of a network or family system and the family as a part of a culturally diverse context. Put simply, the many ways in which homosexuality can be acknowledged and accepted by a family are deeply embedded in a cultural context. In clinical work with a 15-year-old African American male, for example, any inquiry regarding his sexuality needs to be explored in the context of his family relations (including parents, grandparents, siblings, extended family members, and adoptive relatives) and the meaning of his sexual identity in his family, and would also need to take into account issues of class, religion, nationality, geographic region of the country (e.g., North, East, South, West), traditionalism, and family cultural values regarding privacy, sexuality, and relationships. His connection to a youth culture with other Black males and Black teenagers and his relationships to heterosexual female peers and to the gay, lesbian, and bisexual adolescent communities are also important factors.

Among people of African ancestry, for example, it is critical to consider the diversity within the group. Despite their shared oppression and homogeneity in many ways, it is important to note that class, region, nationality, and religious differences can be sources of great diversity among African Americans. Despite the dangers of stereotyping, there are some general considerations that clinicians and re-searchers should observe in working with African Americans and their families. One is to begin with the understanding that there are impor-tant religious differences among African Americans. Black Catholics may respond differently to issues of homosexuality than may Black Baptist or Episcopalian or Pentecostal families. Even within a group of Black Baptists there may be a wide range of responses. Particular interpretations of Scripture can be used by families to penalize or ostracize and disown a lesbian or gay family member. However, Scrip-ture may also be used to justify their acceptance. For instance, the official doctrine of the Catholic Church prohibits sexual activity out-side the sanctity of marriage; because lesbians and gay men cannot be married in the church, their relationships cannot be formally recog-nized. It seems the church does not target gay or lesbian sexual activity alone between members of the same sex exclusively but all premarital sex. Similarly, a church's teaching that one should separate the person from the homosexual behavior and informal norms such as "Don't ask so they won't tell" may allow families to maintain and accept family members who are gay or lesbian without having to address the issue directly or deal with the conflicts that can accompany it.

Therapists cannot assume that they know what their clients' par-ticular family dynamics will be, nor can they assume that their clients will always be aware of the complexity of the religious issues involved in their coming out. Therapists need to raise explicit questions about what their clients' families' religious dictates mean to their clients and the clients' families. For example, some families adopt the position that their love of a family member and the bonds of blood supersede any policy or religious ethic and simply ignore church dictates. In other families, church policy may be used as a way to avoid struggling with more difficult family issues regarding control of the family member that supersede that individual's sexual behavior or sexual orientation. Therapists must also consider the potential for families to use church policy rigidly and as a way of scapegoating a family member or managing a child to whom they do not know how to respond or who they can no longer control. Clinicians can assist clients by exploring the complexity of these issues for individuals and their families as part of the therapeutic process and by not assuming uniformity of religious positions among families.

Other issues therapists should consider exploring about the coming-out process include differences between people of African ancestry born and raised in the United States and those raised in other parts of the world, such as West Indians, Jamaicans, Arubans, Haitians, Trinidadians, Puerto Ricans, and Barbadians. Caribbean traditionalism and colonial influences on family dynamics regarding sex roles and gender role expectations may lead Caribbean Black Americans to report very different values, beliefs, expectations, and experiences. Cultural traditions and family values regarding marriage, having children, and religion would be particularly important issues to consider and explore as well (Newman & Muzzonigro, 1993). Differences in what is considered public versus private information and feelings about the latter can determine what a client or family will disclose to the therapist as well as what material is considered appropriate for open discussion between or among different family members, as well as with a therapist who is not the same sex as the client. The client's degree of acculturation to the dominant culture and the White gay, lesbian, and bisexual culture could also have an impact.

Contextualism and Coming Out

Ethnocentrism is defined as the belief that one's own cultural approach is the normative lens through which to view a situation or experience. The coming out process is described as a White, Western, middle-class phenomenon with little input from other ethnic, religious, or social class groups. Several assumptions are made about the coming-out process that may be salient for White Americans but could be very different for others. There are a number of unexamined assumptions in this research. For example, coming out is assumed to be an individual process, related to a person's self-concept and identity. It is presumed that acknowledging a lesbian, gay, or bisexual sexual orientation is important to heterosexuals in reducing their homophobia by providing positive role models of gay, lesbian, and bisexual people. Failure to acknowledge one's sexual orientation publicly is assumed to represent a form of denial. This is seen as a form of resistance, an indication of self-hatred, shame, embarrassment, or some other negative psychological phenomenon. Many times, coming out is characterized as a dichotomous situation—one is either in or out of the closet—with little notice of what takes place between the two extremes and its psychological complexity. Examples of some of these assumptions are outlined below.

Costs of Multiple Oppressions

The burdens of oppression carried by those living a gay, lesbian, or bisexual lifestyle include stigma, discrimination, and harassment. The costs of coming out are not the same for all groups. In the case of African American lesbians, the burden of oppression based on both race and gender amounts to double jeopardy. Discrimination based on sexual orientation adds yet another burden and level of jeopardy to these women's life experience (Greene, 1994). If their mental resources are already overwhelmed, they may be taxed to the limit or beyond their capacity. If an African American lesbian is also older, or poor, or disabled, her burdens increase again, as may her psychological vulnerability and stigma. It may be argued that, having survived the battles of other forms of oppression over which she has no control or choice, a Black lesbian may proactively choose not to take on yet another hardship by coming out (Greene, 1994; Greene & Boyd-Franklin, 1996). Exercising control over the disclosure of a stigmatized aspect of her identity that she can control may be adaptive. For a White, middle-class, affluent male, coming out may not carry the same kinds of social burdens as it does for the African American lesbian (although this should not be taken to imply that his coming-out process is any less personally painful; see Cerbone, Chapter 6, this volume). For a White male, coming out may be crucial to his individuality, his uniqueness, and his psychological health.

There may also be other reasons individuals choose not to identify as part of a sexual orientation group. For many members of visible ethnic minority groups, racial identity may be a more salient or more primary locus of oppression than their sexual orientation. It may provide them with and represent clearly identifiable cultural connections as well as a source of support against discrimination, and therefore may be a strong basis for their personal identity.

The point here is that it is not the number of oppressions in an individual's life, in an additive sense, that is significant; rather, therapists must take into consideration each individual client's experience and costs of such oppressions.

Internalized Oppression and Personal Choice

In discussions about coming out, an issue frequently raised (as if automatically related) is internalized homophobia. Clients may seek clinical help for a variety of reasons including their unwillingness to accept their attraction to members of the same sex, or because they feel angry about being labelled as members of the other sex like "sissy" or "mannish." These conflicts may be manifested in forms of depression as well as in suicidal ideation. *Internalized oppression* refers to the acceptance and internalization by members of oppressed groups of negative stereotypes and images of their groups, beliefs in their own inferiority, and concomitant beliefs in the superiority of the dominant group. This could be internalized in hurt and anger at being treated badly by members of the dominant group if accompanied by a belief that one deserves such treatment.

Two dynamics create a tension in our understanding of internalized oppression. The dynamics of acts based in self-hatred and those that are conscious strategies for survival is not always clearly distinctive. Behaviors that resemble acceptance of negative stereotypes may have different meanings for the actor. That is, such behaviors can be positive for survival if they are the result of conscious deliberation or strategic choice. For example, there exist many historical stereotypes and beliefs about African Americans' being passive; however, we are aware now that what appeared to be passivity often represented passive resistance at times when overt resistance would have resulted in serious threats to immediate survival. Accepting a job where one is clearly a token—that is, a position as the first and only Puerto Rican, Japanese American, African American—may represent an important opportunity to break the color barrier and, once inside the institution, use whatever means available to open the door for others. Passing, or allowing others to assume that one is a member of the dominant group when one is not, or imitating the behavior of dominant group members, can represent a deliberate method to gain access, to make changes, to open the doors for others—to succeed. All of these can be "adaptive" strategies for responding to oppression of targeted groups. In some cases they represent ways of avoiding exile, isolation, exclusion, or extermination, physically, politically, economically, and socially. Such strategies can be lifesaving alternative routes to self-definition.

Some members of oppressed groups also believe that accepting the dominant view limits their freedom, the choices they can make about their behaviors, thoughts, and feelings. A part of the dynamic of internalized oppression is the recognition that the dominant group sets the agenda about what the oppression is, even so far as defining what the internalizing of oppression means. Interestingly, behaving as an Uncle Tom (behaving as if one is not Black) is not often defined by Whites as internalized oppression. Coming out is often framed as an indicator of self-acceptance and pride. The ability to face the attack of homophobia head-on is described as a sign of homosexual health. We may ask why a major ingredient in coming out emphasizes disclosure to heterosexuals. This can reflect a subtle form of internalized oppression, as the focus is on the dominant group and countering its myths and stereotypes rather than on asking proactive and noncomparative questions about what constitutes self-esteem, self-acceptance, and pride among lesbians, gay men, and bisexuals, independent of what is done in relation to heterosexuals. This lack of free choice in the domain of self-definition is fundamental to a personal sense of self-integrity. Discussions of internalized oppression require a recognition of the difference between particular underlying choices and strategies and self-hatred, especially when the behaviors may look the same.

Individual Behavior Versus Group Identity

Clinicians must remember that behavior is not the sole basis for reference group identity. For a number of Latino and African American men, sexual behavior is not equated with group identity. A man who has sex with another man may draw a distinction between his sexual behavior and his sexual identity. A number of stories about men of color who were married or had ongoing sexual relationships with women but periodically slept with men have found their way into the popular literature (Harris, 1991, 1994). How is it that sexual behavior has come to be seen as such a defining part of an individual's identity? The treatment of sexual behavior as a primary criterion for gender identity represents cultural differences among Blacks, Latinos, Asians, and Whites that require fuller exploration and discussion. A West Indian friend spoke to me about her experience with an informal and unspoken practice of older women initiating younger women into the practice of masturbation. This early "love" relationship is considered a part of healthy female sexual development in a specific cultural context. This expression of sexuality between a younger and older woman is not considered a sign of a lesbian identity; rather, it is seen as a way to develop the younger female's awareness of physical pleasures, needs, and desires in an affirmative way. Similarly, intimacy, dependence, and relational closeness may not be the basis of a lesbian identity for all women. In East Africa, there is a tradition called *mwakamwana*, in which a woman who cannot have children pays the bride-price for a young, childbearing woman. The older woman chooses who will father the children, and full responsibility for the "family." Hence, individual behaviors are not always the basis for a person's group identification.

Self-Disclosure and Self-Acceptance

Some might believe that the ability to disclose personal and private information about the most intimate details of one's life is the primary sign of comfort and self-acceptance. Clinically, disclosure is a common indicator of health and maturity. For many people, however, matters concerning sexual partners or personal relationships are private, and discussing them is not seen as a reflection of pride or self-acceptance. This may be particularly true for people who have had little control over certain aspects of their lives. Information about the self may be one of the few things under an individual's own control. This may be particularly so for people who face multiple levels of discrimination. Such people may treat personal information as personal property, property under their control.

Because of institutional racism, people of color often do not necessarily believe that the principle of safety in disclosure to a therapist will protect them. They have what can be considered an appropriately heightened level of suspicion about how information they disclose about themselves will be used. People of African descent may have different norms about self-disclosure, privacy, and sharing information than do members of other groups (Kochman, 1981). This may be particularly true regarding personal issues such as those concerning sexual behaviors, sexuality, intimate relationships, and family. Among African Americans, talking about who one sleeps with or divulging details about family life may be limited to a few trustworthy people in certain contexts. Discussion of sexuality is not necessarily denied in such contexts; rather, it may be considered impolite and too personal to discuss sexuality publicly. For African Americans who are gay, lesbian, or bisexual, not talking about sexual partners with parents, relatives, or even close friends may be a respectful way of maintaining needed privacy rather than an indication of self-hatred, denial of sexuality, or a sign of struggle with self-acceptance due to shame. In many African American communities the general policy seems to be "Don't ask, don't tell," and may be related to a position of maintaining privacy and respecting boundaries for some of the communities' members rather than to unilateral rejection or hatred.

Since Masters and Johnson (1979) removed discussions about homosexuality from the closet, the emphasis has been on the sexual aspect of homosexuality. However, sexual behavior is not all there is to gay/lesbian/bisexual identity. Among African Americans, sexuality is a complex issue. For instance, sexual attitudes may have little or no relationship to sexual behaviors, just as liberal attitudes do not necessarily result in liberal behaviors and vice versa (Robinson, 1982-1983; Slane, 1981; Staples, 1971). When gay/lesbian and bisexual clients' behaviors and attitudes are contradictory or inconsistent, this may represent an important part of their particular coming-out process. Similarly, clinicians who assume that conservative sexual attitudes are signs of nonacceptance or internalized oppression should observe these assumptions for countertransference bias. For example, a variety of factors influence the sexual attitudes and behaviors of African Americans, including (but not exclusively) church attendance, social class, age, gender, and knowledge about human sexuality and reproduction (Wilson, 1986). Therefore, exploring or experimenting sexually may be a separate and distinctive part of self-identity. Therapists should be aware that more than superficial exploration is necessary to determine whether or not particular sexual behaviors are integral and necessary parts of the coming-out process for African American clients.

Feminism, Lesbianism, and Gender Role Stereotypes

Feminism and lesbianism have sometimes been equated in African American communities, but they are not necessarily related. Feminism as an ideology based on the equal treatment of men and women has different practical implications in the context of racism and classism.

In *Talking Back*, bell hooks (1989) observes that middle-class White feminism has done a disservice to African American women by failing to incorporate race and racism in the feminist agenda. As a result, many Black women avoid the topic of sexism. Other writers have discussed how the absence of class issues has limited the scope of feminism and excluded African American and other women of color (Smith & Smith, 1981). One of the mechanisms of sexism is to tie feminism to lesbianism and to use this as a means of silencing women who might address sexism in the African American community (hooks, 1989). Similarly, negative depictions of lesbians as defective, nonfemale, or sexually deviant "Black bulldaggers" can be a form of gender distortion intended to distract from genuine discussions of sexism (Smith & Smith, 1981). Cornel West (1993) recognizes the dilemma of African American gay men who push the limits of the White and Black communities' definition of macho, aggressive male identity. West points out that Black males are locked into a machismo image, and that the stereotypes of loud, sassy, pushy Black women are not taken seriously. These images become the material used by comedians and the popular culture to laugh at and ridicule lesbians and gay men. Therapists working with Black lesbians and gay men need to be aware of the stress their clients may experience from the potentially damaging limits of gender role stereotypes in the African American community and from pressures to live up or down to White stereotypes of Black gender roles (Wyatt, Strayer, & Lobitz, 1976).

Political Advocacy Versus Sexual Orientation

The history of the civil rights movement suggests that its activists and advocates have been primarily other Black Americans. In this context, civil rights activism has not been a sign of a person's racial identity. Participants have ranged from members of politically conservative (religious and church) groups to members of progressive (Panthers, Nation of Islam) groups. Coming out has been synonymous with advocating for gay rights and gay liberation for many Whites (Dankmeijer, 1993; Phelan, 1993). In this schema of thinking, if an individual does not come out on every occasion with everyone he or she meets, sexual orientation is associated with secrecy, shame, and pathology for that individual. However, activism is not always related to identity. Advocacy of gay liberation need not be related to sexual orientation.

Fighting for gay rights is rooted in activism and political advocacy, which may be reflected in volunteer community work, a paid job, or a career targeted to social change and unrelated to identity. For many African American gay men and lesbians, if forced to choose, political activism around racial causes may be more likely than activism on behalf of gay rights because of the more visible, obvious, overt source of oppression represented by race.

Advocacy for gay liberation or gay pride or work against homophobia does not require a person to be gay, lesbian, or bisexual, just as many civil rights advocates are not African American. There are many different ways to fight oppression; those who are moved to political advocacy should be free to choose their own forms of activism. White lesbian and gay claims of disloyalty and abandonment by Blacks and other people of color can also represent a subtle form of racial prejudice and part of a larger defense system against their own role in maintaining racism.

Afrocentric Coming Out

Members of the gay, lesbian, and bisexual community are often referred to, colloquially, as members of the family. Cultural differences between Black and White gay men and lesbians may begin with the ways African Americans interpret who is a family member. For White lesbians, gay men, and bisexuals, the family in this case refers to the wider lesbian, gay, and bisexual community. Therefore, to come out is to acknowledge one's membership in and to join that group. There are cultural differences in what is defined as coming out, however. Among African Americans, it is not surprising that coming out may be seen as one's family's acceptance and commitment to treat a particular person, one's partner, as if he or she were a member of the biological family, just as the family would treat a spouse, a stepsister, or brother. The act of taking any person home as a family member fits Carol Stack's (1972) concept of fictive kin or non-blood-related people who are taken in as siblings, parents, godparents, aunts, uncles, or grandparents. To take one's partner home to meet one's parents, as a significant other, may for some be the most important sign of self-acceptance and pride. Coming out may be better understood in this context as "taking in" a significant other as if he or she were a member of the biological family.

African American families may display appreciation for the importance of an individual member's partner even in the absence of overt acknowledgment of the label *lesbian* or *gay*. One 30-year-old African American male's partner who was invited to holiday celebrations was asked about his home life, family, and given gifts on birthdays and holidays just as was everyone else in the family. During one visit with the partner's family, there was a brief conversation about their gay lifestyle, but no other conversation was encouraged. It was implicit that he was a member of the family and was never treated otherwise. Emphasizing the strong family ties in this case kept him connected to this family. This man, however, reported the dilemma of feeling accepted and supported by his family while not given license to express his anger at homophobic comments made by family members, as if they did not apply to him. The man's union was treated the same way as all the other family members' marriages, and for this he was grateful and resentful. This family did not appreciate the struggle the two men experienced daily because such topics were not open for discussion. The family's blind acceptance was wonderful in one way, but the man had great difficulty in getting support for the hurts, fears, and anxieties of being Black and gay in America. In this case, coming out in the context of the Black family seems much more related to being taken in and accepted than to being disowned, threatened, or coerced into giving up one's sexual orientation. In this example, the family accepted a family member's gay partner but subtly rejected the identity of the family member as a gay man.

Implications for Therapy

In the previous section I have highlighted a few of the dynamics of African American families and stressed the importance of questioning some of the assumptions made about coming out. I have done so to illustrate how the coming-out process may be different from the perspective of African American families and therefore families from other cultural and religious groups as well. My goals have been to expand the range of ways of understanding this process and to offer alternative explanations for behaviors that clinicians may observe in work with gay, lesbian, or bisexual members of this group. The most critical aspect of coming out for some persons may not be telling their families about their individual sexual orientations, but the relational dynamic of "taking in" partners as new members of the family. Further research into dynamics of families with gay and lesbian members is greatly needed.

The goal for therapy when some family members come out may be limited to educating rather than changing the family's or client's behavior. For some, highlighting family tensions, educating the client, and supporting multiple ways the client can let the family know about how he or she lives are all important and worthy goals. The goal of sexual disclosure might be limited to specific arenas, if it is a goal at all. Clients can give guidance about what is best for them given their families. A successful therapeutic process might include creating an understanding in the family of the complexity of the psychological issues involved in coming out. It may be helpful for therapists to use strategies for working with families that help create family contexts that are supportive of all kinds of differences, whether the issue is interracial partners, disabilities, "poor" relatives, lighter- and darker-skinned partners, or something else.

Other positive therapeutic goals might include building on the strengths of those clients who have positive stories of friends and families who have accepted and affirmed their sexual orientation. Having individuals tell their stories about their families' different ways of being supportive, as opposed to the usual recounting of resistances, is helpful. It is important to remind gay and lesbian clients that, like coming out, being taken into a family is a process that requires different amounts of time for different families. Sometimes fear and anxiety about being rejected, by both the family and the lesbian or gay family member, creates a false sense of urgency about coming out. That fear can lead a lesbian or gay family member to push her or his family to move through the transition before they are ready. Families require time to work through their homophobia and their real or imagined fears and worries about lesbian and gay life when a family member comes out to them. Gay or lesbian persons who are coming out will also require support while their families move through that process as well. If the family has been the major source of emotional support for the gay or lesbian individual, it may be helpful for the therapist to assist the client in developing other supportive networks, as during this difficult period the family may not serve this function as well as it has previously.

Multiple-family therapy groups with a psychoeducational focus can provide families with a forum to share feelings and concerns, ask questions, and openly express their fears. These family therapy sessions can be offered through community churches, as health services through hospitals and clinics, or through community mental health centers. Such sessions can help families to learn about sexual orientation in a supportive atmosphere. In such groups, care should taken that the following points are clear: the purpose of the group; the definition of the family unit (as to who is invited to therapy); and the family structure and values the therapist will raise. The therapists should be aware of gay men's and lesbians' external pressures and strategies for coping, as well as the importance of language used in defining the therapeutic issue and its meaning (i.e., social support versus homosexual behavior); further, they should understand and be sensitive to the issues of gender and sex roles for gay and lesbian clients who come from culturally diverse backgrounds.

Couples Therapy

It is common in treatment to see individual members of a couple at very different places in their coming-out processes. It is important that the therapist be aware of the tensions that can develop from such a situation. The therapist's sensitivity to clients' differences in stages of coming out may require that he or she support one member of the couple in a "holding pattern" while facilitating the other in her or his awareness for a next step. Encouraging a couple to discuss their fears while finding ways to support each other can provide another opportunity for the couple to bond. This is particularly true for interracial couples, for whom other pressures and expectations are already operative. The therapist may need to pay special attention to different expectations and facilitate the couple's ability to talk about them. The degree to which a person identifies with her or his racial/ethnic group is important for the therapist to keep in mind.

Finally, I leave you with a group of vignettes that raise some of the issues previously discussed (names and other identifying information have been altered to maintain confidentiality).

Bruce is an African American male, age 27, who has AIDS and has come to you for therapy. He is struggling with telling his family that he is gay, he has AIDS, and he is dying. He family has been supportive of him and he is afraid of losing their love but does not want to die without telling them about his life.

Javier has come to you because his wife wants a divorce after 18 years of marriage. For the past 5 years, he has been having sexual relations with a man in a another state. His wife found out and is pressing him to choose whether he is gay or "straight." Javier does not want a divorce but also wants to continue his relationship with his male lover. You have agreed to see Javier and his wife for couples therapy. What might be some of the countertransference issues that may emerge for you in working with this couple?

Jack and Leroy are an interracial couple; they have been together for 15 years. Jack is dying of AIDS and the couple has concerns about how the in-laws will respond. Leroy's family has met Jack and welcomed him into their home and hearts. Jack has really felt that his African American in-laws treat him like a son. Leroy has not met Jack's family because Jack fears they will be racially insensitive to Leroy. In addition to issues of death and dying, Jack has come to you for therapy to ease the stress around these issues.

Robert is a 42-year-old African American gay man reporting depression about his work situation. He has been the only African American in his department for 8 years. Recently, he was assigned to a new boss, a 40-year-old African American heterosexual woman. He locates the beginning of his depression around that time and the way his new boss treats him. He does not understand why she is so "angry" with him.

The dilemmas exemplified in the preceding vignettes illustrate the multidimensionality and complexity of coming out under varied circumstances with people from diverse backgrounds, and the need for clinicians to develop a heightened awareness of these issues.

References

Amaro, H. (1978). *Coming out: Hispanic lesbians, their families and communities*. Paper presented at the National Coalition of Hispanic Mental Health and Human Services Organization, Austin, TX.

Boyd-Franklin, N. (1990). *Black families in therapy: A multisystems approach*. New York: Guilford.

Chan, C. (1987). Asian lesbians: Psychological issues in the coming out process. *Asian American Psychological Journal, 12*, 16-18.

Dankmeijer, P. (1993). The construction of identities as a means of survival: Case of gay and lesbian teachers. *Journal of Homosexuality, 24*(3-4), 95-105.

Dempsey, C. L. (1994). Health and social issues of gay, lesbian, and bisexual adolescents. *Families in Society, 75*(3), 160-167.

Espin, O. M. (1984). Cultural and historical influences on sexuality in Hispanic/Latina women: Implications for psychotherapy. In C. Vance (Ed.), *Pleasure and danger: Exploring female sexuality* (pp. 149-163). London: Routledge & Kegan Paul.

Espin, O. M. (1987). Issues of identity in the psychology of Latina lesbians. In Boston Lesbian Psychologies Collective (Ed.), *Lesbian psychologies: Explorations and challenges* (pp. 35-55). Urbana: University of Illinois Press.

Greene, B. (1994). Lesbian women of color: Triple jeopardy. In L. Comas-Diaz & B. Greene (Eds.), *Women of color: Integrating ethnic and gender identities in psychotherapy* (pp. 389-427). New York: Guilford.

Greene, B., & Boyd-Franklin, N. (1996). African American lesbians: Issues in couples therapy. In J. Laird & R. J. Green (Eds.), *Lesbian and gay couples and families: A handbook for therapists* (pp. 251-271). San Francisco: Jossey-Bass.

Harris, E. L. (1991). *Invisible life.* Garden City, NY: Anchor.

Harris, E. L. (1994). *Just as I am: A novel.* Garden City, NY: Anchor.

Harry, J. (1993). Being out: A general model. *Journal of Homosexuality, 26*(1), 25-39.

Hidalgo, H. (1984). The Puerto Rican lesbian in the United States. In T. Darty & S. Potter (Eds.), *Women identified women* (pp. 105-115). Palo Alto, CA: Mayfield.

hooks, b. (1989). *Talking back: Thinking feminist, thinking Black.* Boston: South End.

Hopcke, R. H. (1992). Midlife, gay men, and the AIDS epidemic. *Quadrant, 25*(1), 101-109.

Kanuha, V. (1990). Compounding the triple jeopardy: Battering in lesbian of color relationships. *Women and Therapy, 9*(1-2), 169-183.

Kochman, T. (1981). *Black and White styles in conflict.* Chicago: University of Chicago Press.

Martin, H. P. (1991). The coming out process for homosexuals. *Hospital and Community Psychiatry, 42,* 158-162.

Masters, W. H., & Johnson, V. (1979). *Homosexuality in perspective.* Boston: Little, Brown.

Mays, V. M., & Cochran, S. D. (1988). The Black Women's Relationship Project: A national survey of Black lesbians. In M. Shernoff & W. A. Scott (Eds.), *A sourcebook of gay/lesbian health care* (2nd ed., pp. 54-62). Washington, DC: National Lesbian and Gay Health Foundation.

McGoldrick, M., Pearce, J. K., & Giordano, J. (Eds.). (1982). *Ethnicity and family therapy.* New York: Guilford.

Morales, E. (1989). Ethnic minority families and minority gays and lesbians. *Marriage and Family Review, 14,* 217-239.

Newman, B. S., & Muzzonigro, P. G. (1993). The effects of traditional family values on the coming out process of gay male adolescents. *Adolescence, 28,* 213-226.

Phelan, S. (1993). Coming out: Lesbian identity and politics. *Signs, 18,* 765-790.

Robinson, W. L. (1982-1983). Sexual fantasies, attitudes, and behaviors as a function of race, gender and religiosity. *Imagination, Cognition and Personality, 2,* 281-290.

Slane, S. C. (1981). Race differences in feminism and guilt. *Psychological Reports, 49,* 45-46.

Smith, B., & Smith, B. (1981). Across the kitchen table: A sister to sister dialogue. In C. Moraga & G. Anzaldúa (Eds.), *This bridge called my back: Writings of radical women of color* (pp. 113-127). Watertown, MA: Persephone.

Stack, C. (1972). *All our kin: Strategies for survival in a Black community.* New York: Harper & Row.

Staples, R. (1971). *The Black family: Essays and studies.* Belmont, CA: Wadsworth.

Szapocznik, J., & Kurtines, W. M. (1993). Family psychology and cultural diversity: Opportunities for theory, research, and application. *American Psychologist, 48,* 400-407.

Thompson, C. A. (1992). Lesbian grief and loss issues in the coming out process. *Women and Therapy, 12*(1-2), 175-185.

West, C. (1993). Black sexuality: The taboo topic. In C. West, *Race matters* (pp. 81-91). Boston: Beacon.

Wilson, P. (1986). Black culture and sexuality. *Journal of Social Work and Human Sexuality, 4*(3), 29-46.

Wooden, W. S., Kawasaki, H., & Mayeda, R. (1983). Lifestyles and identity maintenance among gay Japanese American males. *Alternative Lifestyles, 5,* 236-243.

Wyatt, G., Strayer, R., & Lobitz, W. C. (1976). Issues in the treatment of sexually dysfunctioning couples of African American descent. *Psychotherapy, 13,* 44-50.

Somewhere, on the edge of consciousness, there is what I call a *mythical norm*, which each one of us within our hearts knows "that is not me." In America, this norm is usually defined as white, thin, male, young, heterosexual, Christian, and financially secure. It is with this mythical norm that the trappings of power reside in this society. Those of us who stand outside that power often identify one way in which we are different, and we assume that to be the primary cause of all oppression, forgetting other distortions around difference, some of which we ourselves may be practicing.

Audre Lorde, "Age, Race, Class and Sex," in *Sister Outsider: Essays and Speeches* (1984, p. 116). Reprinted by permission of the Crossing Press, Freedom, CA.

Index

303

About the Editor

Beverly Greene is Professor of Psychology at St. John's University and a clinical psychologist in private practice in New York City. She received her Ph.D. (1983) in clinical psychology from the Derner Institute of Advanced Psychological Studies of Adelphi University. She has served as Director of Inpatient Child and Adolescent Psychology Services at Kings County Hospital, in Brooklyn, and Supervising Psychologist-Clinical Assistant Professor of Child Psychiatry at the Outpatient Community Mental Health Center of the University of Medicine and Dentistry of New Jersey at Newark.

Dr. Greene is Associate Editor of the journal *Violence Against Women* and a member of the editorial boards of the *Journal of Feminist Family Therapy* and the *Journal of Lesbian Studies*. She also serves as a guest consulting editor for professional journals and is a coeditor of and an active contributor to a range of professional books and journals on psychotherapy with African Americans; the interactive effects of ethnicity, gender, and sexual orientation in the psychologies of women of color; ethical applications of feminist psychology with diverse populations; and the development of curricula addressing cultural diversity in the delivery of clinical psychological services. She is coauthor of the undergraduate text *Abnormal Psychology in a Changing World* and is currently coediting with Leslie Jackson *Psychotherapy With African American Women: Psychodynamic Perspectives*.

A Fellow of the American Psychological Association and five of the association's divisions, she is a Member at Large of the Division 44 Executive Committee. A recipient of a 1994 Distinguished Humanitarian Award from the American Association of Applied and Preventive

Psychology, she has been awarded the Association for Women in Psychology's 1991 Women of Color Psychologies Publication Award and the 1992 Award for Distinguished Professional Contributions to Ethnic Minority Issues from APA's Division 44. The latter award recognized her development of lesbian affirmative theoretical perspectives and clinical applications with African American women. She is also recipient of a 1995 Psychotherapy With Women Research Award from the Division of the Psychology of Women of APA for the paper "Psychotherapy With African American Women: Integrating Feminist and Psychodynamic Models" and both a 1995 Distinguished Publication Award and 1995 Women of Color Psychologies Publication Award for her coedited book (with Lillian Comas-Diaz) *Women of Color: Integrating Ethnic and Gender Identities in Psychotherapy* (1994), from the Association for Women in Psychology. She was most recently awarded, with Nancy Boyd-Franklin, the 1996 Psychotherapy With Women Research Award for their paper "African American Lesbians: Issues in Couples Therapy" and the 1996 Outstanding Achievement Award from the American Psychological Association's Committee on Lesbian, Gay, and Bisexual Concerns.

About the Contributors

Clarence Lancelot Adams, Jr., is a licensed psychologist in private practice in New York city. He received his Ed.D. in Psychology from the Ferkauf Graduate School of Yeshiva University. Dr. Adams is retired after having served as a Consultant in Special Education to the New York City Board of Education, and a Clinical Psychologist in the Educational Clinic and Supervisor of Counseling and Psychological Services in the CUNY Hunter College Seek Program. His professional activities have also included service as a Clinical Psychologist at the New York Clinic for Mental Health, as a member of the Board of Directors of SAGE (Seniors Action in a Gay Environment) and as faculty in the Psychology department of faculties of Pace University and Bronx Community College of the City University of New York. He is a Fellow of the American Orthopsychiatric Association, and a Diplomate in the International Council of Behavioral Medicine, Counseling and Psychotherapy.

Marta A. Alquijay is Program Director of the Family Preservation Network at California Hospital in the Pico-Union area of Los Angeles and is a clinical psychologist in private practice in Glendale, California. She received her doctoral degree in clinical psychology from the California School of Professional Psychology in Los Angeles, where she specialized in cross-cultural/community psychology. She has taught at CSPP-LA and National University, and has lectured on issues of diversity at the University of California, Los Angeles, and the University of Southern California. She has presented papers at the annual convention of the American Psychological Association, the Association for Women in Psychology, and the Black Gay and Lesbian Leadership Association. She has worked primarily with the Latina/o, African American, and lesbian and gay communities.

Armand R. Cerbone is a clinical psychologist in full-time independent practice in Chicago, with a special focus on sexual orientation issues. He received his B.A. in philosophy from St. John's Seminary in Boston and his Ph.D. in counseling psychology from the University of Notre Dame. He has held academic posts at the University of Illinois at Chicago, Nova University in Florida, and the Illinois School of Professional Psychology. He has been President of Division 44 and Chair of the National Association of Lesbian and Gay Psychologists. In 1986 he founded the Midwest Association of Lesbian and Gay Psychologists. Most recently, he organized the Section for Sexual Orientation Issues within the Illinois Psychological Association. He works very hard for peace among all peoples and at making his Roma tomatoes grow.

Connie S. Chan is Associate Professor of Human Services at the College of Public and Community Service at the University of Massachusetts at Boston, where she is also Codirector of the Institute for Asian American Studies, which conducts research, policy, and curriculum development on Asian American issues. Her research and publications focus upon the intersection of gender, culture, and sexuality issues in Asian American women.

Susan D. Cochran, a clinical psychologist and epidemiologist, is Professor of Epidemiology in the School of Public Health at the University of California, Los Angeles. She has conducted research on the close relationships of lesbians and gay men since 1976. She has served as co-principal investigator of the Black Lesbian Close Relationship Study and of a national study of the intimate relationships and HIV-related behaviors of African American men who have sex with men. Currently she is the principal investigator of a study of lesbian health that examines patterns of utilization, barriers of access to care, and disease prevalence. She is a recent recipient of the President's Award from the National Gay and Lesbian Health Association for her research on lesbians and gay men.

Sari H. Dworkin is Professor of Counselor Education at California State University, Fresno. She is licensed as a psychologist and as a marriage, family, and child counselor. The majority of clients in her part-time practice deal with sexual orientation issues. She also sees clients who struggle with their Jewish identity. She has published and presented widely on gay, lesbian, and bisexual issues, and on the impact of being Jewish in a predominantly non-Jewish world. Her latest project involves research for a book on the construction of bisexual identity in women. Her chapter in this volume is the 1996 recipient of the Jewish Women's Scholarship Award sponsored by the Jewish Women's Caucus of the Association for Women in Psychology.

Oliva M. Espin is Professor of Women's Studies at San Diego State University and part-time core faculty member at the California School of Professional Psychology in San Diego. She has published on psychotherapy with Latinas, immigrant and refugee women, women's sexuality, and other topics. She is coeditor of *Refugee Women and Their Mental Health: Shattered Societies, Shattered Lives* (1992), and her books on immigrant Latina healers and on issues of gender and sexuality with immigrant women are forthcoming. She received a Distinguished Professional Contribution Award from the American Psychological Association in 1991. She is Past President of Division 44 and was recently a Visiting Scholar at the Institute for Research on Women and Gender at Stanford University, where she conducted research on the sexuality of immigrant women.

Leah M. Fygetakis is Director of the Boston University Counseling Center and has a part-time private practice. She received her Ph.D. (1982) in counseling psychology from the Ohio State University. Prior to her Boston University appointment, she was an Associate Director responsible for the University of Rochester's Counseling and Psychology Services internship training program and was an Assistant Professor, part-time, in the Psychology and Women's Studies Departments. She is a Fellow of the Massachusetts Psychological Association, a recipient of the 1991 Distinguished Educational Contribution Award from Division 44 of the American Psychological Association, and represented Division 44 on the APA Council of Representatives from 1992 to 1995. At present, she is serving as Division 44's liaison to the Association of Lesbian and Gay Psychologists of Europe.

Douglas C. Kimmel is Professor of Psychology at City College, City University of New York, where he has been on the faculty since 1970. He is the author of *Adulthood and Aging: An Interdisciplinary Developmental View* (1990; Japanese translation, 1994); coauthor, with Irving B. Weiner, of *Adolescence: A Developmental Transition* (1995); and coeditor, with Linda D. Garnets, of *Psychological Perspectives on Lesbian and Gay Male Experiences* (1993). He was a Fulbright Lecture Professor in Japan (1994-1995). His work in lesbian and gay psychology includes serving as Chair of the Association of Lesbian and Gay Psychologists (1977), Chair of APA's Committee on Lesbian and Gay Concerns (1983), President of the Society for the Psychological Study of Lesbian and Gay Issues (Division 44) of the American Psychological Association (1986-1987), and APA Council Representative for Division 44 (1992-1994). He also served on APA's Board of Social and Ethical Responsibility for Psychology (1984-1986) and as a member of the American Psychological Foundation board of trustees (1996-), with special responsibility for the Wayne Placek Trust. His research on older gay men began in 1976, and he was a cofounder of SAGE (Senior Action in a Gay Environment) in New York City in 1977.

Vickie M. Mays is Professor of Psychology at the University of California, Los Angeles, and a clinical psychologist. She has served as the principal or co-principal investigator of several multiethnic studies investigating the health or mental health of lesbians and gay men. Her areas of research include investigations of behavioral components for the prevention and intervention of HIV risk in women, gay men of color, and heterosexual young adults; the contributions of factors associated with social inequality, such as race, gender, and sexual orientation, to the physical and mental health of ethnic minorities; and cultural/ethnic dimensions of health and mental health service utilization patterns of ethnic minority women. In 1995 she received the Pierre Ludington Service Award for her research on the health of African American lesbians and gay men from the Gay and Lesbian Medical Association and the award for Distinguished Scientific Contributions from Division 44.

Letitia Anne Peplau is a social psychologist and Professor of Psychology at the University of California, Los Angeles. She was President of the International Society for the Study of Personal Relationships. Her research has addressed various aspects of gender and close relationships, including the study of lesbian and gay male relationships, as well as studies of heterosexual dating and same-sex friendship. She is a recipient of an Outstanding Achievement Award from the Committee on Lesbian and Gay Concerns of APA for significant contributions to the mission of CLGC.

Cheryl Potgieter teaches social and community psychology in the Psychology Department at the University of Western Cape, South Africa. A doctoral candidate completing research for her dissertation on Black South African lesbians, she also teaches the course "Sexuality and Social Control" to master's-level graduate students in the Women's Studies Programme and is currently the Academic Coordinator of the Psychology Department's Master's Research Programme. She has published in the area of childhood sexuality, children's economic socialization, and feminist psychology, and has studied at both the University of Western Cape and the University of Cape Town. She has also spent time at the University of St. Louis in Missouri and at the University of Utrecht in the Netherlands as part of staff exchange programs.

Althea Smith is a psychologist whose teaching, research, and therapy focus on the experiences of African Americans, particularly women. She completed her Ph.D. in social psychology at the University of Utah and her postdoctoral work at George Washington University in clinical psychology. She has written and presented on psychological topics by incorporating Black feminist ideology and principles. Some of her writing includes *Racism and Sexism in Black Women's Lives; Feminism and Franz Fanon;* and *The Strength of Marginality: Black Women Leaders.* Her current empirical work is on the mind-body connection for women of African ancestry, including coping with breast cancer and writing on racial identity and body image. As consultant, she travels throughout the United States, the Caribbean, and East Africa to conduct workshops and facilitate groups. She now lives and works in Boston, MA.

Bonnie Ruth Strickland was raised in the South and received her Ph.D. in clinical psychology from the Ohio State University in 1962. She has been on the faculties of Emory University and the University of Massachusetts in Amherst as a teacher, researcher, administrator, clinician, and consultant. A Diplomate in Clinical Psychology and a Fellow of the American Psychological Association, she has been in practice for more than 30 years, and has served as President of the American Psychological Association, the Division of Clinical Psychology, and the American Association for Applied and Preventive Psychology. She was a founder and on the first board of directors of the American Psychological Society. She has been a longtime public advocate for women and minorities, testifying before the U.S. Congress and serving on numerous national boards and committees. She has published more than 100 scholarly works, including two Citation Classics, and is the recipient of numerous national awards for her leadership and distinguished professional contributions. She lives in her lakefront home in the Pioneer Valley with her three cats and her chocolate Labrador, Murphy Brown.

Terry Tafoya of Taos Pueblo and Warm Springs Native heritage, has served as a Professor of Psychology at Evergreen State College and the University of Washington, Seattle. He has also served on the faculties of the Kinsey Institute, Indiana University, Bloomington and the American Psychological Association. He is an internationally acclaimed storyteller and presenter on such topics as cross-cultural communication, substance abuse, AIDS prevention, multicultural education, and psycho-linguistics.

Carla M. Trujillo was born in New Mexico and received a Ph.D. in educational psychology from the University of Wisconsin—Madison. She is the editor of *Chicana Lesbians: The Girls Our Mothers Warned Us About*, an anthology now in its third printing, which won the LAMBDA Book Award for Best Lesbian Anthology and the Out/Write Vanguard Award for Best Pioneering Contribution to the Field of Gay/Lesbian Lifestyle Literature in 1991. She is also the author of various articles on identity, sexuality, and higher education and has just finished editing a book on Xicana theory and consciousness. She works as an administrator and lecturer at the University of California at Berkeley.